We (in industry) use COBOL as a primary programming language, FORTRAN as a secondary language, and PL/I least of all across the whole industry. These are our languages and probably will be our languages forever. Lots of programs are written in COBOL and FORTRAN and won't be changed. So our first problem is that our students sometimes can't talk the language of the streets.

George G. Dodd
General Motors Research Laboratories

WINTHROP COMPUTER SYSTEMS SERIES

Gerald M. Weinberg, *editor*

Future Titles

Robert G. Finkenaur
Northeastern University

COBOL for Students:
A Programming Primer

Winthrop Publishers, Inc.
Cambridge, Massachusetts

Library of Congress Cataloging in Publication Data

Finkenaur, Robert G
  COBOL for students.

  Includes index.
  1. COBOL (Computer program language) I. Title.
QA76.73.C25F54   001.6'424   76-55362
ISBN 0-87626-132-2

Illustrations by Robert F. Rosenberger. Photographs by the author except where otherwise noted.

Acknowledgment

The following acknowledgment is reprinted at the request of the American National Standards Institute, Inc., from their publication, ANSI X3.23-1974, *American National Standard Programming Language COBOL;* May 10, 1974:

> COBOL is an industry language and is not the property of any company or group of companies, or of any organization or group of organizations.

> No warranty, expressed or implied, is made by any contributor or by the CODASYL Programming Language Committee as to the accuracy and functioning of the programming system and language. Moreover, no responsibility is assumed by any contributor, or by the Committee, in connection herewith.

> The authors and copyright holders of the copyrighted material used herein

> > FLOW-MATIC (trademark of Sperry Rand Corporation), Programming for the UNIVAC ® I and II, Data Automation Systems copyrighted 1958, 1959, by Sperry Rand Corporation; IBM Commercial Translator Form No. F 28-8013, copyrighted 1959 by IBM; FACT, DSI 27A5260-2760, copyrighted 1960 by Minneapolis-Honeywell

> have specifically authorized the use of this material in whole or in part, in the COBOL specifications. Such authorization extends to the reproduction and use of COBOL specifications in programming manuals or similar publications.

Contents

7 Your First Program   103

8 A Second Look at the DATA DIVISION: The PICTURE Clause in More Detail   125

9 A Second Look at the PROCEDURE DIVISION: Tne MOVE Verb in More Detail   139

14   An Introduction to Magnetic Tapes   270

15   Processing Data in Magnetic Tape Files   294

Foreword

In the first six months after we announced the Winthrop Computer Systems Series, I personally was offered no fewer than eleven outlines or manuscripts for "Introduction to COBOL." Out of this short dozen, only one had anything to distinguish it from the five dozen COBOL texts already published. That one was Bob Finkenaur's *COBOL for Students*.

Why does *COBOL for Students* represent a true contribution to programming education? Isn't the field adequately covered by the three score texts already in use? Although there are some rather good texts among them, the weaknesses of these existing texts provide the best explanation of the strengths of *COBOL for Students*.

A leading weakness of introductory texts in all languages is their lack of attention to the tenets of good programming style. As a result, some fairly undisciplined programming habits are being taught to students. Kernighan and Plauger, in their *Elements of Programming Style* (McGraw-Hill, 1974), literally shredded scores of examples from FORTRAN and PL/I texts, and could find but two authors with whom they were reasonably satisfied. They have promised to do the same with COBOL texts, and there the shredding job should prove even easier. Finkenaur's text and its examples, however, will stand up well to critical examination from most real programmers. Students are admonished repeatedly that their programs must be written in a style that makes them easily understood and contributes to the ease of their later, inevitable modification. The text's programs demonstrate by example how this is accomplished. The disciplined programming style espoused by this text will leave students well equipped to graduate into the realm of structured programming and the other advanced topics covered in the field's more rigorous literature. It is, for example, completely consistent in spirit with the stylistic approach of the more advanced COBOL text in our series, *High Level COBOL Programming*, making *COBOL For Students* a perfectly suitable introduction for students who might later use that book.

The most serious failing of most introductory texts, however, is the author's " inability to put [himself] in the readers' shoes and write for the average beginner. Too many books seem to have been written with the top student in mind, by authors who either don't realize that most readers are starting at zero, or who seem to assume that the reader is as smart as the writer.*"" Programming is a subject whose full depth has never yet been explored. In writing an introduction to such a deep subject, the author must have an exquisite sense of when to stop exploring and when to start explaining. He must resist the temptation to write a knowing side remark that will impress his colleagues on the tenure board, but will befuddle hundreds of students. He must know when a simplified discussion teaches better than the full gory details, and when saying nothing is better than saying anything at all. Finkenaur, for example, in describing each COBOL program component, wisely chooses to describe it only in its most commonly used form and avoids obscuring its central purpose and usefulness with long lists of seldom used options and seldom violated restrictions.

The level of *COBOL for Students* is right for its audience—beginning students. Some of the programs won't achieve high marks for sophistication, yet the truly sophisticated reader will appreciate that their simplicity is the conscious result of a dedication to effective communication.

It's not enough, unfortunately, to be *dedicated* to effective communication. If that were all there was to it, we'd have sixty wonderful versions of "Introduction to COBOL"—fifty-nine, at least. To write an effective text, one must be able to *write*. Many of the introductory COBOL texts would make excellent casebooks for a freshman English class—providing an abundance of material to be rewritten into effective language. How can one teach programming style when one is unable to write English with any style at all? *COBOL for Students* convinces any skeptic that good writing and good programming are not separate subjects.

Another common failing of introductory texts is in the examples. Publishers commonly boast of the *number* of examples in a text, as if to substitute for the missing *quality*. The experienced teacher who studies Finkenaur's examples will see that each one has a purpose that is specific, significant, and unique. Taken together, the examples cover the subject— but don't bury it.

How does an author arrive at such an ideal set of examples—both for the text and the problem sets? In practice, there can be but one way: through attempting to teach, failing to teach, developing examples to remedy the failure, and testing the examples in actual teaching. Behind each of Finkenaur's examples, there is a former student somewhere who didn't understand something—and raised a hand about it. For a book developed in this humble and interactive manner, what title could be more appropriate than *COBOL for Students*?

The teacher who adopts *COBOL for Students* will find its use full of small pleasures. For one thing, the programs will work in most installations, for they have been tested by machines and by many pairs of eyes. They avoid system-dependent tricks in favor of straightforward style that will work well in almost any sensible installation, and which will prepare a student properly for later courses in programming. And, for those students who will take no other programming course, *COBOL for Students* will not give the common impression that programming is a game for magicians or frustrated Tom Swift's born seventy years too late.

* *Note:* The quoted material is from Stephen B. Gray's article "34 Books on BASIC" in the March–April 1975 issue of *Creative Computing* magazine.

Because of the excellent examples and sensible approach, *COBOL for Students* will encourage students to raise questions of significance, not bit-picking puzzles. What a pleasure for a teacher not to have to apologize for nonsense in a text, and to be able to concentrate on imparting the *wisdom* that an excellent text can suggest, but only an excellent teacher can provide. The problems, for instance, suggest many directions that can be treated more expansively, according to the personal taste, style, and educational philosophy of the instructor.

Some teachers may be momentarily puzzled that *COBOL for Students* does not "cover" all of COBOL—indeed, only about half of the language "features" are presented. Few good instructors (but, unfortunately, the majority of textbook writers) think that complete "coverage" is an important educational objective for an introductory course. Most teachers will be jubilant to discover a text that doesn't submerge students in a bath of advanced terms, technical jargon, and grammatical details—before they've even learned to dog-paddle. No reasonable person believes that a raw student becomes a COBOL programmer in three months or three credits.

COBOL for Students is the proper *size* for a first course. It doesn't intimidate the student with its thickness; it doesn't flood the brain with next semester's material; yet it never gives the impression that you close the subject when you close its covers. It encourages good students to take the next course, but doesn't charge the one-term student for a two-term text—either financially or intellectually.

I hope, however, that someday I will be writing a Foreword to a second Finkenaur text—perhaps, in the Hollywood tradition, entitled *COBOL for Students II*. The material is there, evolving with the full interaction of Bob's students. What we await now is a response from the readers and teachers, telling us that they agree with our assessment of this student-oriented approach—or, if they disagree, giving suggestions for future editions and successors.

Gerald M. Weinberg
Swiss National Holiday, 1976

Preface

This book was written by a person who is a teacher first and a programmer second. It reflects an accumulation of eight years' experience in teaching computer programming to students of every conceivable background and interest. My pupils have represented the full range of the academic spectrum: elective students and reluctant students; bright students and slow students; easy-going liberal artists and regimented military academy cadets; men and women; every known American minority; young full-time day students and adult part-time evening students; and every imaginable major: computer science, engineering, math, business, history, music, astronomy, geology, nursing, physical education, psychology, library science, English, actuarial science, and military science.

Thanks to my students, I have never been allowed to forget that programming does *not* come easily to everyone. What is responsible for the difficulty many students experience in mastering the art of programming a computer?

To be sure, there is the question of "knack." Each of us is stronger in certain talents than in others. You probably know someone who is a good athlete, and someone else who is completely devoid of hand-to-eye coordination and couldn't be taught to play any sport well no matter how many lessons were taken. Yet the latter might be a respectable musician, while the former may not have any musical talents at all, and no amount of music lessons could ever change that. Likewise, there are some who find themselves lacking in the "knack" of organizing their thoughts in the manner necessary to master computer programming with ease, and nothing short of their own superhuman effort will ever make programmers of them.

Another source of difficulty is the manner in which the material is presented. All too often, the teacher of computer programming or the author of programming textbooks is a programmer first and a teacher second (if that). He (or she) is someone to whom the subject *did* come easily and is therefore lacking in the ability to understand why it shouldn't be easy for all. His presentation of the material tends to be overly detailed and rigorous, too rapid, lacking in sufficient examples, and "pitched" to a small group of students who've already had programming experience (though perhaps in another language) and who in the classroom are recognized by their heads nodding in agreement with the instructor, their "Oh, how *right* you are!" smiles, and the types of questions they ask.

There is nothing this book can do to improve your "knack" for computer programming. It is my belief, however, that the book represents a big step forward in improving the manner in which the material is presented.

First, the book is written based on the assumption that you have never even *seen* a computer before. (I may assume that you already know how to *spell* "computer," but not much more.) You will never hear me say, "It is therefore intuitively obvious that . . ." or any other such expression. My students have taught me well the locations of potential points of confusion, and you will see me pausing at each of those troublesome spots to help you through.

My approach to teaching you COBOL programming is what I call a *functional approach.* Having given you the bare skeletal bones of a COBOL program, I'll suggest, one at a time, some additional functions you might want the computer to perform, and having established the motivation for each new function, I'll teach you about only those additional COBOL elements necessary to achieve that additional function. By the time I'm finished, you'll have command of a full set of COBOL programming elements and be able to have the computer produce the fanciest pages of printed results, perform a wide range of calculations, and store, update, and retrieve "tons" of information (or data) on magnetic tape.

Along the road to that end, however, *you* must play *your* part in the learning process. You *must* work the dozen or so Exercises that are presented at the end of each chapter. You *must* study the Example Program that is provided at the end of each chapter starting with Chapter 7. And most important of all, you must work the Student's Program located immediately after each Example Program.

For, like learning to read, learning computer programming is very much a building block process. In reading you must learn your alphabet before you can read words, you must be able to read words before you can read stories. Exactly the same principle applies to the study of computer programming. If one of the blocks is missing, none of the rest will follow. You must assure yourself at the end of each chapter that you have mastered the complete block which that chapter was supposed to provide before you even glance at the next chapter. Only by honestly testing yourself at the end of each chapter with the Exercises, the Example Program, and the Student's Program will you have that assurance.

Before closing, I would like to express appreciation to some people who provided necessary stepping stones along the way to the completion of this book: First comes Colonel Gilbert Kirby, a Professor on the faculty of the U. S. Military Academy at West Point, whose direct order to me (a member of his department at the time; in 1970 to "learn COBOL and get a course going in it!" was responsible for my having learned the language in the first place. Next comes my boss at Northeastern University, Professor Wilfred Rule, who, by inviting me to serve as co-author of his (now our) successful text, *FORTRAN IV Programming,* provided some invaluable experience and inspiration. Both served as catalysts out of which sprang the idea to begin this book. Next are my many students whose repeated prodding ("How's the book going?") did more to *keep* the book going than they can ever imagine. Finally come my wife, Carol, and my teen age son, Bob, who suffered with me through the drudgery of proofreading the final copy.

Robert G. Finkenaur Boston, 1977

1 An Introduction to Digital Computers

1.1 Computers and Their Languages

In this day and age, there is little need to tell students what a computer is or what it does. The word *computer* has become as familiar a part of their household vocabulary as *refrigerator*. Daily we receive through the mail credit card bills, checking account statements, grade reports, etc., all bearing the distinctive "handwriting" of a computer. We know that thousands of others are receiving similar bills and statements, and from that comes our almost intuitive while basically correct understanding of what a computer does—it performs at lightning speed overwhelming numbers of repetitive calculations that at one time would have required countless bookkeepers many hours to perform.

Hand in hand with the word *computer* comes the term *computer programmer*. Most of us have a fairly valid impression of what a computer programmer does. He (or just as often, she) is the person who puts the computer through its paces. He tells it what calculations to make and what to do with the answers to those calculations.

Most people who read this book are doing so because they have decided they would like to become, even if only to a limited degree, computer programmers. In order to program a computer, you must be able to "speak" to it in a language it can understand. There are many languages available for use with the computer, but two are predominant: COBOL and FORTRAN. The latter (whose name is derived from the words "FORmula TRANslation") is best suited for use in science and engineering applications.

This text deals with COBOL, the "COmmon Business Oriented Language," a language designed for use in business applications. COBOL is in fact *the* most widely used language in the computer world today. This is so, because the vast majority of computer users are business firms using the computer to handle basically (though massive) bookkeeping tasks, and COBOL is the best language available for that purpose. A glance through the data processing want ads in any metropolitan newspaper will attest to the popularity of the language and the high level of demand for people who can write programs in it.

Before we begin delving into the details of COBOL programming, let's take an elementary look at how digital computers work. Though there are many who prefer to treat the computer as a "black box," that is, with an "I don't care *how* it does it, as long as it keeps doing it" attitude; this is seldom the best approach for any person who is serious about learning programming. Although a person unfamiliar with the inner workings of a car can still drive it, he can operate it more efficiently and realize better performance if he has some elementary understanding of what actually is happening under the hood. The same can be said of computer programmers.

Read this chapter to gain a general understanding only. It is intended to provide you with a basic feel for what goes on "under the hood" of a computer. It will prepare you to learn the art of computer programming more easily, and result in your becoming a more effective programmer.

1.2   The Digital Computer

The desk top adding machine, so familiar to everyone, is in fact almost a digital computer. Its big shortcoming, however, is that it "can't remember what to do next." It can compute the answer to any problem only as long as you its human operator are on hand to feed it each number and each operation (add, subtract, etc.) one by one and in the proper sequence. Therein lies the key difference between a digital computer and a desk top adding machine: the computer *can* remember "what to do next." It can be given a whole list of operations (or instructions) and a whole list of numbers and remember them all. The operator then simply "pushes the GO button," and the computer takes off entirely on its own, obeying the instructions it has been given beforehand, and solving the whole problem often in less time than it took you to read this sentence.

And that brings us to a second difference between the adding machine and the computer—its extreme speed. An adding machine performs its calculations through a complex set of internal, interconnected gears. The speed with which it performs those calculations is dependent upon the rotational speed of those gears. Within a computer, the components involved in calculations are all electronic circuits, so they are performed at the speed of electricity—the speed of light.

Although the battery-powered, pocket calculators of today do rival the computational speed of digital computers, they still require the presence of the human operator to feed each numerical value and each instruction as it is needed in the course of solving a problem.

It is this list of instructions I keep referring to that is called the program. The scheme which truly sets the computer apart, whereby all instructions are given to the computer and stored in its memory before it begins solving the problem, is therefore called the Stored Program Concept.

1.3   The Organization of the Basic Digital Computer

If I were about to explain to you how an automobile's engine worked, I would use the simplest, most straightforward engine as the basis of my explanation. To make the discussion less difficult to digest, I would omit

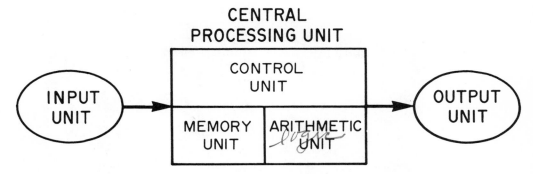

FIGURE 1.1   Organization of a Basic Digital Computer

speaking of such things as fuel injection systems, double-barreled carburetors, emission control systems, and other similarly complicated devices which are so often a part of the most up-to-date engines. Likewise, as I now approach an explanation of how computers are organized and how they function, I will choose the basic or "first generation" digital computer to be the basis of my explanation. Do not fear that you will be getting an inaccurate description. Current generation digital computers have all evolved from the basic digital computer, still retain their principles of operation, and will give the appearance to you of being organized as described here. Only after you have mastered the contents of this book will it be necessary for you to concern yourself with the features built into modern computers which were not available in the simplified version we will be discussing.

As seen in Figure 1.1, the computer is organized into three major units: the input unit, the central processing unit (or "CPU" as the folks down at the computer center call it), and the output unit.

The input unit is the device through which we put information into the computer. The output unit is the device through which the computer puts out for human use the answer to the problem it has solved for us. You may hear the term *peripheral devices,* or simply *peripherals,* being used to lump together the input and output devices as well as any other devices that are connected to but not included in the CPU.

The CPU is further subdivided into three important units: the control unit, the arithmetic unit, and the memory unit.

The arithmetic unit (pronounced a-rith-me'-tic rather than a-rith'-me-tic in computer circles) is the portion of the CPU where all arithmetic operations—adding, subtracting, multiplying, dividing—are performed. If it occurs to you to wonder why the arithmetic unit cannot perform higher-order mathematics such as raising numbers to various powers, or taking square roots or integrating, the answer is that it can, but not directly. Such higher-order operations are accomplished by a clever combination of the four basic operations listed.

The arithmetic unit also provides the computer with the ability to make certain logic decisions such as whether one number is larger than or equal to another, or whether a single number is negative, positive, or zero.

FIGURE 1.2   The Central Processing Unit

Courtesy of Control Data Corp.

You will find such decision-making ability extremely valuable later when you are faced with the necessity to write a program for the computer in which selected instructions are to be omitted under certain numerical circumstances. (Take an example: Under normal circumstances the amount of a check is subtracted from the balance in your checking account. In the hopefully rare instance where the amount of a check is larger than the balance in your account, it should *not* be subtracted from the balance, but rather "bounced" by the bank.) We count as the digital computer's three most valuable talents its Stored Program Concept, its great speed, and this ability provided by the arithmetic unit to make basic logic decisions.

The memory unit is where the computer stores all information it needs to solve the problem it is working on. We will discuss this unit in greater detail in Section 1.6.

The control unit is the boss of the whole operation. Following the instructions it received and stored prior to the operator's "pushing the GO button," it controls the movement of information from the input unit to memory, from memory to the arithmetic unit, from the arithmetic unit back to memory, and from memory to the output unit. Whenever it moves information (numbers) to the arithmetic unit, it tells the arithmetic unit which operation to perform on them (add them or subtract them or whatever), and then it moves the result of the operation, the answer, back to the memory unit.

1.4 The Input Unit

All information that must be provided to the computer falls under one of two categories: instructions or data. *Instructions* are computer deciferable statements which tell the computer which operations to perform in solving the problem and in what order to perform them. *Data* is the word used to describe the actual numbers which must be operated upon in arriving at the solution. (An instruction in a payroll problem might have this appearance: MULTIPLY HOURS-WORKED BY PAY-RATE GIVING GROSS-PAY. That instruction tells the computer *how* to solve for a person's gross pay, but it gives no information about exactly how many hours any one employee worked nor about anyone's particular rate of pay. When later we give the computer some actual numbers to work with—for example, 40.0 and 5.25 as the hours and pay rate of some individual employee—the computer will know what to do with them in order to calculate that employee's gross pay. 40.0 and 5.25 are said to be the data that apply to that employee.)

Several types of devices are available for inputting the necessary information into the computer. The card reader is the most commonly used input device. In a typical digital computer program, the programmer puts his instructions and data on punched cards, or "IBM cards" as they are often called.[1] His cards, assembled into a deck, are fed through a card reader in order to convey their contents to the computer. The card reader passes the punched cards between a light source and some precisely positioned electric eyes and thereby determines the positions of the holes in them and hence the exact contents of each.

Another popular input medium is magnetic tape. The use of magnetic tape will be described in great detail in chapters 14 and 15. Briefly, however, it is the same material as is used in home tape recorders: a very long thin strip of plastic-based tape covered with a thin coat of brown or black iron oxide and stored on large reels. In computer jargon the device itself is called a tape drive rather than a tape recorder. Once information has been recorded on a tape in the form of properly placed magnetic spots, the tape can be mounted on a tape drive, and the drive is ready to perform as an input unit to the CPU.

Magnetic discs are also used as an input medium. They resemble a group of large phonograph records stacked one above another as on an automatic record changer except that there is roughly an inch of space between each disc, and they are all rotating, not just the bottom one. The discs are covered with the same iron oxide that is used on magnetic tape rather than the grooves of a record, and like on tape, information is recorded in the form of properly positioned magnetic spots. Either side of any disc in the

---

[1] Many other companies besides IBM manufacture computer cards. Just as Pepsi Cola objects to its product being called "Coke," the Coca-Cola nickname, so do other manufacturers of computer cards object to their products being referred to as "IBM cards."

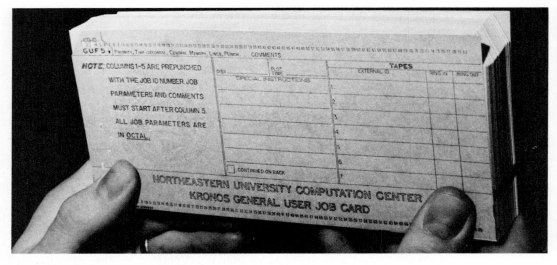

FIGURE 1.3   A Program Deck

stack is available for reading at any time, because each side is equipped with a moveable "read head" reminiscent of the tone arm on a record player.

The magnetic drum is similar in many ways to magnetic disc, except of course that it is shaped like a drum. It also is in continuous rotation. It is equipped with a series of stationary read heads, each aimed at a specific track of information on the magnetic surface of the drum.

These four are the most widely used of a long list of input devices in use today.

1.5   The Output Unit

As is the case with input, there are many different devices which may serve as output units for the computer. Basically, it is the purpose of the output unit to provide a medium upon which the answers to a problem can be recorded, and usually in such a way that they are understandable to the human programmer.

The layman very often imagines all computers writing their answers on electric typewriters. Although electric typewriters are used by computers to print brief, coded technical messages to the computer operator, they are far too slow to be used for general program output. Many student programs can be completely run in the space of time it takes to print one character on an electric typewriter.

For that reason high speed line printers have been developed to handle printed output. A line printer will print a whole line of approximately 130 characters in less time than it takes to typewrite one character. It will fill a 60 line page of computer output paper with answers in half the time it takes to type one line of output on standard typing paper. The line

FIGURE 1.4   The Card Reader

printer will be the output device most commonly used by student programmers. Not equipped with a keyboard, it is not useable as an input
device, although the typewriter is.

A moment of thought should lead even the most inexperienced student
to conclude that the card reader is not suitable for an output device. There
does exist a device, the card punch, which will punch answers on computer
cards. Although faster than an electric typewriter, it is many times slower
than any other output device discussed here, so it is used only when absolutely necessary.

Magnetic tapes, discs, and drums mentioned earlier as possible input
mediums are also useful for the recording of output. They are commonly
used in applications in which the answers to a program being run now are
not needed to be read by any person, but rather are needed for use as input to
another program which will be run later. They are listed in order of increasing speed, but also in order of increasing cost.

1.6   The Memory Unit

The memory unit is where the computer stores instructions and data
brought in from the input unit. It is here that any intermediate answers are

FIGURE 1.5   The High Speed Line Printer

stored pending their use in later final computations. And it is here that the final output is stored just prior to being sent by the control unit to the output unit for printing.

   The memory unit is organized into thousands of elements known as memory locations. It serves as a useful learning device if you will think of each of these memory locations as a post office box, each assigned to one of the data-names in your program, each being equipped with a label and capable of storing one data value. (What is a data-name? Recall that in Section 1.4 I showed you a typical instruction out of a COBOL program: MULTIPLY HOURS-WORKED BY PAY-RATE GIVING GROSS-PAY. In that example we had three data-names, HOURS-WORKED, PAY-RATE and GROSS-PAY.)

   Thus, the instruction

   MOVE 52.5 TO HOURS-WORKED.

in fact says, "Store the value 52.5 in the memory location labelled HOURS-WORKED." The instruction

   SUBTRACT 40.0 FROM HOURS-WORKED GIVING OVERTIME.

says, "Subtract the value 40.0 from the value stored in memory location HOURS-WORKED and store the result in the memory location labelled

FIGURE 1.6   The Programmer Views His Results

OVERTIME.'' Adopting the practice of portraying each memory location as a labelled box, the locations assigned to data-names HOURS-WORKED and OVERTIME would now look like this:

HOURS- WORKED	OVERTIME
52.5	12.5

Consider the effect on the two locations of this instruction:

MOVE 40.0 TO HOURS-WORKED.

Result:

HOURS-WORKED	OVERTIME
40.0	12.5

Note that by storing a new value in location HOURS-WORKED, the former value has been destroyed. This demonstrates the principle of *Destructive Write*. That is, if you store (or write) something into a memory location, whatever was stored there previously will be destroyed and lost.

Now let's make our employee very happy by doing something no employer would ever do, so that I can make a point. Suppose we were to instruct the computer to

MOVE HOURS-WORKED TO OVERTIME.

Result:

HOURS-WORKED	OVERTIME
40.0	40.0

The instruction said, "Store the contents of location HOURS-WORKED in location OVERTIME." What happened to location OVERTIME is another example of a destructive write operation. Note, however, that the contents of location HOURS-WORKED remained unchanged. This was an example of the principle of *Nondestructive Read*. The computer was instructed to do nothing more than to determine or look at (or read) the contents of location HOURS-WORKED, and to move whatever value it found there to location OVERTIME. Since it only "looked at" location HOURS-WORKED, no harm was done to its contents.

The manner in which information is stored in each of these locations will be discussed in the next section. For now it will suffice to say that such storage is accomplished magnetically. A good analogy to the two principles just mentioned can be made by considering the familiar home tape recorder. Music is stored on the recording tape by magnetic impressions made in the iron oxide surface. When the tape is played (or read), the music is heard with no harm done to the recording. No matter how many times the tape is played, the same music will be heard. This is analogous to a nondestructive read operation. If, however, either by mistake or intention, new material is recorded (or written) on a previously recorded tape, the former recording will be erased and lost, and the new material will be recorded in its place. This is analogous to a destructive write operation.

A desk top calculator has one memory location, and it is mechanical in nature. The speed with which we communicate with the location is a factor of the rotational speed of the calculator's moving parts. The memory unit in a computer is of course an electronic device, enabling communication with it as a factor of the speed of light. The world of electronics is rich with relatively simple bi-stable devices. A bi-stable device is one which can take on one of two different states with relative ease: a light bulb is on or off; a switch is closed or open; an iron bar is either magnetized or it is not magnetized. By taking advantage of a number system which uses only two digits, 0 and 1, called the binary system, bi-stable devices are able to be used to store numerical values. The device used is a small donut-shaped iron core. The iron core can be magnetized either clockwise or counterclockwise.

MAGNETIZATION	VALUE REPRESENTED
CW	0
CCW	1

The next section will describe how the binary number system is used to represent any value needed.

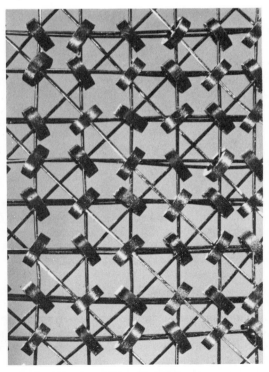

FIGURE 1.7   Magnetic Cores, Greatly Enlarged

Courtesy of Honeywell

1.7 Binary Representation of Data-Values

From the first day of elementary school, the student is taught, drilled, and tested using a number system based on the number 10 and employing ten digits, 0 through 9. It is the decimal system. So ingrained is the decimal system, that it never once occurs to the student to wonder, "Why ten? Why not eight or three or two?"

The object of this section is to demonstrate that the binary system, with its base of two and its two digits, 0 and 1, is equally as good a system for representing numerical quantities as the old familiar decimal system.

All number systems depend on a scheme of positional notation to associate values with what would otherwise be a meaningless string of disconnected digits. When in the decimal system the number 6437 is written, we immediately correctly interpret it as six thousand, four hundred, thirty-seven, because through years of drilling, it now comes as second nature to recognize the 6 as being in the thousands' position, the 4 in the hundreds' position, the 3 in the tens' position, and the 7 in the units' position. Expressed in mathematical symbology,

$$6437 = 6 \times 1000 + 4 \times 100 + 3 \times 10 + 7 \times 1$$

or in another form,

$$6437 = 6 \times 10^3 + 4 \times 10^2 + 3 \times 10^1 + 7 \times 10^0$$

The same scheme of positional notation is used in interpreting numbers in any number system. Consider the octal system with its base of eight and its eight digits, 0 through 7. The octal number 347 is translated into its equivalent decimal value 231, as follows:

$$
\begin{aligned}
\text{Octal } 347 &= 3 \times 8^2 + 4 \times 8^1 + 7 \times 8^0 \\
&= 3 \times 64 + 4 \times 8 + 7 \times 1 \\
&= 192 + 32 + 7 \\
&= \text{Decimal } 231
\end{aligned}
$$

The binary system follows the same pattern. The decimal value 19, is represented in the binary system as 10011, as shown here.

$$
\begin{aligned}
\text{Binary } 10011 &= 1 \times 2^4 + 0 \times 2^3 + 0 \times 2^2 + 1 \times 2^1 + 1 \times 2^0 \\
&= 16 + 0 + 0 + 2 + 1 \\
&= \text{Decimal } 19
\end{aligned}
$$

As mentioned earlier, using the binary system for representing values in the computer memory is what makes it possible to employ simple bistable iron cores in its design. Figure 1.9 demonstrates the configuration of the five cores necessary to represent the value 19.

Even though storage of all information is restricted to a form using the numeric digits, 0 and 1, this does not mean that the computer is unable to store alphabetic information. The computer can also store letters as well as special characters such as the period, comma, dollar sign, etc., but it does

SYSTEM	DECIMAL	OCTAL	BINARY
BASE	10	8	2
DIGITS	0–9	0–7	0–1
Zero	0000	0000	0000
One	0001	0001	0001
Two	0002	0002	0010
Three	0003	0003	0011
Four	0004	0004	0100
Five	0005	0005	0101
Six	0006	0006	0110
Seven	0007	0007	0111
Eight	0008	0010	1000
Nine	0009	0011	1001
Ten	0010	0012	1010
Eleven	0011	0013	1011
Twelve	0012	0014	1100

FIGURE 1.8   Three Number Systems Compared

this by representing all such non-numeric characters numerically in a two digit coded form. For example, an A can be represented by a 21, a B by 22, etc.

1.8   COBOL vs. Machine Language

In the discussion of the design of the memory unit, the point was made that all information stored in memory must be in binary form. Although

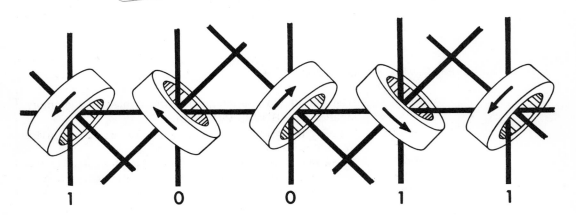

Arrows represent direction of magnetism

FIGURE 1.9   The Value 19 as Stored in Core Memory

the only example given demonstrated the storage of data-values, that is not the only sort of information which must be stored in memory. As I mentioned earlier, there are two basic types of information the computer must be provided by the programmer: instructions and data. Data is often (although not always) in numeric form; however, instructions written in the COBOL programming language are not.

When the term *Stored Program Concept* was introduced in Section 1.2, another important point was made: the entire program—all instructions to be followed in solving the problem—must be stored in the computer's memory before the computer is prepared to execute those instructions and compute the problem's answer(s). The conclusion you should draw is that not only the data values but also the instructions of a program must be transformed into binary form before anything else may be accomplished.

When the student writes his first COBOL program it will contain instruction statements of this form:

MULTIPLY HOURS-WORKED BY PAY-RATE GIVING GROSS-PAY.

Obviously, this is not in binary form. It must be in binary form before it can be stored in the computer's memory, so conversion is accomplished by means of two programs, the compiler program (or compiler) and the assembly program (or assembler).

The compiler is a program which processes a COBOL program and produces from it a version of the program in what is known as *assembly language*. A significant difference between the COBOL and assembly language versions of each instruction, aside from their being in different languages, is that each COBOL instruction results in several assembly language instructions. A single COBOL instruction implies that a whole series of the computer's basic operations must be done. A single assembly language instruction orders a single basic operation to be performed.

Take, for example, the COBOL instruction above. Assuming that HOURS-WORKED had been assigned to memory location number 50, PAY-RATE to location number 53, and GROSS-PAY to location number 57, that instruction would wind up as these three statements in assembly language:

STATEMENT[2]	MEANING
TFA 050	TransFer to the Arithmetic unit the contents of memory location 050 (HOURS-WORKED).
MPY 053	MultiPlY the contents of memory location 053 (PAY-RATE) by what is now in the arithmetic unit.
STA 057	STore the results of the previous operation, now in the Arithmetic unit, in memory location 057 (GROSS-PAY).

[2] There exist as many different versions of assembly languages as there are different models of computers. Every computer model has its own particular version. These statements are intended only as examples of the general form of most assembly language statements.

The program in assembly language is then translated by the assembler into machine language. In machine language each statement appears as a string of binary digits, nearly unintelligible to the human programmer. For example:

010111000101011

might very well be the machine language version of the MPY 053 assembly language instruction, with the first 6 binary digits understood by the computer to represent the command to Multi<u>PlY</u>, and the remaining digits the binary equivalent of the memory location number 053.

By comparison to the task which the compiler accomplishes, that of breaking each of the many COBOL instructions in a program into its several composite assembly language instructions, the assembler performs a relatively trivial task. It simply translates on a one-for-one basis each assembly language instruction into corresponding machine language form.

You can now add two more terms to your expanding vocabulary: *source program* and *object program*. A computer program written in a higher level language such as COBOL is referred to as the source program. In its machine language form, it is referred to as the object program. In view of the much larger role played by the compiler in transforming the source program into the object program, the entire process of compiling and assembling is often lumped together under the single term, *compilation*.

All computer programming languages which require compilation before being useable by the computer are referred to as Compiler Languages. COBOL, the language presented by this book, is by no means the only Compiler Language. FORTRAN is another, but there are many more, each designed with some specific application in mind.

1.9   Hardware vs. Software

A brief word about these two frequently used terms. The computer itself is physically comprised of nuts, bolts, cabinets, wires, resistors, transistors, cores, etc. Just as one might suspect, these items are referred to as its hardware. The term has more significance than that, however.

The arithmetic unit is able to obey an add instruction because there are electric circuits physically wired into it which enable it to add. It is said, therefore, that the computer's ability to add is "a part of its hardware." All of the computer's basic operations, its innate capabilities, are provided through its hardware. For every machine language instruction which the computer is able to obey, there is hardware that gives it that ability.

Each computer comes equipped with prerecorded programs which give it additional capabilities above those provided by its hardware. Such capabilities include its ability to raise to powers, to take sines and cosines, to find roots, to take logarithms, and to compile source programs into object programs, naming just a few. These prerecorded programs are what is referred to by the term software.

EXERCISES

Answers to all exercises in this chapter are given in Appendix A.

1.1 Why must there be special languages for computers?

1.2 What is the term that describes the computer's ability to accept and remember all instructions involved in the solution of a problem, and not just one at a time?

1.3 What are the three major units of the digital computer?

1.4 Which of the three major units are called "peripherals"?

1.5 What is the input unit most commonly used in computer programming?

1.6 How does the computer know what is typed on an IBM card?
   a. It reads the printed information along the top edge of the card.
   b. It reads the holes punched in the card.

1.7 What are the three parts of the CPU?

1.8 The hardware of the arithmetic unit gives it the capability of performing four basic arithmetic operations. What are they?

1.9 What types of information are stored in the memory unit?

1.10 When the arithmetic unit has completed an arithmetic operation involving two numbers, where does the control unit send the result?
   a. Directly to the output unit for printing.
   b. Back to the memory unit for storage.

1.11 The following is a list of peripheral devices. Some are suitable for use only as input units, some only as output units, and some are suitable for either. In the blank following each, indicate its suitability by placing an I (for input-only devices), an O (for output-only devices), or an I/O (for devices that can serve in either capacity).

		I or O or I/O
a.	Electric typewriter	_____
b.	Card reader	_____
c.	Card punch	_____
d.	Line printer	_____
e.	Magnetic tape	_____
f.	Magnetic disc	_____
g.	Magnetic drum	_____
h.	Teletypewriter	_____

1.12 Insert the words "data-name" or "data-value" in the following blanks:
   a. A _____ is used to label a memory location.
   b. A _____ is stored in a memory location.
   c. A _____, once assigned to a memory location, is never changed during the course of processing a program.
   d. A _____, once stored in a memory location, is likely to be changed many times during the course of processing a program.
   e. 6325.4 is a good example of a _____.
   f. COST-OF-CAR is a good example of a _____.

1.13   On the left are shown two memory locations in their initial conditions. On the right are shown the same two memory locations after the computer has executed the instruction: MOVE THIS-STUDENTS-GRADE TO BEST-GRADE-SO-FAR.

THIS-STUDENTS-GRADE	BEST-GRADE-SO-FAR	THIS-STUDENTS-GRADE	BEST-GRADE-SO-FAR
95	89	95	95

Fill in the blanks with the words "destructive write" or "nondestructive read":

   a.   What happened to memory location THIS-STUDENTS-GRADE is an example of a _____ operation.

   b.   What happened to memory location BEST-GRADE-SO-FAR is an example of a _____ operation.

1.14   Express the value twenty-one in the binary number system.

1.15   Translate the binary number 11010 into a decimal number.

1.16   Why did the digital computer designers' decision to use magnetic cores in the memory unit dictate our use of the binary number system within the computer?

1.17   What are the basic differences between a program in the COBOL language and the same program in machine language?

1.18   A COBOL program must be processed by the compiler (the compiler program). Why?

1.19   COBOL is a compiler language. What does that mean?

1.20   Are there any other compiler languages? If so, name one.

1.21   Define these terms:

   a.   Source program

   b.   Object program

2 Programming: A General Description

2.1   Purpose

In Chapter 1 I described some of the internal design and organization of a digital computer. To complete this introductory phase of the book, Chapter 2 will take a quick look at a sample computer program to show what a complete program looks like, how it is presented to the computer, and how the computer processes the program. This chapter should be read for general understanding only, since all of the material presented here will be formally discussed in later chapters.

Specifically, what I want to do in this chapter is to

1. Reinforce your understanding of the terms *compilation* and *execution;*
2. Present an introductory description of the components of a complete COBOL program; and
3. Give you a basic understanding of the way a computer reacts to each of the program components.

2.2   Compilation vs. Execution of a COBOL Program

A tourist receiving directions from a policeman is a good analogy to the computer receiving instructions from a programmer. The policeman might say something like this: "Walk to the end of this block. Turn right. Walk another two blocks, and the bus station will be directly in front of you."

He has given a complete set of instructions to the tourist. What did the tourist do as he received each instruction? Did he obey it before accepting another instruction? Certainly not. He memorized each one as it was given to him, and only after he had all of the policeman's instructions stored in his memory did he follow (execute) them.

Likewise, the computer receives all the instructions it is to follow and "memorizes" them (stores them in its memory unit) before any are obeyed.

One last time, let me re-emphasize the importance of your firmly grasping this concept of computer functioning:

> *THE STORED PROGRAM CONCEPT*
> All instructions of a program are stored in the
> computer's memory before any of them
> are executed (obeyed).

When a program is written, punched onto IBM cards, and assembled into a program deck, it has the appearance of a single deck of cards. In fact, a program deck is divided into two parts: the instruction deck and the data deck. As described in Chapter 1, the instruction deck will contain all instructions to be followed in the solution of the problem (all written in terms of data names), while the data deck will contain the numbers of data values that are to be used in the computations. When the program deck is fed into the computer through the card reader, the first action taken by the computer is to cause the reading of the contents of the instruction deck. At the same time as it is reading the instruction deck, it is compiling it—that is, translating the COBOL instructions into machine language and storing them in the memory unit. The end of the instruction deck is marked by a card containing the phrase END PROGRAM.[1] When the END PROGRAM card is found, then and only then does the computer cease compilation and commence execution of the program.

When are the data cards (the cards in the data deck) read? The programmer will have placed instructions in his instruction deck that tell the computer when it is to go out and fetch the next set of specific data values. Whenever the computer obeys one of these instructions (called READ instructions) it knows that it is to get those data values by reading the next data card in the deck.

THE
PROGRAM
DECK

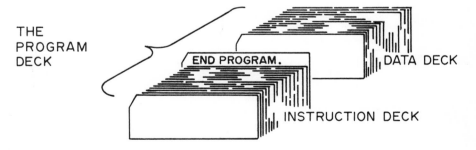

END PROGRAM.   DATA DECK

INSTRUCTION DECK

FIGURE 2.1   The Program Deck

[1] The use of an END PROGRAM card, as such, is not universal; however, all computers *do* require that *some* special card be placed between the Instruction and Data Decks. Ask at your computer center what particular card is required by your computer.

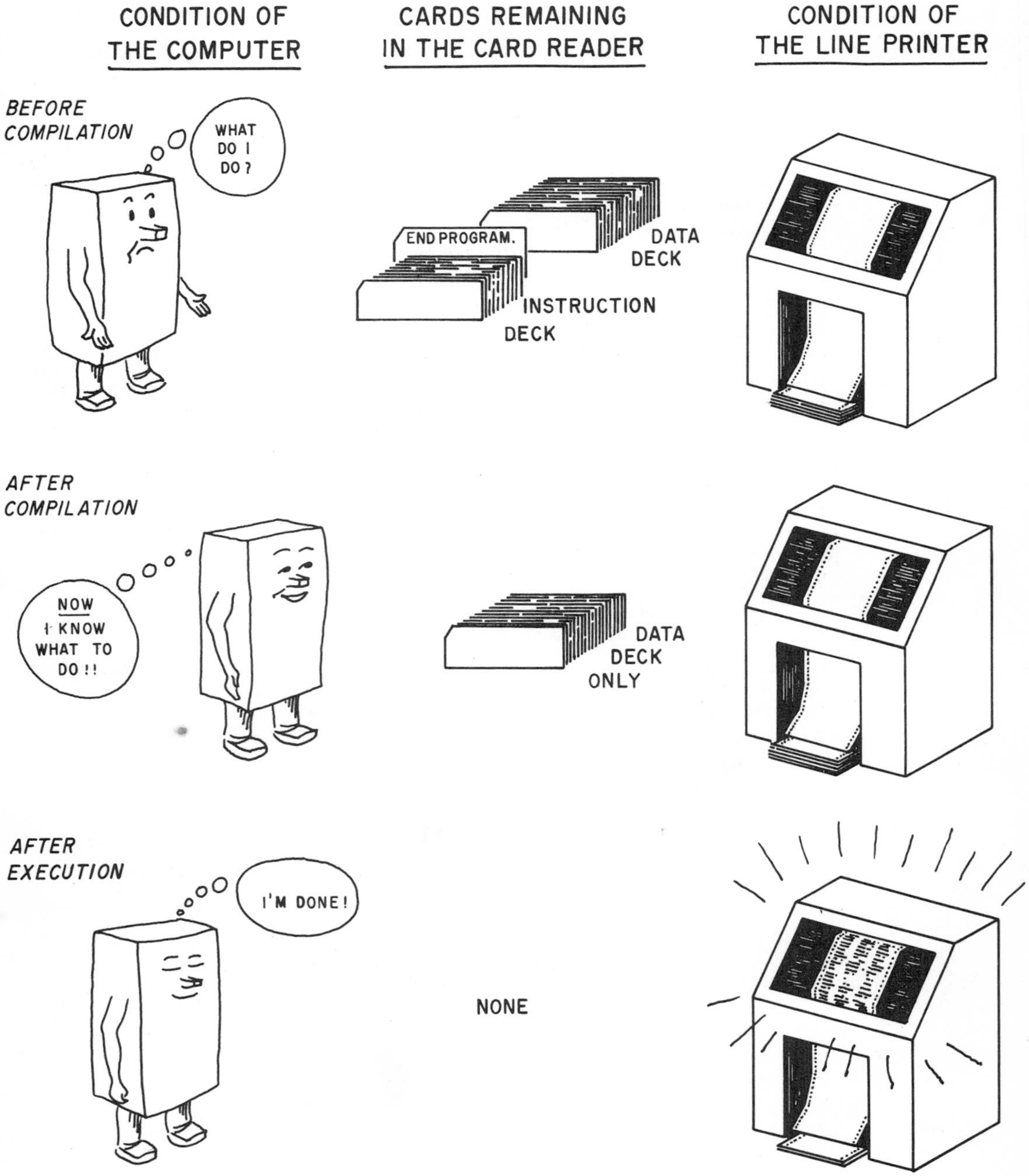

CONDITION OF THE COMPUTER	CARDS REMAINING IN THE CARD READER	CONDITION OF THE LINE PRINTER

FIGURE 2.2   The Compilation and Execution Phases

Note that the instruction deck is "devoured" during compilation, while the data deck is "devoured" during execution.

From this discussion you should have picked up these points. Processing of a computer program in fact occurs in two phases: COMPILATION and EXECUTION. Compilation describes the input, translation, and storing of all the program's instructions in the computer's memory. Detection of the END PROGRAM card is the signal to the computer that it is to cease compilation and to commence execution. Execution is the process of referring to the instructions which, from the computer's view point, are no longer on the cards, but rather are now in its memory, and *obeying them.*

2.3 A Sample Program

Now let's consider what the contents of the instruction deck in a simple COBOL program might look like. Figure 2.3 illustrates a short COBOL program. It is simple enough that you should be able to follow generally what it's intended to do just by reading it.

Notice first that the program is divided into four divisions:

1. The IDENTIFICATION DIVISION.
2. The ENVIRONMENT DIVISION.
3. The DATA DIVISION.
4. The PROCEDURE DIVISION.

All four divisions *must* be present in the instruction deck of a COBOL program, and they *must* occur in that order.

```
IDENTIFICATION  DIVISION.
PROGRAM-ID.     PAY-ROLL.
AUTHOR.         R  G  FINKENAUR.
```

The IDENTIFICATION DIVISION gives information by which the program can be identified. It serves little more than an administrative purpose.

```
ENVIRONMENT  DIVISION.
CONFIGURATION  SECTION.
SOURCE-COMPUTER. HAL-2001.  pop p- / 1
OBJECT-COMPUTER. HAL-2001.
INPUT-OUTPUT  SECTION.
FILE-CONTROL.
     SELECT TIME-CARD-FILE ASSIGN TO CARD-READER.
     SELECT PAY-LISTING ASSIGN TO LINE-PRINTER.
```

In the ENVIRONMENT DIVISION we describe the environment in which the program is designed to run, which computer the program was written for and which of its peripherals (input and output devices) are needed by the program. This program was written to run on the fictitious HAL-2001. It will have two files of data: The first is the TIME-CARD-FILE,

```
IDENTIFICATION DIVISION.
PROGRAM-ID. PAY-ROLL.
AUTHOR.   R G FINKENAUR.

ENVIRONMENT DIVISION.
CONFIGURATION SECTION.
SOURCE-COMPUTER. HAL-2001.
OBJECT-COMPUTER. HAL-2001.
INPUT-OUTPUT SECTION.
FILE-CONTROL.
      SELECT TIME-CARD-FILE ASSIGN TO CARD-READER.
      SELECT PAY-LISTING ASSIGN TO LINE-PRINTER.

DATA DIVISION.
FILE SECTION.
FD  TIME-CARD-FILE; RECORD CONTAINS 80 CHARACTERS; LABEL RECORDS
      ARE OMITTED; DATA RECORD IS TIME-CARD.
01  TIME-CARD.
      02  NAME        PICTURE A(20).
      02  PAY-RATE    PICTURE 99.
      02  MON-HRS     PICTURE 99.
      02  TUE-HRS     PICTURE 99.
      02  WED-HRS     PICTURE 99.
      02  THU-HRS     PICTURE 99.
      02  FRI-HRS     PICTURE 99.
      02  FILLER      PICTURE X(48).
FD  PAY-LISTING; RECORD CONTAINS 136 CHARACTERS; LABEL RECORDS
      ARE OMITTED; DATA RECORD IS PRINTER-LINE.
01  PRINTER-LINE.
      02  FILLER      PICTURE X(5).
      02  NAME        PICTURE A(20).
      02  FILLER      PICTURE X(5).
      02  GROSS-PAY   PICTURE $999.
      02  FILLER      PICTURE X(102).
WORKING-STORAGE SECTION.
77  TOTAL-HRS        PICTURE 99.

PROCEDURE DIVISION.
START-PARAGRAPH.
      OPEN INPUT TIME-CARD-FILE, OUTPUT PAY-LISTING.
      MOVE SPACES TO PRINTER-LINE.
READ-CALCULATE-PRINT-PARAGRAPH.
      READ TIME-CARD-FILE RECORD, AT END GO TO FINAL-PARAGRAPH.
      MOVE NAME IN TIME-CARD TO NAME IN PRINTER-LINE. qualification)
      ADD MON-HRS, TUE-HRS, WED-HRS, THU-HRS, FRI-HRS
            GIVING TOTAL-HRS.
      MULTIPLY PAY-RATE BY TOTAL-HRS GIVING GROSS-PAY.
      WRITE PRINTER-LINE.
      GO TO READ-CALCULATE-PRINT-PARAGRAPH.
FINAL-PARAGRAPH.
      CLOSE TIME-CARD-FILE, PAY-LISTING.
      STOP RUN.
```

FIGURE 2.3   A Sample COBOL Program

a name chosen by the programmer to be associated with his data deck, and which the computer is told here will be found on the card reader. The second is the PAY-LISTING, a name the programmer has given to the "file" of information he will be creating, and which the computer is told here is to be located on the line printer.

But these two divisions take only about a minute for most programmers to write and require a minimum of thought. The two divisions that follow are by far the most important portion of the program.

2.4 The DATA DIVISION

The DATA DIVISION forewarns the computer of all of the data names that will appear in the program. It in effect establishes a glossary of nouns that will be used in the program and gives information about (for example) the maximum size of the data values which will be associated with those data names during the course of executing the program.

Note that there are two sections in the DATA DIVISION, the FILE SECTION and the WORKING-STORAGE SECTION. Let's consider the FILE SECTION first:

```
DATA DIVISION.
FILE SECTION.
FD   TIME-CARD-FILE; RECORD CONTAINS 80 CHARACTERS; LABEL RECORDS
     ARE OMITTED; DATA RECORD IS TIME-CARD.
01   TIME-CARD.
     02  NAME       PICTURE  A(20).
     02  PAY-RATE   PICTURE  99.
     02  MON-HRS    PICTURE  99.
     02  TUE-HRS    PICTURE  99.
     02  WED-HRS    PICTURE  99.
     02  THU-HRS    PICTURE  99.
     02  FRI-HRS    PICTURE  99.
     02  FILLER     PICTURE  X(48).
```

Up to this point we have described the data deck, which in this case the programmer has decided to call the TIME-CARD-FILE. (Recall that earlier, in one of the SELECT sentences of the ENVIRONMENT DIVISION, we told the computer that it would find the TIME-CARD-FILE in the card reader.) We also have announced that each record (each card) in that file will be referred to by the title TIME-CARD. The computer is told that from each TIME-CARD it is to get the following data values: the NAME of each employee whose pay is to be calculated, the hourly PAY-RATE by which he is paid, and the numbers of hours that employee worked on each day of this week (MON-HRS, TUE-HRS, etc.). The PICTURE clauses to the right of the data names forewarn the computer of (for example) the expected size of the data values to be associated with each data name. In this case the computer has been told that the NAME will be no longer than twenty letters, and that the PAY-RATE and the daily hours will be two digit numbers. (For the sake of simplicity in this, your first program, we'll use only whole numbers and forget about decimals.)

Continuing with the FILE SECTION of the DATA DIVISION:

```
FD  PAY-LISTING; RECORD CONTAINS 136 CHARACTERS; LABEL RECORDS
    ARE OMITTED; DATA RECORD IS PRINTER-LINE.
01  PRINTER-LINE.
    02  FILLER      PICTURE X(5).
    02  NAME        PICTURE A(20).
    02  FILLER      PICTURE X(5).
    02  GROSS-PAY   PICTURE $999.
    02  FILLER      PICTURE X(102).
```

Now we have described a second data file, the one we will be creating with this program, the one we've entitled PAY-LISTING, and the one which in a SELECT sentence up in the ENVIRONMENT DIVISION the computer was told to locate on the line printer. We have announced our intention to refer to each record (each line of print) in this file by the title PRINTER-LINE. The computer is told that each PRINTER-LINE is to contain the NAME of each employee whose pay is to be calculated and his GROSS-PAY for the week. Again, the PICTURE clauses specify the maximum size of the values that are going to be printed. The FILLERs appearing here and in the TIME-CARD above, specify areas in the TIME-CARD and in the PRINTER-LINE which are to be filled with blanks. Here we see that each line of print is to consist of five blanks to begin with, then the employee's NAME, then another five blanks, then his GROSS-PAY. The remaining characters on the line are also to be blanks.

The WORKING-STORAGE SECTION of the DATA DIVISION for this program is short. This section has the purpose of describing to the computer any data names that will be used in the program as temporary storage locations for any intermediate results which come up in the course of calculating the final answer.

```
WORKING-STORAGE SECTION.
77  TOTAL-HRS      PICTURE 99.
```

Here we see that this program will use only one such data name, TOTAL-HRS. We will plan to use this data name as a place to store the sum of each employee's daily hours, just prior to multiplying that sum by his pay rate to calculate his gross pay.

Let me make one final but quite important point about the DATA DIVISION before I move on to the PROCEDURE DIVISION. Do you recall our discussion of the memory unit back in Section 1.6? We spoke of memory locations and their association on a one-for-one basis with the data names of a program. As an aid in learning this concept, we used the device of portraying each memory location as a post office box equipped with a label. The most important result of the DATA DIVISION is the assignment of these memory locations, one for each data name described in the division. Only data names that have been assigned to memory locations—that is, only those appearing in the DATA DIVISION—may be used in the instructions which the programmer includes in his PROCEDURE DIVISION.

Figure 2.4 illustrates the memory location assignments which will result from this DATA DIVISION.

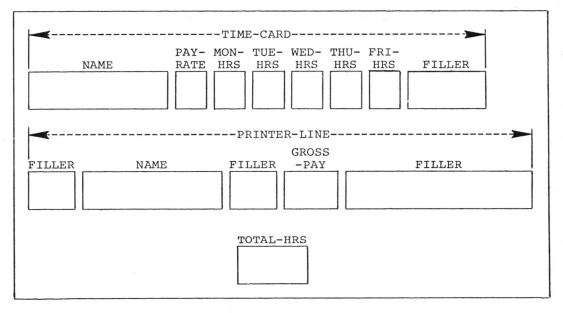

FIGURE 2.4   Memory Locations Assigned by the DATA DIVISION

2.5   The PROCEDURE DIVISION

The PROCEDURE DIVISION is the real meat of the program. It is in this division that we give the computer the actual instructions it needs to know how to calculate the answers to the problem it is to solve.

This PROCEDURE DIVISION is composed of three paragraphs, each with a paragraph title: the START-PARAGRAPH, the MAIN-PARAGRAPH, and the FINAL-PARAGRAPH. Let's look at each paragraph individually:

```
START-PARAGRAPH.
    OPEN INPUT TIME-CARD-FILE, OUTPUT PAY-LISTING.
    MOVE SPACES TO PRINTER-LINE.
```

The two instructions we've put in the START-PARAGRAPH cause some "housekeeping chores" to be performed by the computer. In the OPEN instruction we essentially tell the computer to get our two files ready for use. (If you were going to get information out of a file, you'd have to OPEN it first, wouldn't you?) Recall that we have forewarned the computer of our intention to use these two files in two other places: (1) In the ENVIRON-MENT DIVISION we told it where they'd be (the TIME-CARD-FILE on the card reader; the PAY-LISTING file on the line printer); and (2) in the DATA DIVISION we gave it information about each record in the files (TIME-CARD in the TIME-CARD-FILE; PRINTER-LINE in the PAY-LISTING). In the OPEN instruction we formally announce our intent to use the two files and now we also say *how:* the TIME-CARD-FILE will be used for INPUT, and the PAY-LISTING will be our OUTPUT.

The instruction "MOVE SPACES TO PRINTER-LINE." performs a simple-minded task. We would like to be absolutely sure all our FILLERs contain blanks (or spaces), so we tell the computer to wipe the entire PRINTER-LINE clean by moving SPACES into it. Due to the principle of Destructive Write operations, SPACES being loaded (or "written") into the memory locations which comprise PRINTER-LINE will destroy anything that might be there and replace it with nice, clean SPACES.

```
READ-CALCULATE-PRINT-PARAGRAPH.
    READ TIME-CARD-FILE RECORD, AT END GO TO FINAL-PARAGRAPH.
    MOVE NAME IN TIME-CARD TO NAME IN PRINTER-LINE.
    ADD MON-HRS, TUE-HRS, WED-HRS, THU-HRS, FRI-HRS
        GIVING TOTAL-HRS.
    MULTIPLY PAY-RATE BY TOTAL-HRS GIVING GROSS-PAY.
    WRITE PRINTER-LINE.
    GO TO READ-CALCULATE-PRINT-PARAGRAPH.
```

Let's take the READ-CALCULATE-PRINT-PARAGRAPH an instruction at a time. It contains the real heart of this program, the computational instructions necessary to the calculation of our employees' pays. In order to give you an opportunity to actually see the effect of each instruction, let's consider in detail how the information on the first two data cards in the data deck will be processed by the instructions in the READ-CALCULATE-PRINT-PARAGRAPH during the execution phase. Our data deck is shown in Figure 2.5.

We see the first data card at the front of the deck. On it is the name of our first employee, Bob McGillicudy. Bob is paid $6 per hour. This week he worked eight hours on Monday, eight on Tuesday, ten on Wednesday, eight on Thursday, and four on Friday.

The first instruction in the READ-CALCULATE-PRINT-PARAGRAPH is

READ TIME-CARD-FILE RECORD, (forget the rest for now).

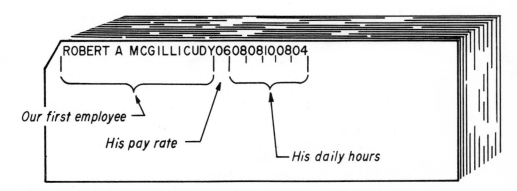

FIGURE 2.5   The Data Deck With the First Card Exposed

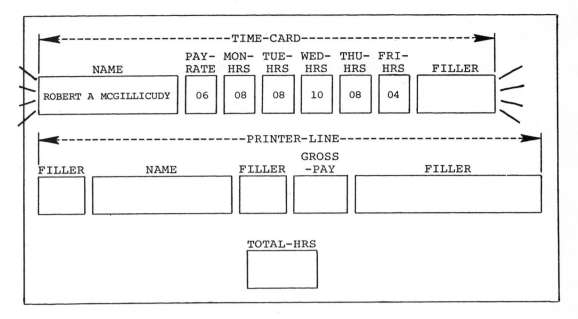

FIGURE 2.6   Memory After Execution of the READ Instruction

This is one of the READ instructions I spoke of in Section 2.2 that tells the computer it is to read one record (a data card) from the TIME-CARD-FILE. From information given in the DATA DIVISION, the computer knows what data values it should find on the data card: the employee's NAME, his PAY-RATE, and his daily hours. Reading the data card automatically results in the correct data values being loaded in the correct memory locations. After the computer has obeyed this command, the first data card will have been read and all the data values pertaining to the first employee, Bob McGillicudy, will have been loaded in memory. Figure 2.6 shows the condition of memory after this READ instruction has been executed.

The next instruction to be executed is

MOVE NAME IN TIME-CARD TO NAME IN PRINTER-LINE.

Reading the data card caused our first employee's name to be loaded into memory location NAME of the TIME-CARD, but we are going to cause the contents of PRINTER-LINE not TIME-CARD to be sent to the line printer for printing. For that reason we have got to move the man's name to memory location NAME of PRINTER-LINE so that when we print *his* amount of pay, *his* name and not somebody else's (or worse nobody's) name will appear next to it. Figure 2.7 shows the condition of memory after this MOVE instruction has been executed.

Did you notice that I said "NAME *IN TIME-CARD*" and "NAME *IN PRINTER-LINE*"? In Section 1.6, I gave you your first exposure to MOVE instructions. In none of them did I ever use prepositional phrases such as "IN TIME-CARD" or "IN PRINTER-LINE." (Actually, only English majors

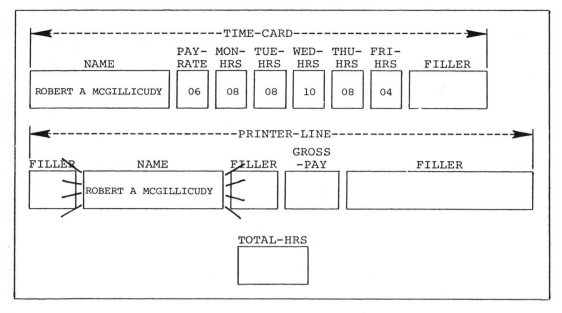

FIGURE 2.7   Memory After Execution of the MOVE Instruction

would refer to those as "prepositional phrases." You will learn to call them "qualifying clauses" as a COBOL programmer.) Why are they necessary now but not before? In the DATA DIVISION of this program we set up two different memory locations labeled NAME. From now on, to avoid "confusing" the computer, we must tell it which location NAME we are referring to by "qualifying" the data name with a phrase such as "IN TIME-CARD" whenever we speak of it. A programmer can save himself from having to use qualifying clauses if he'll avoid giving the same data names to different memory locations.

The ADD instruction is the next to be executed:

ADD MON-HRS, TUE-HRS, WED-HRS, THU-HRS, FRI-HRS GIVING TOTAL-HRS.

Figure 2.8 shows memory after this instruction has been executed. Next to be executed is the MULTIPLY instruction:

MULTIPLY PAY-RATE BY TOTAL-HRS GIVING GROSS-PAY.

You could probably guess the condition of memory resulting from the execution of this instruction. Look at Figure 2.9 and see if you're right.

Perhaps the only surprise you got was the appearance of the dollar sign in memory location GROSS-PAY. Back in the DATA DIVISION, the picture clause of GROSS-PAY told the computer that we wanted a dollar sign loaded into that memory location along with the numeric value.

Although we've moved Bob's name and pay to the part of memory associated with PRINTER-LINE, we have not actually caused it to be

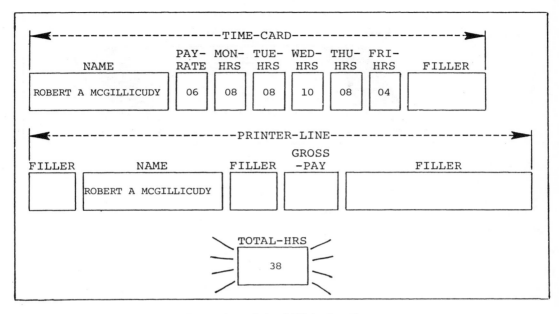

FIGURE 2.8   Memory After Execution of the ADD Instruction

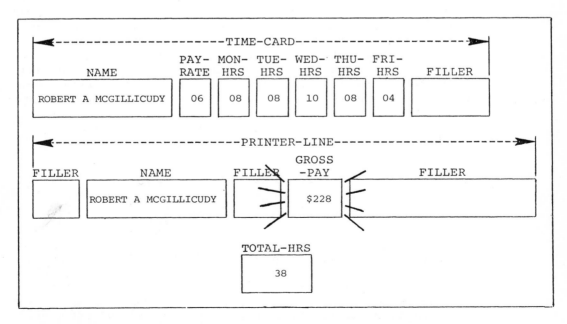

FIGURE 2.9   Memory After Execution of the MULTIPLY Instruction

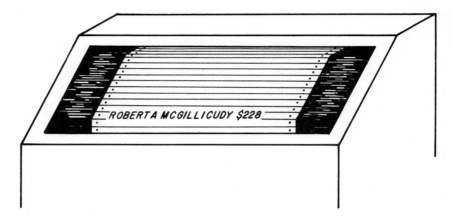

FIGURE 2.10   The Line Printer After Responding to the WRITE Instruction

printed on the line printer yet. The WRITE instruction takes care of that:

WRITE PRINTER-LINE.

The instruction tells the computer to send the contents of the memory locations associated with PRINTER-LINE to the line printer and to have the line printer print them in one line of print. In executing this instruction, the computer "looks at" (or reads) the contents of the PRINTER-LINE memory locations. Because of the Nondestructive Read concept, no change whatsoever is made to the memory location by this action. The only event that occurs as a result of the WRITE instruction, occurs at the line printer where one line of print suddenly appears. This is shown in Figure 2.10.

Now let me ask you a question: In what order did the computer execute the instructions we have considered so far? Without a moment's thought, the answer is on your lips, "Why, it executed them in the same order I read them, of course! First instruction first, second instruction second, third instruction third!"

Correct. But to put it in a single word, they were executed *sequentially.*

ANOTHER COMPUTER CONCEPT
Except when obeying branching instructions, the computer will always execute instructions sequentially.

Branching instructions are important, because they give us the ability to tell the computer we want to do some steps over again without having to write those steps over again in the program. We can simply use a branching instruction to tell the computer to return to an earlier part of the program where the steps are and that we want to repeat. An example of the most elementary branching instruction is given by the next instruction in our program:

GO TO READ-CALCULATE-PRINT-PARAGRAPH.

This instruction is used in order to tell the computer to go back to the beginning of the READ-CALCULATE-PRINT-PARAGRAPH and start through it again. Why would we want to do that? Well, consider what the computer has accomplished after passing through the READ-CALCULATE-PRINT-PARAGRAPH once and obeying each of its instructions only once—it has read the data card describing the first employee, computed his pay, and printed his name and pay on the line printer. But what about the second and third employees, not to mention the 100th or the 1000th?

Having processed the first employee, we would now like the computer to process the second, third, and so on. If our company had 1000 employees and if COBOL had no branching instructions, we would have to repeat the first five instructions 1000 times (making READ-CALCULATE-PRINT-PARAGRAPH 5000 instructions long) in order to process a data deck comprised of 1000 employees' data cards. (Either that or leave the paragraph at five statements, and run the program deck through the card reader 1000 times, each time with a data deck consisting of only one employee's data card—an equally ridiculous idea!)

Because we *are* able to say "GO TO READ-CALCULATE-PRINT-PARAGRAPH." the computer will now return to the beginning of that paragraph and begin sequential execution of its instructions again. Before we start through the paragraph again, however, take a look at the data deck as it now stands. (See Figure 2.11.) We see that our second employee is Dave Duke; he gets $12 an hour; and he isn't our most faithful employee (he didn't even show up for work on Wednesday). Notice the spaces that have been left on the card after his name. In the DATA DIVISION we told the computer that each employee's name would contain twenty letters. Bob McGillicudy's name was exactly twenty characters long (including the two spaces before and after his middle initial), so we could place his pay rate immediately after his name on the card. Dave's name is considerably shorter, however; but we must remain good for our word—we told the computer that employee names will be twenty characters long, so twenty characters they must be; even if, as was the case here, we have to add the necessary number of additional spaces after someone's name to fill up those twenty characters.

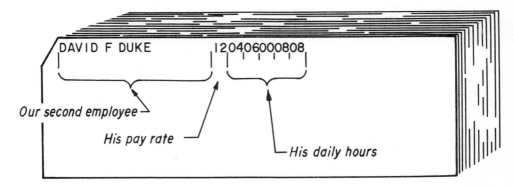

FIGURE 2.11   The Data Deck With the Second Card Exposed

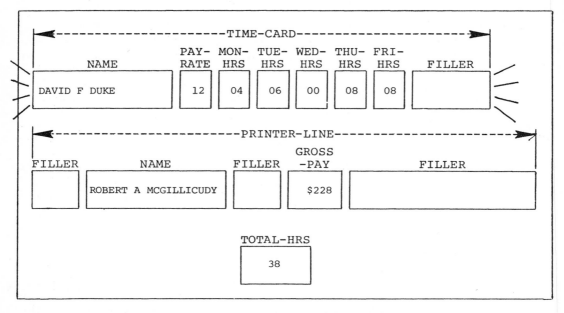

FIGURE 2.12   Memory After the Second Execution of the READ Instruction

The next instruction to be executed will be

READ TIME-CARD-FILE RECORD, etc.

As before, this instruction will cause the reading of one data card, this time Dave Duke's card. As before, the result of this instruction's execution will be the loading of the memory locations associated with TIME-CARD with the data values from Dave's data card. Take a look at Figure 2.12. It shows the condition of memory after this, the second execution of the READ instruction. Be sure to notice that only the memory locations associated with TIME-CARD have new data values stored in them. All others have remained exactly as they were when you saw them last (in Figure 2.9). What happened to the former values that were stored in TIME-CARD? They were destroyed and lost when the computer "destructively wrote" these new data values into those memory locations.

Next to be executed is the MOVE instruction:

MOVE NAME IN TIME-CARD TO NAME IN PRINTER-LINE.

Now take a look at the condition of memory as shown in Figure 2.13. Notice that Dave's name is now down in the PRINTER-LINE, having been "destructively written" over Bob's, but Bob's gross pay is still there. We'd better correct that situation before sending the contents of PRINTER-LINE to the line printer for printing—and we will; just as soon as the ADD and MULTIPLY instructions are executed again.

ADD MON-HRS, TUE-HRS, WED-HRS, THU-HRS, FRI-HRS GIVING TOTAL-HRS.
MULTIPLY PAY-RATE BY TOTAL-HRS GIVING GROSS-PAY.

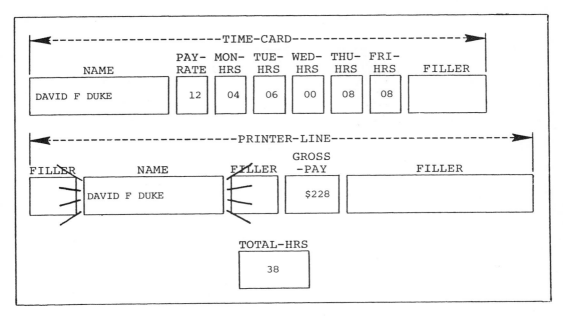

FIGURE 2.13   Memory After the Second Execution of the MOVE Instruction

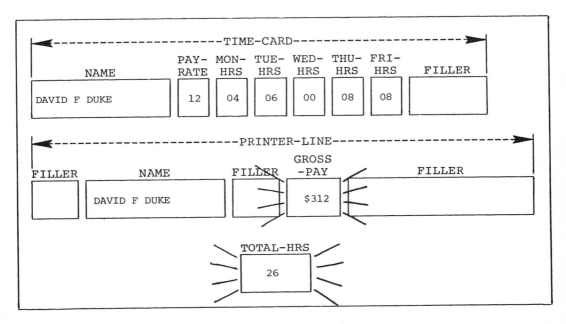

FIGURE 2.14   Memory After the Second Execution of the ADD and MULTIPLY Instructions

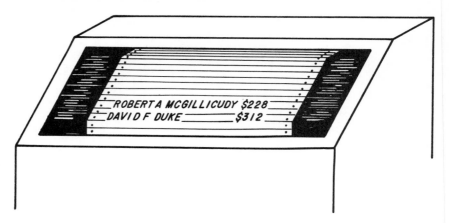

FIGURE 2.15   The Line Printer After Responding a Second Time to the WRITE Instruction

When the ADD instruction is executed, a new value will be loaded into memory location TOTAL-HRS. The MULTIPLY instruction will then compute and load Dave's pay into GROSS-PAY. This is all shown in Figure 2.14.

The final step in computing Dave's pay is writing it on the line printer:

    WRITE PRINTER-LINE.

Again, this instruction causes the contents of PRINTER-LINE to be sent to the line printer for printing. Figure 2.15 shows the line printer after this, the second execution of the WRITE instruction.

This is how the computer processes the first two data cards of the data deck. All remaining cards in the deck will be processed in the same way. The READ-CALCULATE-PRINT-PARAGRAPH will be repeatedly executed until there are no more cards in the data deck. Assuming that there are 1000 employees (and therefore 1000 data cards), the computer will detect the end of the data deck when it starts through READ-CALCULATE-PRINT-PARAGRAPH for the 1001st time. In attempting to obey the READ instruction, it will find no more data cards to read, and the AT END clause of the READ instruction, which we ignored in our earlier discussions, will come into play. Here again is the complete instruction:

    READ TIME-CARD-FILE, AT END GO TO FINAL-PARAGRAPH.

The AT END clause has the function of telling the computer what to do when it runs out of data cards. In this case a branching instruction is given which tells the computer to skip immediately to the FINAL-PARAGRAPH. And when I say "skip," that's exactly what I mean. It skips over all instructions between that point and the FINAL-PARAGRAPH, ignoring them completely, as it obeys the order to GO TO FINAL-PARAGRAPH.

    FINAL-PARAGRAPH.
        CLOSE TIME-CARD-FILE, PAY-LISTING.
        STOP RUN.

Again "housekeeping" chores must be performed as the program comes to an end. We CLOSE the files we've been using, and we tell the computer that it has finished its work on this problem by telling it to STOP the RUN.

2.6   The Sample Program—an Overview

In the previous three sections we have been considering a program written by another programmer. As we read each of the lines in the program, we considered what its effect would be when the program went into the execution phase. That's just the way a programmer *writes* a program. As he composes each line, he does so while considering what effects that line will have when it is executed. As he writes the DATA DIVISION, he envisions the organization of memory locations he is establishing. As he writes each instruction of the PROCEDURE DIVISION, he envisions the action his instruction will cause: the reading of a data card, or the movement of data values between different memory locations, or the arithmetic manipulation of numeric data values, or the movement of data values to the line printer for printing, etc.

Having written his program on a sheet of paper in much the same form as you saw it in Figure 2.3, he then sits down at a typewriter-like device called a keypunch (to be described in detail in Chapter 3) and types each of the lines of the program on a separate IBM card. The program of Figure 2.3 would be typed onto forty-nine cards, including the END PROGRAM card. Those forty-nine cards make up his instruction deck.

He then goes to the company bookkeeper and gets a list of the 1000 employees' names, along with their rates of pay and the hours each of them worked this week. The contents of this list are then typed onto IBM cards, one card for each employee. He must be sure the values are typed on the cards in exactly the arrangement he promised the computer they would be when he wrote the DATA DIVISION. These 1000 cards make up his data deck and are placed behind his instruction deck to complete the program deck.

He then takes his program deck to the computer room and places it in the card reader. He pushes the "GO button" on the computer, and in a little less than three minutes he will have a complete listing on the line printer of this week's gross-earnings of each of the 1000 employees in his company. Go back now and take one last look at Figure 2.2.

Next week the programmer's job will be *much* easier. He can use the same instruction deck he used this week, so he won't have to prepare one. That will save him a good deal of time. He will simply prepare a new data deck based upon next week's hours (and incorporating any pay raises anyone got, of course) and place *that* deck behind his instruction deck in place of this week's. This will give him a new program deck for next week which he will then place into the card reader.

And so it will continue, week after week. No one in this company will ever have to perform those 1000 additions and multiplications weekly again, because their company programmer has done his work.

2.7 Where Do We Go From Here?

You must have noticed that there were numerous elements of the sample program that I did not explain. I omitted those explanations, because you are not yet equipped to understand them. I did want you to see a complete program, however, so I chose to include them despite my intention to ignore them in the discussion.

We have two goals ahead of us now: The first is to get you to the point where you understand all the elements of a COBOL program.

But the second is far more important. You probably found it fairly easy to follow this sample program written by somebody else. (Most anyone would. One of the truly beautiful features of the COBOL language is its English-like quality. It is a quality shared by *no* other programming language.) We must now develop within you an ability to write your *own* programs, and that is what the rest of this book will seek to do.

EXERCISES

Answers to all exercises in this chapter are given in Appendix A.

2.1 Explain in your own words the "Stored Program Concept" and why it distinguishes the computer from other calculators.

2.2 What are the three principal activities associated with the Compilation Phase?

2.3 What portion of the program deck is read during Compilation?

2.4 How does the computer know when it has reached the end of the instruction deck?

2.5 How does the computer know when to cease compilation?

2.6 What portion of the program deck is read during execution?

2.7 Where are the instructions from the instruction deck during execution?

2.8 How does the computer know when it has reached the end of the data deck?

2.9 How does the computer know when to cease execution?

2.10 The following is a list of activities that occur at some time during the processing of a computer program. Some occur during the compilation phase; others occur during the execution phase. Put a C after those that relate to compilation; an E after those that relate to execution.

		C or E
a.	Instruction cards are read	C
b.	Data cards are read	E
c.	Instructions are translated into machine language	E
d.	Data values are stored in memory	C
e.	Instructions are stored in memory	C
f.	Phase terminated by STOP RUN instruction	E
g.	Phase terminated by END PROGRAM card	C
h.	Arithmetic operations performed	E
i.	Branching instructions obeyed	E
j.	Data values printed on the line printer	

2.11 What are the four divisions of a COBOL program?

2.12 Which of the four divisions of a COBOL program are optional?

2.13 TRUE or FALSE? The four divisions of a COBOL program may be in any order.

2.14 TRUE or FALSE? The DATA DIVISION is located in the data deck of a COBOL program.

2.15 When the computer is finished executing an instruction that is not a branching instruction, which instruction does it execute next?

2.16 When the computer executes a branching instruction such as "GO TO CALCULATIONS-PARAGRAPH.", which instruction does it execute next?

2.17   Assume that memory locations ABLE, BAKER, and CHARLIE are initially loaded as follows:

ABLE	BAKER	CHARLIE
24	08	70

Fill the blank memory locations below to show their contents after execution of the instruction:

MOVE ABLE TO CHARLIE.

ABLE	BAKER	CHARLIE
24	68	70

2.18   Assume that memory locations ABLE, BAKER, and CHARLIE are initially loaded as shown in 2.17 above. Fill in the blank memory locations below to show their contents after execution of the instruction:

ADD BAKER, CHARLIE GIVING ABLE.

ABLE	BAKER	CHARLIE
78	08	70

3 An Introduction to COBOL

3.1 An Historical Note

COBOL was born in 1959 in, of all places, the Pentagon. The U. S. Department of Defense, with its innumerable business contacts in the industrial world, was weary of having to remain conversant with the many different computer languages in use by each of those countless business organizations. Wishing they all "spoke" the *same* computer language, it called a meeting in May of that year to consider the "feasibility of establishing a common language for the programming of computers for business-oriented applications." Representatives from computer-using organizations, both in private industry and in government, and computer manufacturers were present. Out of the meeting came an agreement that the project to develop such a language should be undertaken.

By December 1959, COBOL-60 was born. It was a terribly inefficient language, but it did prove that the concept was practical. COBOL-61 evolved a year later. It proved to be much more manageable and became the foundation for the COBOL we use today.

COBOL-61-Extended and COBOL-65 have been developed since then. They kept intact most of what was COBOL-61, but added some of the newer features which are covered in the later chapters of this book.

Today COBOL is *the* official programming language of the U. S. Department of Defense. A Maintenance Committee is in operation whose purpose is to process and consider proposed changes in the language. As evidence of the wide and diverse acceptance of the language, here is a list of some of the firms who are represented on that committee:

Electronics and data processing interests:

Burroughs Corporation	Philco Corporation
Control Data Corporation	RCA
Honeywell, Inc.	Sylvania Electric
IBM Corporation	Univac
NCR Corporation	Westinghouse

Transportation, automotive, and aircraft interests:

Boeing	General Motors
Lockheed	Southern Railway Company

Others:

Allstate Insurance   EXXON Corporation
Owens-Illinois   U. S. Steel

3.2   The Structure of a COBOL Program

As you know from the sample program presented in Chapter 2, a COBOL program is made up of four divisions. Generally speaking:

1. Each division is made up of sections.
2. Each section is made up of paragraphs.
3. Each paragraph is made up of instructions (called sentences).
4. Each sentence is made up of clauses.
5. Each clause is made up of words.
6. Each word is made up of characters.

By way of review, the four divisions are listed here in the order in which they *must* appear in a COBOL program.

1. The IDENTIFICATION DIVISION—identifies the program.
2. The ENVIRONMENT DIVISION—describes the environment in which the program was designed to run, i.e., the computer for which it was written and the input and output devices it needs to use.
3. The DATA DIVISION—sets up all necessary memory locations necessary for the program and describes:
    a. The data files to be manipulated.
    b. The records which make up each file.
    c. The data elements which make up each record.
4. The PROCEDURE DIVISION—describes the steps to be taken (the procedures) in processing the problem.

3.3   The COBOL Character Set

Whenever a student sets out to learn a foreign language, if that language has an alphabet different from that of his own native tongue, he must learn the alphabet of that language before anything else. The same can be said about learning a new programming language, except when speaking in terms of programming languages, we don't call it an alphabet; we call it a character set.

Figure 3.1 shows the COBOL character set. Notice the absence of lower case letters, the colon (:), the ampersand (&), the percent (%), the cent (¢), the conventional multiplication symbol (×), the division symbol (÷), and the double quote ("). In COBOL the asterisk (*) is used for a multiplication symbol, the slash (/) is used as the division symbol, and the apostrophe (') is used as the quote mark.

```
┌─────────────────────────────────────┐
│  THE COBOL CHARACTER SET             │
│  1.  The ten digits (0 through 9).   │
│  2.  The 26 capital letters (A through Z). │
│  3.  The 15 special characters:      │
│         + – * / = < > ( ) ' $ , ; .  │
│         and the space or blank.      │
└─────────────────────────────────────┘
```

FIGURE 3.1   The COBOL Character Set

3.4   COBOL Words—Programmer-Invented-Names

Figure 3.2 outlines the rules governing the "spelling" of COBOL words. For the purpose of our discussion, we will view all COBOL words as falling in two categories:

1. Programmer-invented-names.
2. Reserved words.

Programmer-invented-names are used in many places throughout a COBOL program: Data-names, record-names, and file-names, of which we spoke frequently in discussing the sample program of Chapter 2, are all invented by the programmer. (Examples: PAY-RATE and GROSS-PAY were data-names; TIME-CARD and PRINTER-LINE were record-names; TIME-CARD-FILE and PAY-LISTING were file-names.) Section-names and paragraph-names in the PROCEDURE DIVISION are programmer-invented, as well. (I chose not to divide our sample program's PROCEDURE DIVISION into sections, an option available to the programmer.

```
┌─────────────────────────────────────┐
│        RULES FOR FORMING            │
│          COBOL WORDS                │
│  1.  They may contain only          │
│      a.  letters                    │
│      b.  digits                     │
│      c.  embedded hyphens.          │
│  2.  They may not contain           │
│      a.  embedded spaces            │
│      b.  any special characters.    │
│  3.  They are ended by either       │
│      a.  a space                    │
│      b.  a period   ⎫ followed by   │
│      c.  a comma    ⎬ a space.      │
│      d.  a semi-colon ⎭             │
└─────────────────────────────────────┘
```

FIGURE 3.2   Formation of COBOL Words

```
┌─────────────────────────────────────────────┐
│              RULES FOR FORMING                │
│        A PROGRAMMER-INVENTED-NAME             │
│                                               │
│   1.  Must be a legal COBOL word.             │
│   2.  No longer than 30 characters.           │
│   3.  At least one character must be a letter.│
│   4.  Must not be a Reserved Word.            │
│   5.  Must be unique.                         │
└─────────────────────────────────────────────┘
```

FIGURE 3.3   Formation of Programmer-Invented-Names

Examples of paragraph-names which I invented were START-PARAGRAPH and MAIN-PARAGRAPH.) Figure 3.3 lists the rules governing formation of programmer-invented-names.

Notice rule number 5 which says that programmer-invented-names "must be unique." That means that when you make up, for example, a file-name such as PAY-LISTING, then that name may not be used for anything else in the program except as the name for *that file*. There may be no other file with that name, nor may that name be used as a paragraph-name, a record-name, etc., anywhere else in your program. This rule applies to every programmer-invented-name you make up.

PROGRAMMER-INVENTED-NAMES	VALID OR INVALID?
COST	Valid.
COST OF SALES	Invalid; embedded spaces.
COST-OF-SALES	Valid.
INCOME-TAX-FOR-1975	Valid.
AMOUNT-IN-$	Invalid; special character.
AMOUNT-IN-DOLLARS	Valid.
1976	Invalid; no letters.
1976-INCOME	Valid.
AVERAGE-	Invalid; hyphen not embedded.
AVERAGE-GRADE	Valid.
I.R.S.	Invalid; special characters.
I-R-S	Valid.
CUSTOMER'S-NAME	Invalid; special character.
CUSTOMERS-NAME	Valid.
EMPLOYEE-SOCIAL-SECURITY-NUMBER	Invalid; too many characters.
EMPLOYEE-SOCIAL-SECURITY-NUM	Valid.
PROCEDURE	Invalid; reserved word.
REORDER-PROCEDURE	Valid.

FIGURE 3.4   Examples of Valid and Invalid Programmer-Invented-Names

3.5 The Importance of Descriptive Naming

Before we move on to reserved words, let me give you some advice about names you will be inventing for your programs. The computer does not care what names you invent, as long as you obey the rules of Figure 3.3 when you invent them. I chose the file-name TIME-CARD-FILE for my file of time cards in the Chapter 2 sample program. Even though it was a file-name, I did not *have* to include the word FILE in the name. Even though it was a file of cards, I did not *have* to include the word CARD in the name. In fact I *could* have chosen an entirely nonsensical name for the file, such as ELEPHANT-HERD. Likewise, I did not *have* to choose the record-name PRINTER-LINE for the PAY-LISTING file, either. I could have stayed on my zoological kick and chosen for a record-name, ZEBRA-STRIPE. Both of these absurd names obey the rules of Figure 3.3, and the computer would have been perfectly happy with them. But what would having chosen such names do to the clarity of my program? My PROCEDURE DIVISION would now contain people-confusing statements like this:

```
READ ELEPHANT-HERD RECORD, AT END GO TO FINAL-PARAGRAPH.
WRITE ZEBRA-STRIPE.
```

By the same token, I did not have to choose paragraph-names in my PROCEDURE DIVISION which include the word PARAGRAPH. Many novice programmers, enthralled with this freedom in naming paragraphs will pay homage to their favorite girls by naming their paragraphs CAROL-ANN, MOTHER-MINE, and the like. (It's become the oldest joke in the COBOL book to name one of your paragraphs HELL, so you can later branch to that paragraph with the instruction, GO TO HELL.) Less frivolous perhaps, but just as much open to *my* criticism, is the practice of naming paragraphs PARA-1, PARA-2, PARA-3, etc.

One of the real-life considerations which must be at the forefront of every programmer's mind as he writes a program is the importance of writing the program so that it can be easily understood by somebody else. A company that hires you as a programmer will be extremely unhappy with your work if you write programs that nobody else can follow. Few programs ever remain exactly as they were originally written. Most are added to and improved upon several times during their useful life. The person given the job of changing a program written by somebody else (or one written by himself many months before) is faced with an easy task or a difficult (sometimes impossible) task depending on the degree to which the original programmer made the program self-explanatory. Since you may not be around when your program comes up for change, your Data Processing Manager will demand clarity and a straightforward approach in all your programs.

The clarity of your programs is best served by descriptive naming. If you're inventing a file-name for a file of canceled checks, don't call it INPUT-F; call it CHECK-FILE. If you're inventing a paragraph-name for the paragraph in which most of the calculations are performed, don't call it PARA-2; call it CALCULATIONS-PARA.

3.6 COBOL Reserved Words

There are about 300 COBOL words which are reserved and may not be used as programmer-invented-names. Each of them has a special meaning to the computer and must be used in exactly the way the computer expects it to be used. These are just a few of the reserved words:

ADD	FILE-CONTROL	PROCEDURE
ASSIGN	FILLER	PROGRAM-ID
AUTHOR	GIVING	READ
COBOL	IDENTIFICATION	SECTION
DATA	INPUT-OUTPUT	SELECT
DIVIDE	MOVE	SUBTRACT
DIVISION	MULTIPLY	WORKING-STORAGE
ENVIRONMENT	PICTURE	WRITE
FD		

Every word in that condensed list of reserved words was used properly in the Chapter 2 sample program. The list contains some reserved-names (as opposed to programmer-invented-names), including the four division-names and the section- and paragraph-names used in the first three divisions. Also included in the list are the four arithmetic verbs ADD, SUBTRACT, MULTIPLY, and DIVIDE. There are many, many others that I won't comment on here. A complete list of COBOL reserved words is given in Appendix B.

Don't bother trying to memorize the list. In your first couple of programs, you might check each of your programmer-invented-names against the list to assure yourself you haven't coincidentally used a reserved word. It is unlikely that you ever will. After a couple of scans through the list, you will start to catch on to the types of words that are included, and it will be an easy matter to avoid anything that might smack of those types.

One final point to be made about programmer-invented-names and reserved words: Although the words NEXT and PAGE are reserved words, and alone neither could be used as a programmer-invented-name, the word NEXT-PAGE is not a reserved word and *could* be used. Even though you and I recognize NEXT-PAGE as two reserved words connected by a hyphen, to the computer NEXT-PAGE is one nine character word which is *not* on the reserved word list. The point being made is that although a word such as ADD may be reserved, this does not prevent that group of three characters from being used in any programmer-invented-names such as ADD-PARA or NEW-ADDRESS.

3.7 COBOL Constants—Numeric Literals

A literal is an item of data that has a constant (unchanging) value. Further, the value it has is identical to the characters comprising the item. This is in contrast to a data-name such as GROSS-PAY whose value is anything but constant—it can be $228 at one moment, $312 at the next—and whose value has nothing whatever to do with the characters which make up the data-name. On the other hand, the data-value (or literal) 59 has the constant value of fifty-nine, and its value is identical to the characters which comprise it, 59. There are two types of COBOL literals:

1. Numeric literals.
2. Non-numeric literals.

We'll discuss numeric literals first. They are what you've been calling numeric values all your life. Here are some examples of COBOL numeric literals:

$$150789 \qquad +25.675$$
$$-125.3 \qquad 3.0$$

The rules for forming numeric literals are given in Figure 3.5. Notice the rule that says that a numeric literal may not end in a decimal point (No. 4). This means that the value five may be written as 5 or 5.0, but that writing it as 5. is prohibited. The reason for this is that to the computer a decimal point looks just like a period. The only way that it has to distinguish the two is in how they are used. A period is always followed by a space; a decimal point is always followed immediately by a digit. Suppose the computer were given this instruction: MOVE 5. TO PAY-RATE. It would incorrectly see that as two sentences, each ended by its own period, and each incomplete. The program would not run properly as a result of that error.

RULES FOR FORMING A NUMERIC LITERAL

1. May contain only digits, a plus or minus, and a decimal point.
2. No longer than 18 digits.
3. If no sign is used, it is assumed to be positive.
4. If a decimal point is used, it must *not* be the rightmost character.

FIGURE 3.5   Formation of Numeric Literals

3.8   Non-numeric Literals

Non-numeric literals are frequently used to establish what will be printed as page titles, column headings, and the like. They have other uses but are most often used to dress-up the printed page which is produced on the line printer. As an example, it might have been desired to print MR. or MS. as appropriate, in front of the names listed on the line printer by our sample program in Chapter 2. If so, we could have set up a memory location called SEX-TITLE and then included either of these statements at appropriate spots in the PROCEDURE DIVISION:

```
MOVE 'MR.' TO SEX-TITLE.
MOVE 'MS.' TO SEX-TITLE.
```

```
┌─────────────────────────────────────────────────────┐
│                 RULES FOR FORMING                   │
│                A NON-NUMERIC LITERAL                │
│  1.  May contain any COBOL character except the quote.│
│  2.  No longer than 120 characters.                 │
│  3.  Enclosed in quotes.                            │
└─────────────────────────────────────────────────────┘
```

FIGURE 3.6   Formation of Non-numeric Literals

The 'MR.' and 'MS.' are called non-numeric literals. Here are some other examples of non-numeric literals:

'COMPANY PAYROLL'   'F.I.C.A. DEDUCTIONS'
'CLASS OF 1977 ROSTER'   '$ EQUIVALENT'

Figure 3.6 outlines the rules for forming non-numeric literals. Notice that rule No. 1 says "any character except the quote." That rule says that 'STUDENT'S ADDRESS', for example, is an improper non-numeric literal. The computer, faced with that example, would see a non-numeric literal 'STUDENT' and then be confused by the other ten characters which follow it (S-space-A-D-D-R-E-S-S-').

An important point I wish to make about numeric and non-numeric literals: 12.95 is a numeric literal, but '12.95' is a non-numeric literal. Even though the second example happens to contain only numeric characters, its being bound by quotes makes it a *non*-numeric literal. As such, it may not be involved in any arithmetic calculation. Only *numeric* literals may be used in arithmetic operations.

A question that frequently arises is this: "May reserved words be used within non-numeric literals?" The answer is, "Yes. Any COBOL characters in any arrangement may be used within non-numeric literals." The reason is that the computer makes no attempt at understanding the contents of a non-numeric literal; it obediently but blindly "picks it up" as a (for all it cares) miscellaneous string of characters and "puts it down" intact wherever you say. Since no attempt is made to make sense of the contents of the literal, it never knows if there's a reserved word included in it or not.

3.9 Figurative Constants

One final type of COBOL constant is the figurative constant. Figurative constants are COBOL reserved words which are understood by the computer to have predefined constant values. There are six, but only two receive frequent enough use to merit mentioning here: SPACE and ZERO. (The four I am omitting are ALL, HIGH-VALUE, LOW-VALUE, and QUOTE.)

ZERO or ZEROS or ZEROES is a numeric figurative constant with the value 0. These two statements would have identical results:

MOVE 0.00 TO WEIGHT-TOTAL.
MOVE ZERO TO WEIGHT-TOTAL.

SPACE or SPACES is a non-numeric figurative constant which if printed on the line printer results in spaces or blanks. These two statements would have identical results:

```
MOVE'           'TO PAGE-HEADING.
MOVE SPACES TO PAGE-HEADING.
```

3.10   COBOL Punctuation Rules

The period is the only required punctuation mark in COBOL. As in English, it is used to end a sentence. It has other uses as well which I will explain as we get to them.

Commas and semi-colons will be shown in examples throughout this book, but their use is always optional. Programmers use them to enhance the readability of their sentences. Periods, commas and semi-colons when used must immediately follow a word and must always be followed by a space.

3.11   COBOL Instruction Cards and the COBOL Coding Form

The IBM card I've been speaking of is actually an 80-column computer card used for many purposes. Letters, digits, and special characters are typed and punched onto the card using a machine called a keypunch (more often called a card punch by manufacturers). See Figures 3.7 and 3.8.[1] The keypunch operator uses its typewriter-like keyboard to cause the desired characters to be typed and punched on the 80-column cards. Figure 3.9 demonstrates the keypunched appearance of the ten digits, the 26 letters, and some of the special characters used in COBOL. Note that directly under each typed character are one or more small rectangular holes punched in the card. These are the holes which the computer "reads." The characters typed at the top of the card are invisible to the computer. They are there so that the human programmer will be able to read what is on the card. Although it is not necessary to memorize the hole codes which are used to represent the various characters, it will prove useful if you will note the general pattern followed and remember that digits are represented by single punches, letters by double punches, and only a few special characters involve triple punches.

The bottom of the card is referred to as the "9-edge," for obvious reasons, and the top is the "12-edge." (There are ten rows clearly marked on the card, plus two at the top which are not marked, the eleven and twelve rows.) You will have contact with numerous card processing machines which are labelled with card positioning instructions referencing the card deck's "9-edge" or "12-edge."

[1] Operating instructions for the IBM 029 Card Punch are contained in Appendix C. The older IBM 026 Card Punch, still available in many computer centers, operates very much the same as the Model 029. See Section VII of Appendix C if you will be using a Model 026.

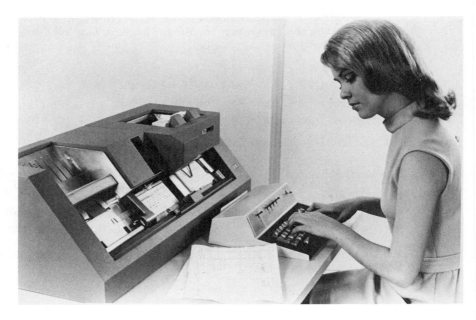

FIGURE 3.7   The IBM 029 Printing Card Punch

Courtesy of IBM Corp.

FIGURE 3.8   The Keyboard of the IBM 029

Courtesy of IBM Corp.

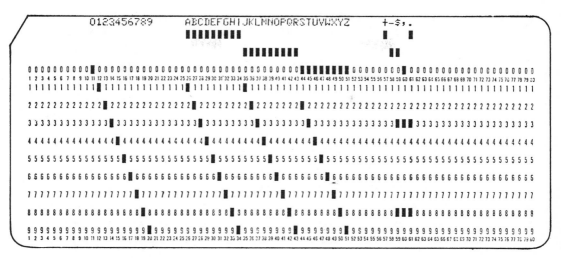

FIGURE 3.9   Character Representation on an 80-column Card

As mentioned above, these cards can be used for many purposes. Depending upon the purpose for which the card is to be used, certain specified columns on the card are reserved for special uses.

In view of the large number of programmers using them for COBOL instruction cards, many computer facilities provide specially printed "COBOL statement" versions. They are over-printed with lines and labels to help the COBOL programmer remember how to use the various columns when she is preparing COBOL instruction cards. Figure 3.10 shows just such a card.

Columns 1–6: Sequence Numbers   Sequence numbers are optional in a COBOL program. You may assign a sequence number to each card in your instruction deck, or you may leave them off. They will prove especially useful if you ever experience the traumatic misfortune of dropping your program deck. Putting the cards back into their proper order is made many times more simple if sequence numbers are on them. Furthermore, if sequence numbers are present, the computer will check them to see that they are in order. A sequence number out of order would mean a card out of order, and that means an *instruction* out of order. As you know, the correct order of the instructions is vital to the successful running of your program. If the computer finds any instruction card whose sequence number shows it to be out of order, it will report this to you by way of a message printed on the line printer. If you choose to use sequence numbers, you'd be wise to assign them initially by tens (the first card a 10, the second a 20, the third a 30, etc.). The computer will check to see only that they are all in ascending order; it doesn't demand that they be consecutive. If you don't take my advice, you may later want to insert a new card between 36 and 37 without disturbing the numerical order of the cards. In order to do that, the new card would have to be numbered 37; the former 37 would have to be *re*numbered 38; and *all* subsequent cards in the deck would have to be renumbered. If

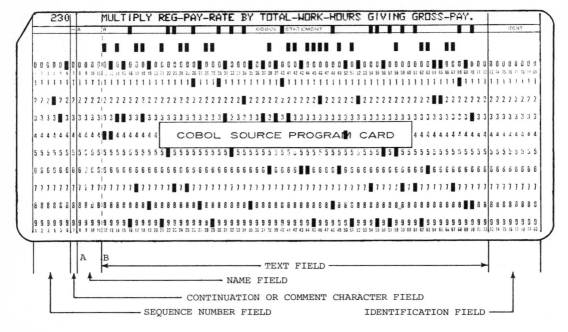

FIGURE 3.10   A COBOL Instruction Card

you *do* take my advice, then when you want to insert a new card between 360 and 370, you can simply number it 365, and no renumbering of *any* other cards will be necessary. (In fact, you still have room for four more cards between 365 and 370.)

We'll skip discussing column 7 for the moment and come back to it shortly.

Columns 8–11: The Name Field   Column 8 is called Margin A. The following items are punched on the card starting at Margin A:

1. Division-names.
2. Section-names.
3. Paragraph-names.
4. Certain items in the DATA DIVISION which we will discuss later.

Items which start at Margin A, do *not* have to remain within the Name Field; they may extend into the Text Field.

Columns 12–72: The Text Field   Column 12 is called Margin B. All sentences are begun and continued at Margin B. No sentence may extend beyond column 72.

Columns 73–80: The Identification Field   On instruction cards (though not on data cards) these final columns are ignored by the computer.

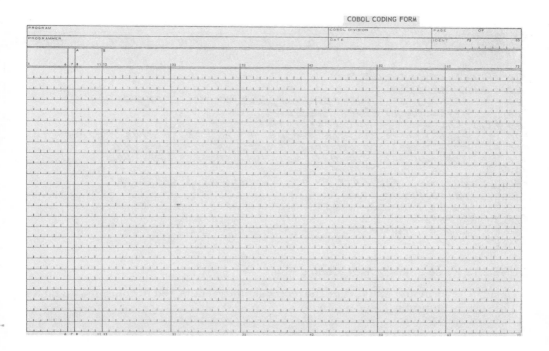

FIGURE 3.11   The COBOL Coding Form

Many a programmer will use this field to type some group of characters which will identify the card as belonging to her program. Then if the traumatic misfortune of the dropped cards involves more than one program deck, the cards can be segregated more easily.

Figure 3.11 shows a COBOL coding form. It is a work sheet used by programmers in writing their programs. Printed on the work sheet are labels and lines to remind them of the format they must follow in preparing each COBOL sentence. Each line on the coding form represents the contents of a single instruction card. Look closely at each line of the coding form, and I think you'll agree that its relationship to the columns on the "COBOL statement" card is obvious. Figure 3.12 shows the PROCEDURE DIVISION of the Chapter 2 sample program as it would be entered on the coding form.

The coding form makes the keypunching job much easier. Unlike the typewriter, the portion of the card that has just been punched is not visible to the operator. He depends upon an indicator on the keypunch to tell him the number of the column which is lined up under the punches at that moment. (If the indicator shows a 17, and he hits the Z button on the keyboard, a Z will be punched in column 17.) If he is distracted or otherwise loses his place while punching a card, he need only glance at the indicator and see that he is aligned on (for example) column 43. He then looks on his coding

COBOL CODING FORM

| PROGRAM | *Chapter 2 Sample Program* | COBOL DIVISION *Procedure* | PAGE *1* OF *1* |
| PROGRAMMER | *R. G. Finkenaur* | DATE *April 5, 1978* | IDENT *PAYROLL* |

```
350  PROCEDURE DIVISION.
360  START-PARAGRAPH.
370      OPEN INPUT TIME-CARD-FILE, OUTPUT PAY-LISTING.
380      MOVE SPACES TO PRINTER-LINE.
390  READ-CALCULATE-PRINT-PARAGRAPH.
400      READ TIME-CARD-FILE RECORD, AT END GO TO FINAL-PARAGRAPH.
410      MOVE NAME IN TIME-CARD TO NAME IN PRINTER-LINE.
420      ADD MON-HRS, TUE-HRS, WED-HRS, THU-HRS, FRI-HRS
430          GIVING TOTAL-HRS.
440      MULTIPLY PAY-RATE BY TOTAL-HRS GIVING GROSS-PAY.
450      WRITE PRINT-LINE.
460      GO TO READ-CALCULATE-PRINT-PARAGRAPH.
470  FINAL-PARAGRAPH.
480      CLOSE TIME-CARD-FILE, PAY-LISTING.
490      STOP RUN.
```

FIGURE 3.12   Use of the COBOL Coding Form

form and finds what character should be punched in column 43, and he has
found his place again.

Column 7: The Continuation Character   Since all sentences *must* be
confined to columns 8 through 72, there often is need to continue a long
sentence from the card where it began to the card or cards following it. This
can be done in one of three ways:

1. The sentence can be broken at a convenient space and con-
    tinued on the next card at or to the right of Margin B. In this case
    no continuation character is needed. An example of this is shown
    in Figure 3.13.

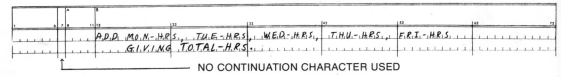

```
        ADD MON-HRS, TUE-HRS, WED-HRS, THU-HRS, FRI-HRS
            GIVING TOTAL-HRS.
```
——————— NO CONTINUATION CHARACTER USED

FIGURE 3.13   Continuation of a Sentence by Breaking It at a Convenient Space

2. If there is no convenient space within a reasonable distance
    of column 72, and you want to conserve card columns, continue
    the sentence all the way to column 72 and break it in the middle of
    a word. On the second card (the card upon which the sentence is to
    be continued), the continuation character, a hyphen, is placed in
    column 7 and the broken word is continued at or to the right of
    Margin B. Figure 3.14 shows an example of this type of continua-
    tion.

3. If you are in the middle of a non-numeric literal at the time
    you discover you're going to run out of columns too soon, continue
    the literal all the way to column 72. On the second card place a

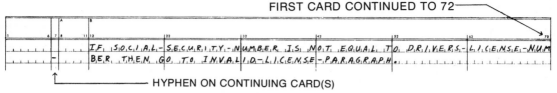

FIRST CARD CONTINUED TO 72

HYPHEN ON CONTINUING CARD(S)

FIGURE 3.14   Continuation of a Sentence by Breaking a Word

hyphen in column 7, a quote at or to the right of Margin B, and continue the literal immediately after the quote. Figure 3.15 shows an example of the continuation of a non-numeric literal.

FIRST CARD CONTINUED TO 72

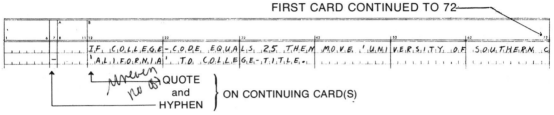

QUOTE and HYPHEN } ON CONTINUING CARD(S)

FIGURE 3.15   Continuation of a Non-numeric Literal

One final note on continuation: You may *not* break in the middle of a *numeric* literal. If a line-threatens to run out in the middle of a numeric literal, you will be forced to break the line at the last space before the literal as described in 1 above.

Column 7: Comment Cards   In longer, more complex programs, experienced programmers habitually include comments written in English, each of which remarks on the purpose of the segment of the program immediately after the comment. Such carefully chosen and properly placed comments can greatly ease the job of understanding a program written by someone else or one that has been on the shelf for several months. The computer would try to interpret these English language comments as COBOL sentences if it were not told otherwise. An asterisk (*) in column 7 identifies each of these "comment cards," and the computer is thereby advised to ignore them during its compilation process. Although "ignored" by the compiler, these comments are reproduced in the *program listing*.

Program listing is a term you haven't seen before. It is a copy of the contents of your instruction deck printed on the line printer by the computer. The computer prints this listing immediately after it finishes compilation (just before it begins execution), so it appears on the line printer paper just prior to the lines of output which the program has caused to be "written." It's the computer's way of saying to you, "Look Mack! Here's what you told me to do! If you don't like the answers I gave you, better look here to see if you told me what you *think* you told me!" The comments' appearing within this listing serves as an immense help to someone trying to make sense of the program, and that is the main reason why programmers use "comment cards."

```
       OVERTIME-PARAGRAPH.
      *THIS PARAGRAPH CALCULATES OVERTIME PAY ONLY FOR THOSE EMPLOYEES
      *WHOSE SUPERVISORS HAVE APPROVED THEIR WORKING OVERTIME.
           MULTIPLY PAY-RATE BY 1.5 GIVING OVERTIME-RATE.
           SUBTRACT 40 FROM TOTAL-HRS GIVING OVERTIME-HRS.
           MULTIPLY OVERTIME-HOURS BY OVERTIME-RATE
               GIVING OVERTIME-EARNINGS.
```

FIGURE 3.16   Use of Comment Cards

Figure 3.16 shows an example PROCEDURE DIVISION paragraph which includes both comment cards and a continued sentence.

3.12   Data Cards

Information on a data card may be located anywhere on the card. All 80 columns may be used without restriction; however, the programmer must tell the computer where he has placed his data on the card. This, you may recall from Chapter 2, is done in the DATA DIVISION. Figure 3.17 shows the actual appearance of a data card. It is the same card that was shown in the sketch of Figure 2.11.

3.13   Punched Cards: One Last Word

Remember that the computer sees nothing on an IBM card but the holes. It is unable to see any over-printing that happens to be on the card. If your

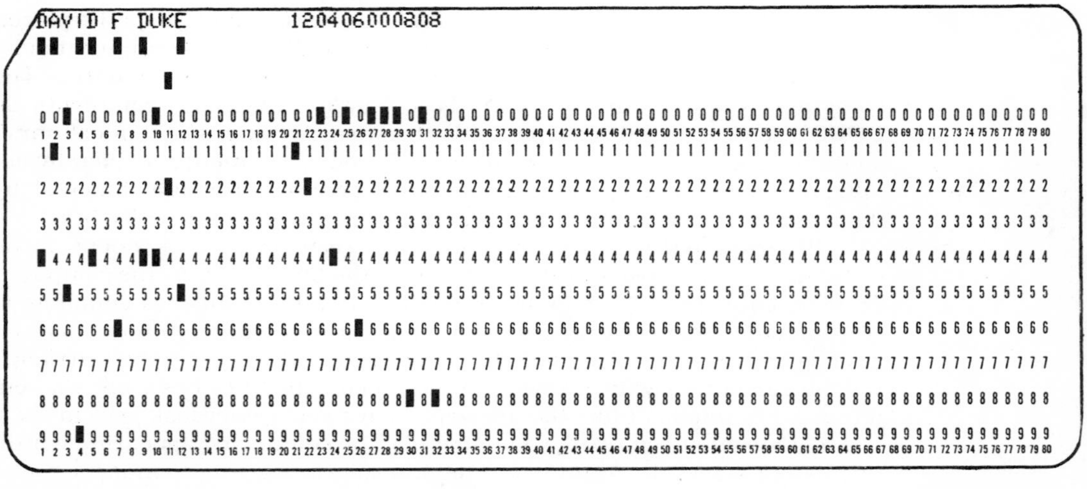

FIGURE 3.17   A Typical Data Card

computer center is out of "COBOL statement" cards on any given day, there is nothing wrong with your using general purpose cards of the type shown in Figure 3.9 for your instruction cards. You might even use cards over-printed as "FORTRAN statement" cards. The *only* essential is that you follow the required format for *COBOL* instruction cards when keypunching, regardless of what card stock you actually are using. Your statements, for example, must begin in column 12, because that's where COBOL statements should begin, and not in column 7 which is where you'd be told to begin them if you happened to be using cards over-printed for use with FORTRAN.

Likewise, there is nothing wrong with using "COBOL statement" or "FORTRAN statement" cards as data cards, as long as you keep the promises you made in the DATA DIVISION about the location of the data values on those cards.

EXERCISES

Answers to all exercises in this chapter are given in Appendix A.

3.1 Put an X through any of the following which are not a part of the COBOL character set:

$$W + \times - \div \# \$ \pounds \& a ; : [\Theta \; Q \; \theta \; \frac{1}{2} \; 5 \; \pi \; * \; \neq \; \tilde{N}$$

3.2 From this list of PROGRAMMER-INVENTED-NAMES, identify those which are invalid and tell what is wrong with them.

    a. TOP-OF-PROCEDURE-DIVISION
    b. 2-STAR-GENERALS
    c. **-GENERALS
    d. U.S.-AIR-FORCE
    e. CLASS-OF-58-GRADUATES
    f. %-OF-RESIGNATIONS
    g. PERCENTAGE-OF-STUDENTS-WHO-FAIL
    h. DATE WRITTEN
    i. DATE-WRITTEN
    j. DATE-WRITTEN-BY-ME
    k. LOST-CARD-NO-

3.3 From this list of NUMERIC-LITERALS, identify those which are invalid and tell what is wrong with them.

    a. −.425
    b. 0.25
    c. .25
    d. 25.0
    e. 25.
    f. 25
    g. 14,263

    h. 1/2
    i. $9.25
    j. 1234567890123456789
    k. −23456789.123456789
    l. 418.
    m. 35MM
    n. '21.4'

3.4 From this list of NON-NUMERIC-LITERALS, identify those which are invalid, and tell what is wrong with them.

    a. '21.4'
    b. 'YOUR ACCOUNT IS PAST DUE.'
    c. 'YOUR CHANGE IN $ AND ¢'
    d. '98.6 DEGREES FAHRENHEIT'
    e. '$100,000.'
    f. 'P. & L. STATEMENT'
    g. 'IT'S IMPOSSIBLE'
    h. 'BLUE CROSS/BLUE SHIELD'

3.5 Which of the following are NOT figurative constants?

    ZERO   ONE   TWO   THREE

3.6 TRUE or FALSE? Whenever a comma is shown in an example in this book, it is a mandatory comma.

3.7 TRUE or FALSE? The computer reads all 80 columns of a data card, but only the first 72 columns of an instruction card.

3.8 TRUE or FALSE? Sequence numbers are not placed on data cards because

they would be mistakenly interpreted by the computer as data-values to be processed by the program.

3.9 What column on a COBOL instruction card is referred to as Margin A? As Margin B? *[handwritten: 12]* *[handwritten: 8]*

3.10 What field begins at each of the following locations on a COBOL instruction card: *[handwritten: seq no field]*
    a. Column 1.
    b. Margin A. *[handwritten: name]*
    c. Margin B. *[handwritten: text]*
    d. Column 73. *[handwritten: ident.]* *[handwritten: Continue comments]*

3.11 Column 7 has two purposes. What are they? *[handwritten: Continue Comments]*

3.12 TRUE or FALSE? Any item which begins at Margin A *must* remain within the Name Field (columns 8–11).

3.13 TRUE or FALSE? Any item which begins at Margin B *must* remain within the Text Field (columns 12–72).

3.14 TRUE or FALSE? The hyphen is not necessary when breaking a continued sentence at a convenient space.

3.15 TRUE or FALSE? When continuing a line by breaking it in the middle of a non-numeric literal, you have the choice of breaking the literal at a convenient space or in the middle of a word.

3.16 If you wanted to include a long comment in your program, so long that it took four cards to hold it all, how many comment characters (asterisks in column 7) would you use?

3.17 TRUE or FALSE? Comment cards are included in an instruction deck to give additional information about your program to the computer.

3.18 TRUE or FALSE? Comment cards may only be included in your PROCE-DURE DIVISION.

3.19 Place the following sentence on a COBOL Coding Form using sequence number 250 for the first line:

    IF NUMBER-OF-PARTS-ON-HAND IS LESS THAN DESIRED-MINIMUM-STOCKAGE-LEVEL, THEN MOVE THE QUANTITY OF THIS PART IS TOO LOW; TIME TO PLACE AN ORDER FOR MORE.' TO SUPERVISORS-MESSAGE.

4 The IDENTIFICATION and ENVIRONMENT DIVISIONS

4.1 This Textbook vs. a *COBOL Reference Manual*

We're about to start the first detailed discussions of the four divisions of a COBOL program and their many component parts. Before we do, let me say a word about the approach I will take.

There are two approaches I *could* take. One would involve presenting 100 percent complete explanations of each of the many program components (sentences, paragraphs, sections and divisions) as we came to them. The discussions of each of these would be complete with descriptions of every last option and restriction associated with it. This approach has serious disadvantages. As you will see, there are a dozen or more options and restrictions associated with each program component. Many of them you will not be equipped even to understand until much later in the book. Others are so obscure that not even an experienced COBOL programmer needs to know about them more often than once in ten years. If they were all presented at your first exposure to each component, you would soon find yourself saturated with long lists of seldom violated restrictions and seldom used options. At the same time you would be failing to develop an understanding of the most frequently used versions of the most important program components.

The other approach, and the one I intend to take, is to present each component in its most easily digestible form first. Then as the text moves along, whenever we find ourselves in a position either requiring some undiscussed option or vulnerable to a violation of an undisclosed restriction, I will present it to you. I will adopt the practice of establishing first a *need* for a more complex version of each component before I reveal the availability of that version.

Remember after all that this is a textbook. Its prime purpose is to present COBOL to you in a way that will make your learning of the language as painless as possible. Although you will probably keep this book to refer back to in later years, it is not primarily a reference book. There *is* a COBOL publication whose prime purpose is to serve as a reference: the *COBOL Reference Manual*.

Back in the early 1960s when COBOL was being developed, it was hoped that the language would evolve into a completely universal one, one that would work in exactly the same form on any and all computers. Unfortunately for us, they were only 90 percent successful in achieving that goal. Although as a general rule COBOL is COBOL no matter what computer you

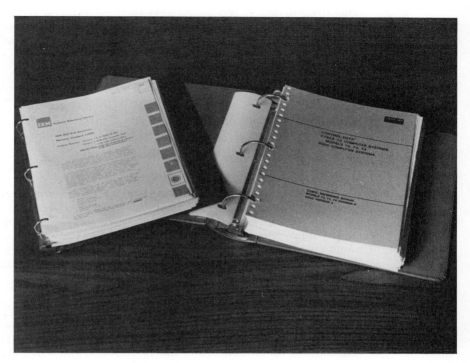

FIGURE 4.1   Sample COBOL Reference Manuals

use it on, there are some minor changes that must be made to any COBOL program which was written to run on one particular model of computer before it can be run on another model. For that reason each computer manufacturer publishes a separate *COBOL Reference Manual* for every model of computer he manufactures. In that manual you can find a description of every program component in the language complete with the long list of options and restrictions that apply to it for that particular model computer. If you were to take out the *COBOL Reference Manual* at your computer center library right now, you'd find it written in a style very nearly impossible for you to comprehend. It was not written with *you* in mind (as this book was). It was written for the experienced programmer and uses the vocabulary of an experienced programmer.

When you finish this book, you then will find yourself equipped to make sense of your center's *COBOL Reference Manual*. Until then your instructor will be the person to turn to for information regarding those few places where the COBOL rules I describe here do not conform exactly with the version in use on your particular computer.

4.2   The IDENTIFICATION DIVISION

Every program starts off with this division whose purpose is simply to give some information about the origin and purpose of the program. Unlike the other three divisions, it does not have sections. It has seven paragraphs each with its own special name. These paragraph-names are *not* programmer-invented-names; they come from the reserved word list. As mentioned in Chapter 3, the paragraph-names are coded at Margin A, and each is followed by a period.

```
PROGRAM-ID.
AUTHOR.
INSTALLATION.
DATE-WRITTEN.
DATE-COMPILED.
SECURITY.
REMARKS.
```

The PROGRAM-ID paragraph is the only paragraph which is *required*. The other six are optional. The PROGRAM-ID paragraph contains the official name of the program. It is a programmer-invented-name and must conform to the rules governing the formation of such names. The name given to the program may not be used anywhere else in the program. (Be sure you notice that the names of this and two later paragraphs contain hyphens.) Example:

```
PROGRAM-ID.
    CREDIT-RATING-PROGRAM.
```

As mentioned above, the remaining six paragraphs are optional. You may include all of them if you like or omit any you wish, but those you use must be in the order presented here. They are not for the use of the computer, but are considered a part of the "documentation" of a program.

Documentation is a term which describes any purely explanatory information provided with a program for the enlightenment of other humans, but is essentially ignored by the computer. Comment cards, described in Chapter 3, are considered a part of a program's documentation. Because of the importance of writing programs so others can understand them, most Data Processing Managers stress the use of documentation, and therefore insist that their programmers include these six optional paragraphs in their IDENTIFICATION DIVISIONs.

Since the contents of the remaining paragraphs are ignored by the computer, there is very little restriction on what they may contain. There are really only two restrictions: They may contain only characters from the COBOL character set, and they must end with a period.

The AUTHOR paragraph provides a place for you to claim your rightful glory as the author of this ingenious program. Example:

```
AUTHOR.
    GARRY A WILLIAMS.
```

In the INSTALLATION paragraph you can give credit to the employer who showed such wisdom in hiring such an ingenious programmer. (Don't forget that there are two L's in this paragraph's name.) Example:

```
INSTALLATION.
    ES+GS COMPUTATION CENTER.
```

In the DATE-WRITTEN paragraph you record the date on which you (what else?) wrote the program. Example:

```
DATE-WRITTEN.
     APRIL 5, 1978.
```

Although you might run your program on the same day you write it, chances are you'll run it many more times on later dates. As you know, every time you run a program it is compiled, and for that reason the next paragraph is entitled DATE-COMPILED. This is a somewhat unusual paragraph. No matter what date *you* might include in it, each time you run the program the computer will replace your date with the date of that run. Suppose you provided a DATE-COMPILED paragraph like this:

```
DATE-COMPILED.
     APRIL 7, 1978.
```

When you ran your program on April 26, this program listing would include this paragraph:

```
DATE-COMPILED.
     78/04/26.
```

Note that the computer provides the date in a format of its own choosing. Each computer has its own form, but they are usually not difficult to decipher whatever their form.

The SECURITY paragraph allows you to stipulate what measure of protection the program is to receive. Many companies keep their prize programs from their competitors and from the general public. In such a case this might be the form of this paragraph:

```
SECURITY.
     ACCESS RESTRICTED TO ES+GS CREDIT DEPT STAFF.
```

In the REMARKS paragraph you usually make some remark regarding the purpose of the program. For example:

```
REMARKS.
     THIS PROGRAM ASSIGNS CREDIT RATINGS TO CUSTOMERS BASED UPON
     SUBSCRIBER PROVIDED DATA SUCH AS PAYMENT RECORDS, PAST DUE
     NOTICES, ETC.
```

Figure 4.2 shows the IDENTIFICATION DIVISION I've been describing in the above examples as it would appear on the coding form. In Figure 4.3 I show an acceptable alternate arrangement for this division. It takes advantage of the fact that the rule presented in Chapter 3 which said, "Sentences must begin at Margin B," is actually somewhat more lenient than that. It allows sentences to begin anywhere, as long as they *don't* begin to the *left* of Margin B. Programmers most often take advantage of this leniency when they write the IDENTIFICATION and ENVIRONMENT DIVISIONs where the sentences are so short. Note that for the sake of

1,0	IDENTIFICATION DIVISION.						
2,0	PROGRAM-ID.						
3,0	CREDIT-RATING-PROGRAM.						
4,0	AUTHOR.						
5,0	GARRY A WILLIAMS.						
6,0	INSTALLATION.						
7,0	E5+G5 COMPUTATION CENTER.						
8,0	DATE-WRITTEN.						
9,0	APRIL 5, 1978.						
10,0	DATE-COMPILED.						
11,0	APRIL 7, 1978.						
12,0	SECURITY.						
13,0	ACCESS RESTRICTED TO E5+G5 CREDIT DEPT STAFF.						
14,0	REMARKS.						
15,0	THIS PROGRAM ASSIGNS CREDIT RATINGS TO CUSTOMERS BASED UPON						
16,0	SUBSCRIBER PROVIDED DATA SUCH AS PAYMENT RECORDS, PAST DUE						
17,0	NOTICES, ETC.						

FIGURE 4.2   The IDENTIFICATION DIVISION

orderly appearance, I've lined all my sentences up on the same column. No official requirement exists for you to do this, but if you do it, be sure you provide for at least one space following the period after every paragraph-name.

Notice also in Figure 4.3 that I have left the DATE-COMPILED paragraph blank. This is what most programmers do since they know the computer's going to fill that in for them anyway.

4.3   The ENVIRONMENT DIVISION

This, the second division of a COBOL program, has the purpose of describing the "environment" in which the program was designed to run. Do you recall my mentioning in Section 4.1 that COBOL is only 90 percent universal and that a program written for one computer will probably require some small changes before it will run on another? In the ENVIRONMENT DIVISION we tell what computer the program was written for. We also announce which input and output devices the program uses and which files of data are going to be on each device.

To begin with, notice that the word *environment* has *three* N's in it. That is a small but important point that many people overlook.

There are two sections in the ENVIRONMENT DIVISION. As mentioned in Chapter 3, the section-names are coded at Margin A. To distinguish these names from paragraph-names, we place the word SECTION after them before the period.

ENVIRONMENT DIVISION.
CONFIGURATION SECTION.
INPUT-OUTPUT SECTION.

```
  1.0  IDENTIFICATION DIVISION.
  2.0  PROGRAM-ID.    CREDIT-RATING-PROGRAM.
  3.0  AUTHOR.        GARRY A WILLIAMS.
  4.0  INSTALLATION.  ES+GS COMPUTATION CENTER.
  5.0  DATE-WRITTEN.  APRIL 5, 1978.
  6.0  DATE-COMPILED.
  7.0  SECURITY.      ACCESS RESTRICTED TO ES+GS CREDIT DEPT STAFF.
  8.0  REMARKS.       THIS PROGRAM ASSIGNS CREDIT RATINGS TO CUSTOMERS
  9.0       BASED UPON SUBSCRIBER PROVIDED DATA SUCH AS PAYMENT RECORDS,
 10.0       PAST DUE NOTICES, ETC.
```

FIGURE 4.3   The IDENTIFICATION DIVISION

It is in the CONFIGURATION SECTION that we announce the model of computer we wrote the program to run on. There are two paragraphs in this section:

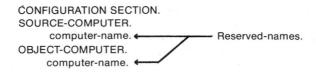

```
CONFIGURATION SECTION.
SOURCE-COMPUTER.
     computer-name. ←——————————— Reserved-names.
OBJECT-COMPUTER.
     computer-name. ←
```

In the SOURCE-COMPUTER and OBJECT-COMPUTER paragraphs you tell the name(s) of the computer(s) on which the source program and the object program are designed to run. (If you've forgotten what the terms source program and object program mean, better go back and take another look at Section 1.8.) Usually these two paragraphs contain the same computer-name, but there are occasions when they do not.

The computer-names are *not* programmer-invented-names; they come from the reserved word list for your particular computer. For your programs, your instructor will have to tell you the exact spelling of the name which your computer "answers to." Example:

```
CONFIGURATION SECTION.
SOURCE-COMPUTER.
     HAL-2001.
OBJECT-COMPUTER.
     HAL-2001.
```

In the INPUT-OUTPUT SECTION (notice the hyphen) there is only one paragraph that we will concern ourselves with in this book, and that is the FILE-CONTROL paragraph:

```
INPUT-OUTPUT SECTION.
FILE-CONTROL.
     select-sentence.
     select-sentence.
     select-sentence.
          etc.
```

In the FILE-CONTROL paragraph are any number of select-sentences of the following form:

These select-sentences have the dual purpose of (1) announcing the names of the files you'll be using and (2) telling on which input or output devices they are located. Up to this point we have only considered two types of data files, a card file (made up of the data deck of your program) and a printer file (the "file" of information generated and printed by your program on the line printer). Later we will discuss data files on magnetic tape and magnetic disc. The names of your files are invented by you, and here is where you announce what they will be.

The device-name is a name from the reserved word list which identifies the input or output device upon which the file you have named in that select-sentence is located. Almost every computer system has a different set of device-names which it uses to designate its various input and output devices. (For example: On the IBM System/360 the card reader goes by the device-name UR-2501-S-CARDS, and the line printer goes by the device-name UR-1403-S-PRINTOUT. The CDC-6600 uses much simpler device-names: INPUT for the card reader, and OUTPUT for the line printer.) This is one of those things you'll have to ask your instructor about for your computer. For the purpose of this textbook and in the interest of simplicity, I will use two fictitious device-names that are used by no computer I know of, but whose meaning will be self-evident: CARD-READER and LINE-PRINTER.

Here is an example INPUT-OUTPUT SECTION:

```
INPUT-OUTPUT SECTION.
FILE-CONTROL.
    SELECT GAS-CHARGES-FILE ASSIGN TO CARD-READER.
    SELECT CUSTOMER-BILLS-LISTING ASSIGN TO LINE-PRINTER.
```

Figure 4.4 shows the ENVIRONMENT DIVISION I've been describing in the above examples as most programmers would place it on the coding form.

```
200  ENVIRONMENT DIVISION.
210  CONFIGURATION SECTION.
220  SOURCE-COMPUTER.  HAL-2001.
230  OBJECT-COMPUTER.  HAL-2001.
240  INPUT-OUTPUT SECTION.
250  FILE-CONTROL.
260      SELECT GAS-CHARGES-FILE ASSIGN TO CARD-READER.
270      SELECT CUSTOMER-BILLS-LISTING ASSIGN TO LINE-PRINTER.
```

FIGURE 4.4   The ENVIRONMENT DIVISION

All of the sections and paragraphs of the ENVIRONMENT DIVISION that I have described here are mandatory. None are optional, and they must appear in the order I have shown.

4.4 Division, Section and Paragraph Headers

Now that you have been exposed to a division which has both paragraphs *and* sections, let me point out explicitly something you may have already noticed yourself. Each of these organizational elements of a COBOL program begins with an identifying header. The headers take the following forms:

	FORM	EXAMPLE
Division Header	division-name DIVISION.	ENVIRONMENT DIVISION.
Section Header	section-name SECTION.	INPUT-OUTPUT SECTION.
Paragraph Header	paragraph-name.	FILE-CONTROL.

All three headers are coded at Margin A. All three end in periods. The computer recognizes a division header by the appearance of the word DIVISION. The word DIVISION is *not* a part of the division-name, and that is why no hyphen is used to connect it to the division-name. Likewise, a section header is recognized by the appearance of the word SECTION, which is also *not* a part of the section-name. A paragraph header is recognized by the absence of either word, DIVISION or SECTION.

All four division-names are reserved-names (names on the reserved word list). All section-names and paragraph-names *except* those in the PROCEDURE DIVISION are reserved-names. Section-names and paragraph-names in the PROCEDURE DIVISION are programmer-invented-names.

EXERCISES

Answers to all exercises in this chapter are given in Appendix A.

4.1 TRUE or FALSE? If your computer center decided to turn in its GE model 225 computer for a GE model 635, your GE-225 COBOL Reference Manual would be perfectly alright for use with the GE-635 since both are GE computers.

4.2 TRUE or FALSE? The COBOL Reference Manual is not written in English.

4.3 TRUE or FALSE? The COBOL Reference Manual is written in English, but it uses terminology which you are not now equipped to understand.

4.4 TRUE or FALSE? The reserved word list in effect for any particular computer can be found in the COBOL Reference Manual for that computer.

4.5 TRUE or FALSE? A COBOL program written for the Honeywell-200 will have to be completely re-written before it will run on the CDC-6400.

4.6 Find the errors in this example IDENTIFICATION DIVISION:

```
10 IDENTIFICATION-DIVISION.
20 PROGRAM ID.    FIRST-PROGRAM.
30 AUTHOR.        JIM HANNON
40 INSTALATION.   U. S. C. COMPUTER CENTER.
50 DATE WRITTEN. APRIL 5, '78.
60 DATE COMPILED.
```

4.7 Find the errors in this example IDENTIFICATION DIVISION:

```
10 IDENTIFICATION  DIVISION.
20 AUTHOR.         MAURICE GUSTIN.
30 INSTALLATION.   SD&B COMPUTATION CENTER.
40 REMARKS.        THIS IS MY FIRST COBOL PROGRAM.
50 DATE-COMPILED.
```

out of place

4.8 Find the errors in this example IDENTIFICATION DIVISION:

```
10 IDENTIFICATION DIVISION.
20 PROGRAM-ID. SECOND PROGRAM.
```

4.9 Find the errors in this example ENVIRONMENT DIVISION:

```
 70 ENVIROMENT  DIVISION.
 80 CONFIGURATION-SECTION.
 90 OBJECT-COMPUTER.  HAL-2001.
100 SOURCE-COMPUTER. HAL-2001.
110 INPUT OUTPUT SECTION.
120     SELECT MY-DATA-FILE ASSIGN TO  CARD-READER.
130     SELECT MY-DATA-FILE ASSIGN TO  LINE-PRINTER.
```

4.10 Find the errors in this ENVIRONMENT DIVISION:

```
 70 ENVIRONMENT DIVISION.
 80 CONFIGURATION SECTION.
 90 SOURCE-COMPUTER HAL-2001.
100 INPUT-OUTPUT SECTION.
110 FILE-CONTROL PARAGRAPH.
120     SELECT THE-OUTPUT-FILE ASSIGN TO LINE-PRINTER.
130     SELECT THE-INPUT-FILE ASSIGN TO CARD-READER.
```

4.11 TRUE or FALSE? Section-names in the IDENTIFICATION DIVI-SION are reserved-names.

4.12 TRUE or FALSE? Section-names in the ENVIRONMENT DIVISION are programmer-invented-names.

4.13 In which division or divisions does the programmer invent his own paragraph-names and section-names?

4.14 Which division or divisions are not and may not be divided into sections?

5 A First Look at the DATA DIVISION: The FILE SECTION

5.1 Introduction

The purpose of this extremely important division is to describe the organization of the data that will be used by the program. The result of this division is the assignment of "post office boxes" (memory locations) in the memory unit to all the various data-names that are to be used in the program.

Remember—if a data-name is not mentioned in the DATA DIVISION, it *may not* be referred to in the PROCEDURE DIVISION. The sentences in the PROCEDURE DIVISION are restricted to referencing only data-names about which the computer has been forewarned in the DATA DIVISION. For that reason many programmers view this as the most vital element of the whole program. They spend the largest portion of their time in writing this division and consider their work 80 percent complete when it's finished.

The DATA DIVISION is made up of two sections:

```
DATA DIVISION.
FILE SECTION.
WORKING-STORAGE SECTION.
```

As you know from Chapter 4, these section-names are reserved-names. Neither section is actually mandatory, per se. (A tricky programmer *could* write a program that used *neither* section, although what that program accomplished wouldn't be worth two cents—unless, of course, the programmer was "tricky" enough to sucker you into betting against him.) As a practical matter, however, any program worth its salt will always have a FILE SECTION, and most will also have a WORKING-STORAGE SECTION. For your purposes, consider the FILE SECTION to be mandatory and the WORKING-STORAGE SECTION to be optional.

Simply speaking, the programmer uses the FILE SECTION to describe all data which comes from files stored externally to the computer. In the WORKING-STORAGE SECTION he describes data which is generated within the computer, such as intermediate results produced by early computational steps that will be used by later computational steps in calculating the final results. (For example: To calculate a person's NET-PAY, you'd first multiply his HOURS-WORKED by his PAY-RATE to get his GROSS-PAY. Then you'd add all his deductions to get his TOTAL-DEDUCTIONS.

Finally, you'd subtract TOTAL-DEDUCTIONS from GROSS-PAY to get NET-PAY. In this example, GROSS-PAY and TOTAL-DEDUCTIONS were *intermediate results* which had to be calculated before you could calculate the final result, NET-PAY. They would both have to be described in the WORKING-STORAGE SECTION.)

A parallel can be drawn between the DATA DIVISION's two sections and the material you use while taking an open-book examination. Your notes, out of which you get needed information, and your test booklet, into which you write your final answers, correspond to things which would be described in the FILE SECTION. Your scratch pad where you perform all your rough calculations corresponds to something which would be described in the WORKING-STORAGE SECTION.

In this Chapter we will discuss only the FILE SECTION. We'll hold the WORKING-STORAGE SECTION until after you've written your first program, one which will use only the FILE SECTION.

I call your attention to my "Note to FORTRAN-Experienced Programmers" in the box that follows. There will be several such boxes throughout the book. If you are learning COBOL as your first programming language, you should completely ignore these boxes. Many people learn COBOL as a second language, however; and most of them learned FORTRAN first. There are many similarities between the two languages, but there are also many places where former FORTRANners might be tempted to assume a similarity existed where in fact there was none. It is the purpose of these boxes to call attention to such illusive dissimilarities.

A Note to FORTRAN-Experienced Programmers—The DATA DIVISION does for a COBOL program essentially what your FORMAT statements as a group did for your FORTRAN programs, with one important difference. In FORTRAN you FORMATed only those variables which were to be input or output. In COBOL you must "FORMAT" *all* variables, even those which are not involved in input or output operations. There is this parallel, however; the variables which are to be input or output will be "FORMATed" in the FILE SECTION, while those which are not will be "FORMATed" in the WORKING-STORAGE SECTION.

5.2 COBOL Data Organization

COBOL views its data as being organized in much the same manner as an office does:

1. Several different FILES.
2. Each file made up of a group of many RECORDS.
3. Each record containing a group of logically associated pieces of information, referred to in computer programming as ITEMS OF DATA.

Think of an office that is familiar to most students, the registrar's office. Within that office are:

1. Several FILES—one for freshmen, one for sophomores, one for juniors, and one for seniors.
2. Within each class file are many RECORDS—one for each student in that class.
3. On each record are many ITEMS OF DATA, all "logically associated" because they all pertain to one student—her name, her address, her phone number, her grades for each course she has taken, etc.

How about a large department store? In its main offices are:

1. Several FILES—one for the furniture department, one for the ladies wear department, one for the sporting goods department, etc.
2. Within each department file are many RECORDS—one for each piece of merchandise sold by that department.
3. On each record are many logically associated ITEMS OF DATA all applying to one piece of merchandise—its stock number, its name, its price, its size, its color, the number on hand in the store, the number on hand in the warehouse, etc.

We use the same terminology in describing the organization of data for a COBOL program, except we go one level deeper and describe in more detail the ITEMS OF DATA. Two terms are used:

GROUP-ITEMS and ELEMENTARY-ITEMS.

A GROUP-ITEM of data is one which is broken down into several ELEMEN-TARY-ITEMS and/or smaller GROUP-ITEMS. An ELEMENTARY-ITEM of data is one which is *not* further broken down. Consider the example record shown in Figure 5.1. It is a data card containing a customer's name, account number, and address.

On this record there are four GROUP-ITEMS of data:

1. NAME
2. ADDR
3. STREET-ADDRESS
4. CITY-ADDRESS

There are eight ELEMENTARY-ITEMS of data:

1. LAST-NAME
2. FIRST-NAME
3. ACCT-NO
4. NO
5. STREET
6. CITY

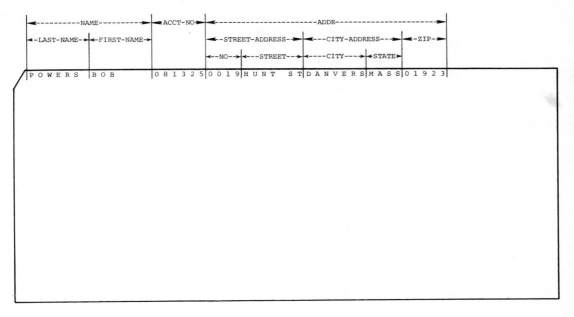

FIGURE 5.1   Items of Data on a COBOL Record

7. STATE
8. ZIP

The rest of this chapter will be devoted to showing you how FILES, RECORDS, and GROUP- and ELEMENTARY-ITEMS of data are described to the computer in the FILE SECTION of the DATA DIVISION.

5.3 File Description

Every file that is used by a COBOL program is described in its FILE SECTION by a File Description (or FD) entry. An FD entry begins with the letters FD coded at Margin A. The remainder of the entry consists of four clauses which are coded at Margin B. This is the form of the FD entry:

```
FD  file-name;
      RECORD CONTAINS integer CHARACTERS;
                          ( OMITTED )
      LABEL RECORDS ARE {    or    } ;
                          ( STANDARD )
            ( RECORD IS   )
      DATA {    or        } record-name-1, record-name-2, etc.
            ( RECORDS ARE  )
```

The file-name makes up the first clause. This must be a file-name which you mentioned in one of the ENVIRONMENT DIVISION's select-sentences.

Next comes the RECORD CONTAINS clause. In this clause you specify how many characters there are on each record in the file. If it were a file of data cards, you'd use a value of 80 for the integer (since a data card is 80 character positions long), and the clause would say

RECORD CONTAINS 80 CHARACTERS

The LABEL RECORDS clause is next. You have the option of saying that they are OMITTED or STANDARD. I'll say very little about this clause now and hold further discussion until later in the book. From now until I tell you otherwise, always use

LABEL RECORDS ARE OMITTED

In the final clause, the DATA RECORD clause, you give the name by which you intend to refer to the records in this file. In most cases all the records in a file will have their items of data in exactly the same arrangement, and when that is so, the clause is used in this form:

DATA RECORD IS GRADE-CARD.

In that example we have announced that all records in the file are of one type, and that we will call each of them by the same record-name, GRADE-CARD.

You will have occasional contact with files made up of records whose data arrangements are *not* all the same. In such cases your DATA RECORD clause will be used in this form:

DATA RECORDS ARE CHARGE-CARD, PAYMENT-RECORD.

In that example we have announced that the file contains records of *two* different types. We'll be referring to one type by the record-name CHARGE-CARD, and the other as PAYMENT-RECORD.

In Figure 5.2 I show an FD entry as it would appear on a coding form. In Figure 5.3 I show the same FD entry in an acceptable alternate arrangement. You'll notice that in one arrangement I chose to include semicolons to enhance readability, but in the other I left them out. If you'll refer back to the outline form of the FD entry I gave at the beginning of this

210	FD.	CUSTOMER-ADDRESS-FILE
220		RECORD CONTAINS 80 CHARACTERS
230		LABEL RECORDS ARE OMITTED
240		DATA RECORD IS CUSTOMER-ADDRESS-CARD.

FIGURE 5.2   An Example File Description Entry

```
2 1 0   FD  CUSTOMER-ADDRESS-FILE; RECORD CONTAINS 80 CHARACTERS; LABEL
2 2 0       RECORDS ARE OMITTED; DATA RECORD IS CUSTOMER-ADDRESS-CARD.
```

FIGURE 5.3   An Alternate Arrangement of the Example File Description Entry of Figure 5.2

section, you'll see I showed that it included semi-colons. Recall that semi-colons are *always* optional punctuation, but that periods are not. The FD entry is ended by a period.

5.4 Record Description

When you describe a record, what you actually do is describe the arrangement of data items on the record. A system of level-numbers is used in COBOL to indicate the so-called "hierarchy" of the items of data. To help me explain what is meant by "hierarchy" in this context, let me refer back to Figure 5.1. There we had a record containing three principal fields of data:

1. NAME
2. ACCT-NO
3. ADDR

Two of these three principal fields were broken down into sub-fields:

1. NAME
   - LAST-NAME
   - FIRST-NAME
2. ADDR
   - STREET-ADDRESS
   - CITY-ADDRESS
   - ZIP

Two of the sub-fields were broken down into sub-sub-fields:

1. STREET-ADDRESS
   - NO
   - STREET
2. CITY-ADDRESS
   - CITY
   - STATE

To convey this "ranked" organization of data to the computer, we use a form of notation shown as it would appear on a coding form in Figure 5.4. The numbers in front of each of the data-names are called the level-numbers. Level-number 01 is reserved for use on the line containing the record-name. You are free to use any other numbers from 02 through 49 as level-numbers for your data-names.

```
01   CUSTOMER-ADDRESS-CARD
     02   NAME
          03   LAST-NAME
          03   FIRST-NAME
     02   ACCT-NO
     02   ADDR
          03   STREET-ADDRESS
               04   NO
               04   STREET
          03   CITY-ADDRESS
               04   CITY
               04   STATE
          03   ZIP
```

FIGURE 5.4   The Use of Level-Numbers in a Record Description

Figure 5.4 illustrates the rules which govern how you communicate a record's data hierarchy to the computer:

1. The *lower* the rank of a data-name in the hierarchy, the *higher* is the level-number assigned to it.

2. The *lower* the rank of a data-name, the *farther to the right* are it and its level-number coded.

3. Data-names of *equal rank* are given the *same level-number* and are coded starting in the *same column*.

The rules governing the format of the record description are also demonstrated in Figure 5.4:

1. Level-number 01 is always coded at Margin A.

2. Level-numbers 02 through 49 are coded at or to the right of Margin B.

3. Two spaces are left between a level-number and its corresponding data-name.

4. Each level-number is coded four columns to the right of the next lower level-number.

You are not required to use consecutive level-numbers in going to each lower level in the data hierarchy as I did (02 then 03 then 04). As long as the level-numbers you use are in ascending order as you proceed down the hierarchy (for example: 02 then 15 then 34), that is sufficient.

210	FD.	CUSTOMER-ADDRESS-FILE; RECORD CONTAINS 80 CHARACTERS; LABEL						
220		RECORDS ARE OMITTED; DATA RECORD IS CUSTOMER-ADDRESS-CARD.						
230	01	CUSTOMER-ADDRESS-CARD.						
240		02 NAME.						
250		03 LAST-NAME						
260		03 FIRST-NAME						
270		02 ACCT-NO						
280		02 ADDR.						
290		03 STREET-ADDRESS.						
300		04 NO						
310		04 STREET						
320		03 CITY-ADDRESS.						
330		04 CITY						
340		04 STATE						
350		03 ZIP						
360		02 FILLER						

FIGURE 5.5   The Relationship Between the File Description and the Record Description Entries

The record description is located in the FILE SECTION immediately after the FD entry to which it applies. This is shown in Figure 5.5. Note that the same record-name appears in both the DATA RECORD clause of the FD entry and the 01 level item of the record description. This is an absolute MUST!

One other point not mentioned so far which pops up in Figure 5.5 is the last line in the record description, the FILLER. FILLER is a reserved word whose purpose is, among other things which we'll discuss as we go along, to describe fields within records which contain blanks or other data about which we have no interest. In this example the record is an 80-column data card. There is useful data on only the first portion of the card. The last portion of the card is empty, and we use the FILLER to forewarn the computer of this fact.

Did you notice that I placed periods after some but not all of the data-names in Figure 5.5? All the data-names who now have their periods are those of GROUP-ITEMS. At this point in the program, the programmer has said all that he is going to say in describing his GROUP-ITEMS of data, so he closes those entries with periods. ELEMENTARY-ITEMS, on the other hand, still need their PICTURE clauses before their entries are complete. (Take another look at Section 5.2 if you've forgotten what GROUP- and ELEMENTARY-ITEMS of data are.)

5.5   The Purpose and Form of the PICTURE Clause

A PICTURE clause is used with every ELEMENTARY-ITEM of data described in the DATA DIVISION. The purpose of the PICTURE clause is to forewarn the computer about the form of the data-values you plan to give to that item of data. It has the following form:

PICTURE character-string

Generally speaking, the PICTURE clause's character-string tells the computer:

1. The SIZE of the item.
2. The CLASS of the item.

The size of an item is the maximum number of characters that its data-values can be expected to have.

There are three classes of data we will consider in this chapter:

CLASS	DATA-VALUE MAY CONTAIN
Numeric (N) Alphabetic (AB) Alphanumeric (AN)	Only digits. Only letters & spaces. Any COBOL characters.

Figure 5.6 demonstrates the use of the terms CLASS and SIZE as they refer to some example data-values.

DATA VALUE	SIZE	CONTENTS	CLASS
127	3	Digits.	N
12 7	4	Digits & space.	AN
1207	4	Digits.	N
12.07	5	Digits & special character.	AN
$12.07	6	Digits & special characters.	AN
1,207	5	Digits & special character.	AN
COD	3	Letters.	AB
C O D	5	Letter & spaces.	AB
C. O. D.	8	Letter, spaces & special characters.	AN
58	2	Digits.	N
058	3	Digits.	N
5 8	3	Digits & space.	AN

FIGURE 5.6   The CLASS and SIZE of Example Data-Values

5.6   The Numeric PICTURE Clause

The character-string of a numeric (class N) PICTURE clause may be made up of one or more of the following characters:

9   V   S   P

You use a 9 to indicate a character position which will contain a digit.

Consider this example entry from the DATA DIVISION of a COBOL program:

    03   ZIP-CODE   PICTURE 99999.

Here the computer has been forewarned that the data-name ZIP-CODE will have data-values given to it, all of which will be five digits long. Consider a second example:

    03   PHONE-NUMBER   PICTURE 9999999.

There we have told the computer that all PHONE-NUMBERs will be made up of seven digits.

This is an equivalent "short-hand" way of writing the last example:

    03   PHONE-NUMBER   PICTURE 9(7).

Whenever you have repeated characters in a PICTURE clause, you may indicate the repetition with that sort of parenthetical notation. Hence:

    PICTURE 9(2). has the same meaning as PICTURE 99.
    PICTURE 9(3). has the same meaning as PICTURE 999.
    PICTURE 9(9). has the same meaning as PICTURE 999999999.
    PICTURE 9(12). has the same meaning as PICTURE 999999999999.

A word of caution—Suppose you had this entry in your DATA DIVISION:

    03   P-O-BOX   PICTURE 9999.

That entry promises the computer that all post office boxes will have four digit numbers. In preparing your data deck, you will then *have* to reserve four columns on each card for the post office box number. Furthermore, since you promised that all four character positions will contain digits, when you come to the person whose post office box number is (for example) 24, you will have to be sure to punch it on the card as 0024.

A Note to FORTRAN-Experienced Programmers—In FORTRAN the computer interprets a space on a data card as a zero. Not so in COBOL! If you leave a space in a field that is supposed to be numeric, you are considered guilty of having placed an alphanumeric character in a field which is supposed to contain only digits. Because of your FORTRAN background, you will be most often tempted to violate this rule in the case of leading zeros. Watch out for it!

In the cases we have discussed so far, all numeric data-values were integers (that is, they had no fractional or decimal part; they were whole numbers). When no mention is made of the position of the decimal point, the computer will assume correctly that you intend the item to contain only integer values.

The PICTURE clause characters V and P are used in connection with numeric data-values that are not integers. The character S is used with numeric data-values that could possibly be negative. We will return to the numeric PICTURE clause in Chapter 8 to discuss these additional characters, which we really do not need at this point.

5.7   The Alphabetic PICTURE Clause

The character-string of an alphabetic (class AB) PICTURE clause may be made up only of A's.

Similar in use to the 9 in a numeric PICTURE clause, the A is used to indicate a character position which will contain a letter or a space. For example, this entry appearing in the DATA DIVISION

    03   MONTH-NAME   PICTURE AAA.

would forewarn the computer that all MONTH-NAMEs will be made up of three letters. The only way the programmer could do that would be if he'd decided to abbreviate all month names down to three letters (JAN, FEB, MAR, etc.).

If he wanted to spell out the month names, he'd have to provide enough room for the longest name, SEPTEMBER, and use an entry like this:

    03   MONTH-NAME   PICTURE AAAAAAAAA.

                    or

    03   MONTH-NAME   PICTURE A(9).

Having promised the computer that all MONTH-NAMEs would be nine letters long, he will have to make good his promise by spelling the seven-letter name JANUARY with two spaces following it, FEBRUARY with one space, MARCH with four spaces, and so on.

Note that although the space is technically a special character, it is the *only* special character that may occur in a character position described by an A. To reiterate a point made in Figure 5.6, a person's name spelled as

    K E GORDON JR

would be acceptable as a class AB item. But if you spelled it

    K. E. GORDON, JR.

it is then a class AN item because of its periods and comma. You run into this same consideration in spelling addresses.

5.8 The Alphanumeric PICTURE Clause

The character-string of an alphanumeric (class AN) PICTURE clause may be made up of one or more of the following characters:

9   A   X

The 9 is used in a class AN PICTURE clause for exactly the same purpose as it was in a class N clause. Likewise, the A is used for exactly the same purpose as it was in a class AB clause.

The X is used to indicate a character position which could be occupied by *any* character in the COBOL set.

Here are some examples of the use of class AN PICTURE clauses: A leading department store uses catalog numbers of this form:

23XW92746F   35XG30428C

(two digits, two letters, five digits, and one letter). A program which uses catalog numbers of that form as one of its items of data would probably include this DATA DIVISION entry:

04   CATALOG-NUMBER   PICTURE 99AA9(5)A.

Consider blood types. They are expressed as

A+   A−   AB   O−

(a letter followed by a letter *or* a plus or minus). If a person's blood type were one of the fields on a data card describing him, this would be a suitable entry to describe that field:

03   BLOOD-TYPE PICTURE AX.

Most people write their social security numbers like this:

081-32-5549   013-30-0500

That would be described with a PICTURE 999X99X9999.

Suppose you wanted to enter dates of birth on all your data cards in this form:

26/APR/71

You could describe that form with the PICTURE 99XAAAX99

If you were reading carefully, you recall my telling you that X's could be used to indicate the positions of not only special characters, but *any* character in the COBOL set. It may have occurred to you to wonder if in the examples given above, the catalog number couldn't have been described with a PICTURE X(9), or the blood type with a PICTURE XX, or the social security number with a PICTURE X(11), or the birth date with a PICTURE X(9). Yes, they could.

My advice, however, has always been to "tell it like it is." If in the case of the date, you used a PICTURE 99XAAAX99 to describe the field, the computer would have been warned of the *exact* form in which it should expect to receive the data-value. If in keypunching one of your data cards, you accidentally omit one of the characters you were supposed to punch, all the characters which come after it will be shifted one position out of place to the left. When the computer gets to that card, it will find a slash (/) in the position where the second digit should be, and another slash in the position where the third letter should be. Since by your PICTURE clause you have given it the ability to know that's wrong, it will notify you of the faulty data card by way of a message printed on the line printer.

If, on the other hand, you had taken the easy way out and described that date field with the simpler PICTURE X(9), you would leave the computer ready to accept any characters whatever that happened to fall in those positions, and you would receive no notice of the faulty card.

There are times, however, when you cannot be more specific and *have* to use PICTURE clauses containing nothing but X's. Consider these addresses:

```
27 CHASE ST., DANVERS, MASS. 01923
3207 IDALIA ST., EL PASO, TEXAS 79930
P. O. BOX 1935, ROCHESTER, N. Y. 14603
```

There is simply no way to predict in those examples where the digits are going to be and where the punctuation is going to be. In every example they are in different positions. There is only one PICTURE clause that can be used to describe all of those address fields: PICTURE X(38).

5.9   The PICTURE Clause in Summary

This table summarizes what we've said about PICTURE clauses so far:

CLASS	DATA-VALUE MAY CONTAIN	PICTURE CLAUSE CHARACTERS
N	Only digits.	9 V S P
AB	Only letters & spaces.	A
AN	Any COBOL characters.	9 A X

Figure 5.7 shows the file and record description entries of Figure 5.5, now complete with the necessary PICTURE clauses.

Notice that all the PICTURE clauses are coded starting in the same column. There is no COBOL requirement that you do this. The only requirement is the obvious one that there be *at least* one space between the data-name and its PICTURE clause. Arranging the clauses one above the

210	FD	CUSTOMER-ADDRESS-FILE; RECORD CONTAINS 80 CHARACTERS; LABEL				
220		RECORDS ARE OMITTED; DATA RECORD IS CUSTOMER-ADDRESS-CARD.				
230	01	CUSTOMER-ADDRESS-CARD.				
240		02 NAME.				
250		03 LAST-NAME PICTURE A(7).				
260		03 FIRST-NAME PICTURE A(7).				
270		02 ACCT-NO PICTURE 9(6).				
280		02 ADDR.				
290		03 STREET-ADDRESS.				
300		04 NO PICTURE 9(4).				
310		04 STREET PICTURE A(7).				
320		03 CITY-ADDRESS.				
330		04 CITY PICTURE A(7).				
340		04 STATE PICTURE A(4).				
350		03 ZIP PICTURE 9(5).				
360		02 FILLER PICTURE X(33).				

FIGURE 5.7   A Complete File and Record Description

other in this way is one of those "good housekeeping" practices that most COBOL programmers adopt in time. It enhances the orderly appearance of the program, and makes any typographical errors you may have made in keypunching the program somewhat easier to spot.

Notice the PICTURE clause I used with the FILLER. It shows the FILLER to be class AN and size 33. Why class AN? Why size 33?

Let's take the last question first. As I've mentioned before, FILLER is being used here to tell the computer that there is a portion of the record it can forget about, because it's blank. We must also tell how big the FILLER portion of the record is. We're dealing with an 80 character record. The PICTURE clauses up to this point have accounted for 47 of the 80 character positions, so that leaves 33 for the FILLER.

Why class AN? This FILLER had as its purpose the marking off of a blank area on the data card, so it could just as easily have been class AB as AN. There are other uses for the FILLER, however. Another is to mark off a segment of a record which contains data-values you don't need and therefore want to skip over. (Sometimes to save yourself from having to punch your own data deck, you'll borrow one punched by someone else for another program. That data deck may contain many items of data, only a few of which are needed by your program. You'd place FILLERs in your record description entries to mark those fields on each data card which are not needed by your program.) Since the data-values you're skipping over could contain any characters, and you don't much care what they are, we customarily use the "all-purpose" character X in the PICTURE clauses for FILLERs.

EXERCISES

Answers to all exercises in this chapter are given in Appendix A.

5.1 Complete these sentences:
   - a. The DATA DIVISION describes the _____ of the data to be used.
   - b. As a result of the DATA DIVISION each _____ is assigned a _____ in the memory unit.

5.2 What is the essential difference between data-names appearing in the FILE SECTION and those appearing in the WORKING-STORAGE SECTION?

5.3 In COBOL's data organization:
   - a. A group of logically associated items of data comprise a _____.
   - b. A group of logically associated records comprise a _____.

5.4 Find the errors in the DATA DIVISION lines given below:

```
300  DATA DIVISION.
310  FILE   SECTION.
320  FD   DRIVERS-LICENSE-FILE.
330       RECORDS CONTAIN 80 CHARACTERS;
340       LABEL RECORDS ARE OMITTED.
350       DATA-RECORD IS APPLICATION-CARD.
360  01   DRIVER-APPLICATION.
370       02 etc.
```

5.5 In describing the contents of a record, level numbers are used to indicate the _____ of the data items.

5.6 Level number 01 is reserved for use with _____.

5.7 TRUE or FALSE? You are free to use any level numbers on your data items from 02 through 99.

5.8 TRUE or FALSE? Principal fields of data are always Group-items.

5.9 TRUE or FALSE? Sub-sub-fields of data are always Elementary-items.

5.10 Given here is enough of a record description for you to be able to distinguish the elementary-items from the group-items of data. Place an E or a G in each blank to the right to indicate whether the item to the left is an elementary- or a group-item.

```
                                            E or G
                                            _____
410  01  CAR-REGISTRATION-APPL.
420      02  OWNERS-NAME             _____
430          03  LAST-NAME           _____
440          03  INITIALS            _____
450              04  FIRST           _____
460              04  SECOND          _____
470      02  CAR-DESCRIPTION         _____
480          03  YEAR                _____
```

490	03	CAR-NAME	_____
500		04 MANUF	_____
510		04 MODEL	_____
520	03	BODY-STYLE	_____
530	03	IDENT-NO	_____
540	03	PRICE	_____
550		04 STICKER	_____
560		05 BASE	_____
570		05 EXTRAS	_____
580		04 SALES-TAX	_____

5.11 Which of the following *always* have PICTURE clauses?
  a. Principal fields of data.   e. 02 level items.
  b. Sub-fields of data.   f. 03 level items.
  c. Sub-sub-fields of data.   g. Group-items.
  d. 01 level items.   h. Elementary-items.

5.12 Of the choices given in problem 5.11, which *never* have PICTURE clauses?

5.13 Here is the description of a record (a data card) used by a television ratings company. Fill in the class and size columns of the chart.

CARD COLUMNS	INFORMATION	EXAMPLE	CLASS	SIZE
1–4	Viewer number.	7794		
5–19	Viewer's last name.	GUSTIN		
20–21	Reporting hour.	10		
22–56	Program being viewed.	M*A*S*H		
57–80	Blank.			

5.14 The maternity department of a large hospital prepares a record on every baby born in that hospital. The contents of each record are transferred to a data card to allow for computer processing of birth data. Here is an example of such a card:

The fields shown on the card are further described as follows:

CARD COLUMNS	INFORMATION	CARD COLUMNS	INFORMATION
1–20	Family name.	49–51	Month.
21–40	Baby's name.	52–53	Year.
21–30	Baby's first name.	54	Sex.
31–40	Baby's middle name.	55–58	Weight at birth.
41–46	Time of birth.	55–56	Pounds.
41–42	AM or PM.	57–58	Ounces.
43–44	Hour.	59–61	Mother's room.
45–46	Minutes.	59	Floor.
47–53	Date of birth.	60–61	Room number.
47–48	Day.	62–80	Blank.

Write a complete record description of these data cards.

5.15 You and a friend work for a local insurance company. Your friend has prepared a data deck for a program she has written. The cards in her data deck contain information in the following arrangement:

CARD COLUMNS	INFORMATION	EXAMPLE
1–8	Policy number.	04198329
9–26	Name of policy holder.	MICHAEL G. HARPER
27–51	Address of policy holder.	12 LEMON ST., GROVER, MD.
52–56	Zip code.	20741
57–66	Phone number.	3017742821
67–71	Amount of insurance.	10000
72–80	Type of insurance.	ORD. LIFE

You have been given the requirement to write a program that will list the names and phone numbers of all customers who live in a given zip code area (01923, for example). You're going to borrow your friend's data deck to save yourself from having to prepare your own. In view of the requirement given you, your program will need only the name, phone number, and zip code fields from the data deck. Write complete FD and record description entries to describe the data deck as it will be used by your program.

5.16 For the program described in problem 5.15, you have decided to print lines of output on the line-printer in this arrangement:

```
3017742821    MICHAEL  G  HARPER
3014987640    PATRICK  O  HARRIGAN
3012469879    TIMOTHY  HAYDEN
3016532758    CONRAD  JANKOWSKI
        23    REGINALD  KILOWATT
```

The fields of each output record (each line of print) can be further described as follows:

PRINTER PAGE POSITION	CONTENTS
1–5	Blanks.
6–15	Phone number.
16–20	Blanks.
21–38	Name of policy holder.
39–136	Blanks.

(This problem assumes a line printer which prints 136 characters per line.) Write complete FD and record description entries to describe the file of output data which will be printed on the line printer by your program.

6 A First Look at the PROCEDURE DIVISION

6.1 Introduction

In the PROCEDURE DIVISION, having dispensed with the preliminaries of the first three divisions, we finally tell the computer exactly what it is we want it to *do*. Here we tell it when to read each of the data cards, what calculations to perform and in what order, and when to print the results of the program (the output) on the line printer.

The commands which we give to the computer and which the computer obeys during the Execution Phase, are expressed as "sentences" in the PROCEDURE DIVISION. The sentences are grouped into paragraphs, and if the programmer wants to, the paragraphs may be grouped into sections. Every sentence must be enclosed in a paragraph; a paragraph may contain one or more sentences; and a section may contain one or more paragraphs.

With regard to sections, recall that the IDENTIFICATION DIVISION is unique as the only division which is not and may not be divided into sections. The ENVIRONMENT and DATA DIVISIONs *are* divided into sections:

```
ENVIRONMENT DIVISION.        DATA DIVISION.
CONFIGURATION SECTION.       FILE SECTION.
INPUT-OUTPUT SECTION.        WORKING-STORAGE SECTION.
```

The PROCEDURE DIVISION is unique as the only division in which sections are *optional*. It is also unique in that all its paragraph- and section-names are programmer-invented. In the first three divisions, paragraph- and section-names are reserved-names from the Reserved Word List.

Here is an example of a PROCEDURE DIVISION which is *not* divided into sections:

```
PROCEDURE DIVISION.
CRANK-UP-ROUTINE.
     Sentence.
     Sentence.
FINISH-THE-JOB-PARA.
     Sentence.
     Sentence.
```

In that example you should recognize CRANK-UP-ROUTINE and FINISH-THE-JOB-PARA as the names of the two paragraphs. Recall that they are coded at Margin A while the sentences which make up the paragraphs are coded at Margin B. (See Figure 3.12 for an example of how the PROCEDURE DIVISION is placed on a COBOL Coding Form.)

Here is an example of a PROCEDURE DIVISION which *is* divided into sections:

```
PROCEDURE DIVISION.
BEGINNING SECTION.
CRANK-UP-ROUTINE.
     Sentence.
     Sentence.
INITIAL-CALCULATIONS.
     Sentence.
     Sentence.
END-OF-JOB SECTION.
PRINT-RESULTS-ROUTINE.
     Sentence.
     Sentence.
WRAP-UP-PARA.
     Sentence.
     Sentence.
```

In that example you should recognize as the two section-names BEGIN-NING and END-OF-JOB. Remember that all these paragraph- and section-names which you make up must conform with the rules governing programmer-invented-names (see Figure 3.3).

Although it is entirely up to you to decide whether or not your PROCE-DURE DIVISION will be divided into sections, there is one rule you must observe: "All or nothing." You must group *all* paragraphs into sections, or *none* of them. Here is an example of a PROCEDURE DIVISION in which the "all or nothing" rule has been violated:

```
PROCEDURE DIVISION.
FIRST-PARA.
     Sentence.
     Sentence.
PRINCIPAL-STEPS SECTION.
IMPORTANT-CALCULATIONS.
     Sentence.
     Sentence.
FINAL-ROUTINE.
     Sentence.
     Sentence.
```

In that example the paragraph named FIRST-PARA is not included within a section, but the IMPORTANT-CALCULATIONS and FINAL-ROUTINE paragraphs are included in the PRINCIPAL-STEPS SECTION. To correct that violation, you would either have to eliminate the single section header, or insert another section header in front of the FIRST-PARA.

The remainder of this chapter will be devoted to describing how some of the most elementary PROCEDURE DIVISION sentences are formed. I will also describe what the computer does in response to each of these sentences.

6.2 The Sentence vs. the Statement

A COBOL statement is a group of words which includes one COBOL verb and directs the computer to execute one operation. A COBOL sentence includes at least one statement, but may contain more. It will not be until much later in the book, however, that we will be using multi-statement sentences, so for the time being you can consider the two words *sentence* and *statement* to be synonymous.

In this chapter we will discuss the four input/output verbs

OPEN   CLOSE
READ   WRITE

and the three processing verbs

MOVE   GO TO   STOP RUN.

6.3 The OPEN Verb

The basic form of the OPEN statement is

$$\text{OPEN} \left\{ \begin{array}{c} \text{INPUT} \\ \text{or} \\ \text{OUTPUT} \end{array} \right\} \left\{ \text{file-name-1, file-name-2, etc.} \right.$$

Before you attempt to use a file in the PROCEDURE DIVISION, you must OPEN it. You must also declare how you intend to use the file: For INPUT? or for OUTPUT?

If you were referring to your data deck by the file-name CARD-FILE, you would have to say

OPEN INPUT CARD-FILE.

before you told the computer to read a card from it. Of course, a data deck can only be used for input, so there can be little question about whether it should be opened for input or output. Magnetic tape, on the other hand, can contain data and be used for input, *or* it can be blank and be used to record your program's output, so you have to give a little more thought to the question in that case. If your program, for example, were going to get some of its input data from data cards (which you'd called CARD-FILE) and some from a magnetic tape (which you'd called OLD-TAPE-FILE), you could open both of them with the single statement:

OPEN INPUT CARD-FILE, OLD-TAPE-FILE.

The line printer is a device that can only be used for output, so again there is little question about *how* to open it. If you were referring to it as the PRINT-FILE, your statement would be:

OPEN OUTPUT PRINT-FILE.

If your program fed some of its results to the line printer (which you'd called PRINT-FILE) and some to a magnetic tape (which you'd called NEW-TAPE-FILE), you could open both in the one statement:

OPEN OUTPUT PRINT-FILE, NEW-TAPE-FILE.

It is possible to combine your OPEN statements into one "compound" statement. Hence, these two statements:

OPEN INPUT CARD-FILE.
OPEN OUTPUT PRINT-FILE.

can be combined into the single statement:

OPEN INPUT CARD-FILE, OUTPUT PRINT-FILE.

Likewise, it would also be possible to combine these two statements:

OPEN INPUT CARD-FILE, OLD-TAPE-FILE.
OPEN OUTPUT PRINT-FILE, NEW-TAPE-FILE.

Combined, they would have this form:

OPEN INPUT CARD-FILE, OLD-TAPE-FILE, OUTPUT PRINT-FILE, NEW-TAPE-FILE.

Be sure that this point has not escaped your attention: The file-names appearing in an OPEN statement in the PROCEDURE DIVISION, must not come as surprises to the computer. They must have already appeared earlier in the program. Do you remember where?

They must have appeared:

1. In the SELECT sentences of the ENVIRONMENT DIVISION, and
2. In the FD entries of the DATA DIVISION.

6.4 The CLOSE Verb

After you are finished with your files you must CLOSE them. The form of the CLOSE statement is as follows:

CLOSE file-name-1, file-name-2, etc.

If you were using files by the names of CARD-FILE and PRINT-FILE in your program, then before the end of the program you would have to be sure to say:

CLOSE CARD-FILE, PRINT-FILE.

Notice that there is no need to say anything about whether the files were input or output files. You simply CLOSE them without any regard for how they were being used in the program.

Though the CLOSE statement may impress you as a relatively trivial part of the program and something that wouldn't be missed if you forgot it, quite the contrary is true. It is an essential part. It serves as a signal to the computer that it may start some necessary, internal tidying-up operations that it must do in order to be ready to handle the next programmer's program. On many computer systems, in fact, the computer checks through your program ahead of time to be sure you've included a CLOSE statement, and if you haven't, it will "punish" you by withholding your output.

6.5   The READ Verb

As mentioned earlier, it is the READ verb that directs the reading of a record from an input file. If the input file is a data deck (which is the only form of input file we will be considering for a while) then the READ verb causes a single data card to be read. The form of a READ statement is as follows:

> READ file-name RECORD, AT END imperative-statement.

The file-name must be that of a file that has been OPENed for INPUT. The file and the arrangement of the data-values on each of its records were described in FD and 01 level entries in the FILE SECTION of the DATA DIVISION. READing of a record from that file results in all the data-values from that record being moved to and stored in the proper memory locations in the computer's memory unit.

The AT END clause of the READ sentence has the function of telling the computer what to do if in attempting to read a data card, it finds there are none left, i.e., if it finds that it is AT the END of the data deck (or input file). The programmer must insert some imperative-statement in the AT END clause that will tell the computer what he wants it to do when that happens. In most cases, this will be a GO TO statement that tells the computer to jump to the end of the program. (A more thorough discussion of the GO TO verb will be presented in Section 6.8.)

Here is an example of a complete READ sentence:

READ CARD-FILE RECORD, AT END GO TO LAST-PARAGRAPH.

Let me reemphasize one point I made earlier: Even though the sentence starts out with the word READ CARD-FILE, the READ statement does *not* direct the reading of the *whole file*. It directs only the reading of *one record* (one data card) from that file.

6.6   The WRITE Verb

A WRITE statement causes one record to be written on the output file. If the output file is the line printer (which is the only form of output file we'll be considering for a while) then the WRITE statement will cause a single line of print to be printed on the line-printer paper. The simplest form of the WRITE statement is as follows:

> WRITE record-name.

Notice that in the WRITE statement, you give a record-name, while in the READ statement you give a file-name. Memorize this catch phrase right now and don't forget it for the rest of your COBOL life:

READ FILES—WRITE RECORDS

Recall that record-names are 01 level entries in the FILE SECTION of the DATA DIVISION. In order for it to be legal to WRITE a record, that record must be a part of a file that has been OPENed for OUTPUT. If you'll assume that the file that was OPENed for OUTPUT was called EMPLOYEE-FILE, and that following the DATA DIVISION's FD entry for EMPLOYEE-FILE was the 01 level entry EMPLOYEE-LISTING, then a proper WRITE statement would look like this:

WRITE EMPLOYEE-LISTING. *Single space after adv 1 line sems*

When a WRITE statement is obeyed, the line printer advances the paper one line and then WRITEs (or prints) whatever record you want written. What you get is what you'd call "single-spacing" on a typewriter. If you want double-spacing, triple-spacing, etc., you use the optional ADVANCING clause of the WRITE statement:

$$
\text{WRITE record-name} \left\{ \begin{array}{c} \text{AFTER} \\ \text{or} \\ \text{BEFORE} \end{array} \right\} \text{ADVANCING} \left\{ \begin{array}{c} \text{integer} \\ \text{or} \\ \text{data-name} \end{array} \right\} \text{LINES.}
$$

You see that you have the option of saying AFTER ADVANCING or BEFORE ADVANCING. If you say AFTER ADVANCING, the line printer will advance the paper and *then* print the record. If you say BEFORE ADVANCING, the line printer will print the record and *then* advance the paper.

Take an example: Suppose the last record that was printed was printed on the tenth line of the printer page. These three statements:

```
WRITE FIRST-RECORD.
WRITE SECOND-RECORD.
WRITE THIRD-RECORD AFTER ADVANCING 2 LINES.
```

would result in the FIRST-RECORD being printed on the eleventh line of the page, the SECOND-RECORD being printed on the twelfth line of the page, and the THIRD-RECORD being printed on the fourteenth line of the page.

Remember that the last record printed was printed on the fourteenth line of the printer page. These two statements:

WRITE FOURTH-RECORD BEFORE ADVANCING 3 LINES.
WRITE FIFTH-RECORD.

would result in the FOURTH-RECORD being printed also on the fourteenth line and the FIFTH-RECORD being printed on the eighteenth line.

Note that if you omit the ADVANCING clause, you will get the same results as if you had said AFTER ADVANCING 1 LINES.[1]

The ADVANCING clause may contain an integer numeric-literal or a data-name to specify the number of LINES you desire advanced. In most instances you will probably use an integer numeric-literal as I did in the examples above. If you ever elect to use a data-name in the clause, it must have an integer numeric value stored in it when you do. Here is an example: Suppose you had the data-name SO-MANY and the record-name PRINT-LINE in your program. You could then say:

WRITE PRINT-LINE AFTER ADVANCING SO-MANY LINES.

If SO-MANY had been given the data-value 5, then that WRITE statement would be interpreted as saying:

WRITE PRINT-LINE AFTER ADVANCING 5 LINES.

The data-name option would be used by a programmer in a WRITE statement that is executed several times in her program where she wants to be able to advance a different number of lines each time it is executed. She would accomplish this by giving the data-name a different value before each execution of the WRITE statement.

6.7 The MOVE Verb

Frequently in the course of writing a program, you will find the need to move new data-values into memory-locations whose data-values are no longer correct. Sometimes those new values will already be in memory but in other memory-locations, and sometimes they will not be in memory at all. The MOVE verb is used to direct such movements. In a MOVE statement you tell the computer to move a data-value from one location (called the "Sending Field") to another location (called the "Receiving Field").

The most elementary forms of the MOVE statement are as follows:

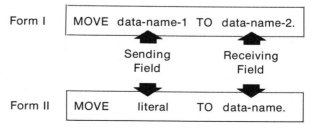

---

[1] A note to IBM computer users: IBM's version of COBOL includes as a requirement that if the ADVANCING clause is used once in a program in connection with a WRITE to the printer file, then it must be used on *all* WRITE statements in the program that cause writing on the printer file.

We'll consider Form I first. Here is an example of a proper Form I MOVE statement:

```
MOVE NUM-ORDERED TO NUM-RECEIVED.
```

In that example, NUM-ORDERED is the Sending Field and NUM-RECEIVED is the Receiving Field.

The statement roughly translates into "MOVE the value stored in NUM-ORDERED to NUM-RECEIVED." It's important, however, that you recognize the difference in meaning between the English verb "move" and the COBOL verb "MOVE." If in English I told you to "Move the chair in the kitchen to the living room," you would *remove* the chair from the kitchen and place it in the living room. When in COBOL I tell you to "MOVE the value in NUM-ORDERED to NUM-RECEIVED," you do *not* actually "remove" the value from NUM-ORDERED.

Here is how it works in COBOL: Let's say that before the MOVE statement is obeyed, memory-locations NUM-ORDERED and NUM-RECEIVED are in this condition:

NUM-ORDERED   NUM-RECEIVED

| 375 | | 239 |

Now the computer executes the statement:

```
MOVE NUM-ORDERED TO NUM-RECEIVED.
```

The result of the execution of that statement is the changing of the two memory locations to this condition:

NUM-ORDERED   NUM-RECEIVED

| 375 | | 375 |

In computer terminology, what happened was this: The computer performed a "nondestructive read" of memory-location NUM-ORDERED to find out what value was stored there (375). It then performed a "destructive write" of that value into memory-location NUM-RECEIVED, "destroying" the value (239) that was previously stored there. Notice that no damage was done to the value stored in NUM-ORDERED by the nondestructive-reading of that value.

I suppose a more correct English verb we could use in describing how the COBOL MOVE verb functions would be "copy." If I told you to "Copy the course number on the blackboard onto your course registration card," you would first read what I had on the board. If you had any other course number on your course registration card, you would erase (or destroy) it and write the correct numbers in its place. Your reading of the value on the blackboard would not have destroyed or disturbed it in any way. It would still be there for the other students to read.

So when you tell the computer to obey the Form I MOVE statement,

```
MOVE NUM-ORDERED TO NUM-RECEIVED.
```

you are really telling it to "*Copy* the value stored in NUM-ORDERED into NUM-RECEIVED."

Here is a *temporary rule* we will observe for the time being: *The Sending Field and the Receiving Field must be of the same class and size.* To put it another way, they must have identical PICTURE clauses. Somewhat later in the book, we will have a thorough discussion of what happens when they do not, but to keep yourself out of trouble until then, always obey this temporary rule.

Now let's talk about Form II of the MOVE statement:

> MOVE literal TO data-name.

Here are two proper examples of Form II MOVE statements:

    MOVE ' JANUARY ' TO THIS-MONTH.
    MOVE 1978 TO THIS-YEAR.

In the first example I used a non-numeric-literal, and in the second I used a numeric-literal. In order for those statements to be acceptable to the computer, entries such as these would have been necessary in the DATA DIVISION:

    02 THIS-MONTH   PICTURE A(9).
    02 THIS-YEAR   PICTURE 9(4).

Again, you should plan to observe the temporary rule I gave above in writing your Form II MOVE statements: Be sure the Receiving Field has a PICTURE that agrees exactly with the literal you place in the Sending Field position of the MOVE statement.

Here's an example to show how the computer would obey MOVE statements such as those above: Assume to start out with, that memory locations THIS-MONTH and THIS-YEAR are in this condition:

THIS-MONTH   THIS-YEAR

| DECEMBER | | 1977 |

Now the computer executes these statements:

    MOVE ' JANUARY ' TO THIS-MONTH.
    MOVE 1978 TO THIS-YEAR.

The result of the execution of those statements would be to change the two memory locations to this condition:

THIS-MONTH   THIS-YEAR

| JANUARY | | 1978 |

Actually just a variation on the Form II MOVE statement, this version is also available:

> MOVE figurative-constant TO data-name.

Recall from Chapter 3 that figurative constants are reserved words which are understood by the computer to have predefined constant values. Only two are used in this text: SPACE and ZERO. ZERO (or ZEROS or ZEROES) is a numeric figurative constant and has the value that its name implies. SPACE (or SPACES) is a nonnumeric figurative constant and represents a string of blank characters.

Suppose that these two entries were in your DATA DIVISION:

```
02 DEPARTMENT PICTURE A(15).
02 SALES-TOTAL PICTURE 9(6).
```

Suppose that as a result of previously executed statements in your PROCE-DURE DIVISION, the two memory locations were in this condition:

DEPARTMENT	SALES-TOTAL
SPARE PARTS	042197

Consider the change in condition of those two memory locations which would be caused by the execution of these two statements:

```
MOVE SPACES TO DEPARTMENT.
MOVE ZERO TO SALES-TOTAL.
```

The two locations would now look like this:

DEPARTMENT	SALES-TOTAL
	000000

6.8 The GO TO Verb

The elementary GO TO statement has this form:

There is a simple, general rule that governs the order in which the computer will execute a series of statements in a COBOL program. It will execute them *sequentially:* the first statement will be executed first, the second statement will be executed second, and so on.

In COBOL there is a family of statements called branching statements. They are employed whenever you wish an exception to be made to the rule of sequential execution. The GO TO statement is the simplest of the branching statements.

Here is an example of a GO TO statement being used in a program to cause the flow of statement execution to jump forward and over a group of sentences:

	Portion of PROCEDURE DIVISION	Order of Execution
	FIRST-PARA.	
	Sentence.	1st
	Sentence.	2nd
	GO TO SECOND-PARA.	3rd
Path of	Sentence.	
Branch	Sentence.	
	SECOND-PARA.	
	Sentence.	4th
	Sentence.	5th
	Sentence.	6th

I can almost hear the questions that are running through your mind right now: "Why would anyone bother to include perfectly good sentences in a program, and then tell the computer not to execute them, but rather to skip over them? Why not just leave them out of the program altogether if you don't want them executed?"

That's a good question. Except when you're forming a loop in your program (to be discussed shortly), you seldom use a GO TO statement as you see it there without some condition attached to it. That way it is obeyed only under the conditions you've specified, while under other conditions it is ignored and the sentences following it are *not* skipped. We'll talk about conditional statements in Chapter 12. However, you have seen one example of the conditional use of a GO TO statement already. In the AT END clause of the example READ statement of Section 6.5, we said GO TO LAST-PARAGRAPH. There we were saying to the computer, "If in your attempt to READ a RECORD from that file, you find yourself AT the END of the file, then do not continue in this paragraph, but GO TO LAST-PARAGRAPH instead."

A GO TO statement can also cause jumping forward over one or more complete paragraphs, as demonstrated here:

	Portion of PROCEDURE DIVISION	Order of Execution
	FIRST-PARA.	
	Sentence.	1st
	Sentence.	2nd
	GO TO THIRD-PARA.	3rd
	Sentence.	
Path of	SECOND-PARA.	
Branch	Sentence.	
	Sentence.	
	THIRD-PARA.	
	Sentence.	4th
	Sentence.	5th

GO TO statements can also cause jumping backward to have the computer *repeat* a portion of the program.

	Portion of PROCEDURE DIVISION	Order of Execution
	FIRST-PARA.	
	Sentence.	1st
	Sentence.	2nd
→	SECOND-PARA.	
	Sentence.	3rd 8th 13th
Path of	Sentence.	4th 9th etc.
Branch	THIRD-PARA.	
	Sentence.	5th 10th
	Sentence.	6th 11th
└─◄	GO TO SECOND-PARA.	7th 12th

In this last example, you see a programming phenomenon known as *looping*. Because of the path of the branch, the computer ends up back at the beginning of the SECOND-PARA again and once again commences sequential execution of the sentences from that point. It eventually gets back down to the GO TO statement again, and again it is sent back to the beginning of the SECOND-PARA. This process occurs again and again, resulting in the computer being caused to "loop" repeatedly through the same portion of the program over and over.

The GO TO statement must always refer to some paragraph- or section-name in the PROCEDURE DIVISION. If the statement refers to a paragraph-name (which is the case in 99 percent of all GO TO's), then the next sentence to be executed will be the first sentence of that paragraph. If the GO TO statement refers to a section-name, then the next sentence to be executed will be the first sentence of the first paragraph of that section. This is the reason why duplicate paragraph- and section-names are prohibited in a program. When told to GO TO CALC-PARA, the computer would be "confused" about where you wanted it to GO if there were more than one CALC-PARA.

6.9 The STOP RUN Statement

Little needs to be said about this short statement. It looks like this:

> STOP RUN.

and its purpose is to tell the computer that you have nothing more for it to do so it can "STOP the RUN."

The word "run" is used in computer lingo in many ways that have nothing to do with its English meaning. You will hear a programmer say, "I'm going down to the Computer Center to run my program." He means that he is going down to have the computer process his program. "My program wouldn't run," is a programmer's lament telling you that there must have been an error in his program, and the computer stopped the processing before it got to the end. "I just had a successful run!!" is an expression of joy which would be shouted if the computer was able to process the whole program and produce the output which the programmer wanted. When you are asked, "What was the run-date on this program?" you are actually being asked, "On what date did you have the computer process this program?"

Hence, when you say "STOP RUN." to the computer, you are saying "Stop the processing of this program," and since the last phase of processing is the Execution Phase, you are actually saying, "Stop executing this program."

Though in most elementary programs, the STOP RUN statement comes as the last sentence in the PROCEDURE DIVISION, there is no absolute requirement for this. In fact in some more complex programs, there are often two or more STOP RUN statements. This would be so in a program which included several alternate sets of circumstances under which the programmer wanted execution to cease.

6.10   A Reminder about END PROGRAM Cards[2]

In Chapter 2, where we discussed for the first time the division of a COBOL program deck into an instruction deck and a data deck, I pointed out that it was the END PROGRAM card that served as the boundary between the two. Though often shown as a part of the PROCEDURE DIVISION, it is technically not a part of *any* division. The statements in the PROCEDURE DIVISION tell the computer what to do during the Execution Phase. The END PROGRAM statement is called a "Compiler Directing Statement." It tells the compiler when it can cease its work and frees the computer to begin execution.

Remember this—(1) The END PROGRAM statement tells the computer to "Cease compilation and begin execution." It *must* be the *last card* in the instruction deck. (2) The STOP RUN statement tells the computer to "Cease execution," and may occur *anywhere* within the PROCEDURE DIVISION.

---

[2] The use of an END PROGRAM card, as such, is not universal; however, all computers *do* require that *some* special card be placed after the Instruction Deck. Ask at your computer center what particular card is required by your computer.

EXERCISES

Answers to all exercises in this chapter are given in Appendix A.

6.1 What are the essential differences between a sentence and a statement?

6.2 Consider the following OPEN statement:

```
OPEN INPUT CARD-FILE, OUTPUT TAPE-FILE PRINT-FILE, INPUT
OLD-DISK-FILE, OUTPUT NEW-DISK-FILE.
```

Which files have been opened for INPUT and which for OUTPUT?

6.3 Assume that these are the first five lines in your PROCEDURE DIVISION:

```
PROCEDURE DIVISION.
FIRST-PARA.
    OPEN INPUT TAPE-FILE, OUTPUT DATA-FILE.
    READ CARD-FILE RECORD, AT END GO TO LAST-PARA.
    READ DATA-FILE RECORD, AT END GO TO LAST-PARA.
```

What errors do you find there?

6.4 What is wrong with this CLOSE statement?

```
CLOSE INPUT CARD-FILE, OUTPUT PRINT-FILE.
```

6.5 Choose the correct response. The statement "READ DATA-FILE RECORD, AT END GO TO LAST-PARA." will cause:
   a. The entire DATA-FILE to be read.
   b. A single record from the DATA-FILE to be read.

6.6 TRUE or FALSE? The AT END clause of the READ statement is optional.

6.7 TRUE or FALSE? The ADVANCING clause of the WRITE statement is optional.

6.8 Suppose that this were the only OPEN statement in your program:

```
OPEN INPUT OLD-DATA-FILE, OUTPUT NEW-DATA-FILE.
```

Would there be anything wrong with the statement "WRITE NEW-DATA-FILE." appearing in your program?

6.9 Consider this an excerpt from your DATA DIVISION:

```
FD  OLD-DATA; RECORD CONTAINS 80 CHARACTERS; LABEL RECORDS ARE
    OMITTED; DATA RECORD IS OLD-CARD.
01  OLD-CARD.
    02  etc.
    02  etc.
FD  LISTING-OF-DATA; RECORD CONTAINS 136 CHARACTERS; LABEL
    RECORDS ARE OMITTED; DATA RECORD IS DETAIL-LINE.
01  DETAIL-LINE.
    02  etc.
    02  etc.
```

Consider this the first sentence in your PROCEDURE DIVISION:

OPEN INPUT OLD-DATA, OUTPUT LISTING-OF-DATA.

Fill in the blanks of these two sentences so that they would be correct statements in your program:

    a. READ _____ RECORD, AT END GO TO LAST-PARA.

    b. WRITE _____ AFTER ADVANCING 2 LINES.

6.10   This is a sentence out of your PROCEDURE DIVISION:

READ PAYROLL-DATA-FILE RECORD, AT END GO TO THE-END.

The file-name PAYROLL-DATA-FILE must have already appeared in three other places in your program. Where?

    a. _____

    b. _____

    c. _____

6.11   Consider these five sentences from your PROCEDURE DIVISION:

MOVE 3 TO THIS-MANY.
WRITE FIRST-RECORD.
WRITE SECOND-RECORD AFTER ADVANCING 4 LINES.
WRITE THIRD-RECORD.
WRITE FOURTH-RECORD AFTER ADVANCING THIS-MANY LINES.

If as a result of the second of those five sentences, the FIRST-RECORD is printed on the 20th line of the printer page, on what lines will these records be printed?

    a. The SECOND-RECORD.

    b. The THIRD-RECORD.

    c. The FOURTH-RECORD.

Problems 6.12 through 6.17 test your understanding of the terms "destructive write" and "nondestructive read" as they apply to the functioning of the computer's memory unit in response to MOVE statements. In problems 6.12 through 6.15 consider these as the initial conditions of the three memory locations:

HIS-PAY	HER-PAY	MY-PAY
495	250	378

6.12   What would be the conditions of the three locations after execution of these two statements:

MOVE HIS-PAY TO HER-PAY.
MOVE HER-PAY TO MY-PAY.

6.13   After execution of these two statements?

MOVE HER-PAY TO MY-PAY.
MOVE HIS-PAY TO HER-PAY.

6.14   After these two?

    MOVE HIS-PAY TO HER-PAY.
    MOVE MY-PAY TO HIS-PAY.

6.15   After these three?

    MOVE MY-PAY TO HER-PAY.
    MOVE HIS-PAY TO MY-PAY.
    MOVE 650 TO HIS-PAY.

In problems 6.16 and 6.17, consider these as the initial conditions of the three memory locations:

HANDSOME	MORE HANDSOME	MOST HANDSOME
SAM	KIP	JOE

6.16   What would be the condition of the three memory locations after execution of these three statements?

    MOVE MORE-HANDSOME TO HANDSOME.
    MOVE MOST-HANDSOME TO MORE-HANDSOME.
    MOVE 'BOB' TO MOST-HANDSOME.

6.17   After these three?

    MOVE 'BOB' TO MOST-HANDSOME.
    MOVE MOST-HANDSOME TO MORE-HANDSOME.
    MOVE MORE-HANDSOME TO HANDSOME.

6.18   Using the sequence numbers to identify each sentence, describe the order in which the sentences in this PROCEDURE DIVISION will be executed.

    700 PROCEDURE DIVISION.
    710 FIRST-PARA.
    720   Sentence.
    730   Sentence.
    740   GO TO THIRD-PARA.
    750 SECOND-PARA.
    760   Sentence.
    770   Sentence.
    780   GO TO FOURTH-PARA.
    790 THIRD-PARA.
    800   Sentence.
    810   GO TO SECOND-PARA.
    820 FOURTH-PARA.
    830   Sentence.
    840   Sentence.
    850   STOP RUN.

6.19 In what order will the sentences of this PROCEDURE DIVISION be executed?

```
700  PROCEDURE DIVISION.
710  FIRST-PARA.
720      Sentence.
730      Sentence.
740      GO TO FOURTH-PARA.
750  SECOND-PARA.
760      Sentence.
770      STOP RUN.
780  THIRD-PARA.
790      Sentence.
800      Sentence.
810      GO TO SECOND-PARA.
820  FOURTH-PARA.
830      Sentence.
840      Sentence.
850      GO TO THIRD-PARA.
```

6.20 What's wrong with this statement?

```
GO TO REQUIRED-CALCULATIONS SECTION.
```

7 Your First Program

7.1 The Program

You now have at your disposal enough of COBOL's basic elements to write a complete, though simple program. Before I begin expanding on those basic elements, let's be sure you've got it all together for as far as we've gone. We'll do that by writing an example program together from start to finish.

The Super Simple Computer Dating Service

For several months you and I have been gathering data on college age people who like to date. We have described each of these people on an IBM card. Our cards are grouped together in two files: a boys' file and a girls' file. Up to this time whenever a boy wanted to look through our files for a suitable date, we'd hand him the stack of girls' cards and he'd search through them until he found one he thought he'd like. He'd note the name and phone number of a girl and return the card to our file. Likewise for girls, except that they'd look through the boys' file.

Each card in the files has information on it in this arrangement:

CARD COLUMN	INFORMATION	EXAMPLE
1–25	Name	
1–15	Last Name	SCHIMMELPFENNIG
16–25	First Name	WILHELMINA
26–55	Address	14 CHESTNUT ST., LACONIA, N.H.
56–58	Height	
56	Feet	4
57–58	Inches	10
59–61	Weight (pounds)	120
62–67	Hair Color	BLONDE
68–77	Phone Number	9146524915
78–80	Blank	

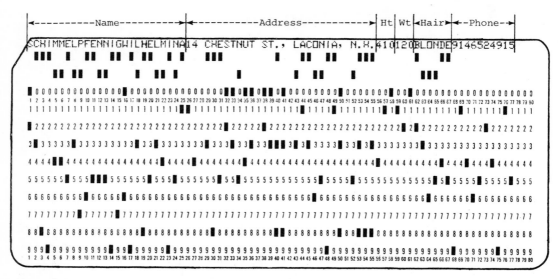

FIGURE 7.1   One of the Dating Service Data Cards

In Figure 7.1 you can see what one of the cards looks like.

With so many people handling our files, the cards have become dog-eared and worn. Some of them are even torn. So we've decided to stop letting people handle the actual card files. We'll keep the cards locked in our file cabinet, adding to the files as we learn of new datable people, and removing cards from the files as we learn of marriages.

In order to provide opportunities for "customers" of our service to look through the contents of the files without actually handling the cards, we plan to use the computer once a week to produce printed lists (one for boys and one for girls) of the contents of the cards on the line printer. We'll hang the lists in our office, and "customers" can search these lists for the names and telephones of people who sound appealing to them.

When we originally planned this system, we thought people would be interested in addresses, so we included addresses on all cards. It's turned out, however, that most of our customers have ignored the addresses, so we'll omit the addresses from the printed lists.

Figure 7.2 shows a portion of one of the lists as we would like it to appear. Our job is to write the COBOL program that will produce these printed lists from our card files.

7.2 The IDENTIFICATION and ENVIRONMENT DIVISIONS

These two divisions are simple enough to write. Figure 7.3 shows the two divisions as they'd appear on coding forms. Notice that in the SELECT sentences of the ENVIRONMENT DIVISION, we have declared our intention to refer to each of our card files as a DATE-CARD-FILE; and our listing on the line printer as the DATE-LISTING-FILE.

WILHELMINA	SCHIMMELPFENNIG	BLONDE HAIR	4 FT 10 IN	120 LBS	PHONE 9146524915
KATE	AMBROSE	BROWN HAIR	4 FT 09 IN	115 LBS	PHONE 6172194283
CAROL	WHALEN	BRUNET HAIR	5 FT 01 IN	105 LBS	PHONE 6177742821
SANDY	THEPERSON	BROWN HAIR	6 FT 04 IN	095 LBS	PHONE 2129743875
CLAUDETTE	WISE	BLACK HAIR	4 FT 11 IN	250 LBS	PHONE 6177749642
SHIRLEY	STURDEVANT	RED HAIR	5 FT 03 IN	120 LBS	PHONE 7135790243
MAE	MCCAULEY	BLONDE HAIR	4 FT 07 IN	195 LBS	PHONE 6177982164
EDITH	DUNKER	GREY HAIR	5 FT 10 IN	145 LBS	PHONE 2124587365

FIGURE 7.2   Desired Form of Dating Program Output

7.3 The DATA DIVISION

The first part of the DATA DIVISION is shown in Figure 7.4. It opens with
the division and FILE SECTION headers (sequence nos. 190 and 200). Following that we describe the DATE-CARD-FILE in an FD entry (sequence
nos. 210 and 220). Notice that in the DATA RECORD clause, we've announced the name by which we will refer to each record in that file:
DATE-CARD.

COBOL CODING FORM

PROGRAM: DATE-SERVICE
PROGRAMMER: R. G. Finkenaur
COBOL DIVISION: IDENT + ENV   PAGE 1 OF 1
DATE: Sept 28, 1978   IDENT: DATE-SVC

```
 1.0  IDENTIFICATION DIVISION.
 2.0  PROGRAM-ID.    DATE-SERVICE.
 3.0  AUTHOR.        R. G. FINKENAUR.
 4.0  INSTALLATION.  NORTHEASTERN UNIV.
 5.0  DATE-WRITTEN.  SEPT 28, 1978.
 6.0  DATE-COMPILED.
 7.0  SECURITY.      FOR UNMARRIED PEOPLE ONLY.
 8.0  REMARKS.       THIS PROGRAM WILL PRODUCE A LISTING OF THE NAMES,
 9.0                 HAIR COLOR, HEIGHT, WEIGHT, AND PHONE NUMBERS OF ALL THE
10.0                 PEOPLE IN MY DATE FILES.
11.0  ENVIRONMENT DIVISION.
12.0  CONFIGURATION SECTION.
13.0  SOURCE-COMPUTER.  HAL-2001.
14.0  OBJECT-COMPUTER.  HAL-2001.
15.0  INPUT-OUTPUT SECTION.
16.0  FILE-CONTROL.
17.0      SELECT DATE-CARD-FILE ASSIGN TO CARD-READER.
18.0      SELECT DATE-LISTING-FILE ASSIGN TO LINE-PRINTER.
```

FIGURE 7.3   The IDENTIFICATION and ENVIRONMENT DIVISIONS

COBOL CODING FORM

| PROGRAM | DATE-SERVICE | | | COBOL DIVISION | DATA | PAGE | 1 | OF | 2 |
| PROGRAMMER | R. G. Finkenaur | | | DATE | Sept. 28, 1978 | IDENT | | DATE-SVC | |

```
 19,0  DATA DIVISION.
 20,0  FILE SECTION.
 21,0  FD  DATE-CARD-FILE; RECORD CONTAINS 80 CHARACTERS; LABEL RECORDS
 22,0      ARE OMITTED; DATA RECORD IS DATE-CARD.
 23,0  01  DATE-CARD.
 24,0      02  LAST-NAME       PICTURE A(15).
 25,0      02  FIRST-NAME      PICTURE A(10).
 26,0      02  FILLER          PICTURE X(30).
 27,0      02  HT-FEET         PICTURE 9.
 28,0      02  HT-INCHES       PICTURE 99.
 29,0      02  WEIGHT          PICTURE 999.
 30,0      02  HAIR-COLOR      PICTURE A(6).
 31,0      02  PHONE           PICTURE 9(10).
 32,0      02  FILLER          PICTURE XXX.
```

FIGURE 7.4   The First Part of the DATA DIVISION

The next step is to write the record description entries that describe to the computer the arrangement of data it should expect to find on each DATE-CARD. Compare sequence nos. 240 through 320 with the description of each card I provided in Section 7.1 and with the picture in Figure 7.1. Notice that the order of the 02 level entries is very important. It is essential that they be in the same order as the corresponding fields on each data card.

The FILLER entry at sequence no. 260 is necessary to alert the computer to the presence of a 30 character field on the data card which we want to be ignored. (It is the address field I spoke of earlier.)

You may wonder why I used all elementary items and no group items. Group items exist for the sake of convenience to the programmer, and are never required. The programmer is free to group his elementary items together into group items if he thinks it will add convenience to his later programming, but he doesn't have to. I simply elected not to do so, because I saw nothing to be gained in doing it in this simple program. You will learn later of the kinds of conveniences which having group items provide. Until then you might as well follow my lead, and use elementary items exclusively.

The remainder of the DATA DIVISION is shown in Figure 7.5. First,

COBOL CODING FORM

| PROGRAM | DATE-SERVICE | COBOL DIVISION | DATA | PAGE | 2 | OF | 2 |
| PROGRAMMER | R. G. Finkenour | DATE | Sept. 28, 1978 | IDENT | | | DATE-SVC |

```
33,0  F,D,  D,A,T,E,-,L,I,S,T,I,N,G,-,F,I,L,E,;  R,E,C,O,R,D  C,O,N,T,A,I,N,S  1,3,6  C,H,A,R,A,C,T,E,R,S,;  L,A,B,E,L
 3,4,0       R,E,C,O,R,D,S  A,R,E  O,M,I,T,T,E,D,;  D,A,T,A  R,E,C,O,R,D  I,S  P,R,I,N,T,-,L,I,N,E,.
 3,5,0  0,1,  P,R,I,N,T,-,L,I,N,E,.
 3,6,0       0,2,  F,I,L,L,E,R           P,I,C,T,U,R,E  X,(,2,7,),.
 3,7,0       0,2,  F,I,R,S,T,-,N,A,M,E,-,O,U,T  P,I,C,T,U,R,E  A,(,1,0,),.
 3,8,0       0,2,  F,I,L,L,E,R           P,I,C,T,U,R,E  X,.
 3,9,0       0,2,  L,A,S,T,-,N,A,M,E,-,O,U,T  P,I,C,T,U,R,E  A,(,1,5,),.
 4,0,0       0,2,  F,I,L,L,E,R           P,I,C,T,U,R,E  X,X,X,.
 4,1,0       0,2,  H,A,I,R,-,C,O,L,O,R,-,O,U,T  P,I,C,T,U,R,E  A,(,6,),.
 4,2,0       0,2,  F,I,E,L,D,-,6         P,I,C,T,U,R,E  X,(,8,),.
 4,3,0       0,2,  H,T,-,F,E,E,T,-,O,U,T  P,I,C,T,U,R,E  9,.
 4,4,0       0,2,  F,I,E,L,D,-,8         P,I,C,T,U,R,E  X,(,4,),.
 4,5,0       0,2,  H,T,-,I,N,C,H,E,S,-,O,U,T  P,I,C,T,U,R,E  9,9,.
 4,6,0       0,2,  F,I,E,L,D,-,1,0       P,I,C,T,U,R,E  X,(,6,),.
 4,7,0       0,2,  W,E,I,G,H,T,-,O,U,T   P,I,C,T,U,R,E  9,9,9,.
 4,8,0       0,2,  F,I,E,L,D,-,1,2       P,I,C,T,U,R,E  X,(,1,3,),.
 4,9,0       0,2,  P,H,O,N,E,-,O,U,T     P,I,C,T,U,R,E  9,(,1,0,),.
 5,0,0       0,2,  F,I,L,L,E,R           P,I,C,T,U,R,E  X,(,2,7,),.
```

FIGURE 7.5   The Remainder of the DATA DIVISION

at sequence nos. 330 and 340, comes the FD entry describing the DATE-LISTING-FILE. (Recall that up in one of the ENVIRONMENT DIVISION's SELECT sentences, we told the computer that we were going to refer to the data file associated with the line printer as the DATE-LISTING-FILE.)

Notice the RECORD CONTAINS clause in this FD entry. It says that there are 136 characters in each record. When you're speaking of a file of IBM cards, the term "record" refers to one of the cards in the file. Each of those "records" contains 80 characters. When you're speaking of the "file" of data being created on the line printer, the term "record" refers to one line of print. A typical line printer has the ability to print 136 characters in one line (one record), so we say RECORD CONTAINS 136 CHARACTERS when we're describing the line printer file.

Having written the FD entry for the DATE-LISTING-FILE, we now turn to the record description entries for its record, which will be called PRINT-LINE in this program.

Consider first one of the lines of output that will be printed on the line printer. From this example line you can see that there are actually 13 different fields involved in the arrangement of each output line that we've decided to use:

|WILHELMINA| |SCHIMMELPFENNING| |BLONDE| HAIR |4| FT |10| IN |120| LBS PHONE |9146524915|

↑ Field 1 ↑ Field 2 ↑ Field 3 ↑ Field 4 ↑ Field 5 ↑ Field 6 ↑ Field 7 ↑ Field 8 ↑ Field 9 ↑ Field 10 ↑ Field 11 ↑ Field 12 ↑ Field 13

That line of output can be described in tabular form as follows:

FIELD	SIZE	CONTENTS OF THE FIELD	CONTENTS TO COME FROM DATA CARD?
1	10	The person's first name.	Yes
2	1	A space to separate the first and last names.	No
3	15	The person's last name.	Yes
4	3	3 spaces.	No
5	6	The person's hair color.	Yes
6	8	A space, the letters HAIR, and 3 spaces.	No
7	1	The feet part of the person's height.	Yes
8	4	A space, the letters FT, and a space.	No
9	2	The inches part of the person's height.	Yes
10	6	A space, the letters IN, and 3 spaces.	No
11	3	The person's weight.	Yes
12	13	A space, the letters LBS, 3 spaces, the letters PHONE, and a space.	No
13	10	The person's phone number.	Yes

In this table I've tried to make the point that some of the data-values that will be appearing in each line of output will come from the data cards, and some will not. The contents of fields 1, 3, 5, 7, 9, 11, and 13 will all be supplied by the data cards. The contents of fields 6, 8, 10, and 12 will not. These fields contain essentially "dress-up" information that enhances the appearance and readability of each line of output.

On a data card there are only 80 columns (or character positions) so we are forced to use as few characters as possible in describing each person. On the line printer there are 136 character positions, so there's plenty of extra room to insert titles, labels, and extra spaces. As you see, that's exactly what we're using fields 2, 4, 6, 8, 10, and 12 for.

For example, in field 6 we want to insert the word HAIR after the hair-color. We want one space between the hair-color and the word HAIR, and we want three spaces to follow the word HAIR to separate it from the next field which has nothing whatever to do with the person's hair. That's a total of 8 characters that have to fit into field 6. In the DATA DIVISION we must set up field 6 to be 8 characters long by an entry such as this:

    02 FIELD-6   PICTURE X(8).

so that the computer will know *how big* we want the field to be. We place that entry among the other output record description entries, right after the hair-color entry and right before the height-in-feet entry so that the computer will know *where* we want it to be. That's all we can do for now. We will have to wait until we get to the PROCEDURE DIVISION before we can tell the computer *what* goes in the field. But to satisfy *your* curiosity now, I'll tell you that in order to get the characters "space-H-A-I-R-space-space-space" stored in field 6, we will use this PROCEDURE DIVISION statement:

    MOVE ' HAIR   ' TO FIELD-6.

The same approach is used for fields 8, 10, and 12. Fields 2 and 4 which contain only spaces are described with FILLERs in the record description entries.

Have you noticed in Figure 7.5 that I've used the suffix "-OUT" on many of our data-names? I've done that to avoid the problems posed by duplicate data-names. In our input record (see Figure 7.4) we have used the data-name LAST-NAME, for example. Since we wanted a last-name field in our output record, as well, we might have been tempted to use the data-name LAST-NAME there, too. If we had, then there'd have been *two* fields called LAST-NAME, and when we told the computer to do something with LAST-NAME, it wouldn't know which one we meant. To avoid having duplicate data-names, I've added -OUT to each of the data-names in our output record.

Fields 1 through 13 of our output record appear as sequence nos. 370 through 490 in Figure 7.5. What are the FILLERs at 360 and 500 for? I've decided that our output lines would look nice centered on the printer page. Fields 1 through 13 account for 82 character positions. There are 136 character positions on the page.

$$136 - 82 = 54$$
$$54 \div 2 = 27$$

If we want those 82 characters centered on the page, then we must place 27 spaces on their left and 27 spaces on their right, and that is what the FILLERs at 360 and 500 do.

```
                                              COBOL CODING FORM

PROGRAM    DATE-SERVICE                        COBOL DIVISION PROCEDURE    PAGE  1  OF  1
PROGRAMMER  R. G. Finkenaur                    DATE Sept. 26, 1978   IDENT   DATE-SVC

  510  PROCEDURE DIVISION.
  520  START-PARA.
  530      OPEN INPUT DATE-CARD-FILE, OUTPUT DATE-LISTING-FILE.
  540      MOVE SPACES TO PRINT-LINE.
  550      MOVE ' HAIR    ' TO FIELD-6.
  560      MOVE ' FT ' TO FIELD-8.
  570      MOVE ' IN   ' TO FIELD-10.
  580      MOVE ' LBS    PHONE ' TO FIELD-12.
  590  READ-DATA-MOVE-AND-PRINT-PARA.
  600      READ DATE-CARD-FILE RECORD AT END GO TO LAST-PARA.
  610      MOVE LAST-NAME TO LAST-NAME-OUT.
  620      MOVE FIRST-NAME TO FIRST-NAME-OUT.
  630      MOVE HAIR-COLOR TO HAIR-COLOR-OUT.
  640      MOVE HT-FEET TO HT-FEET-OUT.
  650      MOVE HT-INCHES TO HT-INCHES-OUT.
  660      MOVE WEIGHT TO WEIGHT-OUT.
  670      MOVE PHONE TO PHONE-OUT.
  680      WRITE PRINT-LINE AFTER ADVANCING 2 LINES.
  690      GO TO READ-DATA-MOVE-AND-PRINT-PARA.
  700  LAST-PARA.
  710      CLOSE DATE-CARD-FILE DATE-LISTING-FILE.
  720      STOP RUN.
```

FIGURE 7.6   The PROCEDURE DIVISION[1]

7.4   The PROCEDURE DIVISION

The PROCEDURE DIVISION is shown in Figure 7.6. It begins with an
OPEN statement which opens our two files. At sequence no. 540, we tell the
computer to clean out the area of memory assigned to PRINT-LINE of any
odds and ends that might be left over from somebody else's program which
may have used the same area of memory. This action is especially important for the purpose of cleaning out the FILLER areas. The other fields
would have been cleaned out anyway by later MOVE commands, but not
the FILLERs. We want to be *sure* they contain SPACES, and the easiest
way to do that is to simply MOVE SPACES TO the entire PRINT-LINE, and
that's what we've done at sequence no. 540.

At sequence nos. 550 through 580 we take care of loading fields
6, 8, 10, and 12 with the titling information we talked about in the last
section.

The READ-DATA-MOVE-AND-PRINT-PARAgraph is the heart of the

---

[1] A note to IBM computer users: In order for this program to work properly on an IBM
computer, the MOVE statements in the START-PARA would have to be moved to the
READ-DATA-MOVE-AND-PRINT-PARA.

program. It accomplishes the three basic steps essential to the transfer of the information on the data cards to the line printer:

1. Reading of each record from the input file. (Sequence no. 600)
2. MOVEment of the data-values from the input record to the output record. (Sequence nos. 610–670)
3. Printing of the output record on the line printer. (Sequence no. 680)

I'd like to reinforce your understanding of those three basic steps. Remember this: when we described the input record (called DATE-CARD) back in the DATA DIVISION (sequence nos. 230-320, Figure 7.4), we were actually telling the computer to set up its memory locations according to the arrangement we described there. There was to be a memory location assigned to LAST-NAME, another assigned to FIRST-NAME, another to HT-FEET, and so on. Not only that, but by the order in which we placed those data-names, we told the computer in what order to expect to find the data-values on the data card. The READ command at sequence no. 600 tells the computer to cause the card reader to read *one card.* When the card is read, all values found on the card will be recorded in the appropriate memory locations: FIRST-NAME will get the person's first name; LAST-NAME will get the person's last name; HT-FEET will get the feet part of the person's height; and so on.

When we described the output record (called PRINT-LINE) back in the DATA DIVISION (sequence nos. 360 through 500, Figure 7.5), we were actually telling the computer to set up another set of memory locations according to the arrangement we described there. There was to be a memory location assigned to FIRST-NAME-OUT, another to LAST-NAME-OUT, another to HT-FEET-OUT, and so on. Not only that, but by the order in which we placed those data-names, we told the computer in what order we wanted their data-values printed in each line on the line printer.

The MOVE commands at sequence nos. 610 through 670 cause the data-values stored in the input record's memory locations to be MOVEd to (or copied into) the appropriate memory locations of the output record. The person's first name, now stored in FIRST-NAME, will be MOVEd to FIRST-NAME-OUT; the person's last name, now stored in LAST-NAME, will be MOVEd to LAST-NAME-OUT; the person's height in feet, now stored in HT-FEET, will be MOVEd to HT-FEET-OUT; and so on.

Having MOVEd all the data-values into the memory locations of the output record (called PRINT-LINE), we still must tell the computer to move those values from memory to the line printer and to cause the line printer to print them. That is what the WRITE command at sequence no. 680 does. Even with all those MOVE commands moving the data-values into PRINT-LINE's memory locations, nothing will actually get printed without a WRITE command.

Now the GO TO command at sequence no. 690: If it weren't for this command, only one data card would be read and only one line of print would be printed. We need this command to tell the computer to go back and start executing the READ-DATA-MOVE-AND-PRINT-PARAgraph again from the beginning. In Section 6.8 I told you about how GO TO statements can be used to branch back in a program and cause "looping" repeatedly through the same portion of a program. That is what's being done here. Because of the presence of the GO TO statement, the computer is in effect being told to:

1. Read the first data card.
2. Move the first set of data-values.
3. Print the first line of print.
4. Read the second data card.
5. Move the second set of data-values.
6. Print the second line of print.
7. Read the third data card.
8. Move the third set of data-values.
9. Print the third line of print.
10. Etc.
11. Etc.

Eventually, the computer, in attempting to obey the READ command, will find no more data cards to read, i.e., it will find itself AT the END of the data deck. At that point it will obey the GO TO LAST-PARA command, the files will be CLOSEd, and the computer will STOP the RUN.

7.5   Preparing the Program to Run: Control Cards

Now that the program is written (or "coded"), it is time to take it to a keypunch and punch it onto cards. Once we have punched all the lines from the coding forms onto cards, we are prepared to run the program, except for one thing which I haven't discussed yet: CONTROL CARDS.

Control cards are a group of IBM cards that are placed at the beginning of the program deck. They are necessary in large computer center operations where programs are not run individually, but rather in "batch runs." The control cards serve several purposes: they separate one programmer's deck from the preceding one; they tell the computer what language the program is written in; they give the account number to which the cost of running the program should be billed; etc.; etc. Programmers wishing to run a program at a computer center must first learn what control cards are required there, what information must be punched on each, and in what order they must be arranged. Any failure to comply exactly with the computer center's control card requirements will result in your program's not being processed.

One other card that is required at most installations is the one placed at the end of the data deck. Called the END OF FILE (or END OF DATA or END OF INFORMATION) card, it is often prepared on red card stock. Computer operators are trained to look for the "Red Card" at the end of all program decks submitted to them for running, and to rcfuse to accept a deck without one. They are necessary because, as mentioned above, programs are not usually run through the card reader one at a time. They are usually stacked in the card reader, one behind the other, six or more at a

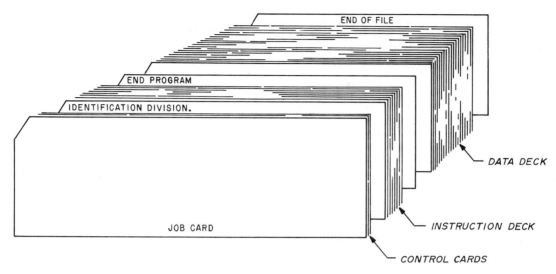

FIGURE 7.7   The Complete Program Deck

time. Without the red END OF FILE card, the operator would have difficulty separating the decks after they had been through the card reader.

Of much greater significance, however, is the need to provide each individual program in a batch of programs with the ability to detect the end of *its* data deck. The END OF FILE card serves that purpose. If a program did not have one, when it reached the end of *its* data deck, it would not stop but rather keep right on reading through the next programmer's control and instruction cards, believing them to be a part of its data deck.

Figure 7.7 shows a program deck ready for running, complete with all control cards and the END OF FILE card.

7.6 Running The Program

Having prepared the control cards, the instruction deck, and the data deck, we are now ready to run the program. We take the program deck to the computer operator; he places it in the card reader and pushes the "START" button. Immediately cards start zipping through the card reader, faster than the eye can follow. In a second or two the line printer starts to chatter. Less than 30 seconds later, all is quiet again; the computer has finished running our program. The operator returns the deck, tears our pages off the line printer, and hands the pages to us.

What did we get? Basically, the line printer gives us three things:

1. The program listing.
2. A list of error messages.
3. The output produced by the program.

```
00001          10 IDENTIFICATION DIVISION.                                      DATE-SVC
00002          20 PROGRAM-ID.    DATE-SERVICE.                                   DATE-SVC
00003          30 AUTHOR.           R G FINKENAUR.                               DATE-SVC
00004          40 INSTALLATION. NORTHEASTERN UNIV.                              DATE-SVC
00005          50 DATE-WRITTEN. SEPT 28, 1978.                                  DATE-SVC
00006          60 DATE-COMPILED.            78/09/28.                           DATE-SVC
00007          70 SECURITY.       FOR UNMARRIED PEOPLE ONLY.                    DATE-SVC
00008          80 REMARKS.        THIS PROGRAM WILL PRODUCE A LISTING OF THE NAMES,  DATE-SVC
00009          90    HAIR COLOR, HEIGHT, WEIGHT, AND PHONE NUMBERS OF ALL THE   DATE-SVC
00010         100    PEOPLE IN MY DATE FILES.                                   DATE-SVC
00011         110 ENVIRONMENT DIVISION.                                         DATE-SVC
00012         120 CONFIGURATION SECTION.                                        DATE-SVC
00013         130 SOURCE-COMPUTER.  HAL-2001.                                   DATE-SVC
00014         140 OBJECT-COMPUTER.  HAL-2001.                                   DATE-SVC
00015         150 INPUT-OUTPUT SECTION.                                         DATE-SVC
00016         160 FILE-CONTROL.                                                 DATE-SVC
00017         170     SELECT DATE-CARD-FILE ASSIGN TO CARD-READER.              DATE-SVC
00018         180     SELECT DATE-LISTING-FILE ASSIGN TO LINE-PRINTER.          DATE-SVC
00019         190 DATA DIVISION.                                                DATE-SVC
00020         200 FILE SECTION.                                                 DATE-SVC
00021         210 FD  DATE-CARD-FILE; RECORD CONTAINS 80 CHARACTERS; LABEL RECORDS  DATE-SVC
00022         220     ARE OMITTED; DATA RECORD IS DATE-CARD.                    DATE-SVC
00023         230 01  DATE-CARD.                                                DATE-SVC
00024         240     02  LAST-NAME        PICTURE A(15).                       DATE-SVC
00025         250     02  FIRST-NAME       PICTURE A(10).                       DATE-SVC
00026         260     02  FILLER           PICTURE X(30).                       DATE-SVC
00027         270     02  HT-FEET          PICTURE 9.                           DATE-SVC
00028         280     02  HT-INCHES        PICTURE 99.                          DATE-SVC
00029         290     02  WEIGHT           PICTURE 999.                         DATE-SVC
00030         300     02  HAIR-COLOR       PICTURE A(6).                        DATE-SVC
00031         310     02  PHONE            PICTURE 9(10).                       DATE-SVC
00032         320     02  FILLER           PICTURE XXX.                         DATE-SVC
00033         330 FD  DATE-LISTING-FILE; RECORD CONTAINS 136 CHARACTERS; LABEL  DATE-SVC
00034         340     RECORDS ARE OMITTED; DATA RECORD IS PRINT-LINE.           DATE-SVC
00035         350 01  PRINT-LINE.                                               DATE-SVC
00036         360     02  FILLER           PICTURE X(27).                       DATE-SVC
00037         370     02  FIRST-NAME-OUT   PICTURE A(10).                       DATE-SVC
00038         380     02  FILLER           PICTURE X.                           DATE-SVC
00039         390     02  LAST-NAME-OUT    PICTURE A(15).                       DATE-SVC
00040         400     02  FILLER           PICTURE XXX.                         DATE-SVC
00041         410     02  HAIR-COLOR-OUT   PICTURE A(6).                        DATE-SVC
00042         420     02  FIELD-6          PICTURE X(8).                        DATE-SVC
00043         430     02  HT-FEET-OUT      PICTURE 9.                           DATE-SVC
00044         440     02  FIELD-8          PICTURE X(4).                        DATE-SVC
00045         450     02  HT-INCHES-OUT    PICTURE 99.                          DATE-SVC
00046         460     02  FIELD-10         PICTURE X(6).                        DATE-SVC
00047         470     02  WEIGHT-OUT       PICTURE 999.                         DATE-SVC
00048         480     02  FIELD-12         PICTURE X(13).                       DATE-SVC
00049         490     02  PHONE-OUT        PICTURE 9(10).                       DATE-SVC
00050         500     02  FILLER           PICTURE X(27).                       DATE-SVC
00051         510 PROCEDURE DIVISION.                                           DATE-SVC
00052         520 START-PARA.                                                   DATE-SVC
00053         530     OPEN INPUT DATE-CARD-FILE, OUTPUT DATE-LISTING-FILE.      DATE-SVC
00054         540     MOVE SPACES TO PRINT-LINE.                                DATE-SVC
00055         550     MOVE ' HAIR   ' TO FIELD-6.                               DATE-SVC
00056         560     MOVE ' FT ' TO FIELD-8.                                   DATE-SVC
00057         570     MOVE ' IN   ' TO FIELD-10.                                DATE-SVC
00058         580     MOVE ' LBS    PHONE ' TO FIELD-12.                        DATE-SVC
00059         590 READ-DATA-MOVE-AND-PRINT-PARA.                                DATE-SVC
00060         600     READ DATE-CARD-FILE RECORD AT END GO TO LAST-PARA.        DATE-SVC
00061         610     MOVE LAST-NAME TO LAST-NAME-OUT.                          DATE-SVC
00062         620     MOVE FIRST-NAME TO FIRST-NAME-OUT.                        DATE-SVC
00063         630     MOVE HAIR-COLOR TO HAIR-COLOR-OUT.                        DATE-SVC
00064         640     MOVE HT-FEET TO HT-FEET-OUT.                              DATE-SVC
00065         650     MOVE HT-INCHES TO HT-INCHES-OUT.                          DATE-SVC
00066         660     MOVE WEIGHT TO WEIGHT-OUT.                                DATE-SVC
00067         670     MOVE PHONE TO PHONE-OUT.                                  DATE-SVC
00068         680     WRITE PRINT-LINE AFTER ADVANCING 2 LINES.                 DATE-SVC
00069         690     GO TO READ-DATA-MOVE-AND-PRINT-PARA.                      DATE-SVC
00070         700 LAST-PARA.                                                    DATE-SVC
00071         710     CLOSE DATE-CARD-FILE DATE-LISTING-FILE.                   DATE-SVC
00072         720     STOP RUN.                                                 DATE-SVC
```

FIGURE 7.8   The Program Listing

The program listing is simply a listing of the contents of the instruction deck. You'll see the four divisions complete, exactly as you punched them onto the cards. You'll see the sequence numbers in a column just to the left of the statements in the program. If you used columns 73–80 of your instruction cards for identifying characters, you'll see these characters appearing repeatedly in a column just to the right of the statements.

The program we have been writing in this chapter is seen in Figure 7.8 as it would appear in a program listing.

Notice the column of numbers just to the left of the sequence numbers. Those are *line numbers*. Line numbers are generated and inserted into the listing by the computer. They are used by the computer in telling you where you made mistakes. If you, for example, leave a hyphen out of a word that is supposed to be hyphenated, the computer will print an error message telling you the number of the *line* in which you made that error. If everybody used sequence numbers, line numbers wouldn't be necessary. Since sequence numbers are optional not everybody uses them, so the computer is programmed not to depend on them. More on error messages in Section 7.8.

If we made no errors in writing or punching our program, there will be no error messages and the next thing after the program listing will be the output produced by the program. A portion of a page of output produced by this program is shown in Figure 7.9.

7.7   Program Errors

I'll present a much more thorough discussion of COBOL programming errors in a later chapter. For now I want to say just enough to get you through your first few elementary programs.

The computer will check your program for errors you may have made in writing or punching the program. Perhaps you're wondering what kinds of errors I'm talking about. Most of the errors you will make in your first programs will fall into two categories:

1.   Spelling errors.
2.   Grammar errors.

```
WILHELMINA  SCHIMMELPFENNIG    BLONDE HAIR    4 FT 10 IN    120 LBS    PHONE 9146524915

KATE        AMBROSE            BROWN  HAIR    4 FT 09 IN    115 LBS    PHONE 6172194283

CAROL       WHALEN             BRUNET HAIR    5 FT 01 IN    105 LBS    PHONE 6177742821

SANDY       THEPERSON          BROWN  HAIR    6 FT 04 IN    095 LBS    PHONE 2129743875

CLAUDETTE   WISE               BLACK  HAIR    4 FT 11 IN    250 LBS    PHONE 6177749642

SHIRLEY     STURDEVANT         RED    HAIR    5 FT 03 IN    120 LBS    PHONE 7135790243

MAE         MCCAULEY           BLONDE HAIR    4 FT 07 IN    195 LBS    PHONE 6177982164

EDITH       BUNKER             GREY   HAIR    5 FT 10 IN    145 LBS    PHONE 2124587365
```

FIGURE 7.9   The Program Output

One of the biggest sources of frustration to new programmers is the detailed accuracy which they must observe in writing a program for the computer. They forget that the computer is a *machine* and incapable of human flexibility in interpreting statements given to it. Humans, when faced with a typographical error in a text, can usually figure out what the author intended to say. Not so with the computer. The slightest misspelling of a word in a program will make that word totally incomprehensible to the computer. If for example you spelled ENVIRONMENT DIVISION as ENVIROMENT DIVISION, you might just as well have spelled it XJVZBQRSNW DIVISION. It knows of no word spelled ENVIROMENT and so it is incapable of comprehending that line of your program. Here are some examples of potential errors you as a beginner must be especially watchful for:

1. *Spelling Errors.*
a. *Missing or Extraneous Hyphens.* Hyphens are as much a part of the spelling of COBOL words as are the letters.

Incorrect	Correct
DATE COMPILED.	DATE-COMPILED.
INPUT OUTPUT SECTION.	INPUT-OUTPUT SECTION.
FILE-SECTION.	FILE SECTION.
DATA-RECORD IS PRINT-LINE.	DATA RECORD IS PRINT-LINE.
READ CARD-FILE-RECORD AT END GO TO LAST-PARA.	READ CARD-FILE RECORD AT END GO TO LAST-PARA.
STOP-RUN.	STOP RUN.

b. *Misspelled Reserved Words and Names.* The simplest misspelling of a reserved word or name will make it unrecognizable to the computer and will result in the function it was to have performed not being performed.

Incorrect	Correct
OPEN OUPUT PRINT-FILE.	OPEN OUTPUT PRINT-FILE.
PROGRAM-I.D.	PROGRAM-ID.
RECORDS CONTAIN 80 CHARACTERS;	RECORD CONTAINS 80 CHARACTERS;
GOTO MAIN-PARA.	GO TO MAIN-PARA.
ID DIVISION.	IDENTIFICATION DIVISION.
DATA DIV.	DATA DIVISION.

c. *Misspelled Programmer-Invented-Names.* You must be absolutely consistent throughout your program in how you spell the names you invent. Suppose in the ENVIRONMENT DIVISION you had said:

SELECT DATE-CARD-FILE ASSIGN TO CARD-READER.

It would then be *incorrect* in the DATA DIVISION to say:

FD   DATE-CARDS-FILE; etc.

It would be likewise *incorrect* in the PROCEDURE DIVISION to say:

OPEN INPUT DATE-KARD-FILE.

or

READ DATA-CARD-FILE RECORD etc.

Suppose this entry were in the DATA DIVISION:

02 HRS-WORKED   PICTURE 99.

It would then be *incorrect* in the PROCEDURE DIVISION to say:

MOVE 40 TO HOURS-WORKED.

Suppose this paragraph heading were in your PROCEDURE DIVISION:

MAIN-PARA.

It would then be *incorrect* to say:

GO TO MAIN-PARAGRAPH.

2. *Grammar Errors.* The rules of COBOL grammar must be followed as closely as the spelling rules. Here are some examples of the kinds of grammar errors you as a beginning programmer are most likely to make:

a. *Forgotten Periods.* As you know, you may continue a long sentence from one line to the next by simply breaking the sentence at a convenient space on the first line and continuing the sentence on the next line. Because of that, if you forget a period at the end of one line, the computer will interpret the next line as a continuation of the first. For example, these two lines:

DATA DIVISION
FILE SECTION.

would be understood by the computer as:

DATA DIVISION FILE SECTION.

That is entirely incomprehensible to the computer. For all it knows, since the thing ends in the word SECTION, you intended that to be the section header of the DATA-DIVISION-FILE SECTION, but you forgot your hyphens. At any rate, whatever it is, the computer can't handle it.

b. *Improper Formation of Sentences.* Sentences must contain only the clauses intended for use with them.

READ CARD-FILE RECORD.

is an *incorrect* sentence, because all READ sentences must have AT END clauses.

WRITE PRINT-REC AT END GO TO LAST-PARA.

is an *incorrect* sentence, because a WRITE sentence may not have an AT END clause.

OPEN CARD-FILE PRINT-FILE.

is an *incorrect* sentence, because it is missing the words INPUT and/or OUTPUT.

    c. *Violations of the READ FILES, WRITE RECORDS Rule.* A READ statement must reference a file-name. A WRITE statement must reference a record-name. In the program we just wrote it would have been incorrect to say:

READ DATE-CARD RECORD AT END GO TO LAST-PARA.

because DATE-CARD is a record-name. Likewise, it would have been *incorrect* to say:

WRITE DATE-LISTING-FILE AFTER ADVANCING 2 LINES.

because DATE-LISTING-FILE is *not* a record-name.

    d. *Failure to OPEN Files Properly.* You may not READ from a file that has not been opened for INPUT (or worse, has not been opened at all). You may not WRITE into a file that has not been opened for OUTPUT.

7.8 Error Messages

Whenever you commit any errors like those outlined above, the computer will give you a set of error messages immediately following your program listing. The messages will tell you where by line number (not by sequence number) each error is located, and it will describe briefly what the nature of each error is.

    Unfortunately, you will find the error descriptions to be worded in such a way as to defy your understanding at first. After having dealt with them for a while, you'll find yourself slowly developing a comprehension of what they're trying to say. In the meantime, however, they will tell you *where* to look for your errors, so they'll prove valuable in that sense right from the start.

    You are going to find that errors have a snowballing effect in terms of the error messages they generate. For example, if you said

OPEN IMPUT CARD-FILE.

that would be a simple spelling error. That simple error, however, makes the entire OPEN statement incomprehensible to the computer, so the result is that CARD-FILE would not get OPENed. If later in the program there were several READ statements such as

READ CARD-FILE RECORD etc.

you would find an error message generated for every one of those READ statements, because you would be telling the computer to READ from a file that hadn't been OPENed. Furthermore, an error message would be generated for every MOVE statement that referenced any data-name in the CARD-FILE's record, since the record had never been read.

The lesson to be learned here is that if you are faced with a long list of error messages, a large number of which reference lines in which you can identify no errors whatsoever, don't despair. Correct the few errors you *do* recognize, and run the program again. You'll be amazed at how many error messages disappear after you've corrected even a small number of the errors that you are able to recognize.

7.9 Before You Go on to Chapter 8

Learning computer programming is very much a building block process. Everything that comes later is dependent upon your complete understanding of everything that went before. For the sake of easing your progress toward becoming a successful COBOL programmer, you must pause at the end of each chapter from here on, and be honest with yourself concerning whether you have mastered the material in that chapter.

To provide an opportunity for self-evaluation, I will give you an Example Program and a Student's Program at the end of each chapter in addition to the Exercises. In each case, you will find the solution to the Example Program given and discussed; however, no solution will be provided for the Student's Program.

My advice to you is that you try solving each Example Program without looking at the solution given. (Just write your solution on coding forms; don't bother to punch and run it.) Then compare your solution with the one given. If they compare favorably (needless to say, they'll *never* agree letter-for-letter), then try to write, punch, *and run* the Student's Program.

Take my advice, and this text will remain uniformly simple throughout. Ignore my advice, and the text will seem to become more and more difficult as you progress into it, to the point that you will finally lose all ability to comprehend it. One of English literature's most quotable quotes says that "he who knows not and knows not that he knows not is a fool." Don't allow yourself to fit that description. Resolve now to make an honest attempt at solving all Student's Programs.

EXERCISES

Answers to all exercises in this chapter are given in Appendix A.

7.1 What are the five parts of a complete COBOL program deck?

7.2 Name the three basic items which you receive from the line printer.

7.3 Place an L or an S after each of the following statements to indicate whether it applies to line numbers or sequence numbers.

L or S

a. Supplied by the programmer. _____
b. Supplied by the computer. _____
c. Always a part of a program listing. _____
d. Not always a part of a program listing. _____
e. Appear as the left-most column in the program listing. _____
f. Referenced in error messages as a means of locating errors. _____

7.4 Complete this sentence: A READ statement must include a _____-name; a WRITE statement must include a _____-name.

7.5 TRUE or FALSE? The AT END clause is a required part of every READ statement.

7.6 TRUE or FALSE? The AFTER ADVANCING clause is a required part of every WRITE statement.

7.7 What two basic events occur as a result of this statement: READ CARD-FILE RECORD AT END GO TO LAST-PARA.

7.8 What event triggers the execution of the AT END clause?

7.9 What two basic events occur as a result of this statement: WRITE PRINT-RECORD.

7.10 Name the two uses for a FILLER that you have been exposed to so far.

7.11 Assume that these lines were the first four record description entries under the FD entry for the PRINT-FILE in the DATA DIVISION.

```
01  PRINT-RECORD.
    02  TITLE-OUT    PICTURE X(3).
    02  FILLER       PICTURE X.
    02  NAME-OUT     PICTURE A(5).
```

Assume for the sake of this exercise that these lines were a part of your PROCEDURE DIVISION.

```
OPEN OUTPUT PRINT-FILE.
MOVE SPACES TO PRINT-RECORD.
MOVE 'MR.' TO TITLE-OUT.
MOVE 'SMITH' TO NAME-OUT.
WRITE PRINT-RECORD.
MOVE 'JONES' TO NAME-OUT.
WRITE PRINT-RECORD.
MOVE 'MS.' TO TITLE-OUT.
WRITE PRINT-RECORD.
MOVE 'KULIK' TO NAME-OUT.
WRITE PRINT-RECORD.
```

What would the four lines look like that would be printed by the line printer as a result of these four WRITE statements?

EXAMPLE PROGRAM

Student Rolls

Write a program which will print a listing of the students who are enrolled in my COBOL course. I have collected their enrollment cards and gathered them into a deck. Each enrollment card is an IBM card containing information in this arrangement:

CARD COLUMNS	INFORMATION	EXAMPLE
1–9	Social Security Number	083223549
10–21	Last name	STANISLOVSKI
22–30	First name	ALEXANDER
31	Middle initial	P
32–33	Graduation Year	76 (1976)
34–80	Blank	

These three lines demonstrate the desired form of each line in the printer listing:

```
ALEXANDER  P STANISLOVSKI    S. S. N. 083-22-3549,  CLASS OF 1976
JOHN       J WHALEN          S. S. N. 064-71-9214,  CLASS OF 1978
DELAINE    M WILLIAMSON      S. S. N. 106-43-2275,  CLASS OF 1980
```

Double space your output on the line printer. Place the first letter of each line in the 2nd character position on the page. Some suggested contents for trial data cards:

```
083223549STANISLOVSKIALEXANDERP76
064719214WHALEN     JOHN     J78
106432275WILLIAMSON DELAINE  M80
279325768POWERS     ROBERT   G81
477934220LIPSETT    CHERYL   T79
376429003ROCK       ALAN     J78
```

Solution

IDENTIFICATION and ENVIRONMENT DIVISIONs omitted.

```
DATA DIVISION.
FILE SECTION.
FD  ENROLLMENT-CARD-FILE; RECORD CONTAINS 80 CHARACTERS; LABEL
    RECORDS ARE OMITTED; DATA RECORD IS ENROLLMENT-CARD.
```

```
01   ENROLLMENT-CARD.
     02   SSN-1-IN              PICTURE 999.
     02   SSN-2-IN              PICTURE 99.
     02   SSN-3-IN              PICTURE 9999.
     02   LAST-NAME-IN          PICTURE A(12).
     02   FIRST-NAME-IN         PICTURE A(9).
     02   INITIAL-IN            PICTURE A.
     02   GRAD-YR-IN            PICTURE 99.
     02   FILLER               PICTURE X(47).
FD   STUDENT-LISTING-FILE; RECORD CONTAINS 136 CHARACTERS; LABEL
     RECORDS ARE OMITTED; DATA RECORD IS PRINT-LINE.
01   PRINT-LINE.
     02   FILLER               PICTURE X.
     02   FIRST-NAME-OUT        PICTURE A(9).
     02   FILLER               PICTURE X.
     02   INITIAL-OUT           PICTURE A.
     02   FILLER               PICTURE X.
     02   LAST-NAME-OUT         PICTURE A(12).
     02   FIELD-6              PICTURE X(12).
     02   SSN-1-OUT            PICTURE 999.
     02   FIELD-8              PICTURE X.
     02   SSN-2-OUT            PICTURE 99.
     02   FIELD-10             PICTURE X.
     02   SSN-3-OUT            PICTURE 9999.
     02   FIELD-12             PICTURE X(13).
     02   GRAD-YR-OUT          PICTURE 99.
     02   FILLER               PICTURE X(73).
PROCEDURE DIVISION.
START-PARA.
     OPEN INPUT ENROLLMENT-CARD-FILE, OUTPUT STUDENT-LISTING-FILE.
     MOVE SPACES TO PRINT-LINE.      ⎫
     MOVE '  S. S. N. ' TO FIELD-6.  ⎪
     MOVE '-' TO FIELD-8.            ⎬ 2
     MOVE '-' TO FIELD-10.           ⎪
     MOVE ', CLASS OF 19' TO FIELD-12. ⎭
READ-DATA-MOVE-AND-PRINT-PARA.
     READ ENROLLMENT-CARD-FILE RECORD, AT END GO TO LAST-PARA.
     MOVE FIRST-NAME-IN TO FIRST-NAME-OUT.
     MOVE INITIAL-IN TO INITIAL-OUT.
     MOVE LAST-NAME-IN TO LAST-NAME-OUT.
     MOVE SSN-1-IN TO SSN-1-OUT.
     MOVE SSN-2-IN TO SSN-2-OUT.
     MOVE SSN-3-IN TO SSN-3-OUT.
     MOVE GRAD-YR-IN TO GRAD-YR-OUT.
     WRITE PRINT-LINE AFTER ADVANCING 2 LINES.
     GO TO READ-DATA-MOVE-AND-PRINT-PARA.
LAST-PARA.
     CLOSE ENROLLMENT-CARD-FILE, STUDENT-LISTING-FILE.
     STOP RUN.
```

[2] A note to IBM computer users: In order for this program to work properly on an IBM computer, the MOVE statements in the START-PARA would have to be moved to the READ-DATA-MOVE-AND-PRINT-PARA.

Discussion

This program is similar to the one discussed in the chapter. The only item worthy of special mention here is the handling of the Social Security Number. The SSN was described as a single field of nine digits on the data card but we were told to print it out in three pieces separated by hyphens. Those nine digits are not welded together. We can handle them in any groupings we like, regardless of how they happened to be described. If you're going to print a field on the line printer in three pieces, you've got to pick it up off the card in three pieces, so that's what was done here.

STUDENT'S PROGRAM

Used Cars

Write a program which will create from a used car dealer's inventory file a
listing on the line printer of all cars which he has on hand for sale. Each
record in the file is an IBM card describing one of the cars in his lot. Each
card contains information in this arrangement:

CARD COLUMNS	INFORMATION	EXAMPLE
1–4	Manufacturer	CHEV
5–14	Body type	2-DR SEDAN
15–16	Year of manufacture	71 (1971)
17–21	Mileage	54321 (54,321)
22	Cylinders	6
23–26	Price	1250 ($1,250)
27–80	Former owner's name & address	GEORGE JONES, etc.

These three lines demonstrate the desired form of each of the lines of the
listing:

```
1971  CHEV  2-DR  SEDAN      6  CYL     $1250      54321  MILES
1970  MERC  STA  WGN         8  CYL     $1500      84762  MILES
1965  FORD  T-BIRD           8  CYL     $2110      62779  MILES
```

Double space and center your output on the printer page. Note that the
dealer does *not* want the former owner's name and address to appear on the
listing. Some suggested contents for trial data cards:

```
CHEV2-DR SEDAN  715432161250GEORGE JONES, 21 MAIN ST., FRANKLIN, N.Y.
MERCSTA WGN     708476281500KIP GORDON, 312 FOURTH AVE., HADDON HTS., N.Y.
FORDT-BIRD      656277982110CHARLEY GLOVER, 213 CAISSON RD., HAMPTON, VA.
PLYMHARDTOP     694216261050GARRY WILLIAMS, 249 BESTEVER DR., CAMBRIDGE, MA.
V W BUG         619914640040MAURY GUSTIN, 42 NONAME LANE, PODUNK, R.I.
CHEVVEGA H.B.   715374241214GLENDA KELLEY, 794 HEIDELBERG ST., ACTON, MA.
```

8 A Second Look at the DATA DIVISION: The PICTURE Clause in More Detail

8.1 Introduction

Up to this point I've limited our discussion of PICTURE clauses to those that handle data values exactly as they come off the data card. We have two basic things to accomplish in this chapter:

1. We must finish up our discussion of the numeric PICTURE clause, so as to release you from the restriction of dealing only with positive, integer values, and
2. We must discuss the editing functions available to us through the PICTURE clause.

By way of review—In Chapter 5 I told you that a PICTURE clause is given to every elementary item of data described in the DATA DIVISION. It tells the class and size of the item. At that time we spoke of only three classes: numeric (N), alphabetic (AB), and alphanumeric (AN). This table, reprinted from Chapter 5, summarizes what has been said so far about Class N, AB, and AN PICTURE clauses:

CLASS	DATA-VALUE MAY CONTAIN	PICTURE CLAUSE CHARACTERS
N	Only digits.	9 V S P
AB	Only letters and spaces.	A
AN	Any COBOL character.	9 A X

This chapter will complete your understanding of the numeric PICTURE clause by discussing the V, S, and P characters, and it will describe class numeric-edited (NE) and alphanumeric-edited (AE).

> *A Note to FORTRAN-Experienced Programmers*—In FORTRAN you were permitted to place decimal points and minus signs in numeric fields on data cards. Not so in COBOL. Decimal points and minus signs are COBOL special characters and as such are forbidden in a Class Numeric (digits-only) field on a data card. Take special note in the following section of how decimal point location and negative values are handled with data cards in COBOL.

8.2   The Numeric Picture Clause

The V Character   In a numeric item that is not to be restricted to integer values, we use the V to indicate the "implied" decimal point location. The word "implied" is used here, because no actual decimal point is placed on the data card. To demonstrate this concept, suppose this entry were in your DATA DIVISION:

    03   UNIT-PRICE   PICTURE 999V99.

Suppose further that the field on the data card holding the data-value for UNIT-PRICE contained these digits—

01495

This would be the result of reading that data card and storing those five digits in memory location UNIT-PRICE:

UNIT-PRICE

Note that I've used the caret (⌃) to indicate the position of the implied decimal point in the memory location. This is a notation I will use for the remainder of the book whenever I want to show an implied decimal point.

The implied decimal point is a necessary evil of COBOL, because of the fact that only "pure" numeric data (Class N) may be involved in arithmetic operations. Recall from the table at the beginning of this chapter that Class N items of data may contain *only* digits. As soon as you include an actual decimal point or any other special character in an otherwise numeric item, it is no longer "purely" numeric; it is alphanumeric and hence not suitable for use in any arithmetic operation.

In determining the size of a Class N item, the V is not counted.

Figure 8.1 will reinforce your understanding of the effect of the V character by presenting some examples of its use.

The P Character   Similar to the V character, the P is used to indicate the location of the implied decimal point. The V character is used when the decimal point location is within the field of the data item; the P character is used when the decimal point is outside the field of the data item. The P is

Characters on the Data Card	PICTURE of the Item	Resulting Value Stored in Memory	Size of Item
137	9V99	1͜37	3
137	99V9	13͜7	3
137	V999	͜137	3
137	999	137͜	3
001275	9V9(5)	0͜01275	6
3645095	9(5)V99	36450͜95	7

FIGURE 8.1   Effect of the V Character in the Class Numeric PICTURE Clause

used most often with very large or very small values in order to eliminate the need to punch long strings of zeros on the data card. To demonstrate the use of the P character, suppose this entry were in your DATA DIVISION.

    03 ANNUAL-SALARY   PICTURE 99PPP.

Suppose further that the field on the data card holding the data-value for ANNUAL-SALARY had the two characters 35 in it. This would be the result of storing that data-value in memory location ANNUAL-SALARY:

ANNUAL-SALARY

35000͜

Like the V character, the P is not counted in computing the size of an item. Note that in a single PICTURE clause, you would use either the V or the P, but not both. Figure 8.2 gives additional examples of the use of the P character.

The S Character   If you ever have a data item whose value may be negative, you must warn the computer of this. You do that by placing an S at the beginning of the PICTURE clause character-string for that item. Don't

Characters on the Data Card	Picture of the Item	Resulting Value Stored in Memory	Size of Item
15	PP99	͜0015	2
326	999P(4)	3260000͜	3
1079	9(4)PP	107900͜	4
6	P(5)9	͜000006	1

FIGURE 8.2   Effect of the P Character in the Class Numeric PICTURE Clause

misunderstand—the S doesn't say that the value *will* be negative; it only says that it *may* be negative. If a negative data-value were given to a field whose PICTURE did not have an S, the negative sign would be ignored and the absolute value would be stored. (In a checking account program, for example, where the programmer failed to put an S in the PICTURE clause for ACCT-BALANCE, if the account holder had $5.00 in her account and wrote a check for $15.00, her ACCT-BALANCE would end up with $10.00 in it.)

As mentioned before, the data-value for a "pure" numeric (Class N) item may contain only digits, but no decimal points nor any other special characters. This restriction applies to minus signs, too. In order to place a negative value on a data card for a COBOL program, you multi-punch[1] a minus sign over the last digit in the field. For example, suppose you had a data-name PROFIT in your program to which you wanted to give a value of −175.82. In your DATA DIVISION you'd need an entry like this:

    03   PROFIT   PICTURE S999V99.

This is how the field on the data card which held the data-value for PROFIT would have to be punched

This would be the result of reading that data card and storing that value in memory location PROFIT:

Note the minus placed over the last digit. This is a notation I will use for the remainder of the book whenever I want to show a negative value stored in Class N form.

Like the V and P, the S character is not counted in determining the size of a Class N item.

Figure 8.3 gives some additional examples of the use of the S, V, and P characters.

8.3   Editing

Suppose you had a program which calculated the total sales for a company. More than likely, you'd have an entry such as this in your DATA DIVISION:

    02   TOTAL-SALES   PICTURE 9(6)V99.

[1] To multi-punch more than one character in a single column on a card, hold down the MULT PCH button on the keypunch's keyboard while hitting the keys of the characters you want in that column.

Characters on the Data Card	PICTURE of the Item	Resulting Value Stored in Memory	Size of Item
564	99V9	564	3
564	S99V9	564	3
564	S99V9	564	3
8	SPP9	008	1
16	S99PPP	16000	2

FIGURE 8.3   Effect of the S, V, and P Characters in the Class Numeric PICTURE Clause

Suppose that as a result of several calculations, your program had computed a value for TOTAL-SALES as shown here:

TOTAL-SALES

| 07458255 |

If you caused the contents of TOTAL-SALES to be printed in that form, it would be printed as 07458255; certainly not what you'd call "fit for human consumption." I think you'll agree that this would be a far more desirable form in which to print that value:

$ 74,582.55

In order to accomplish that transformation from the purely numeric form to the more familiar form including a dollar sign, a comma, and an actual decimal point and excluding the unimportant leading zero, a COBOL process called "editing" is performed.

Editing is accomplished by establishing a second field with an edited PICTURE clause such as this:

02   TOTAL-SALES-OUT   PICTURE $Z99,999.99.

(The $, Z, comma, and decimal point appearing in that PICTURE clause are "editing characters.") Now to have the value printed out as $ 74,582.55 rather than as 07458255, we first say

MOVE TOTAL-SALES TO TOTAL-SALES-OUT.

The Unedited   The Edited
Sending Field   Receiving Field

We then cause the edited value in TOTAL-SALES-OUT rather than the unedited value in TOTAL-SALES to be printed.

Recall this point made in Section 8.2—Numeric values which are being involved in arithmetic operations *must* be kept in pure numeric (unedited) form. You customarily leave such values in their purely numeric (Class N) fields until you are all through with the calculations which involve them, and then just before you have them printed, you MOVE them to edited fields and print the contents of the *edited* fields.

The remainder of this chapter will be devoted to descriptions of the make-up and use of Numeric-edited (Class NE) and Alphanumeric-edited (Class AE) PICTURE clauses.

CLASS	PICTURE CLAUSE CHARACTERS
NE AE	+ − $ Z 9 , . CR DB * B 0 X A 9 B 0

8.4 Numeric Editing

Suppression of Leading Zeros–The Z Character   Z characters are placed starting at the left end of a numeric PICTURE clause in place of 9's to indicate in how many positions you want leading zeros suppressed (replaced by blanks). It is permissible to replace *all* the 9's in a numeric PICTURE clause with Z's. Figure 8.4 demonstrates the functioning of the Zero Suppression Character Z.

Insertion of Decimal Points—The . Character   The . character is placed in an edited PICTURE clause to show that you want an actual decimal point inserted in the same relative position where the implied decimal point was located. Unlike the V character, the . character *is* counted in determining the size of the field. Figure 8.5 demonstrates the functioning of the . character, and gives further examples of the use of the Z character.

THE SENDING FIELD			THE RECEIVING FIELD		
PICTURE of the Item	Item Size	Stored Value	PICTURE of the Item	Item Size	Resulting Value
9999	4	0007	9999	4	0007
9999	4	0007	ZZ99	4	07
9999	4	0027	ZZ99	4	27
9999	4	0327	ZZ99	4	327
9999	4	4327	ZZ99	4	4327
9999	4	0007	ZZZZ	4	7
9999	4	0000	ZZZZ	4	
9999	4	0000	ZZZ9	4	0

FIGURE 8.4   Suppression of Leading Zeros

THE SENDING FIELD			THE RECEIVING FIELD		
PICTURE of the Item	Item Size	Stored Value	PICTURE of the Item	Item Size	Resulting Value
999V99	5	01234	999.99	6	012.34
999V99	5	01234	ZZZ.99	6	12.34
999V99	5	00034	ZZZ.99	6	.34
999V99	5	00000	ZZZ.99	6	.00
9(5)V9	6	315000	Z(5).9	7	31500.0
9(5)V9	6	009755	Z(5).9	7	975.5

FIGURE 8.5   Insertion of Actual Decimal Points

Insertion of Fixed Dollar Signs—The $ Character   The term *fixed dollar signs* is used here to distinguish them from *floating dollar signs* which we will discuss later. A single dollar sign is placed at the left end of an edited PICTURE clause to indicate that you want a dollar sign to appear there when the value is printed out. An important consideration—If your sending field has a PICTURE of 999, it is then possible for it to have a three-digit value such as 564. If you really anticipate a three-digit value, then you'd better allow for that in designing the PICTURE clause of your edited receiving field. A PICTURE of $99 would result in the left-most digit being replaced by a $. A PICTURE of $999 would be preferable.

Figure 8.6 demonstrates the functioning of the fixed $ character. Notice from the figure the existence of this common sense rule: When all the characters to the right of the $ are suppressed, the $ is suppressed.

THE SENDING FIELD			THE RECEIVING FIELD		
PICTURE of the Item	Item Size	Stored Value	PICTURE of the Item	Item Size	Resulting Value
999	3	016	$99	3	$16
999	3	275	$99	3	$75
999	3	275	$999	4	$275
999	3	016	$999	4	$016
999	3	016	$ZZZ	4	$ 16
999	3	000	$ZZZ	4	
999	3	000	$ZZ9	4	$ 0
99V99	4	0500	$99.99	6	$05.00
99V99	4	0500	$ZZ.99	6	$5.00
99V99	4	0000	$ZZ.99	6	$0.00

FIGURE 8.6   Insertion of Fixed Dollar Signs

THE SENDING FIELD			THE RECEIVING FIELD		
PICTURE of the Item	Item Size	Stored Value	PICTURE of the Item	Item Size	Resulting Value
9(8)	8	83246572	99,999,999	10	83,246,572
9(8)	8	00246572	99,999,999	10	00,246,572
9(8)	8	00246572	ZZ,ZZZ,ZZZ	10	246,572
9(8)	8	00006572	ZZ,ZZZ,ZZZ	10	6,572
9(8)	8	00000572	ZZ,ZZZ,ZZZ	10	572
9(5)V99	7	0427538	$99,999.99	10	$04,275.38
9(5)V99	7	0427538	$ZZ,ZZZ.99	10	$4,275.38
9(5)V99	7	0000538	$ZZ,ZZZ.99	10	$5.38
9(5)V99	7	0000000	$ZZ,ZZZ.99	10	$.00

FIGURE 8.7   Insertion of Commas

Insertion of Commas—The , Character   The , character is placed in an edited PICTURE clause to show where you want a comma inserted in the field. More than one , character may be used in an edited PICTURE clause. Figure 8.7 demonstrates their functioning. Notice once again what common sense dictates: When all digits on the left of a comma are suppressed, the comma will be suppressed.

Insertion of Fixed Plus and Minus Signs—The + and − Characters   Again, the term *fixed plus and minus signs* is used to distinguish them from *floating plus and minus signs* which we will discuss later. You place a + or a − character either on the left end (the leading position) or the right end (the trailing position) of an edited PICTURE clause to indicate where you want a + or a − to appear when the value is printed. These two characters operate in a unique manner:

1.   The use of a − will result in the printing of a − if the value is negative and no sign at all (a blank) if the value is positive.

2.   The use of a + will result in the printing of a − if the value is negative and a + is the value is positive.

For those reasons, you find programmers use the − character the most. This table summarizes the two rules I just gave you:

Editing Character Used	Character to be Printed if Value is	
	Negative	Positive
−	−	Blank
+	−	+

THE SENDING FIELD			THE RECEIVING FIELD		
PICTURE of the Item	Item Size	Stored Value	PICTURE of the Item	Item Size	Resulting Value
999	3	123	+999	4	+123
999	3	123	−999	4	123
S999	3	12$\overline{3}$	+999	4	−123
S999	3	12$\overline{3}$	−999	4	−123
S999	3	123	−999	4	123
S999	3	12$\overline{3}$	999+	4	123−
S999	3	12$\overline{3}$	999−	4	123−
S999	3	123	999+	4	123+
S999	3	123	999−	4	123
S999	3	123	+ZZZ	4	+123
S999	3	001	+ZZZ	4	+1
S999	3	000	+999	4	+000
S999	3	000	+ZZZ	4	

FIGURE 8.8   Insertion of + and − Characters

Another way to remember it is this: When you use the − editing character, you're saying, "I want to see a sign *only* if it's a −." When you use the + editing character, you're saying, "I want to see a sign no matter what it is."

Figure 8.8 demonstrates the functioning of the + and − editing characters. It also demonstrates once again that the people who designed COBOL had common sense: Despite what has been said above about the functioning of the + character, when everything else in a field has been suppressed, so will the + be suppressed.

Insertion of Credit and Debit Symbols—The CR and DB Characters These characters are used in accounting applications. The CR and DB symbols are only placed in the trailing (right-most) position of the PICTURE clause; otherwise their functioning is very similar to the − editing character, as shown in the following table and in Figure 8.9.

Editing Symbol Used	Characters to be Printed if Value is	
	Negative	Positive
CR	CR	2 Blanks
DB	DB	2 Blanks

Floating String Characters The $ character, + character, and − character may be used in "fixed mode" (described earlier) or in "floating

THE SENDING FIELD			THE RECEIVING FIELD		
PICTURE of the Item	Item Size	Stored Value	PICTURE of the Item	Item Size	Resulting Value
S9(5)V99	7	0174275	$ZZ,ZZZ.99CR	12	$1,742.75CR
S9(5)V99	7	0174275	$ZZ,ZZZ.99CR	12	$1,742.75
S9(5)V99	7	0174275	$ZZ,ZZZ.99DB	12	$1,742.75DB
S9(5)V99	7	0174275	$ZZ,ZZZ.99DB	12	$1,742.75

FIGURE 8.9   Insertion of CR and DB Symbols

string mode." In floating string mode, you use the character in exactly the same way you use the Z character: in repeated positions starting at the left end of a PICTURE clause character-string to indicate in how many positions you want leading zeros suppressed. In addition to suppressing leading zeros, however, a floating string character will locate itself in the edited field in the position of the last (or right-most) character that was suppressed.

THE SENDING FIELD			THE RECEIVING FIELD		
PICTURE of the Item	Item Size	Stored Value	PICTURE of the Item	Item Size	Resulting Value
99V99	4	0500	$99.99	6	$05.00
99V99	4	0500	$ZZ.99	6	$ 5.00
99V99	4	0500	$$$.99	6	$5.00
99V99	4	1500	$$$.99	6	$15.00
99V99	4	0000	$$$.99	6	$ .00
9(5)V99	7	6457238	$$$,$$$.99	10	$64,572.38
9(5)V99	7	0457238	$$$,$$$.99	10	$4,572.38
9(5)V99	7	0057238	$$$,$$$.99	10	$572.38
S9999	4	8264	− − −99	5	−8264
S9999	4	0264	− − −99	5	−264
S9999	4	0064	− − −99	5	−64
S9999	4	0004	− −−99	5	−04
S9999	4	0004	− − −99	5	04
S9999	4	0004	+ + +99	5	+04
S9999	4	1234	+ + + + +	5	+1234
S9999	4	0004	+ + + + +	5	+4
S9999	4	0000	+ + + + +	5	
S9999	4	0004	− − − − −	5	−4
S9999	4	0000	− − − − −	5	

FIGURE 8.10   Floating String Characters

This will be true whether the last character suppressed was a zero *or* a comma. See Figure 8.10 for some examples of the functioning of the three floating string characters.

Two rules apply to the use of floating string characters:

1. Only one character may be used in floating string mode in a single PICTURE clause. ($---$\$\$\$.99 would be improper, for example, because you tried to use both the $-$ and \$ in floating string mode in the same PICTURE clause.)

2. The character used in floating string mode must be in the left-most position in the PICTURE clause character-string. ($-$\$\$\$.99 would be improper, for example, because the $-$ is to the left of the floating \$. If sometime you want to use a $+$ or a $-$ in the same PICTURE with a floating \$, use a trailing $+$ or $-$.)

*Check Protection—The * Character*   Have you ever received a computer printed check in which the amount appeared in this form?

$*******597.95

The asterisks are placed there to prevent some very clever (and dishonest) person from inserting additional digits to the left of those printed by the computer, and thereby fraudulently increasing the value of the check. The asterisks are therefore referred to as *check protection characters* in this application. They are placed in numeric-edited PICTURE clauses and function exactly like Z's, except that each suppressed character is replaced by a * instead of a blank. For example, if the pure numeric value 00002150 were MOVE'd to an edited field with a PICTURE of $***,***.99, the resulting edited value would be $*****21.50.

8.5   Alphanumeric Editing

All the editing characters described in Section 8.4 are for use only in class NE (numeric-edited) PICTURE clauses. The two characters described in this section, B and 0, may be used in either class NE or AE (alphanumeric-edited) PICTURE clauses.

Blank Insertion—The B Character   B characters are used to cause blanks to be placed at the beginning, at the end, or anywhere in the middle of an edited field.

Zero Insertion—The 0 Character   0 Characters are used to cause zeros to be inserted at any position in an edited field.

Figure 8.11 demonstrates the functioning of the B and 0 editing characters.

THE SENDING FIELD			THE RECEIVING FIELD		
PICTURE of the Item	Item Size	Stored Value	PICTURE of the Item	Item Size	Resulting Value
AAA9999	7	JAN1475	AAAB99B99	9	JAN 14 75
9(9)	9	081325549	999B99B9999	11	081 32 5549
A(6)	6	ENDJOB	AAABAAA	7	END JOB
A(6)	6	ENDJOB	BBBBAAABAAA	11	END JOB
99	2	35	$99000	6	$35000
XXX	3	5CC	X00BXX	6	500 CC
AAA99	5	CDC66	AAAB9900	8	CDC 6600

FIGURE 8.11 Insertion of Blanks and Zeros

8.6 Summary

Now the whole truth can be told. A PICTURE clause's character-string tells the computer:

1. The SIZE of an item.
2. The CLASS of an item.
3. If the item is numeric:
   a. The LOCATION of the DECIMAL POINT.
   b. If it is to be SIGNED (either positive *or* negative).
4. The LOCATION of EDITING CHARACTERS within the item.

Only elementary-items *may* have PICTURE clauses, and all elementary-items *must* have PICTURE clauses. A group item is always considered to be CLASS AN, even if its component elementary-items are all Class N. To determine the size of a group item, you add the sizes of its components.

This table presents in final summary what has been said about PICTURE clauses in Chapters 5 and 8:

CLASS	DATA-VALUE MAY CONTAIN	PICTURE CLAUSE CHARACTERS
N	Only digits.	9 V S P
AB	Only letters and spaces.	A
AN	Any COBOL characters.	9 A X
NE	Digits and any editing characters.	+ $ Z 9 . CR − * B 0 , DB
AE	Any COBOL character and the editing characters B and 0.	9 A X B 0

Data-values are usually placed on data cards with a minimum of fal-deral so as to economize on the use of the mere 80 columns available. Spaces between values, dollar signs, commas, etc. are all considered un-necessary luxuries when a programmer is trying to squeeze what seems to him a person's "life history" into a scant 80 character positions. Editing characters give us the ability to insert those "luxury" characters prior to sending the values to the line printer for printing.

More significant, however, is the need to keep all numeric values in pure numeric (digits-only) form for as long as they are being operated upon arithmetically. Arithmetics completed, the numeric values are then dressed-up (edited) before being displayed for human eyes on the line printer.

The principal COBOL verb involved in the editing process is the MOVE verb. Editing is accomplished by the MOVEment of an unedited data-value from a "sending field" with an unedited PICTURE clause to a "receiving field" which has an edited PICTURE clause.

EXERCISES

Answers to all exercises in this chapter are given in Appendix A.

8.1 Fill in the blanks in this table:

	Characters on the Data Card	PICTURE of the Item	Resulting Value Stored in Memory	Size of Item
a.	539	99V9		
b.	1095	99V99		
c.	00721	S99V999		
d.	40632	S9V9(4)		
e.	927	S9V99		
f.	73.621	X(6)		
g.	426	999P(4)		
h.	93	P(5)99		
i.	00794		00794	
j.	50631		50631	
k.	732		732	
l.	−73.2		−73.2	
m.	77		00077	
n.	598		598	
o.	598		598	

8.2 What purpose does editing accomplish in a COBOL program?

8.3 Fill in the blanks: Editing characters are placed in _____ clauses in the _____ DIVISION; however, the editing process is actually accomplished in the _____ DIVISION through the action of _____ statements.

8.4 When you edit a Class N data-value, you get a Class _____ data-value.
When you edit a Class AB data-value, you get a Class _____ data-value.
When you edit a Class AN data-value, you get a Class _____ data-value.

8.5 There are only three PICTURE clause characters that are permitted in both Class NE and Class AE PICTURE clause character-strings. What are they?

8.6 Assume that you have this elementary item description in your DATA DIVISION:

```
03  HRS-IN     PICTURE 999V99.
```

You would like to have the pure numeric value stored in HRS-IN edited so as to suppress any leading zeros on the left of the decimal point and to replace the implied decimal point with an actual decimal point. You will use the following statement in your PROCEDURE DIVISION to accomplish the editing:

MOVE HRS-IN TO HRS-EDIT.

    a. Write a DATA DIVISION 03 level entry that will describe HRS-EDIT.

    b. Suppose the value stored in HRS-IN prior to the execution of the MOVE statement was 02549. *After* the execution of the MOVE, what would be stored in:

    (1) HRS-IN? _____

    (2) HRS-EDIT? _____

    c. In that MOVE statement, HRS-IN is called the _____ , and HRS-EDIT is called the _____ .

8.7   If you send a *positive* data-value to an edited item containing
    a. the + editing symbol, you'll get a _____ .
    b. the − editing symbol, you'll get a _____ .
    c. the CR editing symbol, you'll get a _____ .
    d. the DB editing symbol, you'll get a _____ .

8.8   If you sent a *negative* data-value to an edited item containing
    a. the + editing symbol, you'll get a _____ .
    b. the − editing symbol, you'll get a _____ .
    c. the CR editing symbol, you'll get a _____ .
    d. the DB editing symbol, you'll get a _____ .

8.9   Tell what is wrong with each of the following incorrect PICTURE clauses:
    a. PICTURE $99V99   e. PICTURE − − − + + +
    b. PICTURE 999−9999   f. PIKTURE $(5).99
    c. PICTURE S999.99   g. PICTURE CR$999.99
    d. PICTURE $99XX   h. PICTURE B(5)$,$$$.99

8.10   Fill in the blanks in this table:

	THE SENDING FIELD			THE RECEIVING FIELD		
	PICTURE of the Item	Item Size	Stored Value	PICTURE of the Item	Item Size	Resulting Value
a.	99V99	4	0304	ZZ.99		
b.	S999V99	5	72129	++++.99		
c.	S99V99	4	0671	−−−.99		
d.	S99V9	3	389	−−−.9		
e.	99V9	3	103	+++.9		
f.	9(4)V99	6	000000	Z,ZZZ.99		
g.	X(4)	4	SSAN	XXBBXX		
h.	999V99	5	02918	$$$$.99		
i.	9(4)V99	6	002635	$Z,ZZZ.99		
j.	9(4)V99	6	118406	$$,$$$.99		

	THE SENDING FIELD			THE RECEIVING FIELD		
	PICTURE of the Item	Item Size	Stored Value	PICTURE of the Item	Item Size	Resulting Value
k.	9(3)V99	5	00000	$(4).99		
l.	S9(4)	4	0067	+(5)		
m.	AAA	3	XYZ	AAABB		
n.	S9(4)V99	6	007239	$Z,ZZZ.99CR		
o.	999V99	5	73204	$$$.99		
p.	S9(4)V99	6	000094	$$,$$$.99DB		
q.	999V99	5	00703	$***.99		
r.	S9(4)V99	6	276148	$$,$$$.$$+		
s.	X(5)	5	77399	XX00XXX		
t.	999V99	5	73204	$(4).99		
u.	99V99	4	0036			$ .36
v.	999V99	5	06492			$64.92
w.	S9(4)V99	6	117466			$1,174.66DB
x.	S9(4)V99	6	000167			$1.67−
y.	A(8)	8	AREACODE			AREA CODE
z.	999V99	5	00003			$.03
aa.	S99V99	4	0045			+0.45
bb.	999V99	5	00000			.00
cc.	9(5)V99	7	0027133			$**271.33
dd.	S99V99	4	0072			−$ .72

EXAMPLE PROGRAM

Blue Cross/Blue Shield

Write a program which will print an edited listing of Blue Cross/Blue Shield individual subscribers. Each input record (data card) is in the following format:

CARD COLUMNS	INFORMATION	EXAMPLE
1–7	Subscriber's Certificate Number.	6752734
8–20	Subscriber's Last Name.	KRISTOFFERSON
21–32	First Name and Middle Initial.	RUTHERFORD P
33–35	Number of claims.	004
36–44	Total amount of claims.	000121653 ($1,216.53)
45–53	Net amount of total payments less claims.	000087131̄ (−$871.31)
54–80	Blank.	

The output is to begin with the title

BC/BS INDIVIDUAL SUBSCRIBERS

centered at the top of the report followed by three blank lines. Each line of the body of the print-out will be an edited copy of the input record. The last name should be followed by at least one space. The middle initial and each subsequent item should be followed by at least five spaces. Center each line of output on the printer page.

This is an example of the desired form of each output line:

KRISTOFFERSON RUTHERFORD P   4 CLAIMS $1,216.53 $871.31−

Solution

IDENTIFICATION and ENVIRONMENT DIVISIONs omitted.

```
DATA DIVISION.
FILE SECTION.
FD  SUBSCRIBER-FILE; RECORD CONTAINS 80 CHARACTERS; LABEL RECORDS
    ARE OMITTED; DATA RECORD IS SUBSCRIBER-CARD.
01  SUBSCRIBER-CARD.
    02  CERT-NR-IN        PICTURE 9(7).
```

```
    02  LAST-NAME-IN      PICTURE A(13).
    02  FIRST-MI-IN       PICTURE A(12).
    02  NR-CLAIMS-IN      PICTURE 999.
    02  CLAIMS-AMT-IN     PICTURE 9(7)V99.
    02  NET-BALANCE-IN    PICTURE S9(7)V99.
    02  FILLER            PICTURE X(27).
FD  ACCOUNT-LIST; RECORD CONTAINS 136 CHARACTERS; LABEL RECORDS
    ARE OMITTED; DATA RECORDS ARE REPORT-HEADING, ACCOUNT-LINE.
01  REPORT-HEADING.
    02  FILLER            PICTURE X(54).
    02  REPORT-TITLE      PICTURE X(28).
    02  FILLER            PICTURE X(54).
01  ACCOUNT-LINE.
    02  FILLER            PICTURE X(29).
    02  LAST-NAME-OUT     PICTURE A(13)B.
    02  FIRST-MI-OUT      PICTURE A(12)B(5).
    02  NR-CLAIMS-OUT     PICTURE ZZ9B.
    02  FIELD-4           PICTURE A(6)B(5).
    02  CLAIMS-AMT-OUT    PICTURE $$,$$$,$$9.99B(5).
    02  NET-BALANCE-OUT   PICTURE $$,$$$,$$9.99-.
    02  FILLER            PICTURE X(29).
PROCEDURE DIVISION.
OPEN-PARA.
    OPEN INPUT SUBSCRIBER-FILE, OUTPUT ACCOUNT-LIST.
PRINT-REPORT-HEADING-PARA.
    MOVE SPACES TO REPORT-HEADING.
    MOVE 'BC/BS INDIVIDUAL SUBSCRIBERS' TO REPORT-TITLE.
    WRITE REPORT-HEADING BEFORE ADVANCING 3 LINES.
READ-DATA-MOVE-AND-PRINT-PARA.
    READ SUBSCRIBER-FILE RECORD AT END GO TO CLOSE-PARA.
    MOVE SPACES TO ACCOUNT-LINE.
    MOVE LAST-NAME-IN TO LAST-NAME-OUT.
    MOVE FIRST-MI-IN TO FIRST-MI-OUT.
    MOVE NR-CLAIMS-IN TO NR-CLAIMS-OUT.
    MOVE 'CLAIMS' TO FIELD-4.
    MOVE CLAIMS-AMT-IN TO CLAIMS-AMT-OUT.
    MOVE NET-BALANCE-IN TO NET-BALANCE-OUT.
    WRITE ACCOUNT-LINE.
    GO TO READ-DATA-MOVE-AND-PRINT-PARA.
CLOSE-PARA.
    CLOSE SUBSCRIBER-FILE, ACCOUNT-LIST.
    STOP RUN.
```

Discussion

This program follows the same logic as Chapter 7's Example Program. The computer loops repeatedly through the READ-DATA-MOVE-AND-PRINT-PARA, reading each card and printing its contents until there are no more cards. However, an additional output record has been added, the heading at the top of the report, necessitating an additional record description in the output file. Note that the heading must be written prior to beginning the repeated executions of the READ-DATA-MOVE-AND-PRINT-PARA, so that it will appear only once before the main body of output.

Notice also the editing characters in ACCOUNT-LINE. The blank spaces achieved by the B's could have also been produced by FILLERs, but FILLERs would have involved additional 02 level entries. The number of claims will have leading zeros suppressed but if any is completely zero, it will appear as a single zero digit. This is more desirable than an empty gap in the output line. The claims amount and net balance will have a $ just left of the most significant digit, and commas will be inserted as indicated. Since the $ is used in floating string mode in NET-BALANCE-OUT, the minus sign must be placed in the trailing position where it will appear in the output if the value is negative. No sign will be printed if the net balance is positive.

STUDENT'S PROGRAM

The Cost of Gasoline

I keep close track of my expenditures for gasoline. Every time I make a purchase, I make a note of the date, the reading on my odometer, the number of gallons I purchased, the cost of the purchase, and whether I paid cash for the purchase or charged it on my credit card. I enter the information from each purchase on a data card:

CARD COLUMNS	INFORMATION	EXAMPLE
1–2	Day of purchase.	10 (10th of the month)
3–8	Odometer reading.	356212 (35,621.2 miles)
9–11	Gallons purchased.	096 (9.6 gallons)
12–15	Cost of purchase.*	0817 ($8.17 paid by credit card)
16–80	Blank.	

* In order to distinguish between a cash and credit card purchase, I place the cost of a credit card purchase on the data card as a negative value.

To save myself some time at the keypunch, I don't place the month and year of each purchase date on every data card. Instead, I place them on a separate card in this format:

CARD COLUMNS	INFORMATION	EXAMPLE
1–10	Month name.	SEPTEMBER
11–14	Year.	1976
15–80	Blank.	

When I assemble my data deck, I place that single "month card" at the beginning of the deck, and place all the "purchase cards" behind it in chronological order.

Write a program that will produce a listing of all my gas purchases. The program will be run at the end of each month, so I want the report to begin with a centered heading which tells the month to which it applies, such as:

SEPTEMBER 1976

(The contents of the heading are to come from the "month card," of course.) Following the heading, there will be one line of output for every "purchase card." Each line of output will be in this form and centered on the printer page:

10   35,621.2 MILES   9.6 GALLONS $8.17CR

The CR symbol is to appear after the cost of any purchase which was paid for by credit card. Provide for zero suppression on all numeric fields and use a floating dollar sign on the cost field. Some suggested contents for trial data cards:

```
JANUARY   1977
052431270840050+
112456381620965
132487922031213
172513811670996
212547732181304
242569101380822
```

9 A Second Look at the PROCEDURE DIVISION: The MOVE Verb in More Detail

9.1 Introduction

I first introduced you to the MOVE verb in Section 6.7. At that time we limited the discussion to its most elementary form:

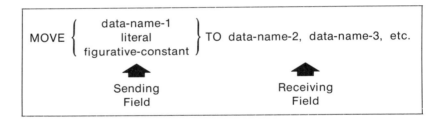

Though I didn't mention it to you at the time, it *is* possible to have more than one receiving field specified in a MOVE statement. When you do, all the receiving fields get the same value. For example, in the solution to the Example Program of Chapter 7, I used the two statements:

```
MOVE '–' TO FIELD-8.
MOVE '–' TO FIELD-10.
```

Since I wanted a dash in both FIELD-8 and FIELD-10, I could have said:

```
MOVE '–' TO FIELD-8, FIELD-10.
```

At the time of your introduction to the MOVE verb, I held you to a temporary rule: The PICTURE clauses of the sending and receiving fields had to be identical. I promised at the time to tell you "later" what happened when they were not identical. Well, later has arrived—that is what this chapter is about.

The result of moving a data-value from a sending field with one PIC-TURE clause to a receiving field with a different PICTURE clause, depends on what type of MOVE it is. There are two types of MOVEs we will be discussing:

1. Numeric MOVEs.
2. Alphanumeric MOVEs.

In addition to those two topics, I'd like to tell you about the MOVE CORResponding verb. It's a real work saver, so I thought I'd do you the favor of giving it to you now rather than waiting until later as many COBOL texts do.

9.2   The Numeric MOVE

A Numeric MOVE is defined as one in which the sending field is Class N and the receiving field is Class N or NE. Stated another way, the only two situations which will produce a Numeric MOVE are these:

1. N to N.
2. N to NE.

Any other kind of MOVE is an Alphanumeric MOVE.

Under the rules of Numeric MOVEs, when the receiving field's PICTURE is different from the sending field's, this is what will happen:

1. The decimal point location of the data-value being MOVEd will be aligned on the decimal point location in the receiving field, and all digits will be located accordingly.
2. Any digits caused to "hang out" of the receiving field by that alignment will be lost (truncated).
3. Any unfilled character positions in the receiving field will be filled with zeros.

Consider this example: Suppose that these two elementary item descriptions are in your DATA DIVISION:

```
02  FIELD-1  PICTURE 9V9999.
02  FIELD-2  PICTURE 999V99.
```

and that as a result of some previous statements, FIELD-1 has been loaded as shown here:

FIELD-1

1	2	3	4	5

Now suppose this is the next statement to be executed:

```
MOVE FIELD-1 TO FIELD-2.
```

Since the sending field, FIELD-1, is Class N, and the receiving field, FIELD-2, is Class N, this is a Numeric MOVE.

Here is what the receiving field looked like before the MOVE:

FIELD-2

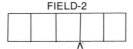

In executing the Numeric MOVE of the contents of FIELD-1 to the memory location of FIELD-2, the computer first loads the digits into the receiving field so that the decimal point locations are aligned:

FIELD-2

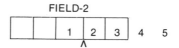

the overhanging digits are truncated:

FIELD-2

and the unfilled positions are filled with zeros:

FIELD-2

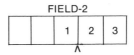

Another example—Let's use these two elementary items this time:

```
02  TOTAL-IN    PICTURE 9(5)V9.
02  TOTAL-OUT   PICTURE 999.999.
```

Consider TOTAL-IN to have been loaded as shown here:

TOTAL-IN

Now consider this as the next statement to be executed:

```
MOVE TOTAL-IN TO TOTAL-OUT.
```

Since the sending field, TOTAL-IN, is Class N, and the receiving field, TOTAL-OUT, is Class NE, this is a Numeric MOVE.

Here is what the receiving field looked like before the MOVE:

TOTAL-OUT

Note that the editing character . does occupy one character position and is the decimal point that will be used in aligning the decimal point locations.

First the computer loads the digits into the receiving field so that the decimal point locations are aligned:

TOTAL-OUT

1	2	3	4	5	·	6		

Next the overhanging digits are truncated:

TOTAL-OUT

3	4	5	·	6		

and the unfilled positions are filled with zeros:

TOTAL-OUT

3	4	5	·	6	0	0

Figure 9.1 gives a more concise summary of the Numeric MOVE rules. In Figure 9.2 I give you a few more examples of how the Numeric MOVE works.

NUMERIC MOVE RULES

1. Decimal point alignment.
2. Overhanging digits lost.
3. Zero fill.

FIGURE 9.1   Numeric MOVE Rules

THE SENDING FIELD			THE RECEIVING FIELD		
PICTURE of the Item	Class	Stored Value	PICTURE of the Item	Class	Resulting Value
999	N	345ᵥ	9999	N	0345ᵥ
999	N	345ᵥ	99	N	45ᵥ
99V9	N	62ᵥ5	999V99	N	06250
99V9	N	62ᵥ5	9999	N	0062ᵥ
999	N	342ᵥ	9999.99	NE	0342.00
99V9999	N	01ᵥ3579	999.99	NE	001.35
9999V999	N	0001ᵥ235	$(5).99	NE	$1.23

FIGURE 9.2   Examples of Numeric MOVEs

9.3 The Alphanumeric MOVE

Any MOVE which is not a Numeric MOVE (an N to N or an N to NE) is an Alphanumeric MOVE. Under the rules of Alphanumeric MOVEs, when the receiving field's PICTURE is different from the sending field's, this is what will happen:

1. The data-value being MOVEd will be loaded into the receiving field starting at its left end (the term "left justified" is used to describe this type of alignment).
2. Any characters which "hang out" the right end of the receiving field will be lost (truncated).
3. Any unfilled character positions in the receiving field will be filled with blanks.

Figure 9.3 presents a more concise statement of these rules. Figure 9.4 demonstrates how they work.

ALPHANUMERIC MOVE RULES
1. Left justification.
2. Overhanging characters lost.
3. Blank fill.

FIGURE 9.3   Alphanumeric MOVE Rules

THE SENDING FIELD			THE RECEIVING FIELD		
PICTURE of the Item	Class	Stored Value	PICTURE of the Item	Class	Resulting Value
A(6)	AB	ENDJOB	A(5)	AB	ENDJO
A(6)	AB	ENDJOB	A(8)	AB	ENDJOB
X(7)	AN	7K-7873	XXBXBXX	AE	7K − 78
999	N	345	XX	AN	34
9(10)	N	9142564100	XXX	AN	914

FIGURE 9.4   Examples of Alphanumeric MOVEs

9.4 Group MOVEs

Everything I've said in Sections 9.2 and 9.3 applies only when the sending and receiving fields are elementary-items. When either the sending field or the receiving field or both are group-items, the MOVE will be performed according to the rules for Alphanumeric MOVEs. This would be so even if the component elementary-items of the group(s) involved were all Class N.

9.5 MOVEs Involving Literals

Recall that the sending field of a MOVE statement may be a numeric literal, a non-numeric literal or a figurative constant. For the purposes of deciding whether a MOVE involving a literal sending field is Numeric or Alphanumeric, we consider a numeric literal to be Class N and a non-numeric literal to be Class AB (if it contains only letters and spaces) or Class AN (if it contains anything else).

For that reason, if you had these two items in your DATA DIVISION:

```
02  BODY-STYLE          PICTURE X(15).
02  COLOR-CODE          PICTURE 9(6).
```

and these two statements were executed:

```
MOVE '2-DR SDN.' TO BODY-STYLE.
MOVE 435 TO COLOR-CODE.
```

then this is the result you'd get in the two memory locations:

```
      BODY-STYLE              COLOR-CODE
┌───────────────────┐      ┌────────┐
│2-DR  SDN.         │      │000435  │
└───────────────────┘      └────────┘
```

Notice that the first MOVE was handled as an Alphanumeric MOVE (left justification with blank fill), and the second MOVE was handled as a Numeric MOVE (decimal point alignment with zero fill).

Likewise, if these had been the MOVEs:

```
MOVE 'TWO-DOOR CONVERTIBLE' TO BODY-STYLE.
MOVE 46791435 TO COLOR-CODE.
```

then this would be the result:

```
      BODY-STYLE              COLOR-CODE
┌───────────────────┐      ┌────────┐
│TWO-DOOR  CONVER   │      │791435  │
└───────────────────┘      └────────┘
```

A somewhat more perplexing situation is posed by the following example. Suppose you had an item in the DATA DIVISION described like this:

```
02  CHANGE-IN-WEIGHT  PICTURE S999V99.
```

and this statement was executed:

```
MOVE -10.5 TO CHANGE-IN-WEIGHT.
```

The result of that MOVE would be this:

CHANGE-IN-WEIGHT

| 010̲50̅ |

You probably recall that the data card fields of Class N items are permitted to contain digits only, and are forbidden to contain actual decimal points or plus or minus signs. That may cause you to wonder about the use of actual decimal points and signs in the numeric literal sending fields of MOVE statements. If you will review Section 3.7, you'll be reminded that numeric literals *are* allowed to contain signs and decimal points along with their digits (as long as the decimal point is *not* on the right end of the literal and the sign *is* on the left end).

This is a messy little problem that the COBOL compiler writers had to grapple with. But grapple they did, so the COBOL compiler now does the troublesome work of stripping such literals of their non-numeric characters and converting their values to purely numeric form with implied decimal points prior to storing them in the memory-location of the receiving field.

9.6   Illegal MOVEs

Now that you are completely free of the "temporary rule" requiring sending and receiving fields to have duplicate PICTURE clauses, it's time for a word of caution. Not all MOVEs are legal. It is illegal, for example, to MOVE the contents of a Class NE field to a Class NE field. It is illegal to MOVE the contents of a Class N field to a Class AE field, unless the Class N field contains a positive integer value.

There are a variety of rules like that. I've chosen a chart as the best way to display them. The MOVEs Chart, as I've called it, is shown in Figure 9.5.

THE MOVES CHART

Sending Item	Receiving Item				
	N	NE	AB	AN	AE
N	OK	OK	No	No(a)	No(a)
NE	No	No(b)	No	OK(b)	OK(b)
AB	No	No	OK	OK	OK
AN	No(a)	No(a)	No	OK	OK
AE	No	No	No	OK	OK

Notes: (a)   OK if sending item is a positive integer.
(b)   Because NE is actually alphanumeric.

FIGURE 9.5   The MOVEs Chart

9.7 Duplicate Data-Names and Qualifying Clauses

Generally speaking, the use of duplicate names in a COBOL program is absolutely forbidden. There *may not* be duplicate paragraph-names (more than one paragraph with the same names); there *may not* be duplicate section-names; there *may not* be duplicate file-names; there *may not* be duplicate record-names.

The rule concerning duplicate data-names is not so stringent. In fact, you *may* have "non-unique" (duplicate) data-names; that is, you may have more than one item of data bearing the same data-name. Non-unique data-names must, however, be a part of a group-item or record which does have a unique name.

If you do have any duplicate data-names, then every time you wish to refer to one of them in a PROCEDURE DIVISION statement, you must specify which of them you are talking about by the use of a "qualifying clause." The form of a qualifying clause is as follows:

$$\text{data-name} \left\{ \begin{matrix} \text{OF} \\ \text{or} \\ \text{IN} \end{matrix} \right\} \left\{ \begin{matrix} \text{record-name} \\ \text{or} \\ \text{group-name} \end{matrix} \right\}$$

To "qualify" a data-name that is non-unique, you give the data-name followed by the word OF or IN and then give the name of the group-item or record of which it is a part. The group- or record-name given must be one that *is* unique (*not* duplicated).

For example, suppose you had two records in your program called CUSTOMER-RECORD and PART-RECORD, and they were organized as shown here (forgetting for the moment about their PICTURE clauses):

```
01  CUSTOMER-RECORD
    02  NAME
    02  ADDR
    02  ACCT-NR
    02  AGE
        03  YR
        03  MO


01  PART-RECORD
    02  NUMBER
    02  NAME
    02  UNIT-PRICE
    02  MFG-DATE
        03  MO
        03  YR
```

If you then wanted to MOVE the customer's name to a receiving field called NAME-OUT, you'd have to say:

```
MOVE NAME IN CUSTOMER-RECORD TO NAME-OUT.
```

If you wanted to move the year that the part was manufactured to a receiving field called YEAR-OUT, you'd have to say:

```
MOVE YR OF MFG-DATE TO YEAR-OUT.
```

The requirement for qualification of duplicated data-names is usually viewed as enough of a pain in the neck that programmers will normally try to keep their data-names unique (as we did in our solution to the Example Program of Chapter 8 with our NAME-IN and NAME-OUT, our AMOUNT-IN and AMOUNT-OUT, etc.).

There *is* a reason, however, why you might *want* to duplicate some data-names—to allow yourself the opportunity to use the MOVE CORResponding verb.

9.8   The MOVE CORResponding Verb

The form of the MOVE CORResponding statement is as follows:

$$
\text{MOVE CORR} \left\{ \begin{array}{c} \text{record-name-1} \\ \text{or} \\ \text{group-name-1} \end{array} \right\} \text{TO} \left\{ \begin{array}{c} \text{record-name-2} \\ \text{or} \\ \text{group-name-2} \end{array} \right\} .
$$

It is used to cause MOVEment of data-values from the elementary-items of one record or group-item to the elementary-items of a second record or group-item. One catch, however—MOVEment will *only* take place between the items whose data-names "correspond," i.e., between items which have exactly the same data-names.

To demonstrate the functioning and usefulness of the MOVE CORResponding verb, suppose you are writing a program which will use data cards, each of which contains these five items of data:

1. A customer's name.
2. Her account number.
3. The number of a check.
4. The date of the check.
5. The amount of the check.

Suppose further that you desire each line of output on the line printer to contain these four items of data:

1. The date of that check.
2. The number of that check.
3. The amount of that check.
4. The balance remaining in the customer's account.

The date, number and amount fields in the output line are to be filled directly from the data card. (We'll presume that the balance field is to be filled as a result of some arithmetic operation which we won't concern ourselves with now.)

Up to this point, your only possible approach would be to describe the data card in terms of unique data-names such as these:

```
01  CARD-RECORD.
    02  CUST-NAME-IN   PICTURE A(20).
    02  ACCT-NR-IN     PICTURE 9(5).
    02  CK-NR-IN       PICTURE 999.
    02  DATE-IN        PICTURE 9(6).
    02  AMT-IN         PICTURE 999V99.
    02  FILLER         PICTURE X(41).
```

and to describe the output line also in terms of unique data-names such as these:

```
01  PRINT-LINE.
    02  FILLER         PICTURE X(47).
    02  DATE-OUT       PICTURE 99B99B99B(5).
    02  CK-NR-OUT      PICTURE ZZ9B(5).
    02  AMT-OUT        PICTURE $$$$.99B(5).
    02  BAL-OUT        PICTURE $(6).99.
    02  FILLER         PICTURE X(47).
```

Your PROCEDURE DIVISION would then have to contain these three separate MOVE statements prior to the WRITE PRINT-LINE statement:

```
MOVE DATE-IN TO DATE-OUT.
MOVE CK-NR-IN TO CK-NR-OUT.
MOVE AMT-IN TO AMT-OUT.
```

The MOVE CORResponding verb allows you to describe your data card as follows:

```
01  CARD-RECORD.
    02  CUST-NAME      PICTURE A(20).
    02  ACCT-NR        PICTURE 9(5).
    02  CK-NR          PICTURE 999.
    02  DATE           PICTURE 9(6).
    02  AMT            PICTURE 999V99.
    02  FILLER         PICTURE X(41).
```

and to describe your output line using some of the very same data-names:

```
01  PRINT-LINE.
    02  FILLER         PICTURE X(47).
    02  DATE           PICTURE 99B99B99B(5).
    02  CK-NR          PICTURE ZZ9B(5).
    02  AMT            PICTURE $$$$.99B(5).
    02  BAL            PICTURE $(6).99.
    02  FILLER         PICTURE X(47).
```

Having used duplicate data-names in the two record descriptions, you can then use a single MOVE CORResponding statement in place of the three separate MOVEs you had before:

MOVE CORR CARD-RECORD TO PRINT-LINE.

That MOVE CORResponding statement will cause the contents of the CARD-RECORD's three sending fields, CK-NR, DATE, and AMT, to be MOVEd to the PRINT-LINE's three receiving fields, CK-NR, DATE, and AMT. The three implied MOVEs will be handled as elementary MOVEs and will be performed according to the rules governing Numeric or Alphanumeric MOVEs as appropriate. The other fields in CARD-RECORD (CUST-NAME and ACCT-NR) which have no corresponding fields in PRINT-LINE will *not* have their contents MOVEd by the MOVE CORResponding statement.

Be sure you've caught this point: Despite the fact that the sending fields and receiving fields of a MOVE CORResponding statement must have the same data-names, there is no requirement for the sending fields to have the same PICTUREs as their corresponding receiving fields. The implied elementary MOVEs are all performed according to the proper MOVE rules (Numeric or Alphanumeric), editing and all.

Figure 9.6 demonstrates graphically the effect of the MOVE CORResponding statement we've been discussing.

Remember, FILLERs are not data-names as such, so they are not affected by the MOVE CORResponding statement.

9.9   Should I or Shouldn't I Use Duplicate Data-Names?

It's entirely up to you, and what you view to be the greater inconvenience. The MOVE CORResponding verb can save you a lot of explicit MOVE statements, but in order to use it, you must have duplicate data-names. If you have duplicate data-names, however, you must use qualifying clauses with them whenever they appear in the PROCEDURE DIVISION.

Using unique data-names throughout your DATA DIVISION can save you from ever having to use any qualifying clauses in your PROCEDURE

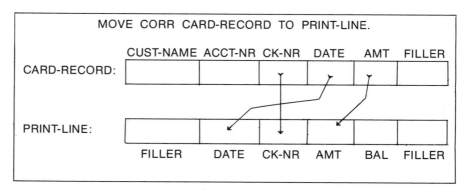

FIGURE 9.6   The Elementary MOVEs Implied by a MOVE CORResponding Statement

DIVISION. If you have all unique data-names, however, you are denied the use of the MOVE CORResponding verb and the benefits it provides.

The decision you will most often make will be a compromise between the two extremes of "all unique" and "none unique." Remember, the use of *some* non-unique data-names does *not* mean that *all* data-names have to be qualified. Qualification is necessary *only* with those data-names that *are* non-unique. So your thoughtful selection of which data-names are to be duplicated and which are to be unique can yield the best of both possibilities.

EXERCISES

Answers to all exercises in this chapter are given in Appendix A.

9.1 An excerpt from a DATA DIVISION looks like this:

```
03  FIELD-1  PICTURE 99.
03  FIELD-2  PICTURE 999.
03  FIELD-3  PICTURE 9.
```

Write *one* COBOL sentence which will load zeros into all three memory locations.

9.2 TRUE or FALSE? There may be more than one Sending Field in a MOVE statement.

9.3 TRUE or FALSE? There may be more than one Receiving Field in a MOVE statement.

9.4 TRUE or FALSE? The Sending Field of a MOVE statement may be a data-name, figurative constant, or a literal.

9.5 TRUE or FALSE? The Receiving Field of a MOVE statement may be a data-name, figurative constant, or a literal.

9.6 After a MOVE operation what happens to the previous contents of
   a. The Sending Field?
   b. The Receiving Field?

9.7 Suppose the following elementary descriptions were in your DATA DIVISION:

```
02  FIELD-A   PICTURE 9999.
02  FIELD-B   PICTURE S9(5)V99.
02  FIELD-C   PICTURE $$$,$$$.99-.
02  FIELD-D   PICTURE A(10).
02  FIELD-E   PICTURE A(5)BA(8).
02  FIELD-F   PICTURE X(11).
02  FIELD-G   PICTURE BX(5)BX(6).
```

Fill in the blanks below. In the Type of MOVE column, use the abbreviations N and AN.

	Class of Sending Field	Class of Receiving Field	Type of MOVE
a. MOVE FIELD-A TO FIELD-B.	_____	_____	_____
b. MOVE FIELD-A TO FIELD-C.	_____	_____	_____
c. MOVE FIELD-A TO FIELD-F.	_____	_____	_____
d. MOVE FIELD-A TO FIELD-G.	_____	_____	_____
e. MOVE FIELD-B TO FIELD-C.	_____	_____	_____
f. MOVE FIELD-C TO FIELD-F.	_____	_____	_____
g. MOVE FIELD-D TO FIELD-E.	_____	_____	_____
h. MOVE FIELD-D TO FIELD-F.	_____	_____	_____
i. MOVE FIELD-F TO FIELD-G.	_____	_____	_____
j. MOVE FIELD-F TO FIELD-A.	_____	_____	_____

9.8 This Exercise is based upon the same elementary-item descriptions as were given in Exercise 9.7. All the MOVEs in Exercise 9.7 were legal. Some of the following are illegal. Identify the illegal MOVEs.

    a. MOVE FIELD-A TO FIELD-D.
    b. MOVE FIELD-A TO FIELD-F.
    c. MOVE FIELD-B TO FIELD-A.
    d. MOVE FIELD-B TO FIELD-F.
    e. MOVE FIELD-C TO FIELD-B.
    f. MOVE FIELD-C TO FIELD-F.
    g. MOVE FIELD-D TO FIELD-G.

9.9 Indicate for each of the following whether it is a characteristic of a Numeric MOVE or an Alphanumeric MOVE or Both.

N or AN or B

    a. Unfilled positions in the receiving field are zero-filled. _____
    b. Unfilled positions in the receiving field are blank-filled. _____
    c. Overhanging characters on the right are truncated. _____
    d. Overhanging characters on the left are truncated. _____
    e. Data-value is left justified in the receiving field. _____
    f. Data-value is aligned on the decimal point location in the receiving field. _____

9.10 Complete this table:

	THE SENDING FIELD		THE RECEIVING FIELD	
	PICTURE of the Item	Stored Value	PICTURE of the Item	Resulting Value
a.	9(5)	12345	9(6)	
b.	99V99	12ˬ34	999V999	
c.	9V99	7ˬ89	9V9	
d.	999V9	678ˬ9	99V99	
e.	99V999	13ˬ579	999V9(4)	
f.	99V999	13ˬ579	9V99	
g.	99V999	13ˬ579	99V9	
h.	9	5	999.99	
i.	9999	0005	99.99	
j.	9999	1234	$ZZZ,ZZZ.99	
k.	99	56	XX	
l.	99	56	XXX	
m.	99	56	999	
n.	XX	AB	XXX	
o.	X(4)	CODE	XXX	
p.	XXX	124	9999	
q.	A(4)	NAME	XXXX	
r.	A(4)	NAME	AAA	
s.	A(4)	NAME	A(5)	
t.	X(6)	I.R.S.	XXBXXB	
u.	AA999	PA654	BXXXBX000	

9.11   Given these elementary-item descriptions:

        03   NUM-1   PICTURE 99V99.
        03   NUM-2   PICTURE 99V9.
        03   NUM-3   PICTURE 9.

What value will be stored in each item after completion of the following MOVE?

        MOVE 37.946 TO NUM-1, NUM-2, NUM-3.

9.12   Select one of the following choices. You have a Group MOVE
        a.   Only when the sending field is a group-item.
        b.   Only when both the sending and receiving fields are group-items.
        c.   When either the sending or receiving field or both are group-items.

9.13   Select one of the following choices. A Group MOVE will be performed according to
        a.   Numeric MOVE rules always.
        b.   Numeric MOVE rules only if all elementary-items of the group-item(s) involved are Class N.
        c.   Alphanumeric MOVE rules always.

9.14   TRUE or FALSE? Paragraph-names must be unique.

9.15   TRUE or FALSE? Record-names must be unique.

9.16   TRUE or FALSE? Data-names must be unique.

9.17   What must be done when a non-unique data-name is referred to in the PROCEDURE DIVISION so the computer will know which one you're talking about?

9.18   The records called OLD-REC and NEW-REC are described in Exercise 9.19 below. Write a statement that will load NEW-REC's LAST-NAME field with spaces.

9.19   Given these record descriptions:

        01   OLD-REC.
            02   LAST-NAME   PICTURE A(10).
            02   FIRST-N   PICTURE A(5).
            02   AGE   PICTURE 99.
            02   SSN   PICTURE 9(9).
        01   NEW-REC.
            02   FIRST-N   PICTURE A(5).
            02   LAST-NAME   PICTURE A(10).
            02   SSN   PICTURE 9(9).

Suppose that as a result of a READ statement OLD-REC had been loaded as shown here:

← - - LAST-NAME - - →	←FIRST-N→	AGE	← - - - SSN - - - →
OLD-REC: F I N K E N A U R	J O H N	3 1	0 8 1 3 2 5 5 4 9

a.   Show the contents of NEW-REC as a result of this statement:

MOVE CORR OLD-REC TO NEW-REC.

|←FIRST-N →|←   -   - LAST-NAME - - -→|←   -   - -SSN - - -→|

NEW-REC:

b.   As a result of this statement:

MOVE OLD-REC TO NEW-REC.

|←FIRST-N →|← -   -LAST-NAME - - -→|←   - - - SSN - - -→|

NEW-REC:

EXAMPLE PROGRAM

YMCA Day Camp

You have just received a final deck of enrollees for the Melrose YMCA Summer Day Camp. A master print out is needed immediately for planning purposes. Each card in the deck follows this format:

CARD COLUMNS	INFORMATION	EXAMPLE
1–15	Last name	INGERSOLL
16–25	First name and middle initial	JONATHAN P
26–35	Telephone number	6173721965
36–37	Age	12
38–60	Address	281 SUMMER ST., SAUGUS
61–75	Dates enrolled	AUG 11 – AUG 24
76–80	Fee paid	03775 ($37.75)

Write a program to provide the desired listing. Allow for each child's data to be divided among several lines of output as follows:

```
JONATHAN P      INGERSOLL      AGE 12
    AUG 11 – AUG 24   PAID     $37.75
    281 SUMMER ST., SAUGUS
    PHONE 617-372-1965
```

Begin the first name in column 5 and indent subsequent lines 3 more spaces. Leave 2 blank lines between child entries. Incorporate the MOVE CORResponding verb in your solution. Here are some sample children to use in a trial data deck:

```
SAMUEL T        BROOKINGS      AGE 11
    JUL 12 – AUG 1    PAID     $7.00
    13 OAK ST., MELROSE
    PHONE 617-475-9960

OSCAR L         ANDERSON       AGE 10
    JUL 12 – JUL 25    PAID    $14.50
    135 TREMONT ST., LYNN
    PHONE 617-481-1163

JOANNE A        GOODPASTER     AGE 9
    AUG 1 – AUG 14    PAID     $21.00
    22C GREENWOOD, SAUGUS
    PHONE 617-372-3962

ALEX X          ROBINSON       AGE 12
    AUG 11 – AUG 24   PAID     $0.00
    6 W MAPLE AVE., MELROSE
    PHONE 617-475-6805
```

Solution

IDENTIFICATION and ENVIRONMENT DIVISIONs are omitted.

```
DATA DIVISION.
FILE SECTION.
FD   CHILD-FILE; RECORD CONTAINS 80 CHARACTERS; LABEL RECORDS ARE
     OMITTED; DATA RECORD IS ENROLL-CARD.
01   ENROLL-CARD.
     02   LAST-NAME           PICTURE A(15).
     02   FIRST-NAME          PICTURE A(10).
     02   PHONE-IN.
          03   AREA-CODE      PICTURE 999.
          03   EXCHANGE       PICTURE 999.
          03   NUMBR          PICTURE 9(4).
     02   AGE                 PICTURE 99.
     02   ADDR                PICTURE X(23).
     02   DATES               PICTURE X(15).
     02   FEE-PAID            PICTURE 999V99.
FD   PRINT-FILE; RECORD CONTAINS 136 CHARACTERS; LABEL RECORDS ARE
     OMITTED; DATA RECORDS ARE NAME-LINE, DATE-LINE, ADDRESS-LINE,
     PHONE-LINE.
01   NAME-LINE.
     02   FILLER              PICTURE X(4).
     02   FIRST-NAME          PICTURE A(10)B.
     02   LAST-NAME           PICTURE A(15)BBB.
     02   NL-FIELD-4          PICTURE X(4).
     02   AGE                 PICTURE Z9.
     02   FILLER              PICTURE X(97).
01   DATE-LINE.
     02   FILLER              PICTURE X(7).
     02   DATES               PICTURE X(15)BBB.
     02   DL-FIELD-3          PICTURE X(5).
     02   FEE-PAID            PICTURE $$$9.99.
     02   FILLER              PICTURE X(99).
01   ADDRESS-LINE.
     02   FILLER              PICTURE X(7).
     02   ADDR                PICTURE X(23).
     02   FILLER              PICTURE X(106).
01   PHONE-LINE.
     02   FILLER              PICTURE X(7).
     02   PL-FIELD-2          PICTURE X(6).
     02   PHONE-OUT.
          03   AREA-CODE      PICTURE 999.
          03   DASH-1         PICTURE X.
          03   EXCHANGE       PICTURE 999.
          03   DASH-2         PICTURE X.
          03   NUMBR          PICTURE 9(4).
     02   FILLER              PICTURE X(111).
 PROCEDURE DIVISION.
 OPEN-PARA.
     OPEN INPUT CHILD-FILE, OUTPUT PRINT-FILE.
 READ-CARD-PARA.
     READ CHILD-FILE RECORD, AT END GO TO CLOSE-PARA.
 PRINT-NAME-LINE-PARA.
     MOVE SPACES TO NAME-LINE.
```

```
    MOVE 'AGE ' TO NL-FIELD-4.
    MOVE CORR ENROLL-CARD TO NAME-LINE.
    WRITE NAME-LINE AFTER ADVANCING 3 LINES.
PRINT-DATE-LINE-PARA.
    MOVE SPACES TO DATE-LINE.
    MOVE 'PAID ' TO DL-FIELD-3.
    MOVE CORR ENROLL-CARD TO DATE-LINE.
    WRITE DATE-LINE.
PRINT-ADDRESS-LINE-PARA.
    MOVE SPACES TO ADDRESS-LINE.
    MOVE ADDR  IN ENROLL-CARD TO ADDR  OF ADDRESS-LINE.
    WRITE ADDRESS-LINE.
PRINT-PHONE-LINE-PARA.
    MOVE SPACES TO PHONE-LINE.
    MOVE 'PHONE ' TO PL-FIELD-2.
    MOVE '-' TO DASH-1, DASH-2.
    MOVE CORR PHONE-IN TO PHONE-OUT.
    WRITE PHONE-LINE.
RETURN-TO-TOP-OF-LOOP-PARA.
    GO TO READ-CARD-PARA.
CLOSE-PARA.
    CLOSE CHILD-FILE, PRINT-FILE.
    STOP RUN.
```

Discussion

The logic involved in this program is basically identical to that used in the programs of Chapters 7 and 8. That is, a card is read, key items of information transferred to the proper output record, and the record printed. But the key feature introduced here is the use of the MOVE CORResponding verb to cut down on the number of elementary MOVEs otherwise required to get the information to the output records. Notice that the child's address could also be MOVEd with a MOVE CORResponding as are other items but instead it was handled as an elementary MOVE to demonstrate how non-unique data-names are qualified. Separating the components of the telephone number with hyphens necessitates their "demotion" to the 03 level so that a MOVE CORResponding can be used.

Of interest here also is the use of multiple output records to achieve four differing printed lines. It might seem terribly inefficient (and it is!) to repeatedly MOVE SPACES and the non-numeric literals 'AGE ', 'PAID ', 'PHONE ', and '−' to their receiving fields in the output records within the read-loop. This is a necessary evil in this program because of the repeated use of all of the multiple record formats in the output file. In the next chapter you will learn that the WORKING-STORAGE SECTION provides a simpler and more efficient approach to this problem.

STUDENT'S PROGRAM

N.F.L. Scouting Report

Write a program for a pro football scouting combine which will read a deck of cards of college prospects and produce a listing of its contents. Each card looks like this:

CARD COLUMNS	ITEM	EXAMPLE
1–15	Player's last name	BRADLEY
16–25	First name and initial	ROBERT G
26–27	Position	QB
28–29	Height	75 (inches)
30–32	Weight	195 (pounds)
33–35	Speed in 100 yard dash	098 (9.8 seconds)
36–51	College	OHIO STATE
52–57	Date of birth	072153 (July 21, 1953)
58–60	Anticipated contract price	055 ($55,000)
61–80	Blank	

The output for each player should appear as follows:

```
QB   ROBERT G   BRADLEY          $55,000
       DOB  7-21-53   COLLEGE — OHIO STATE
       9.8 SEC    195 LBS    75 IN
```

Suppress leading zeros on numeric items and edit as shown. Choose your own spacing but center at the top of the listing the heading:

LIST OF COLLEGE BLUE-CHIPS

Some sample data for trial data cards:

```
BRADLEY          ROBERT G    QB75195098OHIO STATE          072153055
BUONCHRISTIANI   JOHN F      OT77225105NEBRASKA            103052035
CHESNOWSKIS      ALEXANDER   CE72230115SLIPPERY ROCK       021052042
FINKENAUR        JAMES K     LB73180099ARMY                112451041
CERQUA           PAUL J      TE79230100SOUTHERN CALIF      121553065
GUSTIN           MAURICE     RB74190095RENSSELAER POLY     061354050
```

10 The WORKING-STORAGE SECTION and Its Uses

10.1 Introduction

You will recall from Chapter 5 that the DATA DIVISION is made up of two sections:

```
DATA DIVISION.
FILE SECTION.
WORKING-STORAGE SECTION.
```

In general terms, we associate the FILE SECTION with data which come from or are sent to files stored externally: card files, printer files, tape files, and disk files. The WORKING-STORAGE SECTION concerns itself with data which is generated entirely within the computer.

Programmers use the WORKING-STORAGE SECTION for the following purposes: As a place for

1. *Storing intermediate results* in arithmetic calculations,
2. *Building lines of output* prior to sending them to the output file for printing,
3. *Safeguarding input data* which if left in an input record would be prematurely destroyed, and
4. *Building and manipulating tabular data* of the sort involved in income tax calculations.

In this chapter we'll thoroughly discuss only the second and third uses listed above. We'll discuss storage of intermediate results in the chapter on arithmetic verbs. A whole chapter will be devoted to "table manipulation" much later in the book.

All the files to be used by a program are described in its FILE SECTION. Since there are no files described in the WORKING-STORAGE SECTION, it contains no FD entries. It does contain group- and elementary-items of data coded at the 01 level and higher, just as before.

Despite its four uses, your study of the WORKING-STORAGE SECTION in this Chapter will add only two new terms to your COBOL vocabulary:

1. VALUE clauses, and
2. Independent-items (77 level entries).

166

10.2   The VALUE Clause

The VALUE clause may be used only in the WORKING-STORAGE SEC-TION. You place a VALUE clause after the PICTURE clause of an elementary-item when you want to assign an initial value to that item. The form of the VALUE clause is as follows:

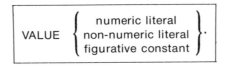

This would be a good time for you to go back for a quick review of the rules governing numeric literals, non-numeric literals and figurative constants in Sections 3.7, 3.8 and 3.9.

Here are two elementary-item descriptions using VALUE clauses:

```
02  DEPT-NO     PICTURE 999    VALUE 1.
02  DEPT-NAME   PICTURE A(15)  VALUE 'AUTO PARTS'.
```

Those two VALUE clauses would have the same effect as these two MOVE statements:

```
MOVE 1 TO DEPT-NO.
MOVE 'AUTO PARTS' TO DEPT-NAME.
```

This is the result they would have in the two memory locations:

DEPT-NO   DEPT-NAME

| 001 | | AUTO PARTS |

Like the literal sending field in a MOVE statement, the literal given in the VALUE clause must be compatible in both *class and size* with the PICTURE clause of the elementary-item involved. They must be of the *same class*, and the size of the literal must be *no larger than* that of the PICTURE clause.

If the Value Clause Contains a	The PICTURE Clause Must Be
Numeric Literal	Class N
Non-Numeric Literal	Class AB or AN
Figurative Constant ZERO	Class N
Figurative Constant SPACE	Class AB or AN

Figure 10.1 demonstrates a variety of properly used VALUE clauses and the results they produce in the memory locations of their elementary-items.

DESCRIPTION OF ELEMENTARY-ITEMS	RESULTS IN MEMORY

02 PAGE-TITLE PICTURE A(14) VALUE 'PAYROLL REPORT'.
 	
   Class of PICTURE Clause: AB
   Content of VALUE Clause: Non-Numeric Literal
	PAGE-TITLE
	| PAYROLL REPORT |

02 COURSE-NUMBER PICTURE X(6) VALUE 'EF-383'.
 	
   Class of PICTURE Clause: AN
   Content of VALUE Clause: Non-Numeric Literal
	COURSE-NUMBER
	| EF-383 |

02 FICA-MAXIMUM PICTURE 999V99 VALUE 772.20.
 	
   Class of PICTURE Clause: N
   Content of VALUE Clause: Numeric Literal
	FICA-MAXIMUM
	| 77220 |

02 EMPLOYEE-COUNTER PICTURE 9999 VALUE ZERO.
 	
   Class of PICTURE Clause: N
   Content of VALUE Clause: Figurative Constant
	EMPLOYEE-COUNTER
	| 0000 |

02 NAME-OF-SPOUSE PICTURE A(16) VALUE SPACES.
 	
   Class of PICTURE Clause: AB
   Content of VALUE Clause: Figurative Constant
	NAME-OF-SPOUSE
	| |

02 GROWTH-RATE PICTURE S9V9999 VALUE −1.0125.
 	
   Class of PICTURE Clause: N
   Content of VALUE Clause: Numeric Literal
	GROWTH-RATE
	| 10125 |

02 COLUMN-HEADING-1 PICTURE X(9) VALUE 'S. S. NO.'.
 	
   Class of PICTURE Clause: AN
   Content of VALUE Clause: Non-Numeric Literal
	COLUMN-HEADING-1
	| S. S. NO. |

FIGURE 10.1   Use of the VALUE Clause

Consider once more the requirement for compatibility of class. Why is this example improper?

        02 ZIP-CODE PICTURE 9(5) VALUE '01923'.

Because the classes of the PICTURE and VALUE clauses are incompatible. The PICTURE clause is CLASS N, but the presence of the quote marks makes the 01923 a non-numeric literal (Class AN). Either of the following *would* be proper:

        02 ZIP-CODE PICTURE 9(5) VALUE 01923.
        02 ZIP-CODE PICTURE X(5) VALUE '01923'.

Before we move on, I'd like to be sure you haven't developed the common misconception that the VALUE clause assigns a "permanent" or unalterable value to a data item. It doesn't! The value assigned is only an *initial* value. It could easily be changed later on in the course of the program, though it doesn't have to be. As an example, consider this entry:

```
02   CREDIT-LIMIT   PICTURE 999V99   VALUE 300.
```

That would have the result of assigning an initial value of 300̭00 to CREDIT-LIMIT. If in executing the PROCEDURE DIVISION of the program, the computer later came to a statement such as

```
MOVE 400 TO CREDIT-LIMIT.
```

the original value (300̭00) of CREDIT-LIMIT would be destroyed and the new value (400̭00) would be stored in its place.

Frequently a programmer will assign a value to an elementary-item that she has no intention of changing. Suppose you were writing a program in which the INTEREST-RATE was fixed at 12.5 percent. You might then have an entry like this:

```
02   INTEREST-RATE   PICTURE V999   VALUE .125.
```

In this case you wouldn't be incorrect in referring to .125 as a "constant" (rather than "initial") value, but is only "constant" because *you* want it to be.

The VALUE clause assigns an initial value only, and that value is just as susceptible to later change as any value you might assign through the action of a MOVE statement. An initial value remains as a constant value only if you elect to leave it unchanged.

10.3   Independent-Items of Data

Independent-items are used only in the WORKING-STORAGE SECTION. They are essentially elementary-items with one additional restriction: they may not be a part of a group-item. They must stand entirely alone. In all other ways independent-items are exactly like elementary-items: they must have PICTURE clauses, and they may have VALUE clauses.

Independent-items are coded at Margin A using level number 77. If you use any 77 level entries in your WORKING-STORAGE SECTION, they must be placed at the beginning of the section, prior to any other entries. Figure 10.2 shows the first four lines of a WORKING-STORAGE SECTION containing 77 level entries.

```
WORKING-STORAGE SECTION.
77  NR-OF-CHECKS     PICTURE 999    VALUE ZERO.
77  SERVICE-CHARGE   PICTURE 99V99.
77  CHARGE-PER-CHECK PICTURE V99    VALUE .25.
```

FIGURE 10.2   Independent Items Described by 77-Level Entries

Independent-items are used primarily as places to store intermediate arithmetic results, so I'll postpone further discussion of them until we get to the chapter on arithmetic verbs.

10.4 Building Lines of Output

The availability of the VALUE clause makes the WORKING-STORAGE SECTION an especially handy place to build lines of output for the line printer.

My recommendation to you, therefore, is that from now on you give up describing the details of your output lines in the FILE SECTION. Reduce the FD and record description entries for your output file to simply this:

```
FD   PRINT-FILE; RECORD CONTAINS 136 CHARACTERS; LABEL RECORDS
     ARE OMITTED; DATA RECORD IS PRINT-LINE.
01   PRINT-LINE  PICTURE  X(136).
```

Describe each line of output, such as the DETAIL-LINE, as a 01 level group-item in the WORKING-STORAGE SECTION. When it comes time to print the contents of DETAIL-LINE on the line printer, simply say:

```
MOVE DETAIL-LINE TO PRINT-LINE.
WRITE PRINT-LINE AFTER ADVANCING 2 LINES.
```

Or you may wish to take advantage of the WRITE FROM verb and say:

```
WRITE PRINT-LINE FROM DETAIL-LINE AFTER ADVANCING 2 LINES.
```

The WRITE FROM statement is a very handy device. In one statement, it produces the same effect as the two statements, MOVE and WRITE, above. The form of the WRITE FROM statement is as follows:

```
WRITE record-name FROM data-name-1
       ⎧ AFTER  ⎫             ⎧ data-name-2     ⎫
       ⎨  or    ⎬ ADVANCING  ⎨      or          ⎬ LINES.
       ⎩ BEFORE ⎭             ⎩ numeric-literal ⎭
       └─────────────────── Optional ──────────────┘
```

"Data-name-1" would normally be the name of a 01 level group-item in the WORKING-STORAGE SECTION. "Record-name" would be the 01 level name under the output file's FD entry in the FILE SECTION. The WRITE FROM statement implies the group MOVE of the contents of "data-name-1" to "record-name" and the printing of the contents of "record-name" on the line printer.

The best way to demonstrate the merits of this approach is through an example: Recall "Your First Program" of Chapter 7, the Super Simple Computer Dating Service? I'll now rewrite that program to demonstrate how well suited the WORKING-STORAGE SECTION is as a place to describe your lines of output.

COBOL CODING FORM

| PROGRAM | DATE-SERVICE-2 | COBOL DIVISION | ID + ENV | PAGE 1 | OF 1 |
| PROGRAMMER | R.G. Finkenaur | DATE | Sept 28, 1978 | IDENT | D.T.-S.V.C-2 |

```
 10  IDENTIFICATION DIVISION.
 20  PROGRAM-ID.    DATE-SERVICE-2.
 30  AUTHOR.        R G FINKENAUR.
 40  INSTALLATION.  NORTHEASTERN UNIV.
 50  DATE-WRITTEN.  SEPT 28, 1978.
 60  DATE-COMPILED.
 70  SECURITY.      FOR UNMARRIED PEOPLE ONLY.
 80  REMARKS.       THIS PROGRAM WILL PRODUCE A LISTING OF THE NAMES,
 90      HAIR COLOR, HEIGHT, WEIGHT, AND PHONE NUMBERS OF ALL THE
100      PEOPLE IN MY DATE FILES.
110  ENVIRONMENT DIVISION.
120  CONFIGURATION SECTION.
130  SOURCE-COMPUTER.  HAL-2001.
140  OBJECT-COMPUTER.  HAL-2001.
150  INPUT-OUTPUT SECTION.
160  FILE-CONTROL.
170      SELECT DATE-CARD-FILE ASSIGN TO CARD-READER.
180      SELECT DATE-LISTING-FILE ASSIGN TO LINE-PRINTER.
```

FIGURE 10.3   The IDENTIFICATION and ENVIRONMENT DIVISIONs

We'll use the same IDENTIFICATION and ENVIRONMENT DIVI-SIONs in this program as we did in Chapter 7. They're shown again in Figure 10.3.

Here again is the description of each of the data cards which will be used with the program:

CARD COLUMNS	INFORMATION	EXAMPLE
1–25	Name	
1–15	Last Name	SCHIMMELPFENNIG
16–25	First Name	WILHELMINA
26–55	Address	14 CHESTNUT ST., LACONIA, N.H.
56–58	Height	
56	Feet	4
57–58	Inches	10
59–61	Weight (pounds)	120
62–67	Hair Color	BLONDE
68–77	Phone Number	9146524915
78–80	Blank	

COBOL CODING FORM

| PROGRAM | DATE - SERVICE - 2 | COBOL DIVISION | DATA | PAGE | 1 | OF | 3 |
| PROGRAMMER | R. G. Finkenaur | DATE | Sept 28, 1978 | IDENT | DT-SVC-2 |

```
190  DATA DIVISION.
200  FILE SECTION.
210  FD  DATE-CARD-FILE; RECORD CONTAINS 80 CHARACTERS; LABEL RECORDS
220      ARE OMITTED; DATA RECORD IS DATE-CARD.
230  01  DATE-CARD.
240      02  LAST-NAME        PICTURE A(15).
250      02  FIRST-NAME       PICTURE A(10).
260      02  FILLER           PICTURE X(30).
270      02  HT-FEET          PICTURE 9.
280      02  HT-INCHES        PICTURE 99.
290      02  WEIGHT           PICTURE 999.
300      02  HAIR-COLOR       PICTURE A(6).
310      02  PHONE            PICTURE 9(10).
320      02  FILLER           PICTURE XXX.
330  FD  DATE-LISTING-FILE; RECORD CONTAINS 136 CHARACTERS; LABEL
340      RECORDS ARE OMITTED; DATA RECORD IS PRINT-LINE.
350  01  PRINT-LINE           PICTURE X(136).
```

FIGURE 10.4   The FILE SECTION

In Figure 10.4 I've shown the FILE SECTION we'll be using for this version of the program. Notice how the output file is described at sequence nos. 330 through 350. That is the result of my following the advice I gave you earlier.

We'll be describing the various output lines themselves in the WORKING-STORAGE SECTION. What kinds of lines might we be describing? Up to this point our printouts have involved nothing more than the essential lines of output. We've made no attempt to dress up the output page with a page heading or column headings. Figure 10.5 describes how we'll

```
                              LIST OF GIRLS NAMES
                              -------------------

             NAME                 HAIR      HEIGHT       WEIGHT      TELEPHONE
WILHELMINA  SCHIMMELPFENNIG      BLONDE    5 FT 10 IN   110 LBS    914 652 4915
KATE        AMBROSE             BROWN     4 FT  9 IN   115 LBS    617 219 4283
CAROL       WHALEN             BRUNET    5 FT  1 IN   105 LBS    617 774 2821
SHIRLEY     STURDEVANT          RED       5 FT  3 IN    95 LBS    713 579 0243
AAAAAAAAAA  AAAAAAAAAAAAAAA     AAAAA     9 AA Z9 AA   Z99 AAA    999 999 9999
```

FIGURE 10.5   Planning the Output Page

dress up our output page this time by the addition of page and column headings.

Figure 10.5 is a demonstration of the kind of layout planning necessary in designing neat looking output. In this case, I've planned my output using a piece of suitably lined scratch paper. There are commercially printed forms you can buy for this purpose.

I want you to notice several things in Figure 10.5. First, notice that I've shown you only the center 75 columns of the total 136 available on the output page. (Everything to the left and right of those 75 columns is blank, and this enabled me to display these essential columns enlarged as much as possible and thereby easier for you to read.) Next, notice that there are four types of output lines shown:

1.   The page heading line,

2.   The line of dashes which serves to underline the page heading,

3.   The line of column headings, and

4.   The lines which make up the essential portion of the output, the so-called "detail-lines."

I'll describe each of these four line types as 01 level entries in the WORKING-STORAGE SECTION. The 01 level entries describing the PAGE-HEADING line, the UNDER-LINE, and the COL-HEADINGS line are shown in Figure 10.6. Spend a moment now comparing Figures 10.5 and 10.6.

COBOL CODING FORM

PROGRAM   DATE - SERVICE - 2
PROGRAMMER   R. G. Finkenaur
COBOL DIVISION   DATA
DATE   Sept 28, 1978
PAGE   2 OF 3
IDENT   DT-SVC-2

```
360   WORKING-STORAGE SECTION.
370   01  PAGE-HEADING.
380   02  PAGE-CONTROL  PICTURE 9.         VALUE 1.
390   02  FILLER        PICTURE X(58).     VALUE SPACES.
400   02  FILLER        PICTURE A(19).     VALUE 'LIST OF GIRLS NAMES'.
410   02  FILLER        PICTURE X(58).     VALUE SPACES.
420   01  UNDER-LINE.
430   02  FILLER        PICTURE X(59).     VALUE SPACES.
440   02  FILLER        PICTURE X(19).     VALUE '------------------'.
450   02  FILLER        PICTURE X(58).     VALUE SPACES.
460   01  COL-HEADINGS.
470   02  FILLER        PICTURE X(43).     VALUE SPACES.
480   02  FILLER        PICTURE A(60).     VALUE 'NAME                        HA
490 -     IR    HEIGHT    WEIGHT   TELEPHONE'.
500   02  FILLER        PICTURE X(33).     VALUE SPACES.
```

FIGURE 10.6   The Beginning of the WORKING-STORAGE SECTION

There are three things in Figure 10.6 that I want to call your attention to:

First, by way of review, notice how I continued the non-numeric literal from one line to another at sequence nos. 480 and 490. If you've forgotten the rule that governs continuation of non-numeric literals, go back and review section 3.11.

Second, notice that I've exposed you to a third use for the reserved-word FILLER. There are three uses for a FILLER, the first two you know about already:

1. To label a field in any record which contains nothing but blanks or spaces,

2. To label a field in an input record (data card) that contains information you don't need, and

3. To label a field in an output record whose value you are establishing with a VALUE clause and have no intention of ever changing. (The wording of report titles, page headings, and column headings are handled this way.)

Third, notice the 02 level entry at sequence no. 380 called PAGE-CONTROL. You'll notice that it is a part of PAGE-HEADING's description. Shouldn't a PAGE-HEADING be printed at the *top* of a page? Of course! But how is that done? This is a question of "carriage control."

The term "carriage control" is a carry-over from the days when computers used electric typewriters as output devices. The two carriage control functions which you will have the most use for are (1) the skipping of lines, and (2) skipping to the top of the next page (referred to also as "page ejection").

Line skipping is accomplished by means of the ADVANCING clause of the WRITE statement.

Page ejection is accomplished in many different ways on many different computers.[1] There is one approach which is nearly universal, and it is the one I'll talk about here. You've had no need to know this up to now, but you must always avoid attempting to print any character in the first (or left-most) character position on the line printer page. This is because the first character position is used to indicate to the line printer what form of carriage control function is desired. For that reason, the line printer will never print any character which happens to fall in that left-most position on its page. There are a variety of carriage control functions available, but the one we're interested in now is the "page eject" function. If you place a 1 in the left-most character position of a line you're going to print, when you tell the computer to WRITE that line, the line printer will respond to the pres-

---

[1] ON IBM computers, page ejection is accomplished by including this paragraph in your CONFIGURATION SECTION: SPECIAL-NAMES. C01 IS TOP-OF-PAGE. In the PROCEDURE DIVISION you say: WRITE PRINT-LINE AFTER ADVANCING TOP-OF-PAGE. Appendix F shows how it is done on several other computers, as well.

ence of that left-most 1 by ejecting the page it is on and printing that line at the top of the next page.

In Figure 10.6, I've taken care of that by the establishment of a one-character numeric field on the left end of PAGE-HEADING called PAGE-CONTROL, and I've given it the VALUE 1. Because I have no intention of changing the value of PAGE-CONTROL, I could just as easily have called that field FILLER, but I wanted to draw your curiosity, so I chose instead a data-name that indicated the purpose of that one-character field.

One last comment about carriage control: If you've decided to achieve carriage control through the use of a line's left-most character, don't use an ADVANCING clause in the WRITE statement which causes that line to be printed. Achieve carriage control by one means or the other; don't attempt to get *two* carriage control functions in *one* print operation. The computer will obey only one of them.

The DETAIL-LINE for this program is shown in Figure 10.7. (The name DETAIL-LINE is a programmer-invented-name that is commonly used by COBOL programmers to identify the line of output that includes the important details of the report being printed. Other output lines are usually

COBOL CODING FORM

| PROGRAM | DATE-SERVICE-2 | | COBOL DIVISION | DATA | PAGE | 3 | OF | 3 |
| PROGRAMMER | R. G. Finkenaur | | DATE Sept 28, 1978 | IDENT | D.T.-S.V.C.-2 |

5 1 0	0 1	DETAIL-LINE.	
5 2 0		0 2 FILLER	PICTURE X(32) VALUE SPACES.
5 3 0		0 2 FIRST-NAME	PICTURE A(10)B.
5 4 0		0 2 LAST-NAME	PICTURE A(15)B(3).
5 5 0		0 2 HAIR-COLOR	PICTURE A(6)B(3).
5 6 0		0 2 HT-FT	PICTURE 9.
5 7 0		0 2 FILLER	PICTURE A(4) VALUE ' FT '.
5 8 0		0 2 HT-IN	PICTURE Z9.
5 9 0		0 2 FILLER	PICTURE A(6) VALUE ' IN '.
6 0 0		0 2 WEIGHT	PICTURE Z99.
6 1 0		0 2 FILLER	PICTURE A(7) VALUE ' LBS '.
6 2 0		0 2 PHONE	PICTURE 999B999B9999.
6 3 0		0 2 FILLER	PICTURE X(31) VALUE SPACES.

FIGURE 10.7   The Remainder of the WORKING-STORAGE SECTION

COBOL CODING FORM

| PROGRAM | DATE-SERVICE-2 | COBOL DIVISION **PROCEDURE** | PAGE **1** OF **1** |
| PROGRAMMER | R. G. Finkenaur | DATE **Sept. 28, 1978** | IDENT **DT-SVC-2** |

```
6.40  PROCEDURE DIVISION.
6.50  OPEN-FILES-PARA.
6.60      OPEN INPUT DATE-CARD-FILE, OUTPUT DATE-LISTING-FILE.
6.70  PRINT-REPORT-HEADINGS-PARA.
6.80      WRITE PRINT-LINE FROM PAGE-HEADING.
6.90      WRITE PRINT-LINE FROM UNDER-LINE.
7.00      WRITE PRINT-LINE FROM COL-HEADINGS AFTER ADVANCING 2 LINES.
7.10  READ-DATA-MOVE-AND-PRINT-PARA.
7.20      READ DATE-CARD-FILE RECORD AT END GO TO LAST-PARA.
7.30      MOVE CORR DATE-CARD TO DETAIL-LINE.
7.40      WRITE PRINT-LINE FROM DETAIL-LINE AFTER ADVANCING 2 LINES.
7.50      GO TO READ-DATA-MOVE-AND-PRINT-PARA.
7.60  CLOSING-PARA.
7.70      CLOSE DATE-CARD-FILE, DATE-LISTING-FILE.
7.80      STOP RUN.
```

FIGURE 10.8   The PROCEDURE DIVISION

just dress-up lines, such as page-headings and column-headings. The real "meat" of any report is printed when you print its DETAIL-LINEs.)

You'll notice I've used names in the DETAIL-LINE that duplicate those in the input record DATE-CARD (see Figure 10.4). This was done to enable me to use the MOVE CORResponding verb.

The PROCEDURE DIVISION of our program is shown in Figure 10.8. Little need be said about this division. Notice how often I've used the WRITE FROM verb. Notice my use of the MOVE CORResponding verb.

Figure 10.9 shows the complete program as it would appear in the program listing from the line printer. Figure 10.10 shows a sampling of the output page produced by this program.

10.5   Safeguarding Input Data

If a data card at or near the beginning of a data deck contains information that will be needed later in the program after other data cards have been read, the information from that earlier data card must be safeguarded by moving it into the WORKING-STORAGE SECTION. If that is not done, the act of reading later data cards will result in the premature destruction of that needed information.

```
 10 IDENTIFICATION DIVISION.
 20 PROGRAM-ID.    DATE-SERVICE-2.
 30 AUTHOR.        R G FINKENAUR.
 40 INSTALLATION. NORTHEASTERN UNIVERSITY.
 50 DATE-WRITTEN. SEPT 28, 1978.
 60 DATE-COMPILED.          78/09/28.
 70 SECURITY.      FOR UNMARRIED PEOPLE ONLY.
 80 REMARKS.       THIS PROGRAM WILL PRODUCE A LISTING OF THE NAMES,
 90     HAIR COLOR, HEIGHT, WEIGHT, AND PHONE NUMBERS OF ALL THE
100     PEOPLE IN MY DATE FILES.
110 ENVIRONMENT DIVISION.
120 CONFIGURATION SECTION.
130 SOURCE-COMPUTER. HAL-2001.
140 OBJECT-COMPUTER. HAL-2001.
150 INPUT-OUTPUT SECTION.
160 FILE-CONTROL.
170     SELECT DATE-CARD-FILE ASSIGN TO CARD-READER.
180     SELECT DATE-LISTING-FILE ASSIGN TO LINE-PRINTER.
190 DATA DIVISION.
200 FILE SECTION.
210 FD  DATE-CARD-FILE; RECORD CONTAINS 80 CHARACTERS; LABEL RECORDS
220     ARE OMITTED; DATA RECORD IS DATE-CARD.
230 01  DATE-CARD.
240     02  LAST-NAME     PICTURE A(15).
250     02  FIRST-NAME    PICTURE A(10).
260     02  FILLER        PICTURE X(30).
270     02  HT-FEET       PICTURE 9.
280     02  HT-INCHES     PICTURE 99.
290     02  WEIGHT        PICTURE 999.
300     02  HAIR-COLOR    PICTURE A(6).
310     02  PHONE         PICTURE 9(10).
320     02  FILLER        PICTURE XXX.
330 FD  DATE-LISTING-FILE; RECORD CONTAINS 136 CHARACTERS; LABEL
340     RECORDS ARE OMITTED; DATA RECORD IS PRINT-LINE.
350 01  PRINT-LINE        PICTURE X(136).
360 WORKING-STORAGE SECTION.
370 01  PAGE-HEADING.
380     02  PAGE-CONTROL  PICTURE 9        VALUE 1.
390     02  FILLER        PICTURE X(58)    VALUE SPACES.
400     02  FILLER        PICTURE A(19)    VALUE 'LIST OF GIRLS NAMES'.
410     02  FILLER        PICTURE X(58)    VALUE SPACES.
420 01  UNDER-LINE.
430     02  FILLER        PICTURE X(59)    VALUE SPACES.
440     02  FILLER        PICTURE X(19)    VALUE '-------------------'.
450     02  FILLER        PICTURE X(58)    VALUE SPACES.
460 01  COL-HEADINGS.
470     02  FILLER        PICTURE X(43)    VALUE SPACES.
480     02  FILLER        PICTURE A(60)    VALUE 'NAME                 HA
490-    'IR      HEIGHT        WEIGHT      TELEPHONE'.
500     02  FILLER        PICTURE X(33)    VALUE SPACES.
510 01  DETAIL-LINE.
520     02  FILLER        PICTURE X(32)    VALUE SPACES.
530     02  FIRST-NAME    PICTURE A(10)B.
540     02  LAST-NAME     PICTURE A(15)B(3).
```

FIGURE 10.9   The Program Listing for DATE-SERVICE-2

```
550        02  HAIR-COLOR        PICTURE A(6)B(3).
560        02  HT-FEET           PICTURE 9.
570        02  FILLER            PICTURE A(4)     VALUE ' FT '.
580        02  HT-INCHES         PICTURE Z9.
590        02  FILLER            PICTURE A(6)     VALUE ' IN   '.
600        02  WEIGHT            PICTURE Z99.
610        02  FILLER            PICTURE A(7)     VALUE ' LBS   '.
620        02  PHONE             PICTURE 999B999B9999.
630        02  FILLER            PICTURE X(31)    VALUE SPACES.
640 PROCEDURE DIVISION.
650 OPEN-FILES-PARA.
660        OPEN INPUT DATE-CARD-FILE, OUTPUT DATE-LISTING-FILE.
670 PRINT-REPORT-HEADINGS-PARA.
680        WRITE PRINT-LINE FROM PAGE-HEADING.
690        WRITE PRINT-LINE FROM UNDER-LINE.
700        WRITE PRINT-LINE FROM COL-HEADINGS AFTER ADVANCING 4 LINES.
710 READ-DATA-MOVE-AND-PRINT-PARA.
720        READ DATE-CARD-FILE RECORD AT END GO TO LAST-PARA.
730        MOVE CORR DATE-CARD TO DETAIL-LINE.
740        WRITE PRINT-LINE FROM DETAIL-LINE AFTER ADVANCING 2 LINES.
750        GO TO READ-DATA-MOVE-AND-PRINT-PARA.
760 LAST-PARA.
770        CLOSE DATE-CARD-FILE, DATE-LISTING-FILE.
780        STOP RUN.
```

FIGURE 10.9   (continued)

To understand this problem better, it will be helpful if you will imagine the computer's memory as being organized as shown in Figure 10.11: an Input Area, a Working Storage Area and an Output Area. The Input Area is established by the FD entry which describes the input file. For example, this FD entry

FD   CARD-FILE; RECORD CONTAINS 80 CHARACTERS; LABEL RECORDS ARE OMITTED; DATA RECORDS ARE CREDIT-LIMIT-REC, CUST-ORDER.

sets up a single Input Area with a capacity of 80 characters. Though this file contains two forms of input records, CREDIT-LIMIT-REC and CUST-ORDER, they will both use the same Input Area. When later, in the PROCEDURE DIVISION, we say

READ CARD-FILE RECORD, AT END etc.

a record (a data card) out of the CARD-FILE will be read by the card reader, and regardless of which form of record it is, its contents will be moved into the single 80-character Input Area.

When we follow an FD entry with more than one 01 level entry, we are not causing more than one Input Area to be established. We are simply telling the computer that we intend to refer to the Input Area by more than one set of data-names.

For example, suppose we followed the above FD entry with these two record descriptions.

```
                       LIST OF GIRLS NAMES
                       -------------------


                NAME            HAIR      HEIGHT       WEIGHT     TELEPHONE

    WILHELMINA SCHIMMELPFENNIG   BLONDE   4 FT 10 IN   120 LBS   914 652 4915

    KATE       AMBROSE           BROWN    4 FT  9 IN   115 LBS   617 219 4283

    CAROL      WHALEN            BRUNET   5 FT  1 IN   105 LBS   617 774 2821

    SANDY      THEPERSON         BROWN    6 FT  4 IN    95 LBS   212 974 3875

    CLAUDETTE  WISE              BLACK    4 FT 11 IN   250 LBS   617 774 9642

    SHIRLEY    STURDEVANT        RED      5 FT  3 IN   120 LBS   713 579 0243

    MAE        MCCAULEY          BLONDE   4 FT  7 IN   195 LBS   617 798 2164

    EDITH      BUNKER            GREY     5 FT 10 IN   145 LBS   212 458 7365
```

FIGURE 10.10   A Portion of the Output from DATE-SERVICE-2

```
01   CREDIT-LIMIT-REC.
     02   ACCT-NO     PICTURE 9(6).
     02   CUST-NAME   PICTURE A(10).
     02   CRED-LIM    PICTURE 9999V99.
     02   FILLER      PICTURE X(58).
01   CUST-ORDER.
     02   CAT-NO      PICTURE 9(7).
     02   ITEM-NAME   PICTURE A(8).
     02   PRICE       PICTURE 99V99.
     02   QUAN        PICTURE 9999.
     02   FILLER      PICTURE X(57).
```

Figure 10.12 demonstrates the effect of these dual record descriptions. The computer now knows that if in the PROCEDURE DIVISION you mention the data-name ACCT-NO, you are referring to the first 6 characters in the Input Area. If you mention CAT-NO, you are referring to the first 7 charac-

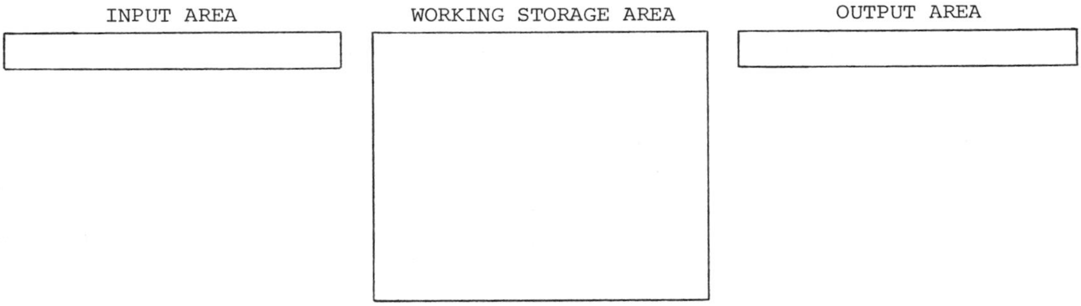

INPUT AREA   WORKING STORAGE AREA   OUTPUT AREA

FIGURE 10.11   Organization of the Memory Unit

FIGURE 10.12   The Effect of Dual Input Record Descriptions

ters in the Input Area. If you mention CUST-NAME, you are referring to the 7th through the 16th characters in the Input Area, but if you mention ITEM-NAME, you are referring to the 8th through the 15th characters.

Suppose the program were one in which you read one card, a CREDIT-LIMIT-REC, which contained in CRED-LIM the maximum amount a given customer was allowed to charge in a single purchase. Suppose that the program then went on to read several orders from that customer, each a CUST-ORDER, and to check each one to see if it exceeded the limit set on the CREDIT-LIMIT-REC.

The reading of the CREDIT-LIMIT-REC would be accomplished by the first occurrence of a READ CARD-FILE RECORD statement. As a result of that READ, the contents of the CREDIT-LIMIT-REC would be stored in the Input Area.

If the program then immediately read a second data card, it would get a CUST-ORDER card, and the contents of that card would also be loaded into the Input Area, overlaying and destroying the contents of the CREDIT-LIMIT-REC stored there just moments before. Then when it turned to comparing the amount of the order with the value of CRED-LIM, it would find the value of CRED-LIM no longer available, having been destroyed by the action of the second READ statement.

To avoid that problem, the programmer should arrange to have the value of CRED-LIM moved into the WORKING-STORAGE SECTION *immediately* after the CREDIT-LIMIT-REC is read so that it will be safe from destruction when the first CUST-ORDER card is read. This could be done by inserting an independent item in the WORKING-STORAGE SECTION such as

```
77  CRED-LIM-WS   PICTURE 9999V99.
```

In the PROCEDURE DIVISION, just after the first READ CARD-FILE RECORD statement the programmer can then say

```
MOVE CRED-LIM TO CRED-LIM-WS.
```

This will cause that value to be moved out of the Input Area and into the Working Storage Area where it will be safe. Now when the second READ CARD-FILE RECORD statement is executed and the CUST-ORDER card is read, the amount of the order can be compared with the value of the credit limit, now available in CRED-LIM-WS.

EXERCISES

Answers to all exercises in this chapter are given in Appendix A.

10.1   TRUE or FALSE? The WORKING-STORAGE SECTION
    a.   Is an optional part of a COBOL program.
    b.   When used, must precede all other sections of the DATA DIVISION.

10.2   TRUE or FALSE? Independent items of data
    a.   Are used only in the WORKING-STORAGE SECTION.
    b.   Must have PICTURE clauses.
    c.   May have VALUE clauses.
    d.   May be subdivided into smaller elementary-items.
    e.   May be a part of a group-item.
    f.   Are coded at the 77 level.
    g.   Must be Class Numeric.

10.3   TRUE or FALSE? 77 Level Entries
    a.   Are an optional part of the WORKING-STORAGE SECTION.
    b.   When used, must precede all other entries in the DATA DIVISION.
    c.   When used, must precede all other entries in the WORKING-STORAGE SECTION.
    d.   Are always coded at Margin B.
    e.   Are used for the description of independent items of data.

10.4   Correct any of the following elementary item descriptions which are incorrect:

```
a.  02  NR-OF-STUDENTS   PICTURE 999      VALUE 125.
b.  02  MAX-SPEED        PICTURE 999      VALUE 55.
c.  02  ACCT-BALANCE     PICTURE S999V99  VALUE −115.75.
d.  02  MIN-WEIGHT       PICTURE 99       VALUE 250.
e.  02  KOUNTER          PICTURE 9(5)     VALUE ZERO.
f.  02  GRAD-YEAR        PICTURE 9999     VALUE '1975'.
g.  02  CREDIT-HRS       PICTURE 99       VALUE SPACES.
h.  02  COURSE-NAME      PICTURE A(10)    VALUE 'ALGEBRA II'.
i.  02  DEPT-NAME        PICTURE A(10)    VALUE 'COMP. SCI.'.
j.  02  MAJOR-FIELD      PICTURE A(10)    VALUE SPACES.
k.  02  CALL-LETTERS     PICTURE X(6)     VALUE 'WBZ-TV'.
l.  02  STATE-ABBREV     PICTURE X(6)     VALUE 'MA.'.
m.  02  BOTTLE-SIZE      PICTURE X(6)     VALUE '4/5TH QT'.
n.  02  FREQUENCY        PICTURE X(3)     VALUE 108.
```

10.5   TRUE or FALSE? If no VALUE clause is used with an elementary-item description in the DATA DIVISION, that item's memory location may be assumed to be loaded with the initial value of zero.

10.6   Consider this excerpt from a DATA DIVISION:

```
FD  PRINT-FILE; RECORD CONTAINS 136 CHARACTERS; LABEL RECORDS ARE
      OMITTED; DATA RECORD IS PRINT-REC.
01  PRINT-REC  PICTURE X(136).
WORKING-STORAGE SECTION.
01  PAGE-HEADING.
    02  FILLER  PICTURE X(62)  VALUE SPACES.
```

```
02  FILLER  PICTURE X(13)  VALUE 'EMPLOYEE DATA'.
02  FILLER  PICTURE X(61)  VALUE SPACES.
```

    a. Give the WRITE FROM statement that will cause the contents of PAGE-HEADING to be printed.

    b. What *two* statements is that WRITE FROM statement equivalent to?

10.7   Consider these two elementary item descriptions:

```
02  FIELD-1  PICTURE 9(5)  VALUE 1.
02  FIELD-2  PICTURE X(5)  VALUE '1'.
```

As the result of those two VALUE clauses, what will be loaded in:

    a. FIELD-1?   b. FIELD-2?

10.8   Suppose this 01 level entry were a part of your program:

```
01  REPORT-TITLE.
    02  FILLER  PICTURE X(61)  VALUE '1'.
    02  FILLER  PICTURE X(14)  VALUE 'PAYROLL REPORT'.
    02  FILLER  PICTURE X(61)  VALUE SPACES.
```

    a. In the first FILLER where will the 1 be loaded, in the 1st character position or in the 61st?

    b. What will be loaded in the other 60 character positions?

    c. Suppose further that that 01 level entry was in your WORKING-STORAGE SECTION and that PRINT-LINE was the record name of your output file. Where would the contents of REPORT-TITLE appear as a result of this statement?

WRITE PRINT-LINE FROM REPORT-TITLE.

    d. Where would the contents of REPORT-TITLE appear as a result of this statement:

WRITE PRINT-LINE FROM REPORT-TITLE AFTER ADVANCING 3 LINES.

10.9   TRUE or FALSE?

    a. An input file may have more than one record-level (01 level) entry.

    b. An input file with two record-level entries will be assigned two input areas in memory.

10.10   When a data card is read, where are its contents stored?

10.11   When a second data card is read, what becomes of the contents of the first data card?

10.12   If you wish to save the contents of the first data card for use *after* the second and subsequent data cards have been read, what steps must you take?

EXAMPLE PROGRAM

The U. S. Census

As a programmer in the Census Bureau, you have been presented a deck of data cards describing U.S. cities, their metropolitan populations, and annual growth rates. Each data card is in this format:

CARD COLUMNS	INFORMATION	EXAMPLE
1–15	City name.	ATLANTA
16–20	State name.	GA
21–24	Urban area.	1727 (1,727 square miles)
25–30	Blanks.	
31–35	Annual growth rate.	00367 (0.0367)
36–40	Blanks.	
41–45	Population in millions.	01390 (1.390 million people)
46–80	Blanks.	

An additional card has been placed at the front of the "city deck" containing the year and region to which the data applies. The format of this "year-region card" is as follows:

1–4	Year.	1960
5–12	Region.	EASTERN (Eastern U.S.)
13–80	Blanks.	

Write a program which will produce a report of these cities so that it appears as follows:

```
MAJOR METROPOLITAN AREAS OF THE EASTERN  UNITED STATES


         CITY          STATE   POPULATION     ANNUAL
                               (MILLIONS)   GROWTH RATE
     ATLANTA            GA        1.390        0.0367
     BOSTON             MASS      3.375        0.0086
     CHICAGO            ILL       6.979        0.0122
     CLEVELAND          OHIO      2.064        0.0081
     DETROIT            MICH      4.200        0.0116
     NEW YORK           N Y      11.529        0.0073
     PHILADELPHIA       PA        4.818        0.0108
     PITTSBURGH         PA        2.401       -0.0002
     WASHINGTON         DC        2.861        0.0386


          DATA AS OF THE YEAR 1960
```

Center the body of the report and center the headings over the columns. Leave 3 blank lines after the title (which should start at the top of a new page). Leave 5 spaces between columns. Center the date line on the third line below the last city. Note that the year and region should be treated as data-values taken from the first card and not as literals. Some suggestions for trial data cards:

```
1960EASTERN
ATLANTA        GA    1727    00367    01390
BOSTON         MASS  1769    00086    03375
CHICAGO        ILL   3720    00122    06979
CLEVELAND      OHIO  1519    00081    02064
DETROIT        MICH  1952    00116    04200
NEW  YORK      N Y   2136    00073    11529
PHILADELPHIA   PA    3553    00108    04818
PITTSBURGH     PA    3049    00002    02401
WASHINGTON     DC    2478    00386    02861
```

└─Col. 1   └─Col. 16   └─Col. 31 └─Col. 41

Solution

IDENTIFICATION and ENVIRONMENT DIVISIONs are omitted.

```
DATA DIVISION.
FILE SECTION.
FD   METRO-DATA-FILE; RECORD CONTAINS 80 CHARACTERS; LABEL RECORDS
     ARE OMITTED; DATA RECORDS ARE LEAD-CARD, CITY-REC.
01   LEAD-CARD.
     02   CENSUS-YEAR      PICTURE 9(4).
     02   REGION-LC        PICTURE A(8).
     02   FILLER           PICTURE X(68).
01   CITY-REC.
     02   CITY             PICTURE A(15).
     02   STATE            PICTURE A(5).
     02   FILLER           PICTURE X(10).
     02   GROWTH-RATE      PICTURE S9V9(4).
     02   FILLER           PICTURE X(5).
     02   POP-MIL          PICTURE 99V999.
     02   FILLER           PICTURE X(35).
FD   REPORT-FILE; RECORD CONTAINS 136 CHARACTERS; LABEL RECORDS
     ARE OMITTED; DATA RECORD IS PRINT-LINE.
01   PRINT-LINE           PICTURE X(136).
WORKING-STORAGE SECTION.
77   DATE-WS              PICTURE 9(4).
01   REPORT-TITLE.
     02   PAGE-EJECT       PICTURE 9        VALUE 1.
     02   FILLER           PICTURE X(40) VALUE SPACES.
     02   FILLER           PICTURE A(32)
          VALUE 'MAJOR METROPOLITAN AREAS OF THE '.
     02   REGION-RT        PICTURE A(8)B.
     02   FILLER           PICTURE A(13) VALUE 'UNITED STATES'.
     02   FILLER           PICTURE X(41) VALUE SPACES.
```

```
01    DETAIL-LINE.
      02   FILLER             PICTURE X(44) VALUE SPACES.
      02   CITY               PICTURE A(15)B(5).
      02   STATE              PICTURE A(5)B(5).
      02   POP-MIL            PICTURE Z9.999B(5).
      02   GROWTH-RATE        PICTURE -9.9(4).
      02   FILLER             PICTURE X(44) VALUE SPACES.
01    COLUMN-HEADING-1.
      02   FILLER             PICTURE X(49) VALUE SPACES.
      02   FILLER             PICTURE X(4)   VALUE 'CITY'.
      02   FILLER             PICTURE X(11) VALUE SPACES.
      02   FILLER             PICTURE X(28)
           VALUE 'STATE      POPULATION     ANNUAL'.
      02   FILLER             PICTURE X(44) VALUE SPACES.
01    COLUMN-HEADING-2.
      02   FILLER             PICTURE X(72) VALUE SPACES.
      02   FILLER             PICTURE X(23)
           VALUE '(MILLIONS)  GROWTH RATE'.
      02   FILLER             PICTURE X(41) VALUE SPACES.
01    BOTTOM-LINE.
      02   FILLER             PICTURE X(56) VALUE SPACES.
      02   FILLER             PICTURE X(20)
           VALUE 'DATA AS OF THE YEAR '.
      02   YEAR-BL            PICTURE 9(4).
      02   FILLER             PICTURE X(56) VALUE SPACES.
01    ERROR-LINE.
      02   FILLER             PICTURE X(21)
           VALUE ' OOPS - NO DATA DECK'.
      02   FILLER             PICTURE X(115) VALUE SPACES.
PROCEDURE DIVISION.
OPEN-PARA.
      OPEN INPUT METRO-DATA-FILE OUTPUT REPORT-FILE.
READ-LEAD-CARD-PARA.
      READ METRO-DATA-FILE RECORD AT END GO TO ERROR-PARA.
MOVE-LEAD-DATA-TO-W-S-PARA.
      MOVE CENSUS-YEAR TO DATE-WS.
      MOVE REGION-LC TO REGION-RT.
PRINT-HEADINGS-PARA.
      WRITE PRINT-LINE FROM REPORT-TITLE.
      WRITE PRINT-LINE FROM COLUMN-HEADING-1
          AFTER ADVANCING 4 LINES.
      WRITE PRINT-LINE FROM COLUMN-HEADING-2.
READ-DATA-MOVE-AND-PRINT-PARA.
      READ METRO-DATA-FILE RECORD
          AT END GO TO PRINT-BOTTOM-LINE-PARA.
      MOVE CORR CITY-REC TO DETAIL-LINE.
      WRITE PRINT-LINE FROM DETAIL-LINE.
      GO TO READ-DATA-MOVE-AND-PRINT-PARA.
PRINT-BOTTOM-LINE-PARA.
      MOVE DATE-WS TO YEAR-BL.
      WRITE PRINT-LINE FROM BOTTOM-LINE AFTER ADVANCING 3 LINES.
CLOSE-PARA.
      CLOSE METRO-DATA-FILE, REPORT-FILE.
      STOP RUN.
ERROR-PARA.
      WRITE PRINT-LINE FROM ERROR-LINE.
      GO TO CLOSE-PARA.
```

Discussion

In this program you must accommodate more than one type of input record. This is done by defining two data records for METRO-DATA. Since the LEAD-CARD is the first card in the deck and since its YEAR contents do not get printed immediately, the program logic ensures that this card is read and the year value thereon safely tucked away in WORKING-STORAGE before proceeding on with the reading of the CITY-REC's. The year is moved to a 77-level entry and then moved again when END-JOB is reached. Actually, that 77-level intermediate resting place for the year is unnecessary; it could have been moved directly from CENSUS-YEAR to YEAR-BL with the same effect. In any event, it must be understood that the year value has to be put somewhere before the next card is read or it will be destroyed.

Hopefully, you did not overlook the fact that Pittsburgh, with its negative growth rate, demands some overpunching and accounting for the minus sign in the PICTURE clause.

With five different formats for output lines, WORKING-STORAGE with its VALUE clause capability becomes the logical place to assemble these lines. The WRITE FROM verb is then used to economize on statements as is MOVE CORResponding. Note also that to ensure that the title begins on a new page, a 1 is inserted in the left-most position of REPORT-TITLE. Another feature of the output in this program is the necessity for *two* 136-character group-items to produce the column headings.

A novelty has been added to this program which is very good procedure for more sophisticated jobs. That is the provision for programmer-invented error messages. In this case, when reading the first card (the "year-region card"), we do not expect the AT END clause to be executed. However, just in case it is (this could only happen if you forgot your data deck) we have provided for the printing of a message which would let us know that problem existed. This approach is one which experienced programmers follow to provide for easier diagnosis of unexpected problems.

STUDENT'S PROGRAM

Mortgage Payments

One of your data processing functions at the Evergreen Savings and Loan Association is to produce an end-of-the-month listing of home mortgage loans and associated statistics. Here is a sample of the desired form of the report:

```
                    STATUS OF HOME MORTGAGE LOANS
                         AS OF SEP 30, 75

                                                   YEAR TO DATE TOTALS
                                                   -------------------
    LOAN     NEXT PAYMENT  PRINCIPAL   ESCROW    ANNUAL    INTEREST   PAYMENTS
   NUMBER        DUE        BALANCE    BALANCE   PCT RATE  PAYMENTS   TO  CITY
 ----------  ------------  ---------  ---------  --------  ---------  ---------
 6 13275 26    AUG  5      $31,746.27   $432.76    7.00   $1,173.84  $1,003.93
 2 73146 33    AUG 12      $35,422.75   $726.23    8.50   $1,562.33    $750.19
 5 44305 21    AUG  9      $19,263.15   $522.91    7.75     $932.56    $681.06
 4 62173 42    AUG 15       $8,531.05   $372.51    6.50     $152.33    $516.43
 7 26905 15    AUG 20      $41,526.84 $1,052.14    7.50   $1,625.71  $1,132.67
 3 76913 11    AUG 17      $32,633.42   $653.25    8.00   $1,202.94    $826.34
```

The data deck consists of cards in this format:

CARD COLUMNS	INFORMATION	EXAMPLE
1–8	Loan number.	61327526 (6 13275 26)
9–10	Day payment is due.	05 (5th of the month)
11–17	Principal balance.	3174627 ($31,746.27)
18–23	Escrow balance.	043276 ($432.76)
24–26	Annual rate of interest.	700 (7.00%)
27–32	Total interest payments to date.	117384 ($1,173.84)
33–38	Total city tax payments to date.	100393 ($1,003.93)
39–80	Blanks.	

There is a single card at the beginning of the deck of account cards which contains information in this format:

1–10	Closing date.	SEP 30, 75
11–13	Name of next month.	AUG
14–80	Blanks.	

The contents of the closing date field are to be used in the second line of the report heading. The name of the next month was placed on this card, so it wouldn't have to be placed on every one of the account cards. Each detail line is to include the due date of the next payment. The month name portion of that date is to come from the lead card. The day portion of that date is to come from each of the account cards as they are processed.

The following are suggested contents for trial data cards:

```
SEP 30, 75AUG
6132752605317462704327670011738410 0393
2731463312354227507262385015623307 5019
5443052109192631505229177509325606 8106
4621734215085310503725165001523305 1643
7269051520415268410521475016257111 3267
3769131117326334206532580012029408 2634
```

11 The COBOL Arithmetic Verbs

11.1 Introduction

A computer that couldn't compute would be like a car without an engine. It would look good sitting there, but it wouldn't be performing the essential function for which it was purchased.

In this chapter we will (at long last, you may say) learn how to write the COBOL instructions that direct the computer to perform arithmetic computations. It seems almost ironic that we've had to wait this long to get to this very fundamental topic. It is a fact, however, that you can't tell the computer to perform arithmetic operations on numbers unless you have given it the numbers upon which it is to operate. Furthermore, I think you'd agree that it would be pointless to have the computer calculate answers and then keep those answers to itself. The answers are worthless to you unless you have the ability to direct their printing on the line printer.

To put it another way, you'd have had no use for COBOL arithmetic instructions if you didn't first have the ability to handle input and output operations. That is what we have been concentrating on up to this point. You now have command of sufficient COBOL instructions to tell the computer what input data to read, what data you want printed on the line printer, in what form, and when. Without this ability, any discussion of COBOL arithmetic instructions would have been a pointless academic exercise.

This chapter will discuss the four basic[1] COBOL arithmetic verbs:

ADD   MULTIPLY
SUBTRACT DIVIDE

It will also discuss the ROUNDED clause, with which you direct the rounding of answers containing more decimal digits than you desire to keep, and the ON SIZE ERROR clause, with which you tell the computer what you want done if it should calculate an answer larger than you had expected

---

[1] A fifth COBOL arithmetic verb, COMPUTE, is discussed in Appendix D. FORTRAN experienced programmers like to use COMPUTE statements because of their similarity to FORTRAN arithmetic statements. If you are studying COBOL as a first programming language, however, you are advised to postpone considering the COMPUTE verb until you are perfectly comfortable with the four basic COBOL arithmetic verbs.

(and therefore larger than you had written your program to properly handle).

There is one principle which runs throughout this chapter and which you must never forget. Any data value which is to be operated upon by an arithmetic verb must be in *purely numeric form*. Any elementary-item with a Class N PICTURE clause will contain only purely numeric data values, and *is* suitable for use in an arithmetic operation. A Class NE item is *not!* Once you have edited a numeric value, it may no longer be used in an arithmetic operation.

Recall also that a numeric literal is considered to be Class N, and therefore *may* be used in an arithmetic operation.

11.2 The ADD Verb

To direct the computer to add two or more values, you use an ADD TO or an ADD GIVING instruction:

Form I: ADD 1st-item(s) TO receiving-item.
Form II: ADD 1st-item(s) GIVING receiving-item.

Rules:
1. There may be more than one 1st-item.
2. Any 1st-item may be a data-name or numeric literal.
3. The receiving-item *must* be a data-name.
4. The 1st-item(s) *must* be Class N.
5. The receiving-item must be:
   a. Class N in Form I.
   b. Class N or NE in Form II.

An ADD TO instruction tells the computer to add the value of the 1st-item(s) to the value of the receiving-item and to store the result in the memory location of the receiving-item. For example, suppose that in your DATA DIVISION, you had two elementary-item descriptions like these:

```
02  BASIC-PAY    PICTURE 999V99.
02  BONUS        PICTURE 99V99.
```

Those would have caused memory locations to be assigned to the data-names BASIC-PAY and BONUS. Suppose that as the result of a READ statement, the two memory locations had been loaded as shown here:

BASIC-PAY   BONUS

12500   1400

Now consider what would happen if the computer executed this statement:

ADD BONUS TO BASIC-PAY.

The computer would send the values stored in BONUS and BASIC-PAY to the arithmetic unit, command the arithmetic unit to add the two values, and then cause the result of that addition to be stored in the receiving-item, BASIC-PAY. This would be the result:

BASIC-PAY

13900

BONUS

1400

Notice that only the receiving-item has its value altered in any way by the action of the ADD statement.

Let's consider that ADD statement in more detail:

ADD BONUS TO BASIC-PAY.

It is an ADD TO statement in which there is only one 1st-item, a data-name, BONUS. The receiving-item is a data-name, BASIC-PAY, as it *must* be. Both the 1st-item and the receiving-item are Class N, as they *must* be. (How do we know they are Class N? Because their PICTURE clauses contain only 9's and V's, and contain *none* of the editing characters that would have made them Class NE.)

Now let's consider in more detail the effect of that ADD statement. It is actually a three step process, as diagrammed in Figure 11.1. Responding to the ADD statement, the computer first (at Step 1) executes non-destructive reads of the two memory locations to determine the values stored in them and transmits those values to the arithmetic unit. It then (at Step 2) commands the arithmetic unit to perform an addition operation on the two values. Finally (at Step 3), it performs a numeric MOVE of the results of the addition operation to the receiving-item, BASIC-PAY, executing a destructive write of that new value into the location and destroying the value that was formerly stored there.

Another example—suppose you had these four memory locations with values stored in them as shown:

AMOUNT-IN-
SAVINGS

156000

CHECK-BOOK-
BALANCE

010500

CASH-IN
HAND

2135

CAPITAL-
ASSETS

100000

What would be the effect of this ADD statement?

ADD   CASH-IN-HAND,   AMOUNT-IN-SAVINGS,   CHECK-BOOK-BALANCE,   TO
CAPITAL-ASSETS.

This is a case where you have more than one 1st-item. (As usual, the com-

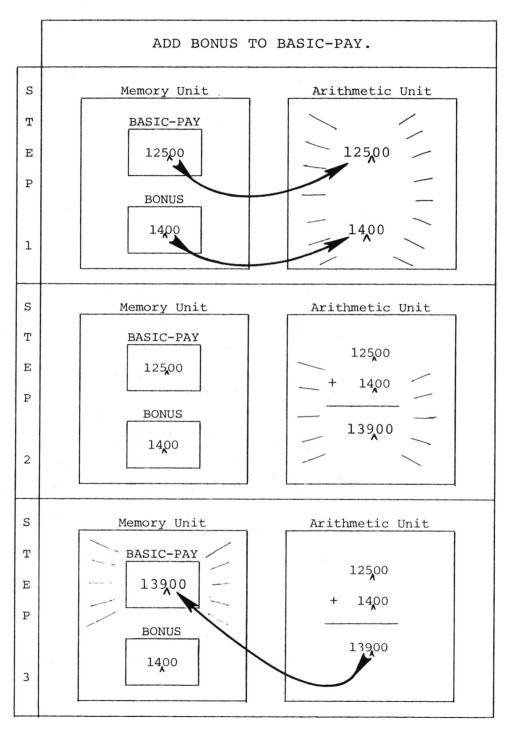

FIGURE 11.1   The Computer Responds to an ADD Instruction

mas shown are optional.) The condition of the memory locations after the execution of that statement would be as follows:

AMOUNT-IN-SAVINGS CHECK-BOOK-BALANCE CASH-IN-HAND CAPITAL-ASSETS

| 1560̤00 | | 01050̤0 | | 21̤35 | | 2686̤35 |

Remember, it *is* permissible for a numeric literal to be the 1st-item or one of the 1st-items. For an example let's start with two memory locations as shown here:

FUEL-CHARGE ELEC-BILL

| 090̤0 | | 12̤00 |

and this as the statement to be executed:

ADD 3.00, FUEL-CHARGE TO ELEC-BILL.

This would be the result:

FUEL-CHARGE ELEC-BILL

| 090̤0 | | 240̤0 |

Of course, it would also be possible for the 1st-item to be a single numeric literal all by itself.

Another point not demonstrated so far is that if a value to be added is negative, it will be added properly, according to the normal rules of algebra. So if the memory locations involved were these:

ADJUSTMENT PRICE

| 012̤5̄ | | 10̤00 |

and the statement to be executed were: ADD ADJUSTMENT TO PRICE. this would be the result:

ADJUSTMENT PRICE

| 012̤5̄ | | 08̤75 |

The ADD GIVING statement is in many ways similar to the ADD TO statement. The principal difference between the two is that in an ADD TO statement the value of the receiving-item *is* included in the actual calculation, whereas in the ADD GIVING statement it is *not*—the receiving-field simply receives the result of the addition but its value is not included in the addition operation.

In an ADD TO statement the receiving-field *must* be Class N, since its value is actually sent to the arithmetic unit for involvement in the addition operation. In an ADD GIVING statement, the value of the receiving-field is *not* used in the addition operation, so the receiving-field may be *either* Class N *or* NE.

To demonstrate the functioning of the ADD GIVING statement, let's take an example. Suppose we started with these three memory locations:

```
    INTEREST-        PRINCIPAL-          TOTAL-
      DUE              DUE              PAYMENT
    ┌──────┐         ┌──────┐         ┌──────┐
    │04000 │         │16000 │         │17500 │
    └──────┘         └──────┘         └──────┘
```

and this as the statement to be executed:

ADD INTEREST-DUE, PRINCIPAL-DUE GIVING TOTAL-PAYMENT.

This would be the result:

```
    INTEREST-        PRINCIPAL-          TOTAL-
      DUE              DUE              PAYMENT
    ┌──────┐         ┌──────┐         ┌──────┐
    │04000 │         │16000 │         │20000 │
    └──────┘         └──────┘         └──────┘
```

What happened? The computer responded to that ADD statement by sending the values of INTEREST-DUE and PRINCIPAL-DUE (but *not* of TOTAL-PAYMENT) to the arithmetic unit. It then directed the adding of the two values, and when that was finished, it stored the result in the receiving-field TOTAL-PAYMENT, destroying the value originally stored there (17500).

Just as with the ADD TO statement, a numeric literal may be one of the 1st-items of an ADD GIVING statement, and all 1st-items *must* be Class N.

Figure 11.2 demonstrates further the functioning of the ADD verb.

One final note before we leave ADD: You will soon learn that each of the COBOL arithmetic verbs except COMPUTE has a preposition which it is customarily associated with. With ADD it is TO. With SUBTRACT it is FROM. With MULTIPLY it is BY. With DIVIDE it is INTO. Notice that we say:

```
    DIVIDE INTO      and     DIVIDE INTO GIVING,
    MULTIPLY BY      and     MULTIPLY BY GIVING,
    SUBTRACT FROM    and   SUBTRACT FROM GIVING,
      ADD TO        but not     ADD TO GIVING.
```

The ADD verb uses ADD TO and ADD GIVING. It is the only one of the four basic arithmetic verbs which looses its preposition in the GIVING form.

	Data-Name: PICTURE:	A 99V9	B 9V99	C V99	D 99V99
ADD A TO B.	Before:	01̬2	6̬31	̬50	10̬00
	After:	01̬2	7̬51	̬50	10̬00
ADD A, C TO D.	Before:	01̬2	6̬31	̬50	10̬00
	After:	01̬2	6̬31	̬50	11̬70
ADD 2.5 TO A.	Before:	01̬2	6̬31	̬50	10̬00
	After:	03̬7	6̬31	̬50	10̬00
ADD 4, C TO D.	Before:	01̬2	6̬31	̬50	10̬00
	After:	01̬2	6̬31	̬50	14̬50
ADD A, B, C GIVING D.	Before:	01̬2	6̬31	̬50	10̬00
	After:	01̬2	6̬31	̬50	08̬01
ADD 5.4, D GIVING A.	Before:	01̬2	6̬31	̬50	10̬00
	After:	15̬4	6̬31	̬50	10̬00
ADD C TO B.	Before:	01̬2	6̬31	̬50	10̬00
	After:	01̬2	6̬81	̬50	10̄00
ADD B TO C.	Before:	01̬2	6̬31	̬50	10̬00
	After:	01̬2	6̬31	̬81	10̬00
ADD B, C GIVING D.	Before:	01̬2	6̬31	̬50	10̬00
	After:	01̬2	6̬31	̬50	06̬81
ADD B, C GIVING A.	Before:	01̬2	6̬31	̬50	10̬00
	After:	06̬8	6̬31	̬50	10̬00

FIGURE 11.2 The ADD Verb

11.3 The SUBTRACT Verb

To tell the computer to perform a subtraction operation, you use a SUB-TRACT FROM or a SUBTRACT FROM GIVING statement:

Form I: SUBTRACT 1st-item(s) FROM receiving-item.
Form II: SUBTRACT 1st-item(s) FROM 2nd-item GIVING receiving-item.

Rules:
1. There may be more than one 1st-item.
2. Any 1st-item or 2nd-item may be a data-name or numeric lateral.
3. The receiving-item *must* be a data-name.
4. The 1st-item(s) and 2nd-item *must* be Class N.
5. The receiving-item must be
   a. Class N in Form I.
   b. Class N or NE in Form II.

A SUBTRACT FROM statement tells the computer to subtract the value of the 1st-item from the value of the receiving-item, and to store the result of that subtraction in the memory location of the receiving-item. If there is more than one 1st-item, the computer will first sum the values of all 1st-items and then subtract *that sum* from the value of the receiving-item.

An example—let's say we start with these three memory locations:

```
                                           ACCT-
     PAYMENT          REFUND              BALANCE
    ┌────────┐       ┌────────┐          ┌────────┐
    │08000   │       │02500   │          │15000   │
    └────────┘       └────────┘          └────────┘
```

and this as the statement to be executed:

SUBTRACT PAYMENT, REFUND FROM ACCT-BALANCE.

This would be the result:

```
                                           ACCT-
     PAYMENT          REFUND              BALANCE
    ┌────────┐       ┌────────┐          ┌────────┐
    │08000   │       │02500   │          │04500   │
    └────────┘       └────────┘          └────────┘
```

Several aspects of the SUBTRACT FROM statement are similar to the ADD TO statement. Since the value of the receiving-item in a SUBTRACT FROM statement *is* involved in the subtraction operation, it *must* be Class N. Also similar is the fact that one or more of the 1st-items of a SUBTRACT FROM statement can be a numeric literal.

The SUBTRACT FROM GIVING statement shares similarities with the ADD GIVING statement. The value of the receiving-item of the SUB-

TRACT FROM GIVING statement is not involved in the subtract operation. The receiving-item simply receives the result of the subtraction with no regard to what its former value was, and for that reason it may be either Class N or NE.

Unlike the ADD GIVING statement, you now have a 2nd-item to contend with in the SUBTRACT FROM GIVING statement. In this case, the value of the 1st-item (or the sum of the values of the 1st-items, if there is more than one) is subtracted from the value of the 2nd-item, and the result is stored in the memory location of the receiving-item.

Another example—we'll begin with these three memory locations:

TOTAL- SEATS	SEATS- RESERVED	VACANT- SEATS
200ˏ	090ˏ	050ˏ

Consider this SUBTRACT statement:

SUBTRACT SEATS-RESERVED FROM TOTAL-SEATS GIVING VACANT-SEATS.

The result would be:

TOTAL- SEATS	SEATS- RESERVED	VACANT- SEATS
200ˏ	090ˏ	110ˏ

Remember, either of the 1st-item(s) or the 2nd-item may be a numeric literal, and although my last example demonstrated only a single 1st-item, it is permissible to have more than one 1st-item in a SUBTRACT FROM GIVING statement.

This would be the appropriate moment to mention something very often overlooked by beginning COBOL programmers. Do you remember when your algebra teacher taught you how to subtract a large number from a smaller number? She showed you how and why $10 - 15 = -5$. Not long after that your bank may have reminded you that when you had $25 in your checking account, you should not write a check for $35, because if you did (and *if* they honored it), your account balance would become a −$10, or $10 overdrawn.

These concerns must also be faced when you're writing a COBOL program, especially when you're describing (in the DATA DIVISION) elementary-items which will be used as the receiving-items of SUBTRACT statements. An elementary-item's memory location is not prepared to receive a negative value unless you have forewarned it of that possibility. You will recall from Section 8.2 that the S character is placed at the left end of a Class N PICTURE clause to identify a SIGNED elementary-item (one that will not always be assumed positive, but may sometimes contain negative values and at other times contain positive values).

Suppose you had these three elementary-item descriptions in your DATA DIVISION:

```
02   COST           PICTURE 99V99.
02   SELLING-PRICE  PICTURE 99V99.
02   PROFIT         PICTURE 99V99.
```

Suppose further that as a result of previous READ statements and calculations, the three memory locations were loaded like this:

COST	SELLING-PRICE	PROFIT
75⌄00	50⌄00	00⌄00

Now we come to the point in the program where we want PROFIT calculated, so we say:

SUBTRACT COST FROM SELLING-PRICE GIVING PROFIT.

The result of the subtraction will be as follows:

COST	SELLING-PRICE	PROFIT
75⌄00	50⌄00	25⌄00

The computer has calculated that we *made a profit* of $25! You and I know that we actually lost $25; that is, we made a profit of −$25. What's the problem here?

The problem is that we never forewarned the computer that PROFIT *could* contain a negative value, despite our hopes that it never would. When the arithmetic unit subtracted the value of COST (75⌄00) from the value of SELLING-PRICE (50⌄00), it got a value of −25. When it tried to MOVE that value to the memory location of the receiving-item, however, it found that location unprepared to receive a negative value, so it stored the 25 without its sign.

In order to overcome this problem, we should have described PROFIT like this:

```
02   PROFIT     PICTURE S99V99.
```

If we had, this would have been the result of the SUBTRACT statement:

COST	SELLING-PRICE	PROFIT
75⌄00	50⌄00	25⌄0̄0

Although this problem arises most often as the result of a subtraction, it can also arise when an addition, multiplication, or division operation involves negative values. So it is important for the programmer always to look ahead to what possible range of values each of her elementary-items may contain, and to be sure to place an S in the PICTURE clause of every item whose range includes negative values. (Many programmers put an S in the PICTURE clause of *every* Class N item, just to be safe.)

Figure 11.3 demonstrates further the functioning of the SUBTRACT verb.

11.4   The MULTIPLY Verb

To tell the computer to perform a multiplication operation, you use a MULTIPLY BY or a MULTIPLY BY GIVING statement:

Form I: MULTIPLY 1st-item BY receiving-item.
Form II: MULTIPLY 1st-item BY 2nd-item GIVING receiving-item.

Rules:
1. There may *not* be more than one 1st-item.
2. The 1st-item or 2nd-item may be a data-name or a numeric literal.
3. The receiving-item *must* be a data-name.
4. The 1st-item and 2nd-item must be Class N.
5. The receiving-item must be
   a. Class N in Form I.
   b. Class N or NE in Form II.

The MULTIPLY statements operate exactly like the SUBTRACT statements, with only two exceptions: The first exception is the obvious one—a MULTIPLY statement directs a multiplication operation instead of a subtraction operation. The second and only noteworthy exception is that a MULTIPLY statement may have *only one* 1st-item.

As an example, consider these two memory locations:

```
         NR-OF-           COOLING-
         ROOMS            REQUIRED
        ┌────┐           ┌──────┐
        │ 11 │           │08000 │
        └────┘           └──────┘
```

and this as the statement to be executed:

MULTIPLY NR-OF-ROOMS BY COOLING-REQUIRED.

This would be the result:

```
         NR-OF-           COOLING-
         ROOMS            REQUIRED
        ┌────┐           ┌──────┐
        │ 11 │           │88000 │
        └────┘           └──────┘
```

		Data-Name: A	B	C	D
		PICTURE: S99V9	9V99	V99	99V99
SUBTRACT A FROM B.	Before:	01∧2	6∧31	∧50	10∧00
	After:	01∧2	5∧11	∧50	10∧00
SUBTRACT A, C FROM D.	Before:	01∧2	6∧31	∧50	10∧00
	After:	01∧2	6∧31	∧50	08∧30
SUBTRACT 4.25 FROM D.	Before:	01∧2	6∧31	∧50	10∧00
	After:	01∧2	6∧31	∧50	05∧75
SUBTRACT 5, A FROM B.	Before:	01∧2	6∧31	∧50	10∧00
	After:	01∧2	0∧11	∧50	10∧00
SUBTRACT D FROM A.	Before:	01∧2	6∧31	∧50	10∧00
	After:	08∧8̄	6∧31	∧50	10∧00
SUBTRACT D FROM B.	Before:	01∧2	6∧31	∧50	10∧00
	After:	01∧2	3∧69	∧50	10∧00
SUBTRACT C FROM B GIVING D.	Before:	01∧2	6∧31	∧50	10∧00
	After:	01∧2	6∧31	∧50	05∧81
SUBTRACT D FROM C GIVING A.	Before:	01∧2	6∧31	∧50	10∧00
	After:	09∧5̄	6∧31	∧50	10∧00
SUBTRACT C, A FROM B GIVING D.	Before:	01∧2	6∧31	∧50	10∧00
	After:	01∧2	6∧31	∧50	04∧61
SUBTRACT 21.4, D FROM B GIVING A.	Before:	01∧2	6∧31	∧50	10∧00
	After:	25∧0̄	6∧31	∧50	10∧00

FIGURE 11.3 The SUBTRACT Verb

Another example—let's start with these three memory locations:

INTEREST-RATE: `^12`
PRINCIPAL: `600^00`
INTEREST-CHARGED: `43^00`

and this as the statement to be executed:

MULTIPLY PRINCIPAL BY INTEREST-RATE GIVING INTEREST-CHARGED.

	Data-Name:	A	B	C	D
	PICTURE:	99V9	9V99	V99	99V99
MULTIPLY D BY A.	Before:	01^2	6^31	^50	10^00
	After:	12^0	6^31	^50	10^00
MULTIPLY 3.67 BY D.	Before:	01^2	6^31	^50	10^00
	After:	01^2	6^31	^50	36^70
MULTIPLY D BY B GIVING A.	Before:	01^2	6^31	^50	10^00
	After:	63^1	6^31	^50	10^00
MULTIPLY 16 BY C GIVING B.	Before:	01^2	6^31	^50	10^00
	After:	01^2	8^00	^50	10^00
MULTIPLY C BY B.	Before:	01^2	6^31	^50	10^00
	After:	01^2	3^15	^50	10^00
MULTIPLY D BY C GIVING B.	Before:	01^2	6^31	^50	10^00
	After:	01^2	5^00	^50	10^00
MULTIPLY D BY C.	Before:	01^2	6^31	^50	10^00
	After:	01^2	6^31	^00	10^00

FIGURE 11.4   The MULTIPLY Verb

This would be the result:

INTEREST-RATE	PRINCIPAL	INTEREST-CHARGED
ͺ12	600ͺ00	72ͺ00

To reiterate a few points: Notice in the above examples that only the receiving-items had their values changed. In the MULTIPLY BY example, the former value of the receiving-item *was* used in the multiplication operation, and for that reason it *had* to be a Class N item. In the MULTIPLY BY GIVING example, the former value of the receiving-item was *not* used, so it *could* have been Class NE.

Also, though neither of my examples demonstrated this, the 1st-item or 2nd-item of a MULTIPLY statement *may* be a numeric literal. Here, for example, is a correct Form II statement which uses a numeric literal as its 1st-item:

MULTIPLY 2.54 BY LENGTH-IN-INCHES GIVING LENGTH-IN-CENTIMETERS.

Be on your guard against the temptation to say "multiply *times*." Ever since you learned to multiply, you've been saying "Multiply A times B," so it will be an easy mistake to make. Remember, in COBOL you say MULTIPLY A *BY* B.

Figure 11.4 demonstrates further the functioning of the MULTIPLY verb.

11.5   The DIVIDE Verb

To tell the computer to perform a division operation, you use a DIVIDE INTO or a DIVIDE INTO GIVING or a DIVIDE BY GIVING statement:

Form I:	DIVIDE 1st-item INTO receiving item.
Form II:	DIVIDE 1st-item INTO 2nd-item GIVING receiving-item.
Form III:	DIVIDE 1st-item BY 2nd-item GIVING receiving-item.

Rules:
1. There may *not* be more than one 1st-item.
2. The 1st-item or 2nd-item may be a data-name or numeric literal.
3. The receiving-item *must* be a data-name.
4. The 1st-item and 2nd-item must be Class N.
5. The receiving-item must be
   a. Class N in Form I.
   b. Class N or NE in Forms II and III.

The DIVIDE statements operate exactly like the MULTIPLY statements except that they direct division to be performed instead of multiplication.

Let's clear up right now any misunderstanding you might have about what "divide into" and "divide by" mean arithmetically. If you "divide 2 *into* 8," you get 4. If you "divide 2 by 8," you get ¼ or .25. "Divide A into B" makes A the divisor and means the same thing as is intended by these mathematical symbols:

$$A\overline{)B} \qquad B \div A \qquad \frac{B}{A}$$

"Divide A by B" make B the divisor and means the same thing as these symbols:

$$B\overline{)A} \qquad A \div B \qquad \frac{A}{B}$$

In addition to concerning yourself with the question of "whom gets divided by whom," in COBOL you must also concern yourself with "where does the resulting value (the quotient) get stored?" As with all other COBOL arithmetic statements, the result will be stored in the memory location of the data-name you specify as the receiving-item.

Some examples—Suppose you had these two memory locations loaded as shown:

NR-OF-
PORTIONS   AMOUNT

5   1$\underset{\wedge}{5}$5

Suppose further that this statement were executed:

DIVIDE NR-OF-PORTIONS INTO AMOUNT.

This would be the result:

NR-OF-
PORTIONS   AMOUNT

5   03$\underset{\wedge}{1}$

Now consider these three memory locations:

GALLONS-   MILES-   MILES-PER-
USED   TRAVELLED   GALLON

20$\underset{\wedge}{0}$ 490$\underset{\wedge}{0}$ 00$\underset{\wedge}{0}$

The execution of either this statement:

DIVIDE GALLONS-USED INTO MILES-TRAVELLED GIVING MILES-PER-GALLON.

or this statement:

DIVIDE MILES-TRAVELLED BY GALLONS-USED GIVING MILES-PER-GALLON.

would produce this result:

GALLONS-USED	MILES-TRAVELLED	MILES-PER-GALLON
200	4900	245

Notice that only with DIVIDE INTO do you have the freedom to use or not to use the GIVING clause. The DIVIDE BY statement *requires* a GIVING clause.

Figure 11.5 demonstrates further the functioning of the DIVIDE verb.

	Data-Name: PICTURE:	A 99V9 ~	B 9V99	C V99	D 99V99
DIVIDE D INTO B.	Before:	012	631	50	1000
	After:	012	063	50	1000
DIVIDE 4 INTO A.	Before:	012	631	50	1000
	After:	003	631	50	1000
DIVIDE C INTO B GIVING D.	Before:	012	631	50	1000
	After:	012	631	50	1262
DIVIDE B BY C GIVING D.	Before:	012	631	50	1000
	After:	012	631	50	1262
DIVIDE 2 INTO C GIVING B.	Before:	012	631	50	1000
	After:	012	025	50	1000
DIVIDE A BY 3 GIVING C.	Before:	012	631	50	1000
	After:	012	631	40	1000

FIGURE 11.5   The DIVIDE Verb

11.6   The ROUNDED Option

Let me demonstrate first why you might want to use the ROUNDED option on an arithmetic statement. Suppose you had these three elementary item descriptions in your DATA DIVISION:

```
02  A  PICTURE 9V99.
02  B  PICTURE 99V9.
02  C  PICTURE 999V9.
```

and that as a result of a READ statement, the three memory locations were loaded as shown here:

Now suppose the next statement to be executed was:

```
MULTIPLY A BY B GIVING C.
```

As a result of that statement, the computer would send the value of A (6̬27) and the value of B (21̬1) to the arithmetic unit and direct that they be multiplied.

$$6̬27 \times 21̬1 = 132̬297$$

Next the computer would perform a numeric move of 132̬297 to C's memory location, and this would be the result:

You may agree with me that if for some reason we've got to stick with only one decimal digit in C, then a more accurate value to store there would have been 132̬3. In other words, it would seem more desirable to *round* the result of the multiplication to one decimal digit than to simply chop off the extra digits without any regard for their value.

You can direct the computer to do that for you by adding the word ROUNDED to any arithmetic statement where you want it done, as shown in these examples:

```
ADD A, C TO D, ROUNDED.
ADD A, C GIVING E, ROUNDED.
SUBTRACT A FROM B, ROUNDED.
SUBTRACT A FROM B GIVING C, ROUNDED.
```

MULTIPLY A BY B, ROUNDED.
MULTIPLY A BY B GIVING C, ROUNDED.
DIVIDE A INTO B, ROUNDED.
DIVIDE A INTO B GIVING C, ROUNDED.
DIVIDE A BY B GIVING C, ROUNDED.

The computer performs rounding according to the usual round-off rules as demonstrated here:

EXAMPLE UNROUNDED VALUE	VALUE ROUNDED TO TWO DECIMAL DIGITS
1.2706	1.27
1.2716	1.27
1.2726	1.27
1.2736	1.27
1.2746	1.27
1.2756	1.28
1.2766	1.28
1.2776	1.28
1.2786	1.28
1.2796	1.28

To state the rule in words—If the right-most digit that you want to retain has a 5, 6, 7, 8, or 9 to *its* immediate right, the retained digit will be rounded up (increased by one). But if that digit is a 0, 1, 2, 3, or 4, the retained digit will *not* be rounded up.

You may find it interesting to know that the way the computer rounds is to simply add a 5 to the left-most digit that's going to be lost. This is done while the value is still in the arithmetic unit and just prior to moving it to the receiving-item's memory location. Consider these two examples, both of which assume a receiving-item of only 2 decimal digits:

Unrounded true values:	1.2746	1.2756
5 added to 3rd dec. digit:	+ 5	+ 5
Values to be moved:	1.2796	1.2806
Values as stored in receiving-item:	1.27	1.28

Figure 11.6 demonstrates further the functioning of the ROUNDED option.

11.7 The ON SIZE ERROR Clause

Let's start out again with an example to point out what a SIZE ERROR is: Suppose you had these three items in your DATA DIVISION:

```
02  A  PICTURE 999V9.
02  B  PICTURE 999V9.
02  C  PICTURE 999V9.
```

	Data-Name: PICTURE:	A 99	B 99V9	C 9V99	D V999
ADD B TO A.	Before:	15,	256	301	,008
	After:	40,	256	301	,008
ADD B TO A, ROUNDED.	Before:	15,	256	301	,008
	After:	41,	256	301	,008
ADD B, C GIVING A.	Before:	15,	256	301	,008
	After:	28,	256	301	,008
ADD B, C GIVING A, ROUNDED.	Before:	15,	256	301	,008
	After:	29,	256	301	,008
ADD C TO B.	Before:	15,	256	301	,008
	After:	15,	286	301	,008
ADD C TO B, ROUNDED.	Before:	15,	256	301	,008
	After:	15,	286	301	,008
DIVIDE 4 INTO A, ROUNDED.	Before:	15,	256	301	,008
	After:	04,	256	301	,008
DIVIDE 4 INTO A GIVING B, ROUNDED.	Before:	15,	256	301	,008
	After:	15,	038	301	,008
DIVIDE 4 INTO A GIVING C, ROUNDED.	Before:	15,	256	301	,008
	After:	15,	256	375	,008
ADD D TO C, ROUNDED.	Before:	15,	256	301	,008
	After:	15,	256	302	,008
ADD D TO B, ROUNDED.	Before:	15,	256	301	,008
	After:	15,	256	301	,008

FIGURE 11.6   The Effect of the ROUNDED Option

and that as a result of a READ statement or earlier arithmetic statements, the three memory locations were loaded like this:

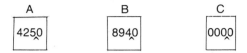

Suppose the next statement to be executed was:

ADD A, B GIVING C.

As a result of that ADD statement, the computer would send the values of A (4250) and B (8940) to the arithmetic unit and direct that they be added:

$$4250 + 8940 = 13190$$

Next the computer would perform a numeric move of 13190 to C's memory location, and this would be the result:

```
      A              B              C
  ┌───────┐      ┌───────┐      ┌───────┐
  │ 4250  │      │ 8940  │      │ 3190  │
  └───────┘      └───────┘      └───────┘
```

The thousands digit was lost! We have here what is called a SIZE ERROR—the receiving-field does not have enough digit positions on the *left* of the decimal point to hold the result of the arithmetic operation.

A SIZE ERROR is a fairly serious thing, because the computer will make no mention of it, and (in the example above) it would proceed on with the remainder of the program believing that the correct value of C was 319 instead of 1319. Imagine the havoc that could play with the accuracy of your program's output!

Most good programmers would never let this sort of thing happen. They would have made generous estimates ahead of time of the maximum size of all values their data-names would have to be able to handle, and as a result would have given their data-names PICTURE clauses of sufficient size.

There may come a time, however, when you feel uncertain about your size estimates for one reason or another. When that happens you will want to tell the computer to keep its "eyes open" for any SIZE ERRORs that might occur. You will also want to tell it what to do in the event that one occurs. The ON SIZE ERROR clause is used for that purpose. It has this form:

> ON SIZE ERROR imperative-statement.

The clause is placed at the end of the arithmetic statement, following ROUNDED if it is used. The imperative statement is where you tell the computer what you want it to do if a SIZE ERROR occurs. An example:

MULTIPLY D BY E GIVING F, ROUNDED, ON SIZE ERROR GO TO LAST-PARA.

The ROUNDED is optional, of course, as are the commas.

11.8   Intermediate Results

In Chapter 10 when I introduced you to the uses of the WORKING-STORAGE SECTION, I pointed out that it was used for the storage of intermediate results. I'd now like to use a simple example program to demonstrate this concept.

Let's write a program to calculate employee pay. For input we'll use data cards, one for each employee, and each card containing data as described here:

CARD COLUMNS	INFORMATION	PICTURE
1–20	Name	A(20)
21–23	Total hours worked	99V9
24–27	Pay rate	99V99
28–80	Blank	X(53)

Or as we will describe it in the DATA DIVISION's FILE SECTION:

```
FD  CARD-FILE; RECORD CONTAINS 80 CHARACTERS; LABEL RECORDS ARE
    OMITTED; DATA RECORD IS EMPLOYEE-CARD.
01  EMPLOYEE-CARD.
    02  NAME-IN     PICTURE A(20).
    02  TOTAL-HRS   PICTURE 99V9.
    02  PAY-RATE    PICTURE 99V99.
    02  FILLER      PICTURE X(53).
```

The detail lines to be printed on the line printer are each to be in this form:

PRINT POSITIONS	INFORMATION	PICTURE
1– 51	Blank	X(51)
52– 76	Name followed by 5 spaces	A(20)B(5)
77– 85	Total pay	$$,$$$.99
86–136	Blank	X(51)

Or as we will describe it in the WORKING-STORAGE SECTION:

```
01  DETAIL-LINE.
    02  FILLER     PICTURE X(51) VALUE SPACES.
    02  NAME-DL    PICTURE A(20)B(5).
    02  TOTAL-PAY  PICTURE $$,$$$.99.
    02  FILLER     PICTURE X(51) VALUE SPACES.
```

Each employee's total pay is to be calculated according to these rules:

1.   Regular wages are to be paid for only the first 40 hours.

2. Overtime wages are to be paid for any hours over 40.

3. The overtime pay rate is equal to 1½ times the regular pay rate.

Those three rules will become the following COBOL arithmetic statements in the PROCEDURE DIVISION of this program:

```
MULTIPLY PAY-RATE BY 40 GIVING REGULAR-EARNINGS.
MULTIPLY 1.5 BY PAY RATE GIVING OVERTIME-RATE.
SUBTRACT 40 FROM TOTAL-HRS GIVING OVERTIME-HOURS.
MULTIPLY OVERTIME-RATE BY OVERTIME-HOURS
     GIVING OVERTIME-EARNINGS.
ADD REGULAR-EARNINGS, OVERTIME-EARNINGS GIVING TOTAL-PAY.
```

Look through those five statements. Notice that they contain data-names from the input record (TOTAL-HRS and PAY-RATE) and a data-name from the detail line (TOTAL-PAY). But those three are not the only data-names you see. In order to go from TOTAL-HRS and PAY-RATE to TOTAL-PAY, we must first calculate REGULAR-EARNINGS, then the OVERTIME-RATE, OVERTIME-HOURS, and OVERTIME-EARNINGS. Only after those intermediate calculations have been made are we able to add REGULAR-EARNINGS and OVERTIME-EARNINGS to get TOTAL-PAY.

The results of such intermediate calculations must be stored somewhere in the memory unit until they are needed. We also are faced with the problem that those arithmetic statements represent PROCEDURE DIVISION sentences which contain data-names not now included in the DATA DIVISION. (Do you remember from Chapter 5 that every data-name you plan to use in your PROCEDURE DIVISION *must* be described somewhere in your DATA DIVISION?) Independent (or 77 level) items are used to fulfill both of those needs. In this example program, we'd need these four 77 level entries:

```
77   REGULAR-EARNINGS    PICTURE 999V99.
77   OVERTIME-RATE       PICTURE 99V99.
77   OVERTIME-HOURS      PICTURE 99V9.
77   OVERTIME-EARNINGS   PICTURE 999V99.
```

IDENTIFICATION and ENVIRONMENT DIVISIONs omitted.

```
300 DATA DIVISION.
310 FILE SECTION.
320 FD   CARD-FILE; RECORD CONTAINS 80 CHARACTERS; LABEL RECORDS ARE
330      OMITTED; DATA RECORD IS EMPLOYEE-CARD.
340 01   EMPLOYEE-CARD.
350      02   NAME-IN         PICTURE A(20).
360      02   TOTAL-HRS       PICTURE 99V9.
370      02   PAY-RATE        PICTURE 99V99.
380      02   FILLER          PICTURE X(53).
390 FD   PRINT-FILE; RECORD CONTAINS 136 CHARACTERS; LABEL RECORDS
400      ARE OMITTED; DATA RECORD IS PRINT-LINE.
410 01   PRINT-LINE          PICTURE X(136).
420 WORKING-STORAGE SECTION.
430 77   REGULAR-EARNINGS    PICTURE 999V99.
```

```
440 77  OVERTIME-RATE      PICTURE 99V99.
450 77  OVERTIME-HOURS     PICTURE 99V9.
460 77  OVERTIME-EARNINGS  PICTURE 999V99.
470 01  DETAIL-LINE.
480     02  FILLER         PICTURE X(51) VALUE SPACES.
490     02  NAME-DL        PICTURE A(20)B(5).
500     02  TOTAL-PAY      PICTURE $$,$$$.99.
510     02  FILLER         PICTURE X(51) VALUE SPACES.
520 PROCEDURE DIVISION.
530 OPEN-PARA.
540     OPEN INPUT CARD-FILE, OUTPUT PRINT-FILE.
550 READ-CALCULATE-PRINT-PARA.
560     READ CARD-FILE RECORD AT END GO TO LAST-PARA.
570     MOVE NAME-IN TO NAME-DL.
580     MULTIPLY PAY-RATE BY 40 GIVING REGULAR-EARNINGS.
590     MULTIPLY 1.5 BY PAY-RATE GIVING OVERTIME-RATE, ROUNDED.
600     SUBTRACT 40 FROM TOTAL-HRS GIVING OVERTIME-HOURS.
610     MULTIPLY OVERTIME-RATE BY OVERTIME-HOURS
620         GIVING OVERTIME-EARNINGS.
630     ADD REGULAR-EARNINGS, OVERTIME-EARNINGS GIVING TOTAL-PAY,
640         ON SIZE ERROR GO TO LAST-PARA.
650     WRITE PRINT-LINE FROM DETAIL-LINE.
660     GO TO READ-CALCULATE-PRINT-PARA.
670 LAST-PARA.
680     CLOSE CARD-FILE PRINT-FILE.
690     STOP RUN.
```

FIGURE 11.7   Program Demonstrating the Use of 77 Level Entries[2]

The program in its entirety is shown in Figure 11.7. It demonstrates the use of 77 level items as well as several other points that have been made in this chapter. I'd like to call those points to your attention.

First, note that all 77 level entries are placed first in the WORKING-STORAGE SECTION. This is a requirement mentioned in Chapter 10 which you may have forgotten.

Second, notice that I have followed the advice I gave you in Chapter 10: I have given a simplified description of my output file and record in the FILE SECTION (at seq. nos. 390–410), described my detail line in WORKING-STORAGE (at seq. nos. 470–510), and used a WRITE FROM statement (at seq. no. 650) for the printing of each line of output.

Third, notice my use of ROUNDED in the MULTIPLY statement at seq. no. 590. I did that because I was multiplying 1.5 times PAY-RATE (which had a PICTURE of 99V99) and giving the result to OVERTIME-RATE (which also had a PICTURE of 99V99). Suppose PAY-RATE had a value like 2.65. If you multiply 1.5 by 2.65 you get 3.975, but the PICTURE of OVERTIME-RATE allows for only two decimal digits. What do we do with the 3rd decimal digit? My using ROUNDED shows that I decided not to simply "amputate" the last digit, but rather to have the value rounded to

[2] This program was written based upon the simplifying assumption that every employee worked at least 40 hours a week. If this were not so, the program would not work.

two decimal digits, a decision which will work in favor of the employee. If the employee's PAY-RATE had been 2.65, he would be paid 3.98 per hour for overtime instead of 3.97.

Fourth, notice my use of an ON SIZE ERROR clause at seq. no. 640. I used it here to cover the rare possibility that a person's pay might greatly exceed my expectations. If such a thing were to occur, this clause would prevent an incorrect result from being printed out by branching to the LAST-PARA where the program would stop.

Finally, notice that at seq. no. 630 you see for the first time an example of a Form II arithmetic statement in which the receiving-item is Class NE. This is the characteristic occasion to do such a thing—when a calculation produces a final result that will not be further involved in other calculations. The GIVING clause of such an arithmetic statement will reference the name of an edited item in the output line, and hence the need for a separate MOVE before printing that value is eliminated.

11.9 The Question of Accuracy

You cannot avoid it. The accuracy of a program's output is ultimately the responsibility of the programmer. In Chapter 7 I mentioned briefly some of the errors a programmer can make in writing a program. They range all the way from the most flagrant down to the most subtle. In Chapter 7 the errors discussed fell in the flagrant category—spelling errors and COBOL grammar errors. They were errors which the computer can detect and for which it will give error messages.

Now that you have arithmetic statements at your disposal, a whole world of much more subtle errors has opened up to you. What's especially troublesome about this category of errors is that the computer is *unable* to detect them and so gives *no* error messages as a result. The only evidence that they have occurred is in the inaccuracy of the answers which are printed on the line printer. I'd like to discuss two of these more subtle errors with you now: Algorithmic Errors and Truncation and Round-off Errors.

Algorithmic Errors   These are the errors which arise out of your having incorrectly instructed the computer in the order or kind of calculations it is to perform.

Remember that the computer is not human. It does not know from its "life's experience" as you and I do that (for example) to calculate a person's weekly pay, you have to *multiply* the person's pay rate by the number of hours she worked. So if you tell the computer to perform this nonsensical calculation:

SUBTRACT PAY-RATE FROM TOTAL-HOURS GIVING TOTAL-PAY.

it will do exactly as it is told to do and the total pay it calculates will be grossly in error. It has no way of knowing that the statement was in error—from its point of view it was *not* in error. There were no misspellings; there were no grammatical errors.

Though it would take a mighty stupid person intentionally to write a statement like that one, it is characteristic of a type of error which many programmers make by accident. Often it occurs because the programmer's mind is wandering to other thoughts while writing his program. Since writing a program onto a coding form is a fairly mechanical process, it is easier than you might imagine for your mind to wander while doing it and for you to copy mindlessly elements of a preceding line into the line you are writing. The best defense against this sort of error is to perform a good "desk check" of your coding forms before you punch their contents onto cards. Proof read them carefully, and blunders such as the one above will stick out like sore thumbs.

It is also possible to make errors such as the one above if you do not yourself understand the way the program *should* be written. If you have no idea how (for example) interest on a mortgage is calculated, you must first learn how to perform the calculations yourself before setting out to write a program which involves such calculations. If you start to write a program to instruct the computer to perform calculations which you don't know how to perform yourself, you are guilty of stupidity equal to that of the person who sits down behind the wheel of a car to take a trip, but doesn't know how to drive the car.

Truncation and Round-Off Errors These are the errors that arise out of your failure to retain all digits generated by an arithmetic operation.

When you perform an intermediate calculation on the computer and then fail to retain every last digit generated by that calculation, you inject a truncation or round-off error into the intermediate result. That error is then carried forward into all subsequent calculations which depend upon that intermediate result. Regrettably, the effect of that error tends to balloon as it is carried forward into more and more subsequent calculations, to the point where it can materially damage the accuracy of the final result.

Here's an example based loosely on the program of the last section: Suppose a worker were paid at the rate of $2.75 an hour, and he worked 25 hours of overtime during the course of a week. To calculate his overtime earnings, we'd first calculate his overtime rate (1½ times his regular rate):

$$1½ \times \$2.75 = \$4.125$$

In the last section we decided to keep only two decimal digits after we'd calculated the overtime pay rate. What should be done with the third decimal digit? Well, we have two choices—truncate it or round it off. If we truncate it we will calculate his overtime earnings to be

$$\$4.12 \times 25 \text{ hrs} = \$103.00$$

If we round it off we will calculate his overtime to be

$$\$4.13 \times 25 \text{ hrs} = \$103.25$$

There's a 25¢ difference between the two. Which approach should we use?

If the worker's a friend of yours, he wants the $103.25 and if you don't give it to him, you might lose a friend. On the other hand, the boss would prefer he be paid the $103.00 and if you don't, you might lose a job. It's not so much that the boss is a cheap so-and-so. He's got hundreds if not thousands of workers on his payroll and if he pays a large number of them 25¢ extra every week, it'll soon amount to a tidy sum. Actually, the best approach and the approach which *no one* can find fault with, is the one which produces the *most accurate* result.

In fact both values, $103.00 and $103.25, were inaccurate to a certain degree. The $103.00 incorporated the effects of a truncation error. The $103.25 incorporated the effects of a round-off error. As I said earlier, such errors tend to balloon as the program moves along. (Round-off errors on the average create smaller inaccuracies than do truncation errors, but they do create inaccuracies nonetheless.)

The best solution to the dilemma is to avoid truncations and round-offs as much as possible, and to postpone those which are unavoidable to as late in the program as possible. Make provisions in your 77 level entries' PICTURE clauses for extra decimal digits so that all digits generated can be retained. Put off your truncation and/or round-offs until the last possible moment.

In the example we've been using here, it would have been wiser to describe OVERTIME-RATE like this:

    77   OVERTIME-RATE   PICTURE 99V999.

since we knew it was possible for the calculation of OVERTIME-RATE to produce three decimal digits. Then when a calculation of an OVERTIME-RATE produced a value with three decimal digits (such as 4125), all three digits would have been kept. Then later OVERTIME-EARNINGS would be calculated like this:

$$4125 \times 25 = 103125$$

which is accurate to the tenth of a penny. This indicates a need for extra decimal digits in OVERTIME-EARNINGS as well:

    77   OVERTIME-EARNINGS   PICTURE 999V999.

If you follow my advice, you will have postponed using the ROUNDED option to the last of the computational steps:

    ADD   REGULAR-EARNINGS,   OVERTIME-EARNINGS   GIVING   TOTAL-PAY,
        ROUNDED.

To be perfectly accurate, you wouldn't even round there except for the practical reality that you don't pay people to the nearest tenth of a penny.

11.10   This Chapter's Example Programs

Unlike the preceding and following chapters, this chapter is followed by *two* Example Programs and a Student's Program. The two Example Programs

are of special importance to you, because in addition to reinforcing the
teaching points of this chapter, they present two programming techniques
which were *not* discussed in the chapter: "Summing" and "Counting."
You'll be using these two techniques frequently as you move forward from
here, so it's important that you master them now.

EXERCISES

Answers to all exercises in this chapter are given in Appendix A.

11.1 TRUE or FALSE
    a. All data items which are operands in arithmetic operations must be Class Numeric.
    b. If the ROUNDED option is not used, truncation of digits which overhang the right end of the receiving-item will occur.
    c. Repeated truncation of intermediate results will have no effect on the accuracy of the final answer.
    d. If in doubt of the algebraic sign of the computed result, an S should be added to the PICTURE clause.
    e. The computer will always provide a message to the programmer if any significant high order digits are lost due to undersized PICTURE clauses.

11.2 Indicate whether the following arithmetic statements are correct or incorrect. If incorrect, write a corrected version.
    a. ADD A AND B TO C.
    b. MULTIPLY EXEMPTIONS BY 750.00.
    c. DIVIDE A BY D.
    d. SUBTRACT $150.00 FROM GROSS-PAY.
    e. SUBTRACT A, C GIVING B.
    f. ADD C, D GIVING G.
    g. MULTIPLY EXEMPTIONS BY 750.00 GIVING EXEMPT ALLOWANCE.
    h. DIVIDE A, B INTO D.
    i. ADD BONUS TO PAY GIVING TOTAL-PAY.
    j. MULTIPLY 2.5 TIMES C GIVING D.
    k. ADD HOURS-WORKED TO 10.
    l. ADD 10. TO HOURS-WORKED.
    m. MOVE TOTAL TO TOTAL-OUT, ROUNDED.

11.3 Given initial values of A, B, and C as shown:

A	B	C
10	20	40

    a. What would be stored as a result of:
ADD A, B TO C

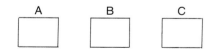

    b. And as a result of:
ADD A, B GIVING C.

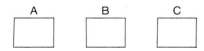

216

11.4 Give two DIVIDE statements that would cause A to be divided by B and the result stored in A.

11.5 Indicate what will be stored in A, B, and C after each of the following arithmetic statements have been executed. Consider the statements to be executed sequentially in a program, that is, the results of one statement are dependent upon the results of the previous statement.

```
77  A   PICTURE 999V9.
77  B   PICTURE 99V99.
77  C   PICTURE 999.
```

	A	B	C
a. MOVE ZERO TO A, B, C.			
b. MOVE 565.8 TO C.			
c. MOVE C TO A.			
d. ADD C TO B.			
e. DIVIDE 2.0 INTO B.			
f. MOVE B TO A.			
g. DIVIDE 2.0 INTO A, ROUNDED.			
h. SUBTRACT 560 FROM C.			
i. MULTIPLY 5 BY B.			
j. ADD 5, A GIVING C.			
k. MULTIPLY C BY 10.0 GIVING A.			
l. SUBTRACT 60.5, C FROM B.			

11.6 Indicate what will be stored in A, B, C, D, and E after each of the following arithmetic statements have been executed:

```
77  A   PICTURE   999       VALUE 100.
77  B   PICTURE   999V99    VALUE 30.15.
77  C   PICTURE   9(4)      VALUE ZERO.
77  D   PICTURE   999V9     VALUE 250.5.
77  E   PICTURE   S999      VALUE -35.
```

a. Show the contents of the memory locations as a result of the VALUE clauses.
b. ADD 55.01, B TO D, ROUNDED.
c. DIVIDE 4 INTO A.
d. MULTIPLY 100 BY A ON SIZE ERROR MOVE E TO A.
e. SUBTRACT A FROM B GIVING C.
f. ADD B, D TO C, ROUNDED.
g. MULTIPLY 2 BY E ON SIZE ERROR MOVE ZERO TO E.
h. DIVIDE D BY 3 GIVING B.
i. SUBTRACT E FROM A.

	A	B	C	D	E
a.					
b.					
c.					
d.					
e.					
f.					
g.					
h.					
i.					

EXAMPLE PROGRAM

Ordering Repair Parts

Each card in a data deck contains a part number, the quantity of that item on hand at the end of the week, the prescribed stockage level, and the cost per part, all in this format:

CARD COLUMNS	ITEM	EXAMPLE
1–5	Part number	P7462
10–13	Quantity on hand	0035 (35 are on hand)
18–21	Prescribed stockage level	0050 (50 should be on hand)
25–30	Cost per item	000451 (They cost $4.51 each)

Write a program which will produce an edited listing with column headings as follows:

PART NUMBER	QUANTITY ON HAND	QUANTITY TO ORDER	TOTAL COST OF ORDER
P7462	35	15	$67.65
T1340	115	0	$ 0.00
Q7613	75	5	$10.75
etc.	etc.	etc.	etc.

At the end of the listing, print a total quantity of all parts to be ordered and the total cost of all such orders:

THE TOTAL COST OF ALL ORDERS IS $XX,XXX,XXX,XXX.XX

Some suggested contents for trial data cards:

P7462	0035	0050	000451
T1340	0115	0115	000063
Q7613	0075	0080	000215
S3891	0026	0030	001550
A6209	0015	0105	000025
C2341	1315	1400	000008
X0043	0063	0065	012530
M1163	0010	0020	007500
H4002	0035	0035	000933

H7310	0016	0020	001175
L0566	0002	0005	023115
J1025	0153	0160	000359
P3334	0081	0095	001860

Solution

IDENTIFICATION and ENVIRONMENT DIVISIONs are omitted.

```
DATA DIVISION.
FILE SECTION.
FD  PART-FILE; LABEL RECORDS ARE OMITTED; RECORD CONTAINS 80
    CHARACTERS; DATA RECORD IS ITEM-CARD.
01  ITEM-CARD.
    02  PART-NUMBER              PICTURE X(5).
    02  FILLER                   PICTURE X(4).
    02  QUANTITY-ON-HAND         PICTURE 9(4).
    02  FILLER                   PICTURE X(4).
    02  STOCK-LEVEL              PICTURE 9(4).
    02  FILLER                   PICTURE X(3).
    02  PART-COST                PICTURE 9(4)V99.
    02  FILLER                   PICTURE X(50).
FD  PRINT-FILE; LABEL RECORDS ARE OMITTED; RECORD CONTAINS 136
    CHARACTERS; DATA RECORD IS PRINT-REC.
01  PRINT-REC                    PICTURE X(136).
WORKING-STORAGE SECTION.
77  QUANTITY-TO-ORDER-WS         PICTURE 9(4).
77  COST-OF-ORDER-WS             PICTURE 9(8)V99.
77  TOTAL-COST-WS                PICTURE 9(11)V99 VALUE ZERO.
01  PAGE-EJECT.
    02  FILLER                   PICTURE X(136) VALUE '1'.
01  HEADING-1.
    02  FILLER                   PICTURE X(37)   VALUE SPACES.
    02  FILLER                   PICTURE X(11)   VALUE 'PART NUMBER'.
    02  FILLER                   PICTURE X(5)    VALUE SPACES.
    02  FILLER                   PICTURE X(8)    VALUE 'QUANTITY'.
    02  FILLER                   PICTURE X(6)    VALUE SPACES.
    02  FILLER                   PICTURE X(8)    VALUE 'QUANTITY'.
    02  FILLER                   PICTURE X(9)    VALUE SPACES.
    02  FILLER                   PICTURE X(10)   VALUE 'TOTAL COST'.
    02  FILLER                   PICTURE X(42)   VALUE SPACES.
01  HEADING-2.
    02  FILLER                   PICTURE X(54)   VALUE SPACES.
    02  FILLER                   PICTURE X(7)    VALUE 'ON HAND'.
    02  FILLER                   PICTURE X(6)    VALUE SPACES.
    02  FILLER                   PICTURE X(8)    VALUE 'TO ORDER'.
    02  FILLER                   PICTURE X(10)   VALUE SPACES.
    02  FILLER                   PICTURE X(8)    VALUE 'OF ORDER'.
    02  FILLER                   PICTURE X(43)   VALUE SPACES.
01  DETAIL-LINE.
    02  FILLER                   PICTURE X(40)   VALUE SPACES.
    02  PART-NUMBER              PICTURE X(5).
    02  FILLER                   PICTURE X(10)   VALUE SPACES.
    02  QUANTITY-ON-HAND         PICTURE ZZZ9.
    02  FILLER                   PICTURE X(10)   VALUE SPACES.
    02  QUANTITY-TO-ORDER-DL     PICTURE ZZZ9.
```

```
    02  FILLER                   PICTURE X(7)    VALUE SPACES.
    02  COST-OF-ORDER-DL         PICTURE $$$,$$$,$$9.99.
    02  FILLER                   PICTURE X(42)   VALUE SPACES.
01  TOTAL-LINE.
    02  FILLER                   PICTURE X(43)   VALUE SPACES.
    02  FILLER                   PICTURE X(32)
        VALUE 'THE TOTAL COST OF ALL ORDERS IS '.
    02  TOTAL-COST               PICTURE $$$,$$$,$$$,$$9.99.
    02  FILLER                   PICTURE X(43)   VALUE SPACES.
PROCEDURE DIVISION.
OPEN-PARA.
    OPEN INPUT PART-FILE, OUTPUT PRINT-FILE.
PRINT-HEADINGS-PARA.
    WRITE PRINT-REC FROM PAGE-EJECT.
    WRITE PRINT-REC FROM HEADING-1 BEFORE ADVANCING 1 LINES.
    WRITE PRINT-REC FROM HEADING-2 BEFORE ADVANCING 2 LINES.
READ-CALCULATE-PRINT-PARA.
    READ PART-FILE RECORD AT END GO TO PRINT-FINAL-LINE-PARA.
    MOVE CORR ITEM-CARD TO DETAIL-LINE.
    SUBTRACT QUANTITY-ON-HAND OF ITEM-CARD FROM STOCK-LEVEL
        GIVING QUANTITY-TO-ORDER-WS.
    MOVE QUANTITY-TO-ORDER-WS TO QUANTITY-TO-ORDER-DL.
    MULTIPLY QUANTITY-TO-ORDER-WS BY PART-COST
        GIVING COST-OF-ORDER-WS.
    MOVE COST-OF-ORDER-WS TO COST-OF-ORDER-DL.
    ADD COST-OF-ORDER-WS TO TOTAL-COST-WS.
    WRITE PRINT-REC FROM DETAIL-LINE.
    GO TO READ-CALCULATE-PRINT-PARA.
PRINT-FINAL-LINE-PARA.
    MOVE TOTAL-COST-WS TO TOTAL-COST.
    WRITE PRINT-REC FROM TOTAL-LINE AFTER ADVANCING 2 LINES.
CLOSE-PARA.
    CLOSE PART-FILE, PRINT-FILE.
    STOP RUN.
```

Discussion

Aside from the computations involved, the logic is similar to that of earlier problems—a card is read, certain items are assembled in the detail-line and printed, and the process is repeated until the card file is empty.

For each part the quantity-to-be-ordered must be computed by subtracting the amount-on-hand from the required stockage level. Here we come to an important point. Although the quantity-to-be-ordered is to be printed in edited form as a part of the detail-line, it is also needed for use in the next computational step (a multiplication operation which calculates the cost-of-the-order) where it must be in purely numeric (unedited) form. To solve this problem we set up a 77-level entry called QUANTITY-TO-ORDER-WS with a purely numeric PICTURE clause and store the value there *in addition* to moving it to the edited field in the detail-line. This way we have the quantity-to-be-ordered available to us in both Class N form for later arithmetic operations as well as in Class NE form for printing on the line printer. (Note that in this case we *first* stored the quantity-to-be-ordered in the Class N item and *then* MOVEd it to the Class NE item. We could not have done it in the reverse order, because an NE to N MOVE is illegal.)

Likewise, in the next step, we need the cost-of-the-order in both Class

N and Class NE forms, so we set up another 77-level entry COST-OF-ORDER-WS with a Class N PICTURE clause. The 02-level entry COST-OF-ORDER-DL in the DETAIL-LINE provides the Class NE field.

The next step represents a programming technique which deserves your careful attention. The technique is called "summing." In this program we wanted to sum all the individual order-costs so that we could print out the grand total at the end of the program. In order to accomplish "summing" in a program, you establish a "summer" as a 77-level item in your DATA DIVISION, and then in your PROCEDURE DIVISION whenever you're ready for the next quantity to be added to the sum, you simply use an ADD TO statement in which the 1st-item is the field whose values you're summing and the receiving-item is the summer. Suppose for example, you were calculating the total weight of all baggage being loaded aboard an aircraft. On your input record you'd probably have a field called WEIGHT and on each record that field would contain the weight of the bag it represented. You'd then set up a 77-level summer called WEIGHT-SUM. In the PROCEDURE DIVISION immediately after reading each record, you'd say ADD WEIGHT TO WEIGHT-SUM. Because of the way an ADD TO statement works, each time you looped through the paragraph in which it was located, the latest value of WEIGHT would be added to the previous value stored in WEIGHT-SUM. As the execution of the program progressed, the value of WEIGHT-SUM would continue to increase as more and more WEIGHT values were added to it, until finally after all cards had been read, its value would represent the total weight of all bags.

One more thing about summing—Since it is an ADD TO statement that actually causes the summing to be performed, and since the value stored in a receiving-item by an ADD TO statement is dependent upon the value previously stored in the receiving-item, we *must* concern ourselves with what value is stored in the summer prior to the *first* occasion that the summing (ADD TO) statement is executed. Unless *you* give an initial value to a memory location, you have no assurance whatsoever of what will be stored there as the program begins execution. In order for a summer to work properly it *must* be loaded with an initial value of zero. (If a summer were by some accident initially loaded with a value of 100, for example, then the grand total it calculated would end up 100 greater than it should be.) You provide for initializing your summer at zero by a VALUE ZERO clause on its 77-level entry in the WORKING-STORAGE SECTION.

In this program our summer is TOTAL-COST-WS. Notice that it has a Class N PICTURE Clause as it *must* have, and that it has a VALUE ZERO clause. Our summing statement is "ADD COST-OF-ORDER-WS TO TOTAL-COST-WS." Summing of the order-costs is complete after the last data card has been processed, and not before, so we do not print the value of the total-order-cost as a part of the READ-CALCULATE-PRINT-PARA. If we had, then a long list of total-order-costs would have been printed, none of which would have been correct except the last. After the last data card has been processed, we branch to the PRINT-FINAL-LINE-PARA, so that is the logical place to include the statements necessary to print the value of TOTAL-COST-WS.

No ROUNDED options were employed in this program, because there was no arithmetic operation which would have generated more than two decimal digits. Since two decimal digits were to be used throughout, there was no need for either truncating or rounding.

EXAMPLE PROGRAM

Course Grades

In several courses I teach, I calculate a numerical course grade for each student based upon the following formulas:

```
Homework Points      = .15 × Homework Average
Midterm Exam Points  = .35 × Midterm Exam Grade
Final Exam Points     = .50 × Final Exam Grade
Course Grade = Homework Points + Midterm Exam Points
                    + Final Exam Points
```

The homework average and the two exam grades can each be up to a maximum of 100 points. The maximum course grade a student can achieve is therefore 100 points.

Write a program that will accept a data deck of unknown size, each card in the deck containing the following information:

CARD COLUMNS	INFORMATION	EXAMPLE
1–20	Student's name.	JAMES P. ALBO
21–23	Homework average.	095 (95 points)
24–26	Midterm Exam grade.	100 (100 points)
27–29	Final Exam grade.	086 (86 points)
30–80	Blank	

The program is to calculate each student's course grade, count the number of students in the class, and calculate the class average. The detail-lines are to be arranged under column headings as shown here:

STUDENT	HOMEWORK AVERAGE	MIDTERM GRADE	FINAL EXAM GRADE	COURSE GRADE
JAMES P. ALBO	95	100	86	92
WILLIAM F. DAUGHERTY	82	90	89	88
FLORA M. DESCENZA	71	81	93	86
etc.	etc.	etc.	etc.	etc.

Following the detail-lines is to be a report-footing in this form:

CLASS CONTAINED XXX STUDENTS. CLASS AVERAGE = XX.X

Some suggested contents for trial data cards:

JAMES P. ALBO	095100086
WILLIAM F. DAUGHERTY	082090089
FLORA M. DESCENZA	071081093
ELIZABETH FINKENAUR	063059071
LELAND G. FREEMAN	100100100
PATTY LOU HALPIN	090075080
JOSEPH HECK	000090090
SUSAN HORNBARGER	094085087

Solution

IDENTIFICATION and ENVIRONMENT DIVISIONs omitted.

```
DATA DIVISION.
FILE SECTION.
FD   STUDENT-FILE; RECORD CONTAINS 80 CHARACTERS; LABEL RECORDS
     ARE OMITTED; DATA RECORD IS GRADE-REC.
01   GRADE-REC.
     02   NAME                 PICTURE A(20).
     02   HW-AVE               PICTURE 999.
     02   MTEX-GRADE           PICTURE 999.
     02   FINEX-GRADE          PICTURE 999.
     02   FILLER               PICTURE X(51).
FD   PRINT-FILE; RECORD CONTAINS 136 CHARACTERS; LABEL RECORDS ARE
     OMITTED; DATA RECORD IS PRINT-LINE.
01   PRINT-LINE               PICTURE X(136).
WORKING-STORAGE SECTION.
77   HW-POINTS                PICTURE 99V99.
77   MTEX-POINTS              PICTURE 99V99.
77   FINEX-POINTS             PICTURE 99V99.
77   COURSE-GRADE-WS          PICTURE 999.
77   GRADE-TOTAL              PICTURE 9(5)   VALUE ZERO.
77   STUDENT-COUNT-WS         PICTURE 999    VALUE ZERO.
01   COL-HEAD-1.
     02   FILLER              PICTURE X(43) VALUE '1'.
     02   FILLER              PICTURE A(16) VALUE 'STUDENT'.
     02   FILLER              PICTURE A(77)
          VALUE 'HOMEWORK    MIDTERM    FINAL EXAM    COURSE'.
01   COL-HEAD-2.
     02   FILLER              PICTURE X(60) VALUE SPACES.
     02   FILLER              PICTURE A(76)
          VALUE 'AVERAGE    GRADE        GRADE        GRADE'.
01   DETAIL-LINE.
     02   FILLER              PICTURE X(37) VALUE SPACES.
     02   NAME                PICTURE A(20)B(4).
     02   HW-AVE              PICTURE Z99B(8).
     02   MTEX-GRADE          PICTURE Z99B(9).
     02   FINEX-GRADE         PICTURE Z99B(8).
     02   COURSE-GRADE-DL     PICTURE Z99.
     02   FILLER              PICTURE X(38) VALUE SPACES.
```

```
01   PAGE-FOOTING.
     02   FILLER                PICTURE X(43) VALUE SPACES.
     02   FILLER                PICTURE X(16)
          VALUE 'CLASS CONTAINED '.
     02   STUDENT-COUNT-PF      PICTURE ZZ9.
     02   FILLER                PICTURE X(28)
          VALUE ' STUDENTS.  CLASS AVERAGE = '.
     02   CLASS-AVE-PF          PICTURE Z99.9.
     02   FILLER                PICTURE X(42) VALUE SPACES.
PROCEDURE DIVISION.
OPEN-PARA.
     OPEN INPUT STUDENT-FILE, OUTPUT PRINT-FILE.
PRINT-HEADINGS-PARA.
     WRITE PRINT-LINE FROM COL-HEAD-1.
     WRITE PRINT-LINE FROM COL-HEAD-2.
READ-CALCULATE-PRINT-PARA.
     READ STUDENT-FILE RECORD AT END GO TO LAST-PARA.
     MOVE CORR GRADE-REC TO DETAIL-LINE.
     MULTIPLY .15 BY HW-AVE IN GRADE-REC GIVING HW-POINTS.
     MULTIPLY .35 BY MTEX-GRADE IN GRADE-REC GIVING MTEX-POINTS.
     MULTIPLY .50 BY FINEX-GRADE IN GRADE-REC GIVING FINEX-POINTS.
     ADD HW-POINTS, MTEX-POINTS, FINEX-POINTS
          GIVING COURSE-GRADE-WS, ROUNDED.
     MOVE COURSE-GRADE-WS TO COURSE-GRADE-DL.
     WRITE PRINT-LINE FROM DETAIL-LINE.
COUNT-STUDENT-PARA.
     ADD 1 TO STUDENT-COUNT-WS.
SUM-GRADES-PARA.
     ADD COURSE-GRADE-WS TO GRADE-TOTAL.
RETURN-TO-TOP-OF-LOOP-PARA.
     GO TO READ-CALCULATE-PRINT-PARA.
LAST-PARA.
     MOVE STUDENT-COUNT-WS TO STUDENT-COUNT-PF.
     DIVIDE GRADE-TOTAL BY STUDENT-COUNT-WS
          GIVING CLASS-AVE-PF, ROUNDED.
     WRITE PRINT-LINE FROM PAGE-FOOTING AFTER ADVANCING 4 LINES.
     CLOSE STUDENT-FILE PRINT-FILE.
     STOP RUN.
```

Discussion

There are several noteworthy points demonstrated by this program. First, notice that in describing the COL-HEAD lines, we took advantage of the fact that when you give a VALUE to a Class AB or AN field where the VALUE contains fewer characters than the field's PICTURE provides for, the characters from the VALUE clause will be loaded into the left end of the field and the remainder of the field will be filled with spaces.

Notice the PICTURE clauses given to the independent-items HW-POINTS, MTEX-POINTS, and FINEX-POINTS. We used PICTUREs of 99V99 because these three fields will get their values from multiplication operations involving a value with two decimal digits and a value with no decimal digits. Such a multiplication will always generate a product which has two decimal digits (for example, $.15 \times 95 = 14.25$), so in keeping with advice given in the chapter, we are making provisions to keep all digits generated.

Once again COURSE-GRADE-WS was needed to provide a Class N location in which to store the course-grade for use in later arithmetic operations, in addition to the Class NE field COURSE-GRADE-DL in the DETAIL-LINE for use in printing it out. No decimal digits are provided for in either of the course-grade fields, because in describing the requirements of the program, we indicated that a whole number grade was desired.

The qualifying clause IN GRADE-REC was necessary in the three MULTIPLY statements because the 2nd-items of those statements were all non-unique data-names.

In the last Example Program we introduced you to the programming technique "summing." Once again, summing is a part of this program. The requirement was to calculate an average. You calculate an average by summing the elements and dividing that sum by the number of elements. GRADE-TOTAL was our summer here. Notice its PICTURE of 9(5). In order to avoid a SIZE ERROR, I made a generous estimate of the largest class I would ever expect to have (200 students). If every one of those 200 students got a course-grade of 100, the total of those course-grades would be 20000, so a PICTURE of 9(5) should be more than sufficient. Notice also the VALUE ZERO clause which is always necessary with summers to assure they start out with a value of zero. The summing statement in this case is "ADD COURSE-GRADE-WS TO GRADE-TOTAL."

The technique which you were promised would be described in this Example Program was "counting." As mentioned above, when you're calculating an average you need not only the sum of the elements but also a count of the number of elements there are. The programming technique of "counting" is a first cousin of "summing." To cause the computer to count anything, you set up a "counter," a 77-level entry in WORKING-STORAGE, and initialize it with a value zero, just like a summer and for the same reason. Then in the PROCEDURE DIVISION you place a counting statement immediately after the event that you want to count. A counting statement takes the form of an ADD TO statement in which you direct the computer to ADD 1 TO your counter.

Suppose that in addition to wanting to know the total weight of baggage being loaded aboard an aircraft, you also wanted to know how many pieces of baggage there were. To provide for that, you could set up a 77-level counter:

```
77  NR-OF-BAGS   PICTURE 9999   VALUE ZERO.
```

Then in the PROCEDURE DIVISION's looping paragraph, you'd place a counting statement:

```
ADD 1 TO NR-OF-BAGS.
```

immediately after the READ statement that caused the baggage data cards to be read. Every time the computer looped through that paragraph, the counting statement would cause the value stored in NR-OF-BAGS to be increased by 1. When the READ statement detected the end of the data deck, its AT END clause would cause branching over the counting statement to some later paragraph in the program, and the value stored in NR-OF-BAGS would represent the number of baggage data cards that had been read and therefore the number of bags.

In this Example Program the counter is STUDENT-COUNT-WS. It has a PICTURE of 999, in keeping with our earlier assumption that the largest number of students I could ever expect to have in a class (and therefore the largest value I would ever expect to store in STUDENT-COUNT-WS) would be 200. It is given an initial VALUE ZERO to be sure the result doesn't incorporate any other numeric value that might happen to be in that memory location when the program commences execution.

The counting statement "ADD 1 TO STUDENT-COUNT-WS." is placed right after the READ STUDENT-FILE RECORD statement where it will count the GRADE-CARDs as they are read. Since each GRADE-CARD represents one student, the result will be that STUDENT-COUNT-WS will contain the actual number of students in the class when the data deck runs out and the AT END clause causes branching to the LAST-PARA.

In the LAST-PARA the division necessary to calculate the average is performed, and the student-count and class-average are moved to the DETAIL-LINE for printing.

STUDENT'S PROGRAM

Real Estate Taxes

Real estate taxes pay the way for schools, services, and other essential activities that are maintained by your community. The annual rate of taxation is usually expressed as a dollar amount per each $1000 of owned property. The total value of the property is the sum of the assessed values of the land and any buildings on it (usually house and garage). For example, if you hold property valued as follows:

Land	$ 8000
Garage	950
House	16300
Total	$25250

Then, if the tax rate is $57 per $1000, your tax bill for the year will equal $1439.25. Make sure you understand this computation. In addition, tax rates are usually expressed as a school rate plus a general rate. In other words, the $57 tax rate used here might consist of $35.50 for schools plus $21.50 general.

Write a program which will compute and print the total taxes for each residential property owned in your town. The input consists of one card with the school and general rates per $1000 in this format:

CARD COLUMNS	ITEM	EXAMPLE	
1–5	School Tax Rate	03550	($35.50)
6–10	General Rate	02150	($21.50)
11–80	Blank		

Subsequent cards contain the assessed property values, each card as follows:

CARD COLUMNS	ITEM	EXAMPLE	
1–5	Lot number	00056	
6–35	Location	63 ELM ST	
36–41	Value of land	008000	($8,000)
42–47	Value of house	016300	($16,300)
48–53	Value of garage and other buildings	000950	($950)
54–80	Blank		

228

The output should contain the information indicated by the following column headings and sample detail line:

ASSESSED VALUES

LOCATION	LOT	LAND	HOUSE	GARAGE	TOTAL	TAXES
63 ELM ST	56	$8,000	$16,300	$950	$25,250	$1,439.25
211 OAK ST	33	$10,000	$35,500	$1,250	$47,250	$2,693.25
etc.	etc.	etc.	etc.	etc.	etc.	etc.

In addition, at the bottom print the total taxes collected for schools, the total collected as general, the average tax bill, and the tax rates contained on card one:

```
TOTAL SCHOOL TAXES    $XXX,XXX,XXX.XX
TOTAL GENERAL TAXES   $XXX,XXX,XXX.XX
AVERAGE TAX BILL           $XX,XXX.XX
BASED ON A TAX RATE PER $1000 OF
        $XXX.XX   SCHOOL
        $XXX.XX   GENERAL
```

Use the following test data:

School tax rate		$35.50		
General tax rate		$21.50		

Lot	Location	Land	House	Garage
56	63 Elm St	$ 8,000	$ 16,300	$ 950
33	211 Oak St	10,000	35,500	1,250
66	17 Franklin Ave	15,000	53,000	1,300
15	15 Woodland Ave	21,500	43,500	1,500
100	367 Douglas Blvd	7,500	13,000	None
25	713 Main St	18,500	29,500	1,100
213	12 Forest Dr	31,000	115,000	2,500
125	333 Lake Ave	12,500	36,500	1,450
150	410 Anderson St	9,500	17,500	None
310	5 Shady Ln	13,000	22,500	1,650
111	78 Clifton Pk	6,200	15,000	730

12 A First Look at Conditional Statements: The IF Statement

12.1 Introduction

In the early chapters of this book, I pointed out that the characteristic which makes a computer truly unique among computing machines is its ability to receive and store all the instructions it will need in the course of solving a complex problem and then to follow those instructions completely independent of human assistance. Actually, that unique ability goes a significant step farther than simply an ability to blindly obey a list of stored instructions. It is even possible to give the computer instructions which cover a variety of conditions it might encounter as it solves the problem, and include a different action for each of those possible conditions.

This type of instruction is called a conditional statement. A conditional statement calls upon the computer to make a decision and then based upon that decision, to take the proper action from among a group of possible actions provided by the programmer.

It is this sort of statement that allows a programmer to write (for example) a checking account maintenance program wherein the computer is told to ascertain first whether the amount of a check is less than the balance remaining in the account prior to processing the check (subtracting its amount from the balance). The computer can be told that if it comes across a check whose amount exceeds the balance in the account, it should not process the check but rather "bounce" it.

Thanks to conditional statements, our programs do not have to be locked into a single set of pre-assumptions, but can be written to handle a variety of unpredictable situations and still leave the computer with its ability to act without human assistance.

The IF statement is not the only conditional statement in COBOL, but it is by far the most frequently used of those available. Here is an example of a correct IF statement:

```
IF ACCOUNT-BALANCE IS LESS THAN AMOUNT-ON-CHECK GO TO BOUNCE-PARA,
ELSE SUBTRACT AMOUNT-ON-CHECK FROM ACCOUNT-BALANCE.
```

This chapter will concern itself exclusively with the IF statement in its most elementary form, concentrating on how its parts are constructed and how the computer reacts to it.

12.2   The Clauses of the IF Statement

The IF statement is actually made up of three clauses:

1.   The IF Clause, which contains the condition to be considered.
2.   The True Clause, which contains the statement to be executed if the condition is true.
3.   The optional False Clause, which contains the statement to be executed if the condition is false.

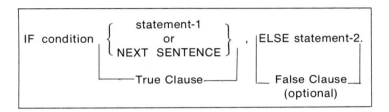

We'll talk about how conditions are written in the next section. For now, just so you'll have an idea of what I mean when I speak of a true or false condition, consider this simple example condition:

A > B

If A had a value of 10 and B had a value of 5, that condition would be true. If, however, A had a value of 5 and B had a value of 10, the condition would be false.

Here in its simplest form is the way an IF statement works: If the condition is true, statement-1 will be executed, statement-2 will be ignored, and the computer will continue on to the next sentence in the program. If the condition is false, statement-1 will be ignored, statement-2 will be executed, and the computer will continue on to the next sentence in the program. Consider these two example sentences from a COBOL program:

IF A > B ADD A TO C, ELSE ADD B TO C.
MOVE C TO D.

Statements to Be Executed If A > B Is	
True	False
ADD A TO C MOVE C TO D	ADD B TO C MOVE C TO D

There is a slight difference in what I said above if the statement executed is a GO TO statement. In that case the computer will not continue on to the next sentence following the IF statement after it executes the GO TO statement. Again, consider some example statements:

```
IF A > B GO TO PARA-2, ELSE ADD B TO C.
    ADD C TO D.
PARA-2.
    MOVE D TO E.
```

Statements to Be Executed If A > B Is	
True	False
GO TO PARA-2 MOVE D TO E	ADD B TO C ADD C TO D MOVE D TO E

There are times when you want the computer to do nothing if the condition is true except to simply move on to the next sentence. If that's what you want, you simply use the NEXT SENTENCE option in the True Clause, like this:

```
IF A > B NEXT SENTENCE, ELSE ADD B TO C.
MOVE B TO D.
```

Statements to Be Executed If A > B Is	
True	False
MOVE B TO D	ADD B TO C MOVE B TO D

(Be sure you've noticed that in the last case, the True Clause simply became NEXT SENTENCE, and *not* GO TO NEXT SENTENCE or NEXT-SENTENCE.)

Likewise, there are times when you want the computer to do nothing if the condition is false except move on to the next sentence. If that's what you want, you simply *omit* the False Clause (that's why it's described as an optional clause).

```
IF A > B ADD A TO C.
MOVE B TO D.
```

Statements to Be Executed If A > B Is	
True	False
ADD A TO C MOVE B TO D	MOVE B TO D

12.3 Conditional Expressions

As you would expect, there are rules governing the writing of the conditions in IF clauses. Referred to officially as "conditional expressions," they are not restricted to use in IF statements, but find use in other statements that we will discuss later.

Conditional expressions take the following form:

$$\left\{ \begin{array}{c} \text{data-name-1} \\ \text{or} \\ \text{literal-1} \\ \text{or} \\ \text{arithmetic-expression-1}^1 \end{array} \right\} \left\{ \text{relational-operator} \right\} \left\{ \begin{array}{c} \text{data-name-2} \\ \text{or} \\ \text{literal-2} \\ \text{or} \\ \text{arithmetic-expression-2}^1 \end{array} \right\}$$

This table lists the 6 relational-operators available in COBOL and their meanings:

Relational Operators	Meaning
> IS GREATER THAN	Is greater than
NOT > IS NOT GREATER THAN	Is not greater than Is less than or equal to
< IS LESS THAN	Is less than
NOT < IS NOT LESS THAN	Is not less than Is greater than or equal to
= IS EQUAL TO	Equals
NOT = IS NOT EQUAL TO	Does not equal

[1] Arithmetic-expressions are discussed in Appendix D along with the COMPUTE verb. Only after you have mastered the COMPUTE verb should you concern yourself with using arithmetic-expressions in IF statements.

Note that you are free either to use the conventional math symbol for each operator or to spell it out. (The symbols < and > are not found on most keypunches, but you can punch the character on a card just the same. What you do is this: Using the MULT (multi-punch) and NUM buttons on the keypunch, multi-punch the arrangement of holes that will be recognized by your computer as the > or the < in the column where you want the symbol to be. On many systems, you get a > by multi-punching the 7, 8, and 11 (or 7, 8, and minus) holes; and a < by multi-punching the 0 and 12 (or zero and plus) holes. Those hole codes are not universal, however, so check with your computer center for the hole codes you should use there.)

On the left and right of the relational-operator go the "operands" of the conditional expression. As indicated earlier, either operand may be a data-name or a literal. Whatever they are, the two operands of a conditional expression should be of the same Class. If you have a Class N data-name on the left, you should have a numeric literal or a Class N data-name on the right (and vice versa). If you have a Class AN data-name on the left, you should have a non-numeric literal or a Class AN data-name on the right (and vice versa).

The following are examples of IF clauses containing correct conditional expressions:

```
IF A IS EQUAL TO B
IF NR-OF-STUDENTS NOT < 100
IF MY-PAY IS NOT GREATER THAN YOUR-PAY
IF 770.40 > FICA-TOTAL
IF TV-NETWORK NOT = 'NBC'
IF CAR-MANUF = 'CHEV'
```

The IF clause with its conditional expressions is used most often to test the relationship of one numeric quantity to another. It is by no means restricted to that use, however. *All* characters in the COBOL character set, not just the digits, have relative ranks. The letter A is considered less than B, which is less than C, etc. Likewise, the name AARONSON is "less than" ABLE, which is "less than" ADAMINSKI. That is why statements such as these are perfectly alright:

```
IF MY-GRADE = 'A' GO TO DEANS-LIST-PARA.
IF MY-GRADE < 'F' GO TO PASSED-PARA, ELSE GO TO FAILED-PARA.
```

assuming that MY-GRADE was given a PICTURE of A back in the DATA DIVISION.

If you wanted to see if two names were in alphabetical order, you could load one name into NAME-1 and the other into NAME-2 and say:

```
IF NAME-2 > NAME-1 GO TO IN-ORDER-PARA, ELSE GO TO OUT-OF-ORDER-PARA.
```

Use the negative relational operators only when you have to. They tend to be troublesome. Consider this example:

A	B
10	12

True or False: A NOT > B

After some mental gymnastics you should conclude that that expression is true. Avoid putting yourself through those gymnastics as much as possible.

12.4 Sign and Class Conditions

The conditions discussed in the last section were "Relation Conditions." There are two other types of lesser used conditional expressions available in COBOL: "Sign Conditions" and "Class Conditions."

The Sign Conditions take this form:

```
┌─────────────────────────────────────────────────────────────┐
│    ⎧  data-name            ⎫ ⎧  IS    ⎫ ⎧ POSITIVE ⎫        │
│    ⎨       or              ⎬ ⎨  or     ⎬ ⎨   or     ⎬        │
│    ⎩ arithmetic-expression ⎭ ⎩ IS NOT ⎭ ⎨  ZERO    ⎬        │
│                                          ⎨   or     ⎬        │
│                                          ⎩ NEGATIVE ⎭        │
└─────────────────────────────────────────────────────────────┘
```

That form of condition permits the use of IF statements such as these:

```
IF ACCOUNT-BALANCE IS NEGATIVE GO TO OVERDRAWN-PARA.
IF TOTAL-DEBTS IS NOT ZERO GO TO DEBTORS-PARA.
IF WEIGHT-CHANGE IS POSITIVE GO TO DIET-PARA.
```

The Class Condition takes this form:

```
┌─────────────────────────────────────────────────────┐
│              ⎧  IS    ⎫ ⎧ NUMERIC    ⎫               │
│  data-name   ⎨  or     ⎬ ⎨   or       ⎬               │
│              ⎩ IS NOT ⎭ ⎩ ALPHABETIC ⎭               │
└─────────────────────────────────────────────────────┘
```

That form of condition is provided for your use when you want to check data being input to be sure it is of the correct form. Some computers make less rigorous checks than others to see if data-values being input conform with the PICTURE clauses describing them. If your computer is one of the less rigorous ones, you might want to check especially those fields that are going to be involved in arithmetic calculations to be sure they contain only Class N data-values. You could say, for example:

```
IF PAY-RATE IS NOT NUMERIC GO TO BAD-DATA-PARA.
```

A Class Condition testing to see if a data-name IS NUMERIC will be false if the data-value being tested contains any letters or special characters. A Class Condition testing to see if a data-name IS ALPHABETIC will be false if the data-value being tested contains anything *but* letters or spaces. (Of course, there is no test for Class ALPHANUMERIC, because that would be a meaningless test—a Class AN field may contain any character, so such a test would *always* be true.)

EXERCISES

Answers to all exercises in this chapter are given in Appendix A.

12.1   Correct any of the following IF statements which are incorrect:

    a.   IF A IS LESS THEN B NEXT-SENTENCE, ELSE GO TO WRAP-UP.
    b.   IF X IS ALPHANUMERIC MOVE C TO D, ELSE GO TO NEXT-PARA.
    c.   IF TOTAL-HOURS IS MORE THAN 40. GO TO OVER-TIME.
    d.   IF KODE = 'E' FINISH-ROUTINE.
    e.   IF ACCOUNT-BALANCE IS NEGATIVE GO TO CREDIT-RTN, ELSE GO TO CHECK-RTN.
    f.   IF ALPHA EQUALS 'DONE' MOVE G TO H.
    g.   IF C EXCEEDS D GO TO NEXT SENTENCE, ELSE GO TO READ-LOOP.
    h.   IF FICA-TOTAL IS GREATER THAN OR EQUAL TO 778.20 GO TO PRINT-PARA.

12.2   Memory locations A, B, C, D, and E are described back in your DATA DIVISION as follows:

    77   A   PICTURE 99V9.
    77   B   PICTURE 999.
    77   C   PICTURE S99.
    77   D   PICTURE S99.
    77   E   PICTURE X(4).

Assume that as the result of some earlier statements in the PROCEDURE DIVISION, those four memory locations are loaded like this:

A	B	C	D	E
17̬0	170	5͞7	33	TEST

Will the following conditions be True or False:

    a.   A IS LESS THAN B   e.   C IS GREATER THAN −58
    b.   C IS LESS THAN D   f.   E IS ALPHABETIC
    c.   C IS NOT POSITIVE   g.   E IS EQUAL TO TEST
    d.   D IS EQUAL TO '33'   h.   A IS EQUAL TO 170

12.3   Write a Conditional statement which will check PRINT-REC to see if its contents are blanks and if so, go to LOOP-PARA.

12.4   Write the statements necessary to put the greatest of three numeric data items, A, B, and C in LARGEST.

12.5   In what order will the sentences of this PROCEDURE DIVISION be executed? Answer the question by listing the sentences' sequence numbers in the order that the sentences would be executed. (The PROCEDURE DIVISION begins at the top of the next page.)

COST	PRICE
0750̬0	1000̬0

```
600 PROCEDURE DIVISION.
610 BEGIN.
620     Sentence.
630     IF COST < 90 NEXT SENTENCE ELSE GO TO MAIN-PARA.
640     Sentence.
650 MAIN-PARA.
660     Sentence.
670     IF COST > PRICE GO TO LOSS-PARA.
680     Sentence.
690     GO TO PROFIT-PARA.
700 LOSS-PARA.
710     Sentence.
720     Sentence.
730 STOP-PARA.
740     Sentence.
750     STOP RUN.
760 PROFIT-PARA.
770     Sentence.
780     SUBTRACT COST FROM PRICE GIVING PROFIT.
790     IF PROFIT > 20 ADD PROFIT TO TOTAL ELSE GO TO POOR-PARA.
800     Sentence.
810     GO TO STOP-PARA.
820 POOR-PARA.
830     Sentence.
840     Sentence.
850     STOP RUN.
```

12.6   Your final letter grade will be assigned based on your final average and the following scheme:

If Your Average Is		Then Your Grade Will Be
Greater Than	But Less Than Or Equal To	
90	100	A
80	90	B
70	80	C
60	70	D
0	60	F

FINAL-AVERAGE and LETTER-GRADE are described by these entries:

```
77   FINAL-AVERAGE   PICTURE 99.
77   LETTER-GRADE    PICTURE X.
```

Write the statements to test the value in FINAL-AVERAGE and put the appropriate letter in LETTER-GRADE.

12.7   Translate this text into COBOL statements:

"If A is less than B and less than C, then go to PARA-1. Otherwise go to PARA-2."

12.8 Given these statements:

```
        MOVE ZERO TO COUNTER.
        MOVE ZERO TO TOTAL-SUM.
LOOP-PARA.
        ADD 2 TO TOTAL-SUM.
        ADD 1 TO COUNTER.
        IF COUNTER IS LESS THAN 5
           GO TO LOOP-PARA.
        STOP RUN.
```

What quantities will TOTAL-SUM and COUNTER contain when execution stops?

12.9 The *Absolute Value* of a number is merely the value of the number with no sign. For example, the absolute value of −19 is 19, and the absolute value of 19 is 19. Write a COBOL statement which will convert the numeric value in TEST-NUMBER to its absolute value.

EXAMPLE PROGRAM

Electric Bills

Almost every bill you receive these days was calculated by a computer. Your electric bill is an example. The heart of a program for computing charges such as an electric bill involves the comparison of a usage factor against a rate schedule by means of a series of IF statements. This program involves such a procedure.

The input consists of a data deck of Bay Area Electric Company user consumption figures for the previous month, each card looking like this:

CARD COLUMNS	ITEM	EXAMPLE
1–8	Account Number	01723662
9–13	Previous Meter Reading (KWH)	55252
14–18	Current Meter Reading (KWH)	55984
19	Water Heater Rental Code	R
20–80	Blank	

The "R" in column 19 indicates an additional charge for rental of a water heater whereas a blank column 19 means there is no rental. KWH means Kilowatt-Hours and is a measure of electricity usage, a figure which is read in the window of your electric meter.

The above readings, for example, indicate that this user consumed 55984 − 55252 or 732 KWH of electricity for which he must pay according to the rate schedule below:

CONSUMPTION CATEGORY	KWH USED	CHARGE
0	0	No Charge
1	1 to 22	$1.72
2	23 to 50	$1.72 + $0.05487 per KWH over 22.
3	51 to 200	$3.26 + $0.03887 per KWH over 50.
4	Over 200	$9.09 + $0.03187 per KWH over 200.

The water heater rental tacks on an additional $5.25 per month. In addition to all of this, a fuel charge is also assessed at a flat rate of $0.01607 per KWH. Therefore, the customer indicated here would pay a total monthly electric bill of $43.05 calculated as follows:

$ 9.09 for first 200 KWH.
 16.95 for remaining 532 KWH @ $0.03187.
 11.76 for fuel charge (732 KWH @ $0.01607).
  5.25 for water heater.
$43.05 Total bill

Write a program which will produce a report listing the electric bills for each customer in the deck with column headings as shown:

BAY AREA ELECTRIC COMPANY
MONTHLY CHARGES

ACCOUNT	OLD	NEW	KWH		CHARGES		
NUMBER	READING	READING	USED	HEATER	ELECT	FUEL	TOTAL

At the end of the listing, write the total number of customers renting water heaters:

NUMBER OF WATER HEATER RENTALS WAS XXX,XXX

Use the test data listed here:

Account Number	Previous Reading	Current Reading	Rental Code
01723662	55252	55984	R
72341833	61257	69871	R
49963542	11298	11654	
80385925	45538	45538	
58693437	63447	63968	R
44867645	39571	44560	R
03640766	55649	55801	
63859675	01933	02645	R
88576453	74403	75134	
86756734	12052	13000	R
25305417	60937	62847	

Solution

IDENTIFICATION and ENVIRONMENT DIVISIONs are omitted.

```
DATA DIVISION.
FILE SECTION
FD  CUSTOMER-FILE; RECORD CONTAINS 80 CHARACTERS; LABEL RECORDS
    ARE OMITTED; DATA RECORD IS KWH-REC.
01  KWH-REC.
    02  ACCOUNT-NUMBER      PICTURE 9(8).
    02  OLD-KWH             PICTURE 9(5).
    02  NEW-KWH             PICTURE 9(5).
    02  RENTAL-CODE         PICTURE A.
    02  FILLER              PICTURE X(61).
FD  CHARGE-FILE; RECORD CONTAINS 136 CHARACTERS; LABEL RECORDS
```

```
        ARE OMITTED; DATA RECORD IS PRINT-LINE.
01   PRINT-LINE               PICTURE X(136).
WORKING-STORAGE SECTION.
77   HEATER-RENT-WS           PICTURE 9V99.
77   NR-OF-RENTALS-WS         PICTURE 9(6)   VALUE ZERO.
77   KWH-USED-WS              PICTURE 9(5).
77   STEP-USE                 PICTURE 9(5).
77   STEP-CHG                 PICTURE 999V99.
77   ELECT-CHG-WS             PICTURE 999V99.
77   FUEL-CHG-WS              PICTURE 999V99.
01   PAGE-SLEW.
     02  FILLER               PICTURE X(136) VALUE '1'.
01   TITLE-1.
     02  FILLER               PICTURE X(56)   VALUE SPACES.
     02  FILLER               PICTURE X(25)
         VALUE 'BAY AREA ELECTRIC COMPANY'.
     02  FILLER               PICTURE X(55)   VALUE SPACES.
01   TITLE-2.
     02  FILLER               PICTURE X(61)   VALUE SPACES.
     02  FILLER               PICTURE X(15)
         VALUE 'MONTHLY CHARGES'.
     02  FILLER               PICTURE X(60)   VALUE SPACES.
01   COL-HEADING-1.
     02  FILLER               PICTURE X(24)   VALUE SPACES.
     02  FILLER               PICTURE X(31)
         VALUE 'ACCOUNT       OLD           NEW'.
     02  FILLER               PICTURE X(42)
         VALUE '          KWH                        CHARGES'.
     02  FILLER               PICTURE X(39)   VALUE SPACES.
01   COL-HEADING-2.
     02  FILLER               PICTURE X(25)   VALUE SPACES.
     02  FILLER               PICTURE X(38)
         VALUE 'NUMBER      READING        READING      '.
     02  FILLER               PICTURE X(48)
         VALUE 'USED        HEATER       ELECT      FUEL       TOTAL'.
     02  FILLER               PICTURE X(25)   VALUE SPACES.
01   DETAIL-LINE.
     02  FILLER               PICTURE X(24)   VALUE SPACES.
     02  ACCOUNT-NUMBER       PICTURE 9(8)B(6).
     02  OLD-KWH              PICTURE 9(5)B(8).
     02  NEW-KWH              PICTURE 9(5)B(6).
     02  KWH-USED-DL          PICTURE Z(4)9B(7).
     02  HEATER-RENT-DL       PICTURE $$.99B(5).
     02  ELECT-CHG-DL         PICTURE $$$9.99B(4).
     02  FUEL-CHG-DL          PICTURE $$$9.99B(3).
     02  TOTAL-CHG-DL         PICTURE $(4)9.99.
     02  FILLER               PICTURE X(23)   VALUE SPACES.
01   BOTTOM-LINE.
     02  FILLER               PICTURE X(47)   VALUE SPACES.
     02  FILLER               PICTURE X(35)
         VALUE 'NUMBER OF WATER HEATER RENTALS WAS '.
     02  NR-OF-RENTALS-BL     PICTURE ZZZ,ZZ9.
     02  FILLER               PICTURE X(47)   VALUE SPACES.
PROCEDURE DIVISION.
INITIAL-ACTIVITIES SECTION.
OPEN-PARA.
```

```
        OPEN INPUT CUSTOMER-FILE, OUTPUT CHARGE-FILE.
PRINT-HEADINGS-PARA.
        WRITE PRINT-LINE FROM PAGE-SLEW.
        WRITE PRINT-LINE FROM TITLE-1.
        WRITE PRINT-LINE FROM TITLE-2.
        WRITE PRINT-LINE FROM COL-HEADING-1, AFTER ADVANCING 3 LINES.
        WRITE PRINT-LINE FROM COL-HEADING-2.
PROCESS-INDIVIDUAL-CUSTOMERS SECTION.
READ-DATA-CARD-PARA.
        READ CUSTOMER-FILE RECORD AT END GO TO FINAL-ACTIVITIES.
CALCULATE-ELEC-CHARGE-PARA.
        SUBTRACT OLD-KWH IN KWH-REC FROM NEW-KWH IN KWH-REC
            GIVING KWH-USED-WS.
        IF KWH-USED-WS > 200 GO TO CAT-4-PARA.
        IF KWH-USED-WS >  50 GO TO CAT-3-PARA.
        IF KWH-USED-WS >  22 GO TO CAT-2-PARA.
        IF KWH-USED-WS >   0 GO TO CAT-1-PARA.
CAT-0-PARA.
        MOVE ZERO TO ELECT-CHG-WS.
        GO TO CALCULATE-FUEL-CHARGE-PARA.
CAT-1-PARA.
        MOVE 1.72 TO ELECT-CHG-WS.
        GO TO CALCULATE-FUEL-CHARGE-PARA.
CAT-2-PARA.
        SUBTRACT 22 FROM KWH-USED-WS GIVING STEP-USE.
        MULTIPLY .05487 BY STEP-USE GIVING STEP-CHG, ROUNDED.
        ADD 1.72, STEP-CHG GIVING ELECT-CHG-WS.
        GO TO CALCULATE-FUEL-CHARGE-PARA.
CAT-3-PARA.
        SUBTRACT 50 FROM KWH-USED-WS GIVING STEP-USE.
        MULTIPLY .03887 BY STEP-USE GIVING STEP-CHG, ROUNDED.
        ADD 3.26, STEP-CHG GIVING ELECT-CHG-WS.
        GO TO CALCULATE-FUEL-CHARGE-PARA.
CAT-4-PARA.
        SUBTRACT 200 FROM KWH-USED-WS GIVING STEP-USE.
        MULTIPLY .03187 BY STEP-USE GIVING STEP-CHG, ROUNDED.
        ADD 9.09, STEP-CHG GIVING ELECT-CHG-WS.
CALCULATE-FUEL-CHARGE-PARA.
        MULTIPLY KWH-USED-WS BY .01607 GIVING
            FUEL-CHG-WS, ROUNDED.
PROCESS-RENTALS-PARA.
        MOVE ZERO TO HEATER-RENT-WS.
        IF RENTAL-CODE IS NOT EQUAL TO 'R'
            GO TO TOTAL-CHARGES-AND-PRINT-PARA.
        MOVE 5.25 TO HEATER-RENT-WS.
        ADD 1 TO NR-OF-RENTALS-WS.
TOTAL-CHARGES-AND-PRINT-PARA.
        ADD ELECT-CHG-WS, FUEL-CHG-WS, HEATER-RENT-WS,
            GIVING TOTAL-CHG-DL.
        MOVE CORR KWH-REC TO DETAIL-LINE.
        MOVE ELECT-CHG-WS TO ELECT-CHG-DL.
        MOVE FUEL-CHG-WS TO FUEL-CHG-DL.
        MOVE HEATER-RENT-WS TO HEATER-RENT-DL.
        MOVE KWH-USED-WS TO KWH-USED-DL.
        WRITE PRINT-LINE FROM DETAIL-LINE AFTER ADVANCING 2 LINES.
RETURN-TO-TOP-OF-LOOP-PARA.
```

```
     GO TO READ-DATA-CARD-PARA.
FINAL-ACTIVITIES SECTION.
PRINT-BOTTOM-LINE-PARA.
     MOVE NR-OF-RENTALS-WS TO NR-OF-RENTALS-BL.
     WRITE PRINT-LINE FROM BOTTOM-LINE AFTER ADVANCING 2 LINES.
CLOSE-PARA.
     CLOSE CUSTOMER-FILE, CHARGE-FILE.
     STOP RUN.
```

Discussion

The solution to this and 99 percent of all data processing problems would be impossible without the ability to test the size of data-values in conditional statements.

You'll notice that we determine whether a customer should be charged for the rental of a water heater by the use of an IF statement. Further, the counting statement to count him as a renter was embedded in an IF statement so that it will only function IF he is a renter.

The interesting feature of this program is the "filtering" process which is used to determine the bracket (or category) into which each customer's electric consumption falls. This is necessary because his charges are calculated dependent upon the consumption category to which he belongs.

The approach to finding the correct kilowatt-hour bracket is very similar to that of a soils-analyst determining the percentage of various size particles in a given volume of soil. He sifts the soil through successive filters or screens, each one having smaller holes in it than the previous screen. The size of the particles which are collected by each screen is dependent upon two factors: the size of the holes in that screen which have allowed the smaller particles to fall through, and the size of the holes in the previous screens which have already filtered out the larger particles. In this program, the IF statements comparing kilowatt-hours-used with the upper boundary of each bracket are the "screens" or "filters." The upper boundary of each bracket is analogous to the size of the holes in each filter. The usage factor passes through each IF filter until it finds one whose "holes" are small enough to stop it. If a usage factor is too large to "pass through" a given IF filter, the program stops dropping through to successive statements, and obeys the GO TO of that IF statement.

Another point I have tried to make in this solution is demonstrated by my CAT-0-PARA, CAT-1-PARA, CAT-2-PARA, CAT-3-PARA, and CAT-4-PARA. Into each of these paragraphs have been grouped the computational steps which are uniquely applicable to the category indicated by the paragraph's name. Once the program has determined the Consumption Category in which the customer belongs, it simply branches to the appropriate paragraph for computation of his charges. I strongly recommend this approach to you as a way to simplify the layout of a program's logic, especially when it is at all complicated. Such a straightforward approach will greatly reduce the possibility of logic errors. If, for example, you are writing a program which processes airline passengers' reservations according to whether they're first-class, tourist-class, or air-shuttle passengers, then I would hope to find you including a FIRST-CLASS-PARA in which you have grouped all computational steps that pertain only to first-class passengers, a TOURIST-CLASS-PARA in which all computational steps unique to tourist-class passengers are grouped, and an AIR-SHUTTLE-PARA containing the steps which uniquely apply to that group. Of course, IF statements earlier in the program would determine for any given passenger which paragraph should be used for processing his particular reservation.

Once again, points made in Chapter 11 are demonstrated in this program. Intermediate results are stored as unedited Class N 77-level items Working-Storage so as to be available and in proper form for involvement in later arithmetic operations. In some cases data-values have to be stored in *both* unedited form (for use in later calculations) *and* in edited form (for immediate printing). ELECT-CHG-WS and ELECT-CHG-DL are examples of unedited and edited memory locations which are established in response to that need.

Notice also the use of the ROUNDED option in the MULTIPLY statements which calculate the step-charges and the fuel-charge. In those cases a value containing 5 decimal digits (.01607, for example) is being multiplied times a value containing no decimal digits (732, for example) and the result is to be stored in a receiving field containing only two decimal places. Such a multiplication generates a result containing 5 decimal digits (.01607 × 732 = 11.76324) which should be ROUNDED before storing it in the two-decimal-digit receiving item.

EXAMPLE PROGRAM

Searching for the Highest and Lowest Grades

You are given a deck of data cards each containing the name of a student and the grade that student got on a test. Write a program to search through that deck and determine which students got the highest and lowest grades. (We'll make the simplifying assumption that no two students got the same grade.) The format of each data card is as follows:

CARD COLUMNS	INFORMATION	EXAMPLE
1–20	Student's name.	MARY ELLEN CLEMENS
21–23	Test grade.	084
24–80	Blank.	

Print the results of your search in two lines in this form:

```
THE  96 OF KATHRYN ZIMMERMAN   WAS THE HIGHEST  GRADE.
THE  42 OF HENRY SCHARPENBERG  WAS THE LOWEST   GRADE.
```

Some suggested contents for trial data cards:

MARY ELLEN CLEMENS	084
DONALD FOWLER	079
MARILYN GUSTIN	091
GLENN HARPER	093
KEITH JONES	061
PAUL LALIBERTE	082
SUE OELKE	073
HENRY SCHARPENBERG	042
LUCY SPENCER	095
WILLIAM TAYLOR	088
KATHRYN ZIMMERMAN	096

Solution

IDENTIFICATION and ENVIRONMENT DIVISIONs omitted.

```
DATA DIVISION.
FILE SECTION.
FD  GRADE-FILE; RECORD CONTAINS 80 CHARACTERS; LABEL RECORDS ARE
    OMITTED; DATA RECORD IS GRADE-REC.
01  GRADE-REC.
```

```
     02   NAME                    PICTURE A(20).
     02   GRADE                   PICTURE 999.
     02   FILLER                  PICTURE X(57).
FD   PRINT-FILE; RECORD CONTAINS 136 CHARACTERS; LABEL RECORDS ARE
     OMITTED; DATA RECORD IS PRINT-LINE.
01   PRINT-LINE                   PICTURE X(136).
WORKING-STORAGE SECTION.
77   BEST-GRADE-SO-FAR            PICTURE 999        VALUE ZERO.
77   BEST-STUDENT-SO-FAR          PICTURE A(20).
77   POOREST-GRADE-SO-FAR         PICTURE 999        VALUE 999.
77   POOREST-STUDENT-SO-FAR PICTURE A(20).
01   DETAIL-LINE.
     02   FILLER                  PICTURE A(5)       VALUE ' THE '.
     02   GRADE-DL                PICTURE ZZ9.
     02   FILLER                  PICTURE A(4)       VALUE ' OF '.
     02   NAME-DL                 PICTURE A(20).
     02   FILLER                  PICTURE A(9)       VALUE ' WAS THE '.
     02   LABEL-DL                PICTURE A(7)       VALUE 'HIGHEST'.
     02   FILLER                  PICTURE X(88)      VALUE ' GRADE.'.
PROCEDURE DIVISION.
OPEN-PARA.
     OPEN INPUT GRADE-FILE, OUTPUT PRINT-FILE.
READ-CARD-PARA.
     READ GRADE-FILE RECORD AT END GO TO PRINT-RESULTS-PARA.
TEST-FOR-BEST-PARA.
     IF GRADE IS NOT > BEST-GRADE-SO-FAR
         GO TO TEST-FOR-POOREST-PARA.
     MOVE GRADE TO BEST-GRADE-SO-FAR.
     MOVE NAME TO BEST-STUDENT-SO-FAR.
TEST-FOR-POOREST-PARA.
     IF GRADE IS NOT < POOREST-GRADE-SO-FAR
         GO TO READ-CARD-PARA.
     MOVE GRADE TO POOREST-GRADE-SO-FAR.
     MOVE NAME TO POOREST-STUDENT-SO-FAR.
     GO TO READ-CARD-PARA.
PRINT-RESULTS-PARA.
     MOVE BEST-GRADE-SO-FAR TO GRADE-DL.
     MOVE BEST-STUDENT-SO-FAR TO NAME-DL.
     WRITE PRINT-LINE FROM DETAIL-LINE.
     MOVE 'LOWEST' TO LABEL-DL.
     MOVE POOREST-GRADE-SO-FAR TO GRADE-DL.
     MOVE POOREST-STUDENT-SO-FAR TO NAME-DL.
     WRITE PRINT-LINE FROM DETAIL-LINE.
CLOSE-PARA.
     CLOSE GRADE-FILE, PRINT-FILE.
     STOP RUN.
```

Discussion

This brief example program is provided to introduce you to another important programming technique: identifying the largest (or smallest) value in a set of values.

Let's first discuss searching for the largest value. The technique involves the establishment of a special memory location (called LARGEST-

VALUE, for example) in which to store each larger value as it is found. The program's logic repeatedly compares subsequent values to the value stored in LARGEST-VALUE. If any value is found to be larger than the value stored in LARGEST-VALUE, that new, larger value is MOVEd into LARGER-VALUE, destroying the smaller value formerly stored there. When the program has completed its work, the value remaining in LARGEST-VALUE will be just what the data-name implies—the LARGEST-VALUE in the set.

In this example program, the special memory location is called BEST-GRADE-SO-FAR. If the intent of the program had been to search only for the highest grade (and not for the lowest, as well) then the contents of the TEST-FOR-BEST-PARA would be simply this:

```
TEST-FOR-BEST-PARA.
    IF GRADE IS NOT > BEST-GRADE-SO-FAR GO TO READ-CARD-PARA.
    MOVE GRADE TO BEST-GRADE-SO-FAR.
    MOVE NAME TO BEST-STUDENT-SO-FAR.
    GO TO READ-CARD-PARA.
```

As the search for the best grade progresses, the computer is told to compare each new grade as it is read off a data card with the value stored in BEST-GRADE-SO-FAR. If a more recently read grade is found to be greater than the value in BEST-GRADE-SO-FAR, then *it* (and *not* the value in BEST-GRADE-SO-FAR) is really the better grade, so the computer is told to:

```
MOVE GRADE TO BEST-GRADE-SO-FAR.
```

In this case we want to keep track of not only what the BEST-GRADE-SO-FAR is, but also who got that grade. To take care of that, we provide a memory location called BEST-STUDENT-SO-FAR, and whenever a grade higher than the BEST-GRADE-SO-FAR is found, in addition to recording that higher grade in BEST-GRADE-SO-FAR, we also record that student's name in BEST-STUDENT-SO-FAR:

```
MOVE NAME TO BEST-STUDENT-SO-FAR.
```

If, on the other hand, a more recently read grade is found that is *not* greater than the value stored in BEST-GRADE-SO-FAR, the computer is told to simply go back and get the next data card. It does *nothing* to either BEST-GRADE-SO-FAR or BEST-STUDENT-SO-FAR, and thereby simply leaves them containing the values they had.

When the end of the data deck is found, the grade stored in BEST-GRADE-SO-FAR will be *the* best grade in the whole set of grades, and the name stored in BEST-STUDENT-SO-FAR will be that of the student who earned the best grade.

So you see, the process of finding the highest value in a set of values is a looping process in which each new value is compared with the largest value that has been found up to that point. One *important* question *must* be answered: What happens the *first* time through the loop? What happens when the *first* value is compared? What is that first value going to be compared with?

The fact of the matter is that we really do not want to perform a comparison when that *first* value is read. We simply want that first value loaded directly into our LARGEST-VALUE memory location. Our concern, then, is how to cause that to happen without changing the logic already set up within the search loop? (Of course, we could write some special statements *just* to handle the first value, but why do that if we don't have to?)

The solution to that dilemma is to simply "fake the computer out" and "dupe" it into concluding that the first value it receives is the LARGEST-VALUE it has seen up to that point. This is done by giving LARGEST-VALUE an initial, phony VALUE far less than any realistic value that will be processed by the program. In this case, we gave BEST-GRADE-SO-FAR the initial VALUE of ZERO, far less than any grade that would be reasonably in the running for the title of best grade. As a result, the computer will be asked to compare the first real grade it gets with that phony grade value of zero. It quite naturally will conclude that the first grade is larger than the zero value is BEST-GRADE-SO-FAR, so it will load that first grade into BEST-GRADE-SO-FAR—exactly what we want it to do.

The technique for identifying the smallest value from among a set of values is exactly similar. It is a looping process wherein each new value is compared with whatever is stored in the SMALLEST-VALUE memory location up to that point. If a more recent value is smaller than the SMALLEST-VALUE so far, then the new smaller value is loaded into SMALLEST-VALUE. Again we must face the question of how to "fake" the computer into the proper conclusion that the first value it gets should be directly loaded into SMALLEST-VALUE. And again, we do this by giving SMALLEST-VALUE an initial, phony value far greater than any reasonable value that the program is expected to process.

In this example program, the SMALLEST-VALUE memory location is called POOREST-GRADE-SO-FAR. It is given the phony, initial value of 999. If the intent of the program had been to search only for the lowest grade (and not for the highest, as well) then this TEST-FOR-POOREST-PARA would have been used *instead* of the TEST-FOR-BEST-PARA:

```
TEST-FOR-POOREST-PARA.
    IF GRADE IS NOT < POOREST-GRADE-SO-FAR GO TO READ-CARD-PARA.
    MOVE GRADE TO POOREST-GRADE-SO-FAR.
    MOVE NAME TO POOREST-STUDENT-SO-FAR.
    GO TO READ-CARD-PARA.
```

Note the use of the memory location POOREST-STUDENT-SO-FAR into which the name of each student with a subsequently poorer grade is loaded.

In order to combine the logic of the highest and lowest value searches, we employ *both* the TEST-FOR-BEST-PARA *and* the TEST-FOR-POOREST-PARA, and make the appropriate modifications to the TEST-FOR-BEST-PARA so that *every* grade will be subjected to both tests (for best *and* for poorest):

```
READ-CARD-PARA.
    READ GRADE-FILE RECORD AT END GO TO PRINT-RESULTS-PARA.
TEST-FOR-BEST-PARA.
    IF GRADE IS NOT > BEST-GRADE-SO-FAR
        GO TO TEST-FOR-POOREST-PARA.
```

```
        MOVE  GRADE  TO  BEST-GRADE-SO-FAR.
        MOVE  NAME  TO  BEST-STUDENT-SO-FAR.
TEST-FOR-POOREST-PARA.
        IF  GRADE  IS  NOT < POOREST-GRADE-SO-FAR
            GO  TO  READ-CARD-PARA.
        MOVE  GRADE  TO  POOREST-GRADE-SO-FAR.
        MOVE  NAME  TO  POOREST-STUDENT-SO-FAR.
        GO  TO  READ-CARD-PARA.
```

STUDENT'S PROGRAM

Charge Accounts

A data deck contains information on charge customers of SAV-MOR Department Stores as follows:

CARD COLUMNS	ITEM	EXAMPLE
1–16	Name	JAMES SCHMEDLAP
17–24	Account Number	43729162
25–30	Last Month's Balance	003015 ($30.15)
31–36	Payments	001500 ($15.00)
37–42	Charges during current month	002493 ($24.93)
43–79	Blank	
80	Employee code	E if employee; blank if not.

Write a program which will print a report showing each customer's balance as of the current month using these formulas:

Remaining Balance = Old Balance − Payments
Service Charge = 0.015 × Remaining Balance
New Balance = Remaining Balance + Service Charge
+ Monthly Charges

Do not impose a service charge on a customer who is also a company employee (indicated by an "E" in column 80).
The output should look like this:

SUMMARY OF CHARGE ACCOUNTS

ACCOUNT NUMBER	CURRENT BALANCE
XXXXXXX	$X,XXX.XX

Assume all cards to be in numerical order by account number. If one is out of order, have the computer print the contents of that card and an error message, and immediately stop the run. The error message should read as follows:

ERROR   PREVIOUS CARD NOT IN SEQUENCE.

Hint: In order to check for the proper numerical sequence of account numbers, you will have to establish a memory location (called PREV-ACCT-NO, for example) whose purpose will be to "remember" the immediately previous account number that was processed. Each time the computer gets a new account number, the program, using an IF statement, should check to see that this latest account number IS GREATER THAN PREV-ACCT-NO, and take an appropriate action if it is not. PREV-ACCT-NO should be initialized with a value of ZERO, and then each time just before branching back to process the next account card, the account number that was just processed should be loaded into PREV-ACCT-NO. This way the computer will be able to know during each pass through the loop what account number was processed during the previous pass through the loop.

Use the following as test data:

NAME	ACCOUNT NUMBER	OLD BALANCE	PAY-MENTS	CHARGES	EM-PLOYEE?
JUDITH MARK	00421671	$ 0.00	$ 0.00	$17.50	Yes
JAMES SCHWARTZ	00671192	561.35	100.17	25.00	Yes
MARY SMITH	01932165	39.99	15.50	30.00	No
RALPH ROGERS	07344005	63.47	0.00	10.73	No
JANE RICH	30215708	2455.63	235.50	56.33	No
ALFRED JOHNSON	45121372	43.85	5.00	0.00	Yes
STANLEY MORRIS	53468731	573.45	25.00	36.73	No
JULIA COMMONS	51611289	31.25	5.00	10.50	No
JOHN THOMAS	55961320	95.00	0.00	0.00	Yes
ALEX ALLEN	61342715	15.35	15.35	0.00	No

13 More Branching Statements

13.1 Introduction

The computer always executes program statements sequentially, except when obeying a branching statement. You've known that since Chapter 6. Up to this point there's been only one branching statement in your life—the simple GO TO statement.

In this chapter we'll discuss the GO TO DEPENDING statement and the remarkable PERFORM statement in its most elementary form.

13.2 The GO TO DEPENDING Statement

The simple GO TO statement can name only one destination. The GO TO DEPENDING statement can name several destinations, and the one it will use at any particular time will depend upon the value of a data-name given at the end of the statement. Confused? Read on!

The form of the GO TO DEPENDING statement is as follows:

```
GO TO para-name-1, para-name-2, . . . , para-name-n
     DEPENDING ON data-name.
```

The data-name given must have an integer numeric value:

If that value is 1, the program will GO TO the 1st paragraph named.
If that value is 2, the program will GO TO the 2nd paragraph named.
If that value is 3, the program will GO TO the 3rd paragraph named.
     etc.   etc.   etc.

If the value of the data-name is either less than one or greater than the number of paragraphs named in the statement, the computer will simply ignore the statement and move on to the next sentence in the program.

Consider this example statement:

```
GO TO CALC-PARA, PRINT-PARA, LAST-PARA, MAIN-PARA
     DEPENDING ON JOB-COUNTER.
```

That one statement would accomplish the same thing for you as these four IF statements:

```
IF JOB-COUNTER = 1 GO TO CALC-PARA.
IF JOB-COUNTER = 2 GO TO PRINT-PARA.
IF JOB-COUNTER = 3 GO TO LAST-PARA.
IF JOB-COUNTER = 4 GO TO MAIN-PARA.
```

In this case, if JOB-COUNTER had a value of less than 1 or greater than 4, the entire GO TO statement would have been ignored.

A Note to FORTRAN-Experienced Programmers—You will recognize the GO TO DEPENDING statement as a first cousin of FORTRAN's computed GO TO statement. In FORTRAN, however, it was considered an *error* if you allowed the indexing variable to take on any value less than 1 or greater than the number of statement numbers included. That is *not* considered an error in COBOL. In fact, many COBOL programmers program to take advantage of the COBOL feature that the statement will be ignored in such cases.

The GO TO DEPENDING statement is especially handy in situations where the program must recognize in which of several categories a data card's contents belong, and the programmer (as is so often done) has used a 1 digit code to indicate the category of each card. (A single digit category code is far better than spelling out the name of the category when you're trying to fit as much information as possible into a meager 80 columns.) Suppose for example, each person's religion were indicated on a data card by such a code, and you wanted to process members of each religion in a separate paragraph. If the codes were assigned like this:

CODE	RELIGION
1	Buddhist
2	Catholic
3	Jewish
4	Mormon
5	Protestant

you could then use this statement:

```
GO TO BUDD-PARA, CATH-PARA, JEW-PARA, MORM-PARA, PROT-PARA DEPEND-
    ING ON KODE.
```

(Code was spelled KODE because CODE is a reserved word.)

Though it may seem so, there is no restriction against a paragraph-name's appearing more than once in a GO TO DEPENDING statement. Consider this example:

```
GO TO ODD-PARA, EVEN-PARA, ODD-PARA, EVEN-PARA DEPENDING ON DEPT-
    NO.
```

In that case the program would branch to the ODD-PARA if DEPT-NO had a value of 1 or 3, and to the EVEN-PARA if DEPT-NO had a value of 2 or 4.

13.3 An Introduction to the PERFORM Verb

The PERFORM statement is available in several forms. We will consider it initially in only its most basic form:

PERFORM para-name.

Similar to a GO TO statement, the PERFORM statement will cause the computer to branch to the paragraph named. The difference between the two lies in the question of what happens when the computer finishes executing the paragraph to which it branched. If a GO TO statement were used, when the computer is finished executing the subject paragraph, it simply continues sequential processing and moves on to the next paragraph. If, however, a PERFORM statement were used, when the computer finishes executing the paragraph to which it was branched, it *automatically branches back* to the sentence just following the PERFORM statement that sent it down there.

The branching paths of a GO TO statement compared with those of a PERFORM statement are diagrammed in Figure 13.1.

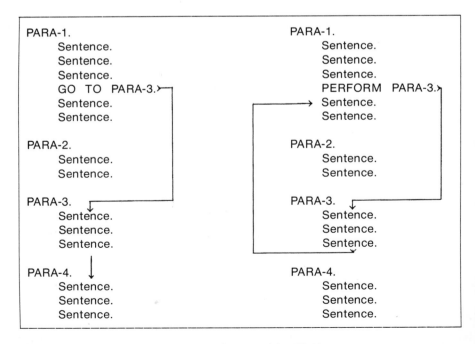

FIGURE 13.1   Comparison of GO TO and PERFORM Branching Paths

How might you use a PERFORM statement? Well, an especially suitable opportunity for its use occurs when you have a handful of sentences that recur several times in your program. You take that group of recurring sentences and place them all in one paragraph by themselves. Then in every spot where those sentences used to be, you simply replace them with a PERFORM statement which references their paragraph.

I have diagrammed that approach in Figure 13.2. Notice first the program on the left, written without PERFORM statements. I've indicated a group of four sentences (sentence-A, sentence-B, sentence-C, and sentence-D) which recur three times in the program. That version of the program required 21 sentences to write.

On the right you see the program with the four recurring sentences grouped into their own paragraph, the ABCD-PARA. Wherever you found

```
Program Without                    Program With
  PERFORM                            PERFORM
 Statements                        Statements

PARA-1.                          PARA-1.
    Sentence.                        Sentence.
    Sentence.                        Sentence.
    Sentence-A.                      PERFORM    ABCD-PARA.
    Sentence-B.                      Sentence.
    Sentence-C.
    Sentence-D.                  PARA-2.
    Sentence.                        Sentence.
                                     Sentence.
PARA-2.                              PERFORM    ABCD-PARA.
    Sentence.
    Sentence.                    PARA-3.
    Sentence-A.                      Sentence.
    Sentence-B.                      Sentence.
    Sentence-C.                      PERFORM    ABCD-PARA.
    Sentence-D.                      Sentence.
                                     STOP  RUN.
PARA-3.
    Sentence.                    ABCD-PARA.
    Sentence.                        Sentence-A.
    Sentence-A.                      Sentence-B.
    Sentence-B.                      Sentence-C.
    Sentence-C.                      Sentence-D.
    Sentence-D.
    Sentence.
    STOP  RUN.

Total:  21 sentences         Total:  16 sentences
```

FIGURE 13.2   Advantageous Use of the PERFORM Statement

those four sentences on the left, they are now replaced with a single PER-FORM statement. This version required only 16 sentences to write—a savings of 24 percent.

All too often, students faced with that example are troubled over whether the computer will know which sentence to branch back to since the three PERFORM statements look exactly alike. You can put your mind at ease! Thanks to some very clever people who wrote the COBOL software[1], the computer *is* able to keep track of which PERFORM statement it is obeying at any given time, and therefore which sentence it should return to when it's finished.

And speaking of software, you must be sure never to "violate" the software that oversees the functioning of the PERFORM verb. As I mentioned in the last paragraph, there is software whose job it is to keep track of where the computer should return to after it is finished PERFORMing a paragraph. It is considered a violation of that software if in the middle of a paragraph to be PERFORMed, you have a GO TO statement. Figure 13.3 diagrams the conflicting situation created for the computer by such a violation. Although you may get away with such a violation once in a program, your violation will have "messed up" the PERFORM software for the rest of that program, and if there are any other PERFORM statements later in the program, they will not work properly for you.

On the other hand, it *is* permissible to have another *PERFORM* statement within a paragraph that is being PERFORMed. The reason that's OK is diagrammed on the left in Figure 13.3: The first PERFORM statement starts the PERFORMance of PARA-3. In the middle of PARA-3, we come to a second PERFORM statement which causes the computer to pause in the PERFORMance of PARA-3 while it branches down to PERFORM PARA-5. After PARA-5's PERFORMance is completed, the computer returns to *complete* the PERFORMance of PARA-3, after which it returns to the sentence following the first PERFORM statement. Since all PERFORM statements were allowed to "run their full course," none were "violated."

A PERFORM statement may also give a section-name. When it does then the entire section named including all its paragraphs will be PER-FORMed.

13.4 The THRU Option in PERFORM Statements

The THRU option is available in the basic and all other forms of the PER-FORM statement:

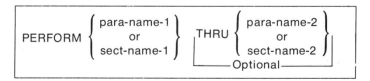

You use the THRU clause when you want *several*[2] sequential paragraphs or

---

[1] Have you forgotten what software is? Go back and review Section 1.9.

[2] Anything more than one.

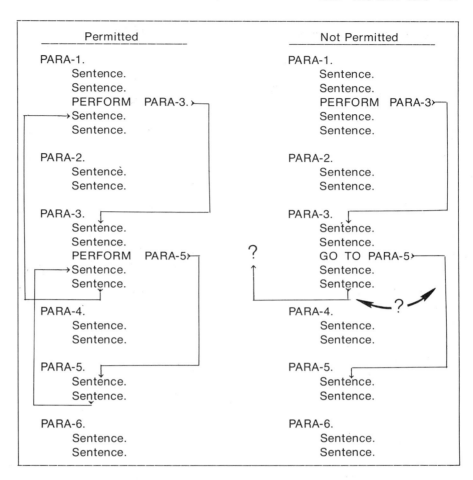

FIGURE 13.3   Branches From Within a PERFORMed Paragraph

sections PERFORMed. Figure 13.4 diagrams the branching path of a PER-FORM statement which uses the THRU option.

When you are using the THRU option, you *are* permitted to have a GO TO statement within one of the paragraphs or sections being PERFORMed. However, your GO TO statement's branch must remain *within the group* of paragraphs or sections being PERFORMed. Figure 13.5 diagrams a situation which complies with this rule.

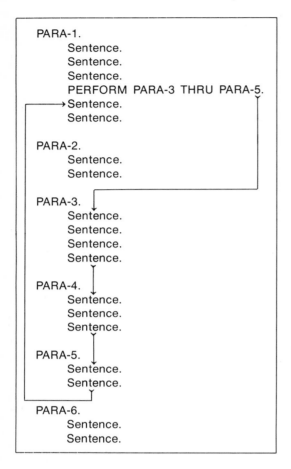

FIGURE 13.4   The Effect of a
PERFORM THRU Statement

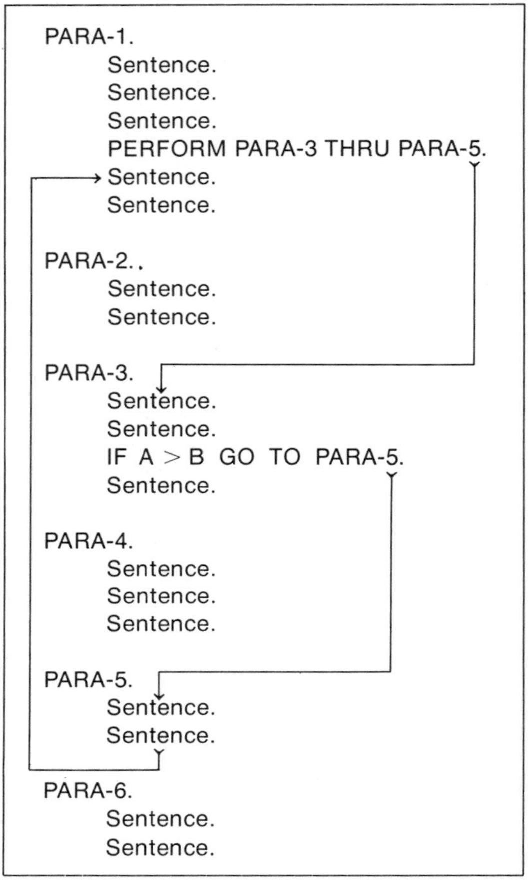

FIGURE 13.5   Permissible Branching
Within PERFORMed Paragraphs

13.5   The EXIT Verb

The EXIT statement is a real prima donna. It may contain only one word,
EXIT, and it must be in a paragraph by itself.

```
Para-name.
  EXIT.
```

Joking aside, the EXIT statement is provided to solve a specific programming problem that comes up occasionally: You have a paragraph or section
you want PERFORMed; however, there are conditions under which you
wish only the first part of that paragraph or section to be PERFORMed and
the remainder to be ignored.

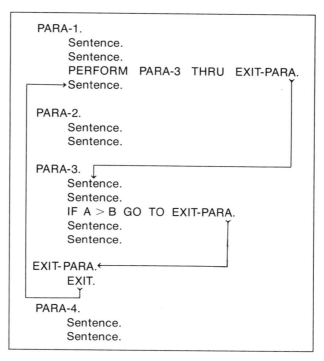

FIGURE 13.6   Use of the EXIT Statement

     As demonstrated in Figure 13.6, this is done by placing the EXIT statement in a paragraph following the paragraph you want PERFORMed. (Programmers usually call the EXIT statement's private paragraph the EXIT-PARA.) You then use a PERFORM para-name THRU EXIT-PARA statement instead of a simple PERFORM statement. An IF statement in the middle of the PERFORMed paragraph determines when the entire paragraph will be PERFORMed and when it will not.[3]

     The EXIT statement has no meaning except when used in the context described here. If the computer came upon an EXIT statement while *not* under the control of a PERFORM THRU statement which referenced its paragraph, the EXIT statement would be ignored. The computer would pass right through it, as if it weren't there, and move on to the next statement in the program.

---

[3] Another possible approach would be to place PARA-3, the EXIT-PARA and any paragraphs that came between them in a section, and then say simply "PERFORM section-name."

EXERCISES

Answers to all exercises in this chapter are given in Appendix A.

13.1　What is wrong with this statement?

> GO TO PARA-3, PARA-7, PARA-4, PARA-2 DEPENDENT UPON TRANS-CODE.

13.2　Write a COBOL statement that will branch to PARA-A if COUNTER = 1 or 3; to PARA-B if COUNTER = 2; and to PARA-C if COUNTER = 4.

13.3　Assuming PRICE has a PICTURE of 9V99, is there anything wrong with the following statements?

> MOVE 4.95 TO PRICE.
> GO TO ROUTINE-A, ROUTINE-B, ROUTINE-C DEPENDING ON PRICE.

13.4　Consider the following excerpt from a PROCEDURE DIVISION:

> PARA-1
> 　　Sentence.
> 　　SUBTRACT 1 FROM CNTR-1 GIVING CNTR-2.
> 　　GO TO PARA-3, PARA-4, PARA-5 DEPENDING ON CNTR-2.
> PARA-2.
> 　　Sentence.
> 　　Etc.

Tell which paragraph would be the next to be executed after the GO TO statement for each of the following values of CNTR-1.

	If CNTR-1 had a value of	The next paragraph executed would be
a.	1	
b.	2	
c.	3	
d.	4	
e.	5	
f.	6	

13.5　Write the statements (including a GO TO DEPENDING statement) necessary to accomplish the following branch: TO RTN-1 if PREFIX = 4, to RTN-2 if PREFIX = 5, to RTN-3 if PREFIX = 6, otherwise to LAST-PARA.

13.6 In what order will the sentences of the PROCEDURE DIVISION on the right be executed? Answer the questions by listing the sentences' sequence numbers in the order of their execution.

```
700 PROCEDURE DIVISION.
710 PARA-1.
720     Sentence.
730     Sentence.
740     PERFORM PARA-3.
750     Sentence.
760 PARA-2.
770     Sentence.
780     PERFORM PARA-3.
790     Sentence.
800     GO TO PARA-4.
810     Sentence.
820 PARA-3.
830     Sentence.
840     Sentence.
850 PARA-4.
860     Sentence.
870     Sentence.
880     STOP RUN.
```

13.7 In what order will the sentences of the PROCEDURE DIVISION on the right be executed?

```
700 PROCEDURE DIVISION.
710 PARA-1.
720     Sentence.
730     Sentence.
740     PERFORM PARA-3.
750     Sentence.
760 PARA-2.
770     Sentence.
780     Sentence.
790     STOP RUN.
800 PARA-3.
810     Sentence.
820     Sentence.
830     PERFORM PARA-4.
840     Sentence.
850 PARA-4.
860     Sentence.
870     Sentence.
```

13.8 In the PROCEDURE DIVISION on the right, how many times will the following paragraphs be executed?

    a. A-RTN: _____ times.
    b. B-RTN: _____ times.
    c. C-RTN: _____ times.
    d. D-RTN: _____ times.
    e. E-RTN: _____ times.

```
PROCEDURE DIVISION.
A-RTN.
     Sentence.
     PERFORM E-RTN.
     Sentence.
B-RTN.
     Sentence.
     Sentence.
C-RTN.
     Sentence.
     PERFORM D-RTN.
     Sentence.
D-RTN.
     Sentence.
     PERFORM B-RTN.
     Sentence.
```

E-RTN.
    Sentence.
    Sentence.
LAST-RTN.
    Sentence.
    STOP RUN.

13.9 In the PROCEDURE DIVISION excerpt on the right, there is a violation of the rule concerning branching within PERFORMed paragraphs. Rewrite the excerpt to eliminate that violation.

PROCEDURE DIVISION.
RTN-A.
    Sentence.
    Sentence.
    PERFORM RTN-C THRU RTN-D.
RTN-B.
    Sentence.
RTN-C.
    Sentence.
    IF A > B GO TO RTN-B.
    Sentence.
RTN-D.
    Sentence.
RTN-E.
    Sentence.
    Etc.

13.10 Given the program excerpt on the right, what values will be stored in memory locations A and B when execution ceases?

WORKING-STORAGE SECTION.
77 A PICTURE 9   VALUE ZERO.
77 B PICTURE 99 VALUE ZERO.
PROCEDURE DIVISION.
PARA-1.
    IF A IS GREATER THAN 5 GO TO
      PARA-2.
    PERFORM PARA-2 THRU PARA-4.
    GO TO PARA-1.
PARA-2.
    ADD 1 TO A.
PARA-3.
    ADD A TO B.
    IF B IS GREATER THAN 5 GO TO
      PARA-4.
    GO TO PARA-3.
PARA-4.
    EXIT.
PARA-5.
    STOP RUN.

EXAMPLE PROGRAM

The Increasing Cost of Gasoline

The energy crisis—who's ripping us off the worst? We'd like to know if any of the major oil companies is more guilty than its competitors. We have made a survey of 500 gas stations in the greater Boston area. On January 15th, we visited each of them and noted the price they were selling regular gas for. On July 15th, we visited them all again to note their most recent prices for regular gas.

We have prepared a data deck containing 500 cards, one for each gas station we visited. Each data card contains information in the following format:

CARD COLUMNS	INFORMATION	PICTURE
1	Brand-Code	9
2–4	Gas price on January 15th	99V9
5–7	Gas price on July 15th	99V9
8–80	Blank	

Brand-Code indicates which brand was being sold by the station.

A 1 in column 1 means Exxon.
A 2 in column 1 means Gulf.
A 3 in column 1 means Texaco.

Write a program to compute and print the average increase in price over the six months' period by all Exxon stations, by all Gulf stations, and by all Texaco stations. Have the computer print the averages in detail lines of this format:

Brand-name INCREASED XX.X CENTS PER GALLON.

Next, have the computer test to determine which company increased the most, and print out the results of that test in a line of this format:

THE COMPANY WITH THE LARGEST INCREASE WAS Brand-name.

Use the following test data:

Brand-Code	January Price	July Price
2	58.4	60.9
1	57.8	62.3
3	59.0	63.1
1	57.5	64.9
3	58.0	63.7
2	60.1	65.3
2	59.9	61.3
1	61.1	66.7
3	60.0	64.5
1	59.0	60.9
2	65.6	67.9
3	62.1	65.0

Solution

IDENTIFICATION and ENVIRONMENT DIVISIONs are omitted.

```
DATA DIVISION.
FILE SECTION.
FD  PRICE-FILE; RECORD CONTAINS 80 CHARACTERS; LABEL RECORDS
    ARE OMITTED; DATA RECORD IS PRICE-CARD.
01  PRICE-CARD.
    02  BRAND-CODE          PICTURE 9.
    02  OLD-PRICE           PICTURE 99V9.
    02  NEW-PRICE           PICTURE 99V9.
    02  FILLER              PICTURE X(73).
FD  REPORT-FILE; RECORD CONTAINS 136 CHARACTERS; LABEL RECORDS
    ARE OMITTED; DATA RECORD IS PRINT-LINE.
01  PRINT-LINE              PICTURE X(136).
WORKING-STORAGE SECTION.
77  INCREASE               PICTURE S99V9.
77  EXXON-SUM              PICTURE S9(6)V9  VALUE ZERO.
77  GULF-SUM               PICTURE S9(6)V9  VALUE ZERO.
77  TEXACO-SUM             PICTURE S9(6)V9  VALUE ZERO.
77  NR-OF-EXXON            PICTURE 999      VALUE ZERO.
77  NR-OF-GULF             PICTURE 999      VALUE ZERO.
77  NR-OF-TEXACO           PICTURE 999      VALUE ZERO.
77  AVE-INCR-WS            PICTURE 99V9.
77  WORST-INCREASE-SO-FAR  PICTURE 99V9     VALUE ZERO.
77  WORST-COMPANY-SO-FAR   PICTURE A(6).
01  DETAIL-LINE.
    02  FILLER             PICTURE X        VALUE SPACES.
    02  BRAND-DL           PICTURE A(6).
    02  FILLER             PICTURE A(11)        VALUE ' INCREASED '.
    02  AVE-INCR-DL        PICTURE Z9.9.
    02  FILLER             PICTURE X(114)
        VALUE ' CENTS PER GALLON.'.
01  WORST-LINE.
    02  FILLER                 PICTURE X(43)
        VALUE ' THE COMPANY WITH THE LARGEST INCREASE WAS '.
    02  BRAND-WL               PICTURE A(6).
    02  FILLER                 PICTURE X(87)     VALUE SPACES.
```

```
PROCEDURE DIVISION.
TABULATE-THE-DATA SECTION.
OPEN-INPUT-PARA.
    OPEN INPUT PRICE-FILE.
READ-PRICE-CARD-PARA.
    READ PRICE-FILE RECORD AT END GO TO PREPARE-THE-REPORT.
CALCULATE-INCREASE-PARA.
    SUBTRACT OLD-PRICE FROM NEW-PRICE GIVING INCREASE.
SELECT-BRAND-AND-TALLY-PARA.
    IF BRAND-CODE = 1 PERFORM TALLY-EXXON-PARA.
    IF BRAND-CODE = 2 PERFORM TALLY-GULF-PARA.
    IF BRAND-CODE = 3 PERFORM TALLY-TEXACO-PARA.
RETURN-TO-TOP-OF-LOOP-PARA.
    GO TO READ-PRICE-CARD-PARA.
TALLY-EXXON-PARA.
    ADD INCREASE TO EXXON-SUM.
    ADD 1 TO NR-OF-EXXON.
TALLY-GULF-PARA.
    ADD INCREASE TO GULF-SUM.
    ADD 1 TO NR-OF-GULF.
TALLY-TEXACO-PARA.
    ADD INCREASE TO TEXACO-SUM.
    ADD 1 TO NR-OF-TEXACO.
PREPARE-THE-REPORT SECTION.
CLOSE-INPUT-OPEN-OUTPUT-PARA.
    CLOSE PRICE-FILE.
    OPEN OUTPUT REPORT-FILE.
EXXON-PRINT-AND-COMPARE-PARA.
    MOVE 'EXXON' TO BRAND-DL.
    DIVIDE EXXON-SUM BY NR-OF-EXXON GIVING AVE-INCR-WS.
    PERFORM PRINT-PARA THRU COMPARE-EXIT-PARA.
GULF-PRINT-AND-COMPARE-PARA.
    MOVE 'GULF' TO BRAND-DL.
    DIVIDE GULF-SUM BY NR-OF-GULF GIVING AVE-INCR-WS.
    PERFORM PRINT-PARA THRU COMPARE-EXIT-PARA.
TEXACO-PRINT-AND-COMPARE-PARA.
    MOVE 'TEXACO' TO BRAND-DL.
    DIVIDE TEXACO-SUM BY NR-OF-TEXACO GIVING AVE-INCR-WS.
    PERFORM PRINT-PARA THRU COMPARE-EXIT-PARA.
REVEAL-THE-WORST-PARA.
    MOVE WORST-COMPANY-SO-FAR TO BRAND-WL.
    WRITE PRINT-LINE FROM WORST-LINE AFTER ADVANCING 2 LINES.
CLOSE-PARA.
    CLOSE REPORT-FILE.
    STOP RUN.
PRINT-PARA.
    MOVE AVE-INCR-WS TO AVE-INCR-DL.
    WRITE PRINT-LINE FROM DETAIL-LINE AFTER ADVANCING 2 LINES.
COMPARE-PARA.
    IF AVE-INCR-WS NOT > WORST-INCREASE-SO-FAR
        GO TO COMPARE-EXIT-PARA.
    MOVE AVE-INCR-WS TO WORST-INCREASE-SO-FAR.
    MOVE BRAND-DL TO WORST-COMPANY-SO-FAR.
COMPARE-EXIT-PARA.
    EXIT.
```

Discussion

This program contains further examples of summing and counting, searching for the largest value among a group of values, using IF statements to determine the category of the data on each record, and grouping computational steps by categories into separate, appropriately named paragraphs.

The unique feature demonstrated by this program is the use of the PERFORM verb. In the READ-CARD-PARA you see PERFORM statements used as the "True Clauses" of IF statements. These IF statements are being used to determine which category (which brand) the data on each data card belong to. They cause the appropriate brand paragraph (EXXON-PARA, GULF-PARA, or TEXACO-PARA) to be PERFORMed depending on the value of BRAND-CODE. Because of the automatic return feature of PER-FORM statements, it is *not* necessary to end each of the brand paragraphs with a GO TO statement in order to provide for branching back to the READ-CARD-PARA.

The program could have made good use of a GO TO DEPENDING statement in place of those three IF statements due to the existence of the BRAND-CODE. If we'd chosen to use a GO TO DEPENDING statement, the last 15 lines of the TABULATE-THE-DATA SECTION would have looked like this:

```
SELECT-BRAND-AND-TALLY-PARA.
    GO TO TALLY-EXXON-PARA, TALLY-GULF-PARA, TALLY-TEXACO-PARA,
        DEPENDING ON BRAND-CODE.
TALLY-EXXON-PARA.
    ADD INCREASE TO EXXON-SUM.
    ADD 1 TO NR-OF-EXXON.
    GO TO READ-PRICE-CARD-PARA.
TALLY-GULF-PARA.
    ADD INCREASE TO GULF-SUM.
    ADD 1 TO NR-OF-GULF.
    GO TO READ-PRICE-CARD-PARA.
TALLY-TEXACO-PARA.
    ADD INCREASE TO TEXACO-SUM.
    ADD 1 TO NR-OF-TEXACO.
    GO TO READ-PRICE-CARD-PARA.
```

That required 15 lines of coding—exactly the same number we needed in the original solution. The reduction in lines realized by not needing three separate IF statements, was offset by the need to provide each of the TALLY paragraphs with a final GO TO statement. Either solution is quite satisfactory, however.

In the PREPARE-THE-REPORT SECTION, you see the statement

```
PERFORM PRINT-PARA THRU EXIT-PARA.
```

used three times. That saved us from having to write the five sentences of the PRINT-PARA and COMPARE-PARA three times.

The PRINT-PARA contains the steps necessary for the printing of the detail line. The COMPARE-PARA contains the logic necessary for the comparison of the latest average-increase calculated and the WORST-INCREASE-SO-FAR. When a value of AVE-INCR-WS is found to be greater than the WORST-INCREASE-SO-FAR, then that larger value of AVE-INCR-WS is MOVEd into WORST-INCREASE-SO-FAR, and the company's name is MOVEd into WORST-COMPANY-SO-FAR. In the case where a calculated value of AVE-INCR-WS is *not* greater than WORST-INCREASE-SO-FAR, we do *not* want the two MOVE statements executed, and that is why we have had to include the use of an EXIT statement in conjunction with the COMPARE-PARA.

Why did we need two separate fields for average increase, the unedited AVE-INCR-WS in addition to the edited AVE-INCR-DL? Clearly, the edited AVE-INCR-DL was needed for use in printing the value. The average increase is not involved in a later arithmetic operation, so why do we also need the unedited AVE-INCR-WS? Notice that later in the program, the value of average-increase for each brand is compared with WORST-INCREASE-SO-FAR in the conditional expression of an IF statement. Recall from Chapter 12 the rule that requires both operands of a conditional expression to be of the same Class. Since WORST-INCREASE-SO-FAR is a Class N data-name, we need average-increase stored in Class N form as well to enable a proper comparison to be made. AVE-INCR-WS provides the Class N memory location we need for that purpose.

STUDENT'S PROGRAM

Is There Sex Discrimination in the Payroll?

The XYZ Chapter of the Women's Liberation Association would like some information about how wages paid to male employees at the XYZ Manufacturing Co. compare with wages paid to female employees. You have assembled a deck of data cards each containing pay information on the employees of the XYZ Co. The format of each card is as follows:

CARD COLUMNS	INFORMATION	PICTURE
1–10	Name	A(10)
11	Sex (0 = Male, 1 = Female)	9
12–20	Social Sec. No.	9(9)
21–22	Department	99
23–31	Blank	
32–35	Hourly Pay Rate	99V99
36–41	Blank	
42–44	Regular Hours	99V9
45–47	Overtime Hours	99V9
48–70	Blank	
71	Overtime Code	9
72–80	Blank	

A person can earn overtime pay only if his or her department chief has authorized it. Authorized overtime is indicated by a 1 in column 71 of the card. Regular earnings will be paid for overtime work if the overtime has not been authorized. A zero will be in column 71 if the person has not been authorized to work overtime.

Pay is computed according to the following formulas for people who are authorized to work overtime:

Regular earnings = regular hours × pay rate
Overtime earnings = 1½ × pay rate × overtime hours
Total earnings = regular earnings + overtime earnings

For people not authorized to work overtime, pay is calculated as follows:

Total earnings = total hours × pay rate

Write a program that will print a report showing the wages earned by the XYZ employees. For each employee, print out the name preceded by the title MR. or MS. as appropriate, the social security number, the department number, and the total wages earned by that individual. The report should be in this format:

NAME	SSN	DEPT	HOURLY PAY RATE	REGULAR HOURS	OVERTIME HOURS	OVERTIME AUTH	TOTAL PAY
MR. ABBOTT	098 67 4587	1	$1.25	40.0	0.0	YES	$ 50.00
MS. BERGSTROM	178 00 8079	1	$1.50	40.0	2.0	YES	$ 64.50
MS. CAMERON	876 41 3512	2	$2.55	40.0	0.0	NO	$102.00
Etc.	Etc.	Etc.	Etc.	Etc.	Etc.	Etc.	Etc.

Have your program determine and print the name of the person (preceded by the appropriate title) who received the highest pay and the person who received the lowest pay. For example:

MR. MURPHY   EARNED THE HIGHEST PAY.
MS. COHEN   EARNED THE LOWEST PAY.

Have your program also compute and print the average of all wages paid to men and all wages paid to women. For example.

THE AVERAGE MALE   PAY IS $144.51
THE AVERAGE FEMALE PAY IS $135.89

Some suggested contents for trial data cards:

ABBOTT	009867458701	0125	400000	1
BERGSTROM	117800807901	0150	400020	1
CAMERON	187641351202	0255	400000	0
CLARK	143876584602	0200	400000	0
COHEN	151652883102	0100	400000	0
COVITZ	079427580903	0560	400000	0
DEVLADAR	075057190404	0250	400000	0
DOLSON	026862750106	0145	400000	0
DONAVAN	088287221810	0275	400050	1
EMOND	123882079610	0265	400000	0
GALLAGHER	151758535610	0125	400200	1
GETZOFF	023896632810	0295	400000	0
GOODRIDGE	194078413811	0160	400000	0
GOULD	040373513711	0180	400000	0
GRANATO	133414699711	0210	400100	0
GRAZULIS	173622003311	0305	400000	0
GREENBURG	136824675112	0210	400000	0
HALPERN	136952170012	0150	400050	0
HECK	079516604413	0175	400000	0
HOBERMAN	046997282213	0200	400060	0
KELLEY	035159230114	0450	400000	0
KOBRENSKI	199407086415	0600	400000	0
LAVERS	164881141116	0700	400200	0
MOSGOFIAN	132693554517	0800	400000	0
MURPHY	074242488618	0900	400100	1

As a check of the accuracy of your program, you should have calculated a salary for Mr. Donavan of $130.63 and for Ms. Gallagher of $87.50.

14 An Introduction to Magnetic Tapes

14.1   The Advantages of Magnetic Tape for Bulk Data Storage

In the typical student's program, the amount of data that must be processed is relatively small. In every program you've written so far, the data that was to be manipulated could be easily stored in a data deck of less than one hundred cards. In the real world of data processing, it is far more likely that programs will be handling literally tons of data—so much data that it is simply not practical to consider storing that data solely on data cards.

FIGURE 14.1   The Tape Files of the Social Security Administration

Photograph by Bruce Dale, © 1970 National Geographic Society

FIGURE 14.2   An Internal Revenue Tape File Containing 25,000 Tax Returns

Courtesy of The Boston Globe

Magnetic tape provides a vast improvement in storage efficiency over data cards. A box of IBM cards holds 2000 cards. It is possible to store the data from 100 boxes of cards on one 12 inch reel (holding 2400 feet) of tape. One person can carry such a reel under one arm, yet one hundred card boxes would be an impossible load for any human.

Tape also provides a significant improvement in input/output speed, an important factor when dealing with super-huge files of data. One hundred boxes of data cards (200,000 cards) would take one hundred minutes to read on the fastest card reader available. That same amount of data could be read off a tape in six minutes.

Frequently a program will produce output data that will be used as the input data for another program. When that is the case, it is clearly impossible to use our old friend the line printer as the output device for the first program, because of the obvious fact that printer paper cannot be used for input. There is an output device, the card punch, which will punch the output from a program onto IBM cards. The cards it punches can be used for input; however, first a person must lift them out of the card punch (which is strictly an output device) and load them into the card reader. Since the card punch is a very slow device, this is seldom done.

The device that handles magnetic tape, called a tape drive, represents the first peripheral device you have had contact with which can serve *both* as an output device *and* as an input device. After writing (or recording) data on tape, you can simply command the computer to rewind the tape. After the tape is rewound, it is immediately ready to be read as input, and it can be left on the same tape drive where it was recorded. One hundred boxes of data cards can take as much as 400 minutes to punch on a card punch. An equivalent amount of data can be written on tape in only six minutes.

FIGURE 14.3   A Magnetic Tape Drive

Magnetic disc provides an improvement in input/output speed over tape, so disc is used in preference to tape when that is the paramount consideration. Disc does *not*, however, provide an improvement in storage capacity. A disc pack of six discs, somewhat larger in overall size than the reel of tape we've been discussing, can hold only half as much data.

Tape gives you a lot more storage space for your money, too. You pay about $30 for a 2400 foot reel of tape, while a disc pack costs in the neighborhood of $300. When you consider that a disc pack holds only half as much data as a reel of tape, you can see that when you go with disc, you pay twenty times more for the equivalent storage capacity.

14.2 The Management of Data Files

This chapter on tape and the chapters on disc which will follow in a later edition of the book have one thing in common—they all concern themselves with the topic of Data File Management. The management of data files (or tape files as they will be called in this chapter) involves six operations:

1. File Building
2. Searching
3. Updating ⎫
4. Purging ⎭ also called File Maintenance Operations.
5. Sorting
6. Merging

File Building   The first act in the life of a tape file is the creation (or building) of the file. This frequently entails taking data which was originally on data cards, and storing it on the tape.

Searching   The act of looking (or searching) through a tape file in order to find a particular record or group of records which fit certain criteria.

File Maintenance   The next two operations, updating and purging, can be lumped together under this single heading. They both have as their purposes the elimination of incorrect data in the file.

Updating   The correction of out-of-date or erroneous data in any of the file's records.

Purging   The removal of out-of-date or cancelled records from the file.

Sorting   The rearrangement of records in the file into some order different from their original order.

Merging   The addition of new records to a file so that they are in the proper relative order with respect to records that were already in the file.

14.3   The Tape and Tape Drives

The magnetic tape used by computers is very similar to that used by the tape recorders and players found in so many homes and cars today. It is a plastic base tape coated with an iron-oxide material and stored on reels. It is of better quality, however, than the tape used in homes; it is one-half inch wide and usually in reels of 2400 feet. Data tape runs at a speed roughly 30 times faster than the music tape used at home.

A tape drive is also similar to the tape recorder you use at home. It is equipped with read/write and erase heads and all the other necessary mechanisms to provide for the movement of the tape at the proper speed in front of those heads. Information can only be recorded on the tape while it is in motion, and the speed of that motion (approximately six miles per hour on some models) is critical to the accurate recording and reading of information on the tape.

There is a length of stronger, uncoated white plastic leader attached to both ends of a reel of tape for the operator to use in threading the tape through the tape drive. Just after the tape's beginning leader and just before its trailing leader are polished, metallic, adhesive strips called the load point and trailer markers, respectively. Because they are shiny, the markers provide the tape drive the ability to optically detect the "official" beginning and ending of the tape. When an operator has mounted a reel of tape on the tape drive and threaded it, he reels the tape forward past the load point marker and pushes a button to turn control of the tape drive over to the Control Unit. As soon as the button is pushed, the tape is rewound to the load point marker and stops. Only after the marker has been located does the computer consider the tape ready for use. The load point marker also has the function of indicating where the tape drive should stop during a rewind commanded by the program. Complete unreeling of the tape is thereby prevented.

The trailer marker likewise serves as a warning device to mark the end of the usable portion of the tape. If a trailer marker is found during a data recording operation, it means your file is too big for that tape. Unless the file you're recording has been declared a multiple reel file (to be discussed in Section 15.8), this would be an error.

As a safeguard against the accidental erasing of valuable data, each reel is equipped with a "write permit ring." Unless that ring is in place on the reel at the time it is mounted on the tape drive, writing (recording) of new data on the tape is automatically prevented. "No ring; no write!" is how the saying goes.

14.4   The Arrangement of Data on Tape

If you could see the magnetic impressions on the tape (but you can't), you'd see that each character is recorded as a group of magnetic spots aligned vertically on the tape in an arrangement reminiscent of the holes in an IBM card.

Records can be written individually on the tape, but usually they are not. They are normally grouped together into what are called record blocks.

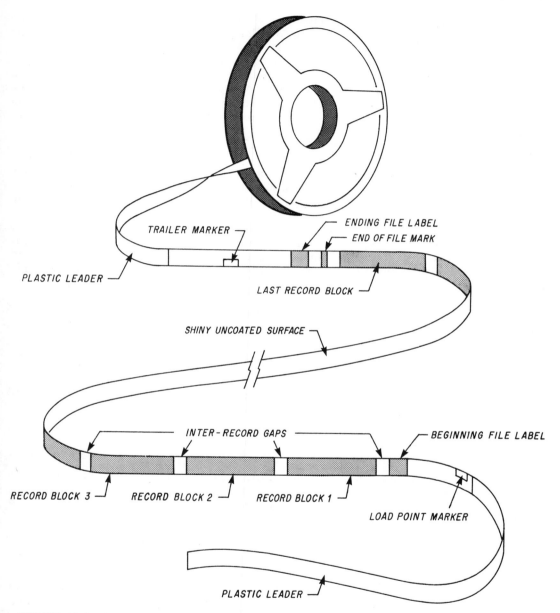

FIGURE 14.4   The Arrangement of Data in a Magnetic Tape File

The only time the tape actually moves under the read/write heads is when the computer writes or reads a record block, or when it rewinds the tape. At all other times the tape remains motionless. Prior to writing or reading a record block, the tape must be accelerated from a dead standstill to in excess of 100 inches per second. In order for the characters of each record block to be properly spaced, the tape must be read or written upon only when the tape is moving at full speed. The tape drive can bring the tape from a stop to full speed in 0.3 of an inch, and it can also bring the tape to a full stop in 0.3 of an inch. Therefore, any record block which will be read or written must have 0.3 inch of blank tape on the leading end as a starting space, and 0.3 inch of blank tape after the last character as a stopping space. Since record blocks come one after the other, the stopping space of one record adds to the starting space of the next to create an inter-record gap (IRG) of 0.6 inch in length.

When you create a tape file, it is possible to record only one record (the contents of one data card, for example) in every record block. This is sometimes referred to as recording "card images" or "unit records" on tape. The image of a data card with all 80 columns filled takes up about 0.1 inch on magnetic tape. When you use the unit record approach, your file is made up of short record blocks (only 0.1 inch long) each followed by an inter-record gap (0.6 inch long). Hence, $^6/_7$ths or 85 percent of the tape is wasted to empty inter-record gaps. If you group your records two to a block, then your file is made up of somewhat longer record blocks (0.2 inch long) each paired with a 0.6 inch inter-record gap. The fraction of wasted tape is thereby reduced to $^6/_8$ths or 75 percent. If the records are grouped 20 to a block, the fraction of wasted tape is reduced to $^6/_{26}$ths or 23 percent.

Blocking of records also results in a requirement for less total tape. Consider 5000 records recorded at 1 per block. They would consume

$$5000 \times .1 + 5000 \times .6 = 3500 \text{ inches.}$$

Blocked at 20 per block, they would result in only 250 record blocks and hence only 250 inter-record gaps, and the file would consume only

$$5000 \times .1 + 250 \times .6 = 650 \text{ inches.}$$

So you see, when you put the largest possible number of records into your record blocks, you not only improve the efficiency with which the available space on your tape is used; you also decrease the total amount of tape you need.

Blocking of your records also improves input/output time. The more frequently the tape must be started and stopped in the reading of a given number of records, the more time that reading operation will consume. If ten records are recorded one per record block, the tape will have to be started and stopped ten separate times in the reading of those records. If all ten are grouped into one record block, the tape will have to be started and stopped only once.

Obviously, the more records that can be included in a record block, the more efficient the operation will become. But how far can this process of maximizing the length of record blocks be carried? What's to prevent us from placing the entire file in *one* tremendously long record block? Recall that a record block contains all the data that is recorded in one movement of the tape, and that the recording of a record block on tape is triggered by a write command in the program. By this point in the text, it comes as second nature to you to realize that if you tell the computer to write something on the line printer, the information that will be printed will come from core memory. Likewise, if you tell the computer to write (record) something on magnetic tape, the information that will be recorded there will come from core memory. Hence, the factor that limits the size of a record block is the amount of core memory available for accumulating the records that will go into each block. (I will demonstrate the calculations that go into the determination of the blocking factor later in this chapter.)

There exists one other constraint on the size of a record block which on some occasions takes precedence. Many computers are limited by their hardware as to the maximum number of characters that may be transferred to or from a tape drive at one time, and therefore the maximum number of characters that may be in a single record block. On one model, for example, that limit is roughly 5000 characters. You should take precautions to avoid exceeding that limit for your computer. Since the size of this limitation is so much a function of the individual computer's design, it will not be considered further in this text.

14.5   File Labels and the End of File Mark

The first record in every tape file (as shown in Figure 14.4) is a Beginning-File-Label. At the end of each file is an Ending-File-Label. These labels contain information about the file which is needed by any computer which will be reading from the file, such as the name of the file, the date the file was created, the date after which the file is no longer valid, the record blocking factor that was used in creating the file, etc.

You will recall that card files and printer files had no file labels so we always said in their FD entries:

LABEL RECORDS ARE OMITTED

Tape and disc files do have file labels, and the ones most commonly used are those specified as standard by each computer manufacturer. For that reason we will now say:

LABEL RECORDS ARE STANDARD

See your computer's COBOL Reference Manual if you are burning to know what your system's standard labels include. Some COBOL compilers give you the option of designing your own labels—another feature you'll find described in your Reference Manual if it's available to you.

The End of File (EOF) mark (also shown in Figure 14.4) is always recorded immediately after the last record block in the file. It serves the same purpose as the End of File card at the end of a data card file. If you direct the computer to READ a record from the tape file and instead of a record block the computer comes up with the EOF mark, the AT END clause of the READ statement will be executed.

Here's a question for you to think about: When you are going to create a tape file, do you OPEN it for INPUT or OUTPUT? You OPEN it for OUT-

PUT, and for the same reason that you always OPENed the printer file for OUTPUT—because you are going to be sending data from core memory *out* to it to be written. When you are going to be reading a tape file, you OPEN it for INPUT, for the same reason that you always OPENed a data card file for INPUT—because you're going to be reading from it in order to bring data *into* core memory.

The act of OPENing a tape file for OUTPUT causes the Beginning-File-Label to be recorded. The act of CLOSEing a tape file that has been OPEN for OUTPUT causes both the EOF mark and the Ending-File-Label to be recorded.

One other thing happens when you CLOSE a tape file (regardless of whether it is OPEN for INPUT or OUTPUT)—it is rewound back to the load point marker.

The act of OPENing a tape file for INPUT causes the Beginning-File-Label to be read and checked by the computer. By doing this the computer is able to be sure that the correct reel of tape has been mounted on the tape drive. (When you OPEN a tape file, if it is not already rewound, the computer will also rewind it.)

14.6   COBOL's "Automatic" Blocking Routine

In the next section, I will present an example of a tape file building program. Before I do, I'd like to tell you about a truly marvelous feature of the COBOL language—its provision for "automatic" record blocking.

In Section 14.4 I told you why it is so important to record your records on tape in blocks rather than to record them individually. To cause records to be blocked in a tape or disc file, you simply include a BLOCK CONTAINS clause in the FD entry for that file.:

> BLOCK CONTAINS integer RECORDS

and *that is all you have to do!!* You write your PROCEDURE DIVISION as if you were recording your record individually (one per record block) on the tape.

When you tell the computer to WRITE a record that is supposed to be grouped with others into a record block, it does not actually write the record on the tape. It loads that record into an area in memory called a file buffer—an area established in response to your BLOCK CONTAINS clause. Only after that file buffer is full does any actual writing on the tape take place. After one buffer load has been written on the tape, the computer then commences loading the buffer from the top again in response to the WRITEs in your program.

Suppose you had a file described as follows:

```
FD   TAPE-FILE; BLOCK CONTAINS 10 RECORDS; RECORD CONTAINS 34 CHAR
 -      ACTERS; LABEL RECORDS ARE STANDARD; DATA RECORD IS TAPE-REC.
     01   TAPE-REC.
          02   NAME       PICTURE A(16).
          02   ACCT-NO    PICTURE 9(9).
          02   BALANCE    PICTURE 9(7)V99.
```

←————NAME————→	←— ACCT-NO —→	←— BALANCE —→
Record No. 1		∧
Record No. 2		∧
Record No. 3		∧
Record No. 4		∧
Record No. 5		∧
Record No. 6		∧
Record No. 7		∧
Record No. 8		∧
Record No. 9		∧
Record No. 10		∧

FIGURE 14.5   The File Buffer Established by the BLOCK CONTAINS 10 RECORDS Clause

Figure 14.5 demonstrates the file buffer that would be established by that FD entry—big enough for 10 records of 34 characters each.

The first time the WRITE TAPE-REC statement is executed, the contents of TAPE-REC (contrary to what the statement seems to be directing) will *not* be written on the tape. It will be loaded into the first record position of the file buffer. The second time the WRITE TAPE-REC statement is executed, the contents of TAPE-REC will be loaded into the second record position. This process will continue in a similar fashion until the 10th execution of that WRITE statement.

Immediately after the 10th record position in the buffer has been filled, the computer will move the contents of the buffer (all 10 records; all 340 characters) to the tape drive and cause them to be written on the tape as Record Block #1.

On the 11th execution of the WRITE statement, the contents of TAPE-REC will again be loaded in the *first* record position of the buffer. On the 20th execution, the 10th record position will be filled and Record Block #2 will be recorded on the tape.

A similar process is employed by the computer when you're reading records from a blocked tape file. As soon as you OPEN that file for INPUT, the computer (after checking the Beginning-File-Label) reads Record Block #1 and loads its contents into the file buffer. The first time your READ TAPE-FILE RECORD statement is executed, the computer obeys that command by "reading" (or "accessing") the first record in the buffer. On the second execution of the READ statement, the second record in the buffer is accessed. This continues until the last record in the buffer has been accessed. At that point, the computer reads the next record block off the tape, loading its contents into the file buffer. The next time the READ statement is executed, the computer returns to the top of the buffer and once again begins accessing records starting at the first record position.

But the remarkable feats don't end there. In order to make the above discussion of file buffers somewhat simpler to digest, I have postponed this additional revelation until now—in fact, all blocked COBOL files are actually *double* buffered! Each has not one, but *two* file buffer areas assigned to it in memory. The purpose of double buffering is to minimize the effect on total processing time of the comparatively slow input and output operations.

When you're creating a tape file, as soon as the first buffer is full, the computer without delay switches to the second buffer and immediately begins filling it. At the same time it releases the contents of the first buffer to be moved to the tape drive and written on the tape as Record Block #1. The recording of the contents of the first buffer and filling of the second buffer take place simultaneously. As soon as the second buffer is full, the computer switches back to the first buffer again and starts filling it while releasing the second buffer's contents to be output to the tape. This process of flip-flopping back and forth between buffers continues until the entire file is created.

When you're reading a tape file, Record Block #1 is loaded into the first buffer, and Record Block #2 is loaded into the second buffer. The computer accesses records from the first buffer until it reaches the bottom of that buffer. It then switches without hesitation to the second buffer and begins accessing records there. Simultaneously, Record Block #3 is read from the tape and loaded into the first buffer. Again, this back and forth process continues until the entire file is read.

The use of double buffers provides a considerable savings in processing time. As you have seen, it allows two operations to be progressing in the same space of time. The computer is always accessing or loading records in one buffer while simultaneously reading or recording the contents of the other buffer as (or from) a record block on the tape. This process is referred to as "I/O Overlap" in official computer jargon.

The complex buffering routines described above are presented with an implied "count your blessings" message. I emphasize again that thanks to some very clever COBOL software, you are completely free of the burden of having to program these complicated input/output operations. Having declared to the computer (in a BLOCK CONTAINS clause) that you want your records blocked, you simply return to your old familiar one-record-at-a-time style of programming and the computer will take care of the messy business involved in blocking records for you.

14.7 Building a Data File on Tape

Let's use an example program to demonstrate the file building operation. A university registrar desires his card file on all students to be transferred to magnetic tape to cut down on its bulk. Presently the file is made up of one card on each of the school's 15,564 students. Each card contains the following information:

CARD COLUMNS	INFORMATION	PICTURE
1–24	Name.	A(24)
25–52	Address.	X(28)
53–61	Social security number.	9(9)
62–63	Graduation year (last two digits).	99
64–65	Major (two letter abbreviation).	AA
66–68	Total credit hours taken to date.	999
69–72	Total grade points earned to date.	9999
73–76	Current grade point average.	9V999
77–80	Blank.	

The first decision to be made in this problem is what blocking factor to use. As I pointed out before, the fewer record blocks there are on the tape, the fewer inter-record gaps and the less waste of tape there will be. The more records that can be fitted into each record block, the larger will each record block be, and the fewer will be the total number of record blocks in the tape file. Since a record block is the amount of data that is written on the tape during one movement of the tape, the maximum size of a record block (that is to say, the maximum number of records that can be contained in any one record block) is determined by the amount of core memory which can be devoted to the file buffers in which the records will be accumulated prior to their being recorded.

So the first question which must be answered is, "How many words of core memory can be devoted to the file buffers?" The answer to that question is usually arrived at by a simple scratch pad subtraction problem. From the computer center, you find out how many words of memory are going to be allotted to your entire program, and of those how many will be needed for the compiler program. Based upon experience (either yours or that of one of the systems programmers at your computer center), you estimate the number of words which will be used up by the *largest* program which will *ever* use this tape file. The remainder is the number of words that will be available for your file buffers.

The following represents a typical computation:

11,000	words for the entire program.
− 6,000	words for the compiler program.
5,000	
− 4,000	words for the longest program that will use this file.
1,000	words remaining for file buffers and other program data.

Using that example computation, we now know that the buffers for the registrar's tape file must be limited to 1000 words of core memory. As mentioned in Section 14.6, each file has two buffers associated with it, so we must divide that figure by two—leaving 500 words that can be used for each buffer in this example.

In order to calculate the number of records we can load into each file buffer (and hence, into a record block), we need to know how many words of memory are required for each record. To do this we first count the number of characters that will be recorded in each record. In this case there are 76.[1]

The next question is, "How many characters can fit into a word of memory?" The answer to that depends upon the computer you're going to be using. The number varies, but for the purpose of this example, let's assume that each word of memory can hold no more than 4 characters.

$$\frac{76 \text{ characters per record}}{4 \text{ characters per word}} = 19 \text{ words per record}$$

In a previous paragraph we concluded that the buffer can be no larger than 500 words of memory, so from that we know that the record block will have to contain no more data than can be stored in 500 words of memory.

$$\frac{500 \text{ words per record block}}{19 \text{ words per record}} = 26 \text{ records per record block}$$

Remembering that there will be some data used by the program which will not be stored on tape, we must be sure not to plan to use 100 percent of the available memory for file buffers. With that in mind it's a good idea to round the results of that calculation down to the next lower "convenient" figure—20, for example. So we have now decided to use a blocking factor of 20 records per record block. In the FD entry for this file we'll say

    BLOCK CONTAINS 20 RECORDS

The program to build the tape file is shown in Figure 14.6. Let me point out to you now the unique features of this program.

First look at the ENVIRONMENT DIVISION. In the FILE-CONTROL paragraph, you find the SELECT sentence for the tape file:

    SELECT TAPE-FILE ASSIGN TO TAPE-1.

By way of review, recall that the form of the SELECT sentence is

    SELECT file-name ASSIGN TO device-name.

where file-name is a programmer-invented-name, and device-name is one of the set of reserved-names peculiar to each individual computer by which it identifies its peripheral devices. You'll have to find out what device-names indicate the tape drives on your computer system. For the purposes of this book I'll use TAPE-1, TAPE-2, etc., to indicate the tape drives. While there is usually only one card reader and only one line printer, there are *several* tape drives available for the computer to use. For that reason, the device-names for tape drives must provide you the ability to tell which one(s) you have mounted your tape(s) on. In my fictitious device-names for tapes, I'll use a numerical suffix for that purpose.

[1] Note that the 4 blank characters at the end of each data card are *not* going to be recorded in each tape record. That would be a waste of tape space. For that reason, the tape records in this program will be only 76 characters long.

IDENTIFICATION DIVISION omitted.

```
ENVIRONMENT DIVISION.
CONFIGURATION SECTION.
SOURCE-COMPUTER.        HAL-2001.
OBJECT-COMPUTER.        HAL-2001.
INPUT-OUTPUT SECTION.
FILE-CONTROL.
     SELECT CARD-FILE ASSIGN TO CARD-READER.
     SELECT TAPE-FILE ASSIGN TO TAPE-1.
DATA DIVISION.
FILE SECTION.
FD   CARD-FILE; RECORD CONTAINS 80 CHARACTERS; LABEL RECORDS ARE
     OMITTED; DATA RECORD IS STUDENT-CARD.
01   STUDENT-CARD.
     02   NAME           PICTURE A(24).
     02   ADDR           PICTURE X(28).
     02   SSN            PICTURE 9(9).
     02   GRAD-YR        PICTURE 99.
     02   MAJOR          PICTURE AA.
     02   TOTAL-CR-HRS   PICTURE 999.
     02   TOTAL-GR-PTS   PICTURE 9999.
     02   GR-PT-AVE      PICTURE 9V999.
     02   FILLER         PICTURE X(4).
FD   TAPE-FILE; BLOCK CONTAINS 20 RECORDS; RECORD CONTAINS 76 CHAR
-    ACTERS; LABEL RECORDS ARE STANDARD; DATA RECORD IS TAPE-REC.
01   TAPE-REC.
     02   NAME           PICTURE A(24).
     02   ADDR           PICTURE X(28).
     02   SSN            PICTURE 9(9).
     02   GRAD-YR        PICTURE 99.
     02   MAJOR          PICTURE AA.
     02   TOTAL-CR-HRS   PICTURE 999.
     02   TOTAL-GR-PTS   PICTURE 9999.
     02   GR-PT-AVE      PICTURE 9V999.
PROCEDURE DIVISION.
OPEN-PARA.
     OPEN INPUT CARD-FILE, OUTPUT TAPE-FILE.
READ-CARDS-WRITE-TAPE-PARA.
     READ CARD-FILE RECORD AT END GO TO CLOSE-PARA.
     WRITE TAPE-REC FROM STUDENT-CARD.
     GO TO READ-CARDS-WRITE-TAPE-PARA.
CLOSE-PARA.
     CLOSE CARD-FILE, TAPE-FILE.
     STOP RUN.
```

FIGURE 14.6   A Program to Build a Tape File from Cards

Notice the FD entry for TAPE-FILE:

```
FD   TAPE-FILE; BLOCK CONTAINS 20 RECORDS; RECORD CONTAINS 76 CHAR
     ACTERS; LABEL RECORDS ARE STANDARD; DATA RECORD IS TAPE-REC.
```

You see the BLOCK CONTAINS clause we developed earlier. Notice that you're seeing for the first time a RECORD CONTAINS clause that specifies something other than 80 or 136 characters. The records on tape can be any size you want them to be. If the data you want to store in each tape record amounts to only 76 characters, then go ahead and make the record 76 characters long. On the other hand, if you need a record of 100 characters, that's alright, too. Cards and printer lines are the only data records for which you have to include a FILLER at the end to account for the character positions up to a mandatory total of 80 or 136. Also notice that we are declaring that LABEL RECORDS ARE STANDARD now.

The PROCEDURE DIVISION is relatively short. It begins with:

```
OPEN-PARA.
     OPEN INPUT CARD-FILE, OUTPUT TAPE-FILE.
```

Since this is a program which writes records on the TAPE-FILE, we OPEN it for OUTPUT. OPENing the tape file for OUTPUT causes the Beginning-File-Label to be written on the tape. It also causes the tape to be rewound back to its Load Point Marker if for some reason it hadn't been.

Take special note of the READ-CARDS-WRITE-TAPE-PARA. The use of the WRITE FROM statement might trouble you. I could have written the paragraph this way:

```
READ-CARDS-WRITE-TAPE-PARA.
     READ CARD-FILE RECORD AT END GO TO CLOSE-PARA.
     MOVE CORR STUDENT-CARD TO TAPE-REC.
     WRITE TAPE-REC.
     GO TO READ-CARDS-WRITE-TAPE-PARA.
```

(Note that I said WRITE TAPE-REC and *not* WRITE TAPE-FILE. You *read files*, but you *write records*—and don't ever forget it!!) Since the first 76 columns of STUDENT-CARD are exactly the same as TAPE-REC, there was really no need to put the computer through the extra work that a MOVE CORResponding entails. We could just as easily have used a Group MOVE of STUDENT-CARD to TAPE-REC. Recall that a Group MOVE is always executed according to Alphanumeric MOVE Rules—a character-for-character MOVE from left to right. (Had there been any disagreement in the order or size of the corresponding fields on the STUDENT-CARD and the TAPE-REC, then a MOVE CORResponding *would* have been necessary.) In this case the paragraph could have been simplified to

```
READ-CARDS-WRITE-TAPE-PARA.
     READ CARD-FILE RECORD AT END GO TO CLOSE-PARA.
     MOVE STUDENT-CARD TO TAPE-REC.
     WRITE TAPE-REC.
     GO TO READ-CARDS-WRITE-TAPE-PARA.
```

But since a WRITE FROM sentence implies just the Group MOVE we want anyway, a further simplification is possible:

```
READ-CARDS-WRITE-TAPE-PARA.
     READ CARD-FILE RECORD AT END GO TO CLOSE-PARA.
     WRITE TAPE-REC FROM STUDENT-CARD.
     GO TO READ-CARDS-WRITE-TAPE-PARA.
```

Finally we have the brief closing paragraph of the division:

```
CLOSE-PARA.
    CLOSE CARD-FILE, TAPE-FILE.
    STOP RUN.
```

CLOSEing the TAPE-FILE: (1) releases the final buffer load to be recorded as the final record block; (2) causes the EOF mark to be written on the tape; (3) causes the Ending-File-Label to be written on the tape, and; (4) rewinds the tape back to the load point marker.

And that's all there is to it!

14.8 Reading Data from a Tape File

The reading of tape files is an important topic for us to consider for several reasons: (1) After a tape file is first created, you will want to be sure that the data was recorded as you intended it to be. (2) You as a programmer will frequently be required to produce periodic (weekly and/or monthly) reports on the line printer from the contents of selected tape files. (3) The reading of tape files is fundamental to *all* of the remaining tape operations which we'll be discussing in this book.

Again, I'll use an example program to demonstrate the tape reading process. The program, shown in its entirety in Figure 14.7, simply reads the data off the registrar's tape file and causes it to be printed on the line printer. This will enable us to be sure that the data was recorded properly on the tape.

The program is fairly straightforward. There are a couple of points worthy of calling your attention to, however. Notice that the TAPE-FILE is OPENed for INPUT, because we are going to read records from it. Once again, we are able to write the program as if the records had been individually recorded on the tape, which they were not. The BLOCK CONTAINS clause in the TAPE-FILE's FD entry forewarns the computer that the records are blocked. The computer responds to that information by setting up the proper buffers, and starting in motion the necessary internal processes to provide for reading entire record blocks from the tape into the buffers while allowing you to access records from those buffers on an individual basis.

Remember that it is the detection of the EOF mark at the end of the file that activates the READ statement's AT END clause. CLOSEing the TAPE-FILE causes the Ending-File-Label to be checked and the tape file to be rewound back to the Load Point Marker.

IDENTIFICATION DIVISION omitted.

```
ENVIRONMENT DIVISION.
CONFIGURATION SECTION.
SOURCE-COMPUTER.        HAL-2001.
OBJECT-COMPUTER.        HAL-2001.
INPUT-OUTPUT SECTION.
```

FIGURE 14.7   A Program to Read and Print the Contents of a Tape File

```
FILE-CONTROL.
     SELECT TAPE-FILE ASSIGN TO TAPE-1.
     SELECT PRINT-FILE ASSIGN TO LINE-PRINTER.
DATA DIVISION.
FILE SECTION.
FD  TAPE-FILE; BLOCK CONTAINS 20 RECORDS; RECORD CONTAINS 76 CHAR
-   ACTERS; LABEL RECORDS ARE STANDARD; DATA RECORD IS TAPE-REC.
01  TAPE-REC.
     02  NAME            PICTURE A(24).
     02  ADDR            PICTURE X(28).
     02  SSN             PICTURE 9(9).
     02  GRAD-YR         PICTURE 99.
     02  MAJOR           PICTURE AA.
     02  TOTAL-CR-HRS    PICTURE 999.
     02  TOTAL-GR-PTS    PICTURE 9999.
     02  GR-PT-AVE       PICTURE 9V999.
FD  PRINT-FILE; RECORD CONTAINS 136 CHARACTERS; LABEL RECORDS ARE
    OMITTED; DATA RECORD IS PRINT-LINE.
01  PRINT-LINE          PICTURE X(136).
WORKING-STORAGE SECTION.
01  DETAIL-LINE.
     02  NAME            PICTURE BA(24)B(5).
     02  ADDR            PICTURE X(28)B(5).
     02  SSN             PICTURE 999B99B9999B(5).
     02  FILLER          PICTURE XX                  VALUE '19'.
     02  GRAD-YR         PICTURE 99B(5).
     02  MAJOR           PICTURE AAB(5).
     02  TOTAL-CR-HRS    PICTURE ZZ9B(5).
     02  TOTAL-GR-PTS    PICTURE ZZZ9B(5).
     02  GR-PT-AVE       PICTURE 9.999.
     02  FILLER          PICTURE X(19)               VALUE SPACES.
PROCEDURE DIVISION.
OPEN-PARA.
     OPEN INPUT TAPE-FILE, OUTPUT PRINT-FILE.
READ-TAPE-AND-PRINT-PARA.
     READ TAPE-FILE RECORD AT END GO TO CLOSE-PARA.
     MOVE CORR TAPE-REC TO DETAIL-LINE.
     WRITE PRINT-LINE FROM DETAIL-LINE.
     GO TO READ-TAPE-AND-PRINT-PARA.
CLOSE-PARA.
     CLOSE TAPE-FILE, PRINT-FILE.
     STOP RUN.
```

FIGURE 14.7   (continued)

EXERCISES

Answers to all exercises in this chapter are given in Appendix A.

14.1 TRUE or FALSE: An individual tape record
   a. *Must* contain less than 80 characters.
   b. *Must* contain 80 characters.
   c. May contain 160 characters.
   d. May be any length you want.

14.2 TRUE or FALSE: A record block must contain more than one individual tape record.

14.3 List three advantages of recording records on tape in blocks of more than one.

14.4 Using the length approximations given in Section 14.4, how many feet of tape would you need to store the contents of 45,000 full data cards if the records were recorded with a blocking factor of:
   a. 1 record per block.
   b. 25 records per block.

14.5 In exercise 14.4b, how many feet of tape would you need if only 40 columns of each card contained data?

14.6 Given the following FD entry:

    FD   TAPE-FILE; BLOCK CONTAINS 30 RECORDS; RECORD CONTAINS 160 CHAR
    -      ACTERS; LABEL RECORDS ARE STANDARD; DATA RECORD IS TAPE-REC.

How long (in feet of tape) will this file be if there are 60,000 individual records?

14.7 Given the file described in exercise 14.6, what is the maximum number of this file's individual records that could be recorded on a 2400 foot reel?

14.8 Figure 14.3 shows a 2400 foot reel which contains 25,000 tax return records. Assume that the records on the tape were recorded at 1 per block. How many characters are in each record?

14.9 You are about to write a program which creates a tape file containing mortgage account information. Each record in the file will be in this format:

    01   MORTGAGE-RECORD.
         02   ACCT-NO   PICTURE 9(5).
         02   NAME-OF-MORTGAGE-HOLDER PICTURE X(25).
         02   MAILING-ADDRESS   PICTURE X(40).
         02   HOME-PHONE   PICTURE 9(10).
         02   BUSINESS-ADDRESS   PICTURE X(40).
         02   BUSINESS-PHONE   PICTURE 9(10).
         02   MORTGAGE-BALANCE   PICTURE 9(5)V99.
         02   INTEREST-RATE   PICTURE V999.

   a. How many characters will be in each tape record?
   b. Assuming that each word of memory can hold 4 characters, how many words will be required to store the contents of each of these tape records?

14.10 Based upon the following information, decide upon a blocking factor for the file described in exercise 14.9:

  (1) 13,000 words of memory are allocated for your use.
  (2) 6,000 words of memory will be consumed by the COBOL compiler.
  (3) Tape files are double buffered.
  (4) Three programs will use this file. For storage of their object code, each of the programs needs different amounts of memory: One requires 4,000 words; the second requires 4,800 words; and the third requires 3,000 words.

  a. How many words of memory are available for storage of your buffers?
  b. What blocking factor will you use?

14.11 Quoting from Section 14.4—"Many computers are limited by their hardware as to the maximum number of characters that may be transferred to or from a tape drive at one time, and therefore the maximum number of characters that may be in a single record block. On one model, for example, that limit is roughly 5000 characters." If your computer had that limitation (no more than 5000 characters per input or output operation), what block size would that dictate for the file of exercise 14.9?

14.12 Considering the block size you calculated in exercise 14.10 and the one you calculated in 14.11, which would you use?

14.13 Write the FD entry for the file we've been discussing in the last four exercises.

14.14 Because the mortgage file's records are 140 characters long, you will have to use a pair of data cards to contain the data for each tape record. You'll place the first 80 characters on the first card of each pair, and the remaining 60 characters on the second card. This is the DATA DIVISION you'll use in the program to create the MORTGAGE-FILE we've been discussing:

```
DATA DIVISION.
FILE SECTION.
FD  CARD-FILE; RECORD CONTAINS 80 CHARACTERS; LABEL RECORDS ARE
    OMITTED; DATA RECORDS ARE FIRST-CARD, SECOND-CARD.
01  FIRST-CARD.
    02  ACCT-NO                     PICTURE 9(5).
    02  NAME-OF-MORTGAGE-HOLDER     PICTURE X(25).
    02  MAILING-ADDRESS             PICTURE X(40).
    02  HOME-PHONE                  PICTURE 9(10).
01  SECOND-CARD.
    02  BUSINESS-ADDRESS            PICTURE X(40).
    02  BUSINESS-PHONE              PICTURE 9(10).
    02  MORTGAGE-BALANCE            PICTURE 9(5)V99.
    02  INTEREST-RATE               PICTURE V999.
    02  FILLER                      PICTURE X(10).
FD  MORTGAGE-FILE; BLOCK CONTAINS 30 RECORDS; RECORD CONTAINS
    140 CHARACTERS; LABEL RECORDS ARE STANDARD; DATA RECORD IS
    MORTGAGE-RECORD.
```

```
01   MORTGAGE-RECORD.
     02   ACCT-NO                        PICTURE  9(5).
     02   NAME-OF-MORTGAGE-HOLDER        PICTURE  X(25).
     02   MAILING-ADDRESS                PICTURE  X(40).
     02   HOME-PHONE                     PICTURE  9(10).
     02   BUSINESS-ADDRESS               PICTURE  X(40).
     02   BUSINESS-PHONE                 PICTURE  9(10).
     02   MORTGAGE-BALANCE               PICTURE  9(5)V99.
     02   INTEREST-RATE                  PICTURE  V999.
```

Write the PROCEDURE DIVISION of the program to create the MORTGAGE-FILE on tape.

14.15   When you OPEN a tape file for OUTPUT, what two events take place?

14.16   When you CLOSE a tape file that has been open for output, what four events take place?

14.17   When you OPEN a tape file for INPUT, what three events take place?

14.18   When you CLOSE a tape file that has been open for input, what two events take place?

EXAMPLE PROGRAM

Electronic Parts Supply

The AC-DC Electronics Supply Company stocks 250,000 electronics parts (tubes, wires, bulbs, relays, etc.). They have for years kept track of their inventory on punched cards, but have only just decided to computerize the system. To get things started, you are to write a program for them that will store the contents of their card inventory file on magnetic tape.

Each card is in the following format:

COLUMNS	INFORMATION	PICTURE
1–10	Part number	9(10)
11–25	Part name	X(15)
26–30	Unit price	999V99
31–34	Quantity on hand	9999
35–80	Blank	X(46)

Write a program that will record the data from these cards in a tape file using a blocking factor of 10 records per block. After the program has recorded the file, have it rewind the file and as a check of its correctness, have it read and print the data from the tape on the line printer.

Here are some suggested contents for test data cards:

```
0019246789RECEIVING TUBE 004950020
0035742169CIRCUIT BREAKER012300030
0059051643FUSE BOX       007250040
0088767423TERMINAL STRIP 000950125
0124916401POTENTIOMETER  029450241
0249248770DIG. VOLT METER110550005
0367066952TV PICTURE TUBE175000009
0585184034G-F INTERRUPTER045250057
0713392216THERMOSTAT     025950110
0931570488DI-POLE ANTENNA073210032
1058751661FM ADAPTER     068370000
1776933843CEILING FIXTURE 012500150
2194215925PHOTO-ELEC CELL019850070
```

Solution

IDENTIFICATION DIVISION omitted.

```
ENVIRONMENT DIVISION.
CONFIGURATION SECTION.
SOURCE-COMPUTER.  HAL-2001.
```

```
OBJECT-COMPUTER. HAL-2001.
INPUT-OUTPUT SECTION.
FILE-CONTROL.
     SELECT CARD-FILE ASSIGN TO CARD-READER.
     SELECT PRINT-FILE ASSIGN TO LINE-PRINTER.
     SELECT INVENTORY-TAPE-FILE ASSIGN TO TAPE-1.
DATA DIVISION.
FILE SECTION.
FD   CARD-FILE; RECORD CONTAINS 80 CHARACTERS; LABEL RECORDS ARE
     OMITTED; DATA RECORD IS INVENTORY-CARD.
01   INVENTORY-CARD         PICTURE X(80).
FD   PRINT-FILE; RECORD CONTAINS 136 CHARACTERS; LABEL RECORDS ARE
     OMITTED; DATA RECORD IS PRINT-LINE.
01   PRINT-LINE             PICTURE X(136).
FD   INVENTORY-TAPE-FILE; BLOCK CONTAINS 10 RECORDS; RECORD CONTAI
-    NS 34 CHARACTERS; LABEL RECORDS ARE STANDARD; DATA RECORD IS
     INVENTORY-TAPE-REC.
01   INVENTORY-TAPE-REC.
     02   PART-NUMBER        PICTURE 9(10).
     02   PART-NAME          PICTURE X(15).
     02   UNIT-PRICE         PICTURE 999V99.
     02   QUANTITY-ON-HAND   PICTURE 9999.
WORKING-STORAGE SECTION.
01   DETAIL-LINE.
     02   PART-NUMBER        PICTURE B9(10)B(5).
     02   PART-NAME          PICTURE X(15)B(5).
     02   UNIT-PRICE         PICTURE $$$$.99B(5).
     02   QUANTITY-ON-HAND   PICTURE ZZZ9.
     02   FILLER             PICTURE X(84)          VALUE SPACES.
PROCEDURE DIVISION.
CREATE-TAPE-FILE SECTION.
OPEN-PARA-1.
     OPEN INPUT CARD-FILE, OUTPUT INVENTORY-TAPE-FILE.
READ-CARDS-WRITE-TAPE-PARA.
     READ CARD-FILE RECORD AT END GO TO CLOSE-PARA-1.
     WRITE INVENTORY-TAPE-REC FROM INVENTORY-CARD.
     GO TO READ-CARDS-WRITE-TAPE-PARA.
CLOSE-PARA-1.
     CLOSE CARD-FILE, INVENTORY-TAPE-FILE.
CHECK-TAPE-FILE SECTION.
OPEN-PARA-2.
     OPEN INPUT INVENTORY-TAPE-FILE, OUTPUT PRINT-FILE.
READ-TAPE-AND-PRINT-PARA.
     READ INVENTORY-TAPE-FILE RECORD AT END GO TO CLOSE-PARA-2.
     MOVE CORR INVENTORY-TAPE-REC TO DETAIL-LINE.
     WRITE PRINT-LINE FROM DETAIL-LINE.
     GO TO READ-TAPE-AND-PRINT-PARA.
CLOSE-PARA-2.
     CLOSE INVENTORY-TAPE-FILE, PRINT-FILE.
     STOP RUN.
```

Discussion

This program is based directly on the tape file building and reading programs of Figures 14.6 and 14.7. Several new ideas are presented, however.

First, notice that in the ENVIRONMENT DIVISION, we have for the first time *three* SELECT sentences instead of the two we've become so accustomed to seeing. This is necessary because we now have a program that uses *three* files—the data card file, the file of inventory records on tape, and the file of data to be printed on the line printer. In the DATA DIVISION's FILE SECTION, you see the FD entries for those three files.

Next, notice the organization of the fields in the tape record. It is an exact duplicate of the organization of the fields on the data card (except for the unused 46 spaces at the end of the card.) As in Section 14.7, I chose that organization to enable me to load the tape record from the data card with a group MOVE. Since I wanted a blind "transplant" of the first 34 characters of the data card to the tape record, there was no need to explicitly name the fields which make up the card. I saved myself some time at the keypunch, and described the card as a record comprised of one 80 character field. (Of course, the group MOVE of the 80 characters in the INVENTORY-CARD to the 34 character memory location of the INVENTORY-TAPE-REC will result in the loss of the card's last 46 characters, but they are just useless spaces anyway, so who cares?)

In the PROCEDURE DIVISION, notice that I've grouped the paragraphs into appropriately named SECTIONs.

There is one other unusual feature you ought to notice. For the first time you're seeing a file (the INVENTORY-TAPE-FILE) being CLOSEd and then re-OPENed in the same program. In the CREATE-TAPE-FILE SECTION, the INVENTORY-TAPE-FILE was OPENed for OUTPUT so we could read from it. We had to CLOSE the file at the end of the first section for two reasons:

1. You can't re-OPEN a file that is already OPEN. If you want it OPEN for another purpose, you must CLOSE it first.

2. We needed the tape we'd just recorded rewound back to its beginning before we could read what we'd written on it. When a tape is CLOSEd, it gets rewound.

STUDENT'S PROGRAM

Motor Vehicle Registration

You have been hired by the data processing department of your state's Registry of Motor Vehicles. Your first assignment is to build a magnetic tape file from their file of vehicle registration cards.

Each card is in this format:

COLUMNS	INFORMATION	PICTURE
1–7	License plate no.	X(7)
8–11	Make of car	A(4)
12–13	Year of manufacture	99
14–28	Motor serial no.	X(15)
29–48	Name of owner(s)	X(20)
49–73	Address of owner(s)	X(25)
74–78	Zip Code	9(5)
79–80	Blank	XX

Write a program that will record the data from these cards in a tape file using a blocking factor of 10 records per block. After the program has recorded the file, have it rewind the file and as a check of its correctness, have it read and print the data from the tape on the line printer.

Some suggested contents for trial data cards:

```
3A-2843CHEV 7715-7421642-4216 NEIL + ANN O'DONOVAN  59 SUMMER ST, NAHANT, MA 01908
3C-5692OLDS 75798416 3742 98   PATRICK J. KENNEDY    10 OLD FARM RD, ESSEX, MA01929
4B-3474BUIC 6449/72/406/79     THEODORE G. KYRAZIS   306 MOULTON ST, ASTOR, MA02123
5D-2256FORD 735907643-7        CAROLYN SWEENEY       5 CHAPEL RD, REVERE, MA   02151
5G-1938MERC7500041987602143    DAVID ACKERMAN        9 COLBY AVE, WINTHROP, MA02152
5H-0710V W  71123123123123     BOB + BARBARA JAMES   8 PURDON LN, QUINCY, MA   02169
6C-2538SAAB 690469-70-416      BETTY-ANN HICKS       57 GARDNER ST, MILTON, MA02186
6N-4659VLVO 771-664-217986     STEPHEN NAWORSKI      4 ARDMORE DR, READING, MA01867
7G-6376MZDA76124796            GERRY MUNROE          6 GOODYEAR ST, LOWELL, MA01854
7H-8194BMW 750961740619723-7   THOMAS TAYLOR         7 LAUREL ST, WOBURN, MA   01801
7K-7873TOYO 6A-46-273-Z        BUD + BARBARA REMON   14 OAK ST, SWAMPSCOTT, MA 01907
8L-9652DATS 772179-476721      MARTHA DONOVAN        53 CARTER ST, BELMONT, MA 02178
8N-5430PONT 7493-0462-8753-94  JOHN HIEBER           3 MARNE AVE, ANDOVER, MA01810
9B-3212CADI 68217659843-BA     DAVID HOAG            43 BAY VIEW DR, SALEM, MA 01970
9M-1034AMC 73K2-469-4986-CJ7   JOHN J. FINKENAUR     3 SUNSET LN, ROCKPORT, MA 01966
```

15 Processing Data in Magnetic Tape Files

15.1 Searching for Particular Records in a Tape File

In the example program of Section 14.8, the *entire* contents of a tape file were read and printed on the line printer. That was an indiscriminate operation which literally "dumped" every last one of the file's records to the printer.

Frequently, the desire is not to blindly print the entire contents of a file, but rather just a selected record or group of records which meets some specific criteria. When that's what you want, you perform a search operation.

As an example of the simplest form of a search—one that finds *all* records that fall into a given category—suppose the registrar wanted a list of all students who are eligible for the Dean's List, that is, all students whose grade point averages are 3.500 or better. The list is to include the name, class and major of each student selected. Figure 15.1 shows the program necessary to search the tape file for all such Dean's List students.

Notice the FILLERs in the record description for TAPE-REC. They are included to indicate areas of the TAPE-REC which contain data that will not be needed by this program.

IDENTIFICATION and ENVIRONMENT DIVISIONs omitted.

```
DATA DIVISION.
FILE SECTION.
FD   TAPE-FILE; BLOCK CONTAINS 20 RECORDS; RECORD CONTAINS 76 CHAR
-    ACTERS; LABEL RECORDS ARE STANDARD; DATA RECORD IS TAPE-REC.
01   TAPE-REC.
     02   NAME          PICTURE A(24).
     02   FILLER        PICTURE X(37).
     02   GRAD-YR       PICTURE 99.
     02   MAJOR         PICTURE AA.
     02   FILLER        PICTURE X(7).
     02   GR-PT-AVE     PICTURE 9V999.
FD   PRINT-FILE; RECORD CONTAINS 136 CHARACTERS; LABEL RECORDS ARE
     OMITTED; DATA RECORD IS PRINT-LINE.
01   PRINT-LINE        PICTURE X(136).
```

FIGURE 15.1   A Program to Search for a Particular Category of Records in a Tape File

```
WORKING-STORAGE SECTION.
01   PAGE-HEADING.
     02   FILLER          PICTURE X               VALUE '1'.
     02   FILLER          PICTURE X(135)          VALUE 'DEANS LIST'.
01   DETAIL-LINE.
     02   NAME            PICTURE BA(24)B(5).
     02   FILLER          PICTURE X(11)           VALUE 'CLASS OF 19'.
     02   GRAD-YR         PICTURE 99B(5).
     02   MAJOR           PICTURE AA.
     02   FILLER          PICTURE X(86)           VALUE SPACES.
PROCEDURE DIVISION.
OPEN-PARA.
     OPEN INPUT TAPE-FILE, OUTPUT PRINT-FILE.
     WRITE PRINT-LINE FROM PAGE-HEADING.
READ-TAPE-PARA.
     READ TAPE-FILE RECORD AT END GO TO CLOSE-PARA.
PRINT-SELECTED-RECORDS-PARA.
     IF GR-PT-AVE IS LESS THAN 3.500 GO TO READ-TAPE-PARA.
     MOVE CORR TAPE-REC TO DETAIL-LINE.
     WRITE PRINT-LINE FROM DETAIL-LINE.
     GO TO READ-TAPE-PARA.
CLOSE-PARA.
     CLOSE TAPE-FILE, PRINT-FILE.
     STOP RUN.
```

FIGURE 15.1   (continued)

The logic of the program is fairly simple to follow. The heart of the logic is in these two paragraphs:

```
READ-TAPE-PARA.
    READ TAPE-FILE RECORD AT END GO TO CLOSE-PARA.
PRINT-SELECTED-RECORDS-PARA.
    IF GR-PT-AVE IS LESS THAN 3.500 GO TO READ-TAPE-PARA.
    MOVE CORR TAPE-REC TO DETAIL-LINE.
    WRITE PRINT-LINE FROM DETAIL-LINE.
    GO TO READ-TAPE-PARA.
```

The IF statement does the real work of determining who will be "accepted" as a member of the Dean's List and who will be "rejected." It "rejects" a student if his GR-PT-AVE IS LESS THAN 3.500 by branching immediately back to read the next tape record without having allowed his name, class, and major to be printed. If the student is "accepted," his name, etc., *are* printed before the program branches back to read the next tape record.

The search operation becomes somewhat more complex when the job is to find a particular record that satisfies some unique criteria, for example, the one record which contains the Social Security Number 081325549.

Suppose that the registrar wanted the ability to obtain the current grade point average on any particular student in the file. He tells us that anytime he needs a student's average, he'll give us a data card which contains that student's Social Security Number (SSN). The program to search for any given student's record based upon his SSN is shown in Figure 15.2.

IDENTIFICATION DIVISION omitted.

```
ENVIRONMENT DIVISION.
CONFIGURATION SECTION.
SOURCE-COMPUTER.  HAL-2001.
OBJECT-COMPUTER.  HAL-2001.
INPUT-OUTPUT SECTION.
FILE-CONTROL.
    SELECT CARD-FILE ASSIGN TO CARD-READER.
    SELECT TAPE-FILE ASSIGN TO TAPE-1.
    SELECT PRINT-FILE ASSIGN TO LINE-PRINTER.
DATA DIVISION.
FILE SECTION.
FD  CARD-FILE; RECORD CONTAINS 80 CHARACTERS; LABEL RECORDS ARE
    OMITTED; DATA RECORD IS SSN-CARD.
01  SSN-CARD.
    02  DES-SSN      PICTURE 9(9).
    02  FILLER       PICTURE X(71).
FD  TAPE-FILE; BLOCK CONTAINS 20 RECORDS; RECORD CONTAINS 76 CHAR
-   ACTERS; LABEL RECORDS ARE STANDARD; DATA RECORD IS TAPE-REC.
01  TAPE-REC.
    02  NAME         PICTURE A(24).
    02  FILLER       PICTURE X(28).
    02  SSN-T        PICTURE 9(9).
    02  FILLER       PICTURE X(11).
    02  GR-PT-AVE    PICTURE 9V999.
FD  PRINT-FILE; RECORD CONTAINS 136 CHARACTERS; LABEL RECORDS ARE
    OMITTED; DATA RECORD IS PRINT-LINE.
01  PRINT-LINE       PICTURE X(136).
WORKING-STORAGE SECTION.
01  DETAIL-LINE.
    02  NAME         PICTURE BA(24)B(5).
    02  GR-PT-AVE    PICTURE 9.999.
    02  FILLER       PICTURE X(101) VALUE SPACES.
01  ERROR-LINE.
    02  FILLER       PICTURE X(21) VALUE ' NO STUDENT WITH SSN '.
    02  SSN-EL       PICTURE 999B99B9999.
    02  FILLER       PICTURE X(104) VALUE ' IN THIS FILE.'.
PROCEDURE DIVISION.
START-PARA.
    OPEN INPUT CARD-FILE, TAPE-FILE; OUTPUT PRINT-FILE.
READ-SSN-PARA.
    READ CARD-FILE RECORD AT END GO TO STOP-PARA.
SEARCH-PARA.
    READ TAPE-FILE RECORD AT END GO TO ERROR-PARA.
    IF SSN-T = DES-SSN GO TO FOUND-STUDENT-PARA,
        ELSE GO TO SEARCH-PARA.
FOUND-STUDENT-PARA.
    MOVE CORR TAPE-REC TO DETAIL-LINE.
    WRITE PRINT-LINE FROM DETAIL-LINE.
    GO TO STOP-PARA.
ERROR-PARA.
    MOVE DES-SSN TO SSN-EL.
    WRITE PRINT-LINE FROM ERROR-LINE.
STOP-PARA.
    CLOSE CARD-FILE, TAPE-FILE, PRINT-FILE.
    STOP RUN.
```

FIGURE 15.2   A Program to Search For One Particular Record in a Tape File

Once again we have an ENVIRONMENT DIVISION with *three* SELECT sentences (as we did in the Example Program for Chapter 14). In the DATA DIVISION's FILE SECTION, you see the FD entries which describe those three files.

In the WORKING-STORAGE SECTION, I've provided two forms of output lines—a DETAIL-LINE to be used when we find the desired student; and a so-called ERROR-LINE to be used in case we get a SSN which cannot be found in the file.

Notice the suffix -T used on the SSN-T field in the tape record. That was done to distinguish it from the other two SSN fields in the program: the DES-SSN (for desired SSN) in the card record and the SSN-EL in the ERROR-LINE (which is what the -EL suffix stands for).

Now consider the PROCEDURE DIVISION. I first OPEN the files:

```
OPEN INPUT CARD-FILE, TAPE-FILE; OUTPUT PRINT-FILE.
```

Both the CARD-FILE and the TAPE-FILE are OPENed for INPUT, because I will be reading data records from both of them—from the CARD-FILE to determine the SSN I'm to search for, and from the TAPE-FILE as I look for the record with that SSN in it.

In the READ-SSN-PARA, I tell the computer to READ the single data card which contains the SSN of the desired student (the DES-SSN):

```
READ CARD-FILE RECORD AT END GO TO CLOSE-PARA.
```

The SEARCH-PARA contains the heart of the program's logic:

```
SEARCH-PARA.
     READ TAPE-FILE RECORD AT END GO TO ERROR-PARA.
     IF SSN-T = DES-SSN GO TO FOUND-STUDENT-PARA,
         ELSE GO TO SEARCH-PARA.
```

This is the paragraph which will be looped through repeatedly, causing the computer to read record after record after record from the tape until one of two possibilities occurs:

1. The record containing the desired student is found, in which case the computer will branch to the FOUND-STUDENT-PARA where the student's name and grade point average will be printed; or
2. The end of the tape file will be reached, indicating that the search was unsuccessful—the desired SSN was not found in the file—and in that case the computer will branch to the ERROR-PARA where that fact will be reported.

In either case, the program then CLOSEs the files and STOPs the RUN. (Even in the case where the student *is* found, there is no reason to continue with the search. We designed the program assuming it would perform a search for only one student during each run.)

To introduce the next more complex search, suppose the registrar has just asked to be relieved of this one-student-at-a-time restriction. In other words, he wants to be able to hand us a deck of data cards, each containing the SSN of a student whose grade point average he wants, and have us list those students all in one run of the program.

To do this in the most efficient way, we'd first want to assure ourselves that the records in the file were in numerical order by SSN's. (If they weren't, we could easily have them sorted into that order by use of COBOL's SORT verb, which we'll discuss later. For now, let's assume the file's records are in the desired order.) Next we'd sort the data deck into that same order. (This can also be done easily and quickly on a mechanical card sorter, available in all data processing centers.)

We now have a problem involving sufficiently complex logic to merit the use of a flowchart in the design of the program. (If you are unfamiliar with flowcharts, you should pause here to study the discussion of flow diagramming in Appendix E.) I'll present the flowchart for this program piece by piece in Figures 15.3a, 15.3b, and 15.3c to give you a better opportunity to be sure you understand each of its elements. (This, by the way, is how flowcharts are developed by programmers—piece by piece.) Make a special effort to digest the reasoning behind each element of this flow chart and the program which is based upon it (Figure 15.4). Every flowchart and program

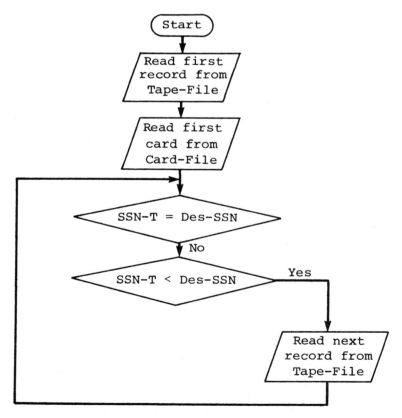

FIGURE 15.3a   Beginning the Search Operation: Searching for the First Record to be Printed

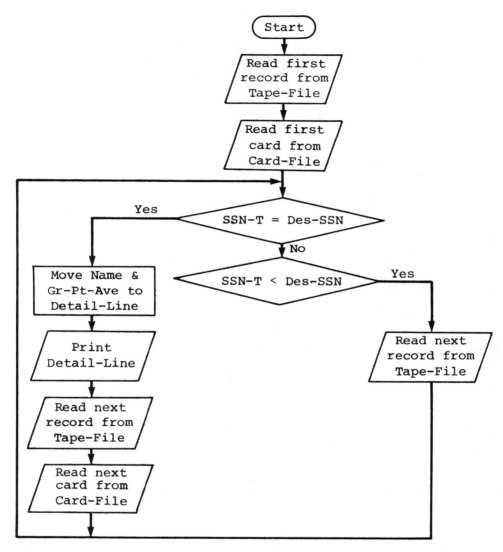

FIGURE 15.3b   The Search Operation: Finding the First Record and Commencing the Search for the Next Record

to follow in this chapter is an extension of this flowchart and program. You will never understand them, if you don't understand these.

Consider first Figure 15.3a. The search process is "primed" (like a pump) by having the computer read the first record from each of the two input files—the tape file and the card file. Reading the first card record reveals the SSN of the first student we're to search for.

Next in the flowchart are two decision symbols in which we tell the computer to compare the value of SSN-T (the SSN in the tape record) with

```
                          ┌──────────┐
                          │  Start   │
                          └────┬─────┘
                          ┌────┴─────┐
                          │Read first│
                          │record from│
                          │Tape-File │
                          └────┬─────┘
                          ┌────┴─────┐
                          │Read first│
                          │card from │
                          │Card-File │
                          └────┬─────┘
                               │        (Compare-SSN-Para)
                          ◇────┴────◇
             Yes         ╱ SSN-T = Des-SSN ╲
        ┌───────────────╱                   ╲
        │               ╲                   ╱
        │                ◇─────────────────◇
        │                      │ No
        │  (Found-Para)   ◇────┴────◇        Yes
   ┌────┴─────┐          ╱SSN-T < Des-SSN╲──────────┐
   │Move Name &│         ╲                ╱          │
   │Gr-Pt-Ave to│         ◇──────────────◇          │
   │Detail-Line │              │ No                  │
   └────┬─────┘          (Error-Para)    (Continue-Search-Para)
   ┌────┴─────┐          ┌─────┴────┐      ┌─────┴────┐
   │  Print   │          │  Move    │      │Read next │
   │Detail-Line│         │Des-SSN to│      │record from│
   └────┬─────┘          │Error-Line│      │Tape-File │
   ┌────┴─────┐          └─────┬────┘      └─────┬────┘
   │Read next │          ┌─────┴────┐            │
   │record from│         │  Print   │            │
   │Tape-File │          │Error-Line│            │
   └────┬─────┘          └─────┬────┘            │
   ┌────┴─────┐    at    ┌─────┴────┐   at        │
   │Read next │    end   │Read next │   end       │
   │card from │───→ (A)  │card from │──→ (A)       │
   │Card-File │          │Card-File │             │
   └────┬─────┘          └─────┬────┘             │
        │                      │                  │
```

FIGURE 15.3c   The Complete Search Operation

the value of DES-SSN (the desired student's SSN). The computer will be faced with three possible situations:

1. The SSN-T could be less than (<) the DES-SSN (as diagrammed in Figure 15.3a). If that were so, it would mean that the student in the first tape record is not the student we're looking for. Because of our assumption that all records (card records as well as tape records) are in ascending numerical order, this would also mean that

if the student is in the file at all, his record is located somewhere farther down the tape beyond the record we've just read. So we tell the computer to read the next tape record. (Notice that we *don't* tell it to read another data card at this point. We won't do that until we've found the student whose SSN was on the first card.) The computer is then sent back to do another comparison of SSN's.

2. The SSN-T could be equal to (=) the DES-SSN. (See Figure 15.3b.) This would mean that we've found the student we've been looking for, so we tell the computer to move his name and grade point average to the DETAIL-LINE and print it. The computer is then told to commence searching for the *next* desired student. As before, the search is "primed" by having the computer read the next record from each of the input files—the tape file and the card file. As before, reading the next card record reveals the SSN of the next student we're to search for.

3. The third (and least likely) possibility is that the SSN-T would be greater than (>) the DES-SSN. (See Figure 15.3c.) This would only happen if the SSN we were searching to find (and therefore the desired student) were not on the tape. (The student could have dropped out of school last term. Or maybe an error was made in punching the SSN on the card, and hence we're looking for a SSN that *never was* in the file.) Suppose for example that we were looking for the record of a student whose SSN was 36. (Pardon me while I for the sake of simplicity use only two-digit SSN's.) Now suppose we read a series of tape records and came up with these SSN's:

Des-SSN	SSN-T
	21
	25
	28
	32
36	34
	37

As soon as we came up with the 37, we would know something was wrong. Had there been a 36 on the tape, it should have been located *between* 34 and 37. Since it wasn't *there*, we can conclude that it isn't *anywhere* on this tape (since all records on the tape are in numerical order). In terms of the logic of this program, we want the computer to conclude that the DES-SSN it has been looking for (36) is not on the tape the moment that it comes upon a value for SSN-T (37) which is *greater* than (or in the terms of our flowchart, not = and not <) that DES-SSN. As soon as the determination has been made that a record we've been searching for is not on the tape, the computer is told to inform us by moving the non-existent SSN to the ERROR-LINE and printing the ERROR-LINE. It then is to read the next card to get the next DES-SSN. We do *not* want it to read the next tape record, however, because (using my set of example SSN's above) the next SSN we'll be looking for *might be* 37, and we don't want to move on past 37's tape record until we're sure.

This search program has finished its work when the end of the card file is detected.

Now spend some time looking through the program of Figure 15.4 and seeing how this flowchart is translated into a COBOL PROCEDURE DIVISION.

This would be the appropriate moment to introduce you to another important data processing term: the "key field." The key field of a tape record is the field which is used to uniquely identify each record in the file and upon which the order of the records is based. (In this last program, the key field was the SSN field.) The logic of the search operation is dependent upon the assumption that each record will have its own unique key field value and that the records will be in order according to those values. An inventory file would probably use the catalog number or part number as the key field. A charge account or bank account file would probably use the account number. Since the search operation is fundamental to all operations that follow, you can expect to see the term key field again.

5.2   File Maintenance: the Update Operation

A tape file once created seldom remains unchanged for very long. There are usually changes that must be made to records in the file on a fairly regular basis.

Consider the charge account files in a large department store. Each record in such a file would no doubt contain the account number, name, address, phone, and account balance for one customer. That customer will move and change addresses occasionally. Whenever she does, the address field in her record must be changed (updated). *Much* more often, however, updates of her record will be required because she has charged another purchase or made another payment on her account. In such cases, it is the account balance field in her record which will have to be updated. In a store with fairly active accounts, charge account tape files must be updated at least once a week, and in some places, once a day.

If it were possible to do so, the process of updating an out-of-date record in a tape file would involve four simple steps: (1) searching for the record that needed updating, (2) correcting the incorrect fields of the record after they'd been read into core memory, (3) backspacing the tape one record, and (4) rewriting the corrected version of the record in exactly the same position where the out-of-date version had been recorded. (Needless to say, the act of recording the corrected or updated version of the record in the same location where the incorrect or out-of-date version had been recorded would result in the destruction of the out-of-date version, which of course is exactly what we'd want.) However, such a process would require the ability to READ from and WRITE onto the tape within the same procedure, so it would be necessary to have the tape file OPEN for *both* INPUT *and* OUTPUT at the same time. That is not possible, so the update of a tape file always involves the use of *two* tapes—one (the original tape file) which is OPENed for INPUT and from which the computer READs the original versions of the records; and the other (referred to as the new tape file) which is OPENed for OUTPUT and onto which the computer WRITEs the corrected or updated versions of those records.

IDENTIFICATION, ENVIRONMENT and DATA DIVISIONs same as in Figure 15.2.

```
PROCEDURE DIVISION.
START-PARA.
    OPEN INPUT CARD-FILE, TAPE-FILE; OUTPUT PRINT-FILE.
    READ TAPE-FILE RECORD AT END GO TO STOP-PARA.
    READ CARD-FILE RECORD AT END GO TO STOP-PARA.
COMPARE-SSN-PARA.
    IF SSN-T = DES-SSN GO TO FOUND-PARA.
    IF SSN-T < DES-SSN GO TO CONTINUE-SEARCH-PARA.
ERROR-PARA.
    MOVE DES-SSN TO SSN-EL.
    WRITE PRINT-LINE FROM ERROR-LINE.
    READ CARD-FILE RECORD AT END GO TO STOP-PARA.
    GO TO COMPARE-SSN-PARA.
FOUND-PARA.
    MOVE CORR TAPE-REC TO DETAIL-LINE.
    WRITE PRINT-LINE FROM DETAIL-LINE.
    READ TAPE-FILE AT END GO TO STOP-PARA.
    READ CARD-FILE AT END GO TO STOP-PARA.
    GO TO COMPARE-SSN-PARA.
CONTINUE-SEARCH-PARA.
    READ TAPE-FILE RECORD AT END GO TO STOP-PARA.
    GO TO COMPARE-SSN-PARA.
STOP-PARA.
    CLOSE CARD-FILE, TAPE-FILE, PRINT-FILE.
    STOP RUN.
```

FIGURE 15.4   A Program to Search for Several Particular Records in a Tape File

If I now gave you the requirement to write a program which would update a tape file, with the information you have right now, you would probably make this characteristic though understandable mistake—you'd write a program which transferred to the new tape only those records which required updating by the program, and you'd *fail* to transfer to the new tape any records which *didn't* require updating. The impractical result of such a mistake would be the need to retain *both* tapes—the new tape containing the records that had been changed, and the old tape containing not only the out-of-date versions of the changed records, but more importantly, all the rest of the original records in the file. If you later performed another update in this way, you'd then need to retain three files—the new tape, the old tape, and the old-old tape—in order to avoid having lost any of the original records.

Clearly that would be an impractical approach. To avoid it, we write an update program so that the new tape ends up containing *all* the records from the original file and *not* just those which have been updated. This way we only have to retain *one* file—the one which is most current.

Once again, I'll use an example to demonstrate how a tape update works: The registrar wants a program that will post changes of address to his tape file. Input to the program will be a deck of change-of-address cards, each card containing the SSN of a student whose address has changed, and his new address. All cards in the deck will be in numerical order by SSN. (We'll continue with our assumption that the records in the tape file are also in numerical order by SSN.)

Before we get to the logic of this program, let's consider its ENVIRONMENT and DATA DIVISIONs. They are shown in Figure 15.5. There are several new program features to call your attention to in these DIVISIONs.

First, notice that I have provided for *two* separate tape files in both the ENVIRONMENT DIVISION and the DATA DIVISION. In the SELECT

```
ENVIRONMENT DIVISION.
CONFIGURATION SECTION.
SOURCE-COMPUTER. HAL-2001.
OBJECT-COMPUTER. HAL-2001.
INPUT-OUTPUT SECTION.
FILE-CONTROL.
     SELECT CARD-FILE ASSIGN TO CARD-READER.
     SELECT PRINT-FILE ASSIGN TO LINE-PRINTER.
     SELECT OLD-TAPE ASSIGN TO TAPE-1.
     SELECT NEW-TAPE ASSIGN TO TAPE-2.
DATA DIVISION.
FILE SECTION.
FD   CARD-FILE; RECORD CONTAINS 80 CHARACTERS; LABEL RECORDS ARE
     OMITTED; DATA RECORD IS CHANGE-CARD.
01   CHANGE-CARD.
     02   SSN-CC             PICTURE 9(9).
     02   NEW-ADDRESS        PICTURE X(28).
     02   FILLER             PICTURE X(43).
FD   PRINT-FILE; RECORD CONTAINS 136 CHARACTERS; LABEL RECORDS ARE
     OMITTED; DATA RECORD IS PRINT-LINE.
01   PRINT-LINE             PICTURE X(136).
FD   OLD-TAPE; BLOCK CONTAINS 20 RECORDS; RECORD CONTAINS 76 CHARA
-    CTERS; LABEL RECORDS ARE STANDARD; DATA RECORD IS OT-REC.
  01 OT-REC.
     02   NAME-OT            PICTURE A(24).
     02   ADDR-OT            PICTURE X(28).
     02   SSN-OT             PICTURE 9(9).
     02   GRAD-YR-OT         PICTURE 99.
     02   MAJOR-OT           PICTURE AA.
     02   TOTAL-CR-HRS-OT    PICTURE 999.
     02   TOTAL-GR-PTS-OT    PICTURE 9999.
     02   GR-PT-AVE-OT       PICTURE 9V999.
FD   NEW-TAPE; BLOCK CONTAINS 20 RECORDS; RECORD CONTAINS 76 CHARA
-    CTERS; LABEL RECORDS ARE STANDARD; DATA RECORD IS NT-REC.
  01 NT-REC                 PICTURE X(76).
WORKING-STORAGE SECTION.
  01 ERROR-LINE.
     02   FILLER PICTURE X(21)         VALUE ' NO STUDENT WITH SSN '.
     02   SSN-EL PICTURE 999B99B9999.
     02   FILLER PICTURE X(104)        VALUE ' IS IN THE FILE.'.
```

FIGURE 15.5   The ENVIRONMENT and DATA DIVISIONs of a Tape File Update Program

sentences I have announced that the original tape file, to be called OLD-TAPE in this program, is located on tape drive #1. I have also announced that the reel of blank tape upon which I wish to record the contents of the NEW-TAPE file is located on tape drive #2. (Of course, it is now of paramount importance that I actually load my tapes on the correct tape drives according to the association established by those two SELECT sentences.)

Next, notice the simplified record description I have given following NEW-TAPE's FD entry:

    01   NT-REC   PICTURE X(76).

For reasons I'll discuss later, it is important that the characters of data within each record in the new tape file be in *exactly* the same arrangement as they were in the old tape file. The easiest approach to providing for that duplicate arrangement is to simply describe NT-REC (the new tape record) as being a single field of 76 characters. When it comes time to transfer the contents of an OT-REC (an old tape record) to the new tape, we use a group MOVE of the 76 characters in OT-REC to NT-REC, and then WRITE the contents of NT-REC directly onto the new tape:

    MOVE OT-REC TO NT-REC.
    WRITE NT-REC.

or in the equivalent but shorter form:

    WRITE NT-REC FROM OT-REC.

Notice the ERROR-LINE provided in the WORKING-STORAGE SECTION. It will be printed on the line printer (via the PRINT-FILE's PRINT-LINE) whenever a card turns up in the data deck which contains an erroneous SSN. (A complete discussion of what might produce erroneous SSN's and why and how they should be reported was included in Section 15.1.) It is for this reason that the ENVIRONMENT and DATA DIVISIONs include SELECT and FD entries for the PRINT-FILE.

And finally, notice my practice of assigning the suffix -OT to all the data names associated with the old tape, -CC to the SSN field in the CHANGE-CARD, and -EL to the SSN field in the ERROR-LINE. The adoption of this system of suffixes will prove helpful when we get to the PROCEDURE DIVISION. (There is no field called simply SSN, for example. Had there been, whenever we came to the mention of SSN in the PROCEDURE DIVISION, we'd have to strain to recall which of the three SSN fields was being referred to. Since each SSN data-name comes equipped with its own identifying suffix, no such "straining" will ever be necessary.)

The logic for this program is really just an extension of the logic used in the last search program (Figures 15.3 and 15.4). In fact the search operation forms the heart of an update operation—you can't update a record until you've searched for and found it. The principal difference between a search operation and an update operation lies in the fact that in a search operation, when you read a tape record which isn't the one you're searching for, you

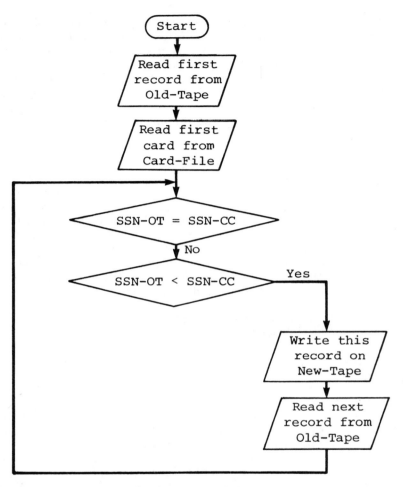

FIGURE 15.6a   Beginning the Update Operation: Searching for the First Record to be Updated

simply ignore it and proceed on to read the next tape record. In an update operation, we have the responsibility to guarantee that every record that was on the original tape will be transferred to the new tape, *even* those that are *not* changed in any way. For that reason, when you're in an update operation and you read a record off the old tape which isn't the one you're searching for to correct, you *cannot* simply ignore it. You *must* be sure that that record gets transferred to the new tape before you read the next record off the old tape.

As mentioned above, the logic of this update program is based heavily on the logic of the search program whose flowchart was given in Figure 15.3. Imitating the approach I took in developing the search logic for you, I will now present the update program's flowchart "piece by piece" in Figures 15.6a, 15.6b, 15.6c, and 15.6d.

Figure 15.6a shows how the update operation gets underway. Its first task is to search through the old tape for the record of the first student whose address is to be changed. As before, the search process is "primed" by having the computer read the first record off the old tape and card files. Reading the first card record reveals the SSN of the first student whose record is to be updated. (Recall that the data card contains not only the student's SSN but also his new address.) The computer then commences the search for that student's record on the old tape—it compares the SSN from the first tape record with the SSN it got from the first card. Figure 15.6a shows the

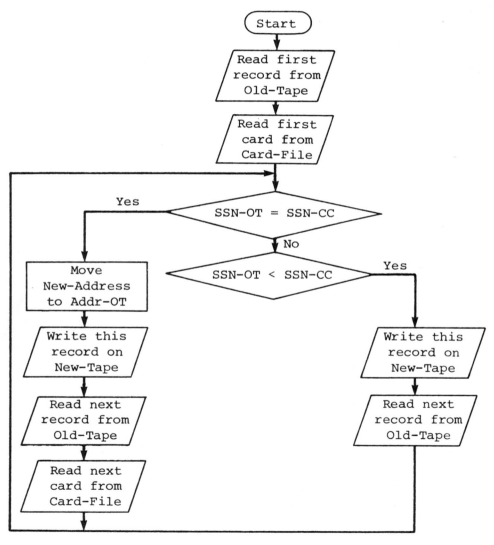

FIGURE 15.6b   The Update Operation: Updating a Record and Searching for the Next Record to be Updated

branch that will be made if they do not agree and if the SSN on the tape is less than the SSN from the card. As discussed earlier, in an update operation *all* records must be transferred to the new tape. So in this case, when the computer finds a disagreement between the SSNs, it *first* transfers that tape record onto the new tape and *then* reads the next record off the old tape.

In Figure 15.6b, elements have been added to the flowchart to show what must take place when a tape record to be updated is found. First the computer is told to update the address in the old tape record by moving the NEW-ADDRESS into it, and then it is told to write that tape record (now

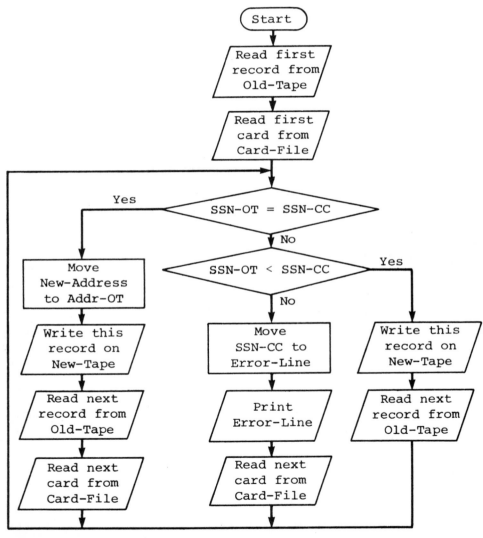

FIGURE 15.6c   The Update Operation: Reporting Erroneous SSN's Found in the Card File

updated) onto the new tape. Having searched for, found, and updated the first student's record, we now begin the search for the *next* student who needs his record updated. Once again the search is "primed" by reading the next record from each of the old tape and card files. Having read the next card (and learned the SSN of the next student needing his address changed), the computer then returns to the process we discussed in connection with Figure 15.6a—searching for the next tape record to be updated while simultaneously transferring the unchanged records to the new tape as it searches.

Figure 15.6c adds the elements of the flowchart necessary to provide for the occurrence of a SSN in the card deck for which there was no record in the old tape file. This problem of an erroneous SSN in the card deck is handled in an update program *exactly* like it was in a search program. Since it was discussed thoroughly in the last section, I won't repeat that discussion here.

The update operation described in the several preceding paragraphs will continue to function until the end of the data card deck is reached. When that happens we know there are no more students in the old tape file who need their records updated, so for all intents and purposes the update operation is finished. There is one remaining task to be performed, however. While there are no more students' records on the old tape which need their addresses updated, it *is* very likely that there are still some records on the old tape which, though their addresses may be correct, must nevertheless be transferred to the new tape. Remember—the new tape *must* contain *all* records from the old tape! So we must now provide some steps that will transfer the remaining old tape records onto the new tape.

In Figure 15.6d you see that the "AT END clauses" have been added to the two READ CARD-FILE statements. They direct the program to a small loop at the bottom of the flowchart where the computer is put through the paces of transferring the remaining records from the old tape onto the new tape. Reaching the end of the old tape file will signal the completion of the entire operation, so it is the "AT END clause" of the READ OLD-TAPE statement in that final loop that sends us to the STOP-PARA.

The PROCEDURE DIVISION that is based upon the flowchart of Figure 15.6d is given in Figure 15.7.

In this section we've been considering a type of update operation made somewhat simpler by the fact that each record we were to update had only one change that had to be made to it—in this case, the change of the contents of the address field. For any record in the old tape file that had to be updated, there was only one change record in the data deck. The logic of the program was built around the assumption that there *would* be only one change to be posted to any record in the file, so we'd have to alter the logic if we wanted to alter that assumption. Before we leave the subject of update operations, we will have to consider the problem of so-called "multiple update operations"—those in which the data deck *may* contain more than one change record for each tape record that is to be updated. (I'll use the term "simple update operation" from now on to refer to the type of update we've been discussing in this section in order to distinguish it from a "multiple update operation.")

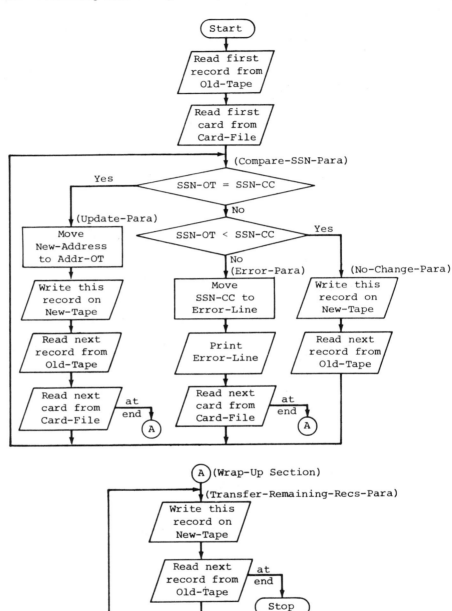

FIGURE 15.6d   The Simple Update Operation: Final Modification

Before we move on to multiple updating, however, I want to tell you about the purge operation. It is so *very* similar to the simple update operation, that you will have a much easier time following it if I present it now while that subject is still fresh in your mind. After my discussion of the purge operation, we'll get back to the discussion of multiple updates.

ENVIRONMENT and DATA DIVISIONs given in Figure 15.5.

```
PROCEDURE DIVISION.
UPDATE SECTION.
START-PARA.
    OPEN INPUT CARD-FILE, OLD-TAPE; OUTPUT NEW-TAPE, PRINT-FILE.
    READ OLD-TAPE RECORD AT END GO TO STOP-PARA.
    READ CARD-FILE RECORD AT END GO TO WRAP-UP.
COMPARE-SSN-PARA.
    IF SSN-OT = SSN-CC GO TO UPDATE-PARA.
    IF SSN-OT < SSN-CC GO TO NO-CHANGE-PARA.
ERROR-PARA.
    MOVE SSN-CC TO SSN-EL.
    WRITE PRINT-LINE FROM ERROR-LINE.
    READ CARD-FILE RECORD AT END GO TO WRAP-UP.
    GO TO COMPARE-SSN-PARA.
UPDATE-PARA.
    MOVE NEW-ADDRESS TO ADDR-OT.
    WRITE NT-REC FROM OT-REC.
    READ OLD-TAPE RECORD AT END GO TO STOP-PARA.
    READ CARD-FILE AT END GO TO WRAP-UP.
    GO TO COMPARE-SSN-PARA.
NO-CHANGE-PARA.
    WRITE NT-REC FROM OT-REC.
    READ OLD-TAPE RECORD AT END GO TO STOP-PARA.
    GO TO COMPARE-SSN-PARA.
WRAP-UP SECTION.
TRANSFER-REMAINING-RECS-PARA.
    WRITE NT-REC FROM OT-REC.
    READ OLD-TAPE RECORD AT END GO TO STOP-PARA.
    GO TO TRANSFER-REMAINING-RECS-PARA.
STOP-PARA.
    CLOSE CARD-FILE, OLD-TAPE, NEW-TAPE, PRINT-FILE.
    STOP RUN.
```

FIGURE 15.7 The PROCEDURE DIVISION of a Tape File Simple Update Program

15.3   File Maintenance: the Purge Operation

The purge operation, like the update operation, has as its object the bringing up to date of a file which contains records that are out of date. In an update, you correct the file by correcting the incorrect fields in the out-of-date records. In a purge, however, you correct the file by *tossing out* or deleting the out-of-date records. You would perform a purge operation, for example, if you wanted to clear a charge account file of records describing accounts that have been closed. You would perform a purge operation if you wanted to scrub from an inventory file the records describing items you no longer wished to stock.

Like a simple update, the purge involves a data deck in which there will only be one card for each record that is to be purged. Each card gives the key field value (account number, part number, or catalog number, etc.) of a record you want purged.

Purging is an act of omission—it is not what you *do* to a record that purges it; it's what you *don't* do to the record that results in its being

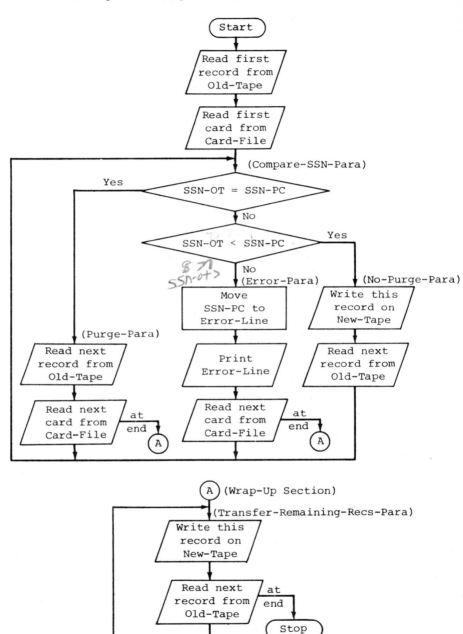

FIGURE 15.8　The Purge Operation

```
ENVIRONMENT DIVISION.
     .
     .
DATA DIVISION.
FILE SECTION.
FD  CARD-FILE; RECORD CONTAINS 80 CHARACTERS; LABEL RECORDS ARE
    OMITTED; DATA RECORD IS PURGE-CARD.
01  PURGE-CARD.
    02  SSN-PC            PICTURE 9(9).
    02  FILLER           PICTURE X(71).
FD  PRINT-FILE; . . . . . . . .
     .
     .
FD  OLD-TAPE; . . . . . . . . .
     .
     .
FD  NEW-TAPE; . . . . . . . . .
     .
     .
WORKING-STORAGE SECTION.
01  ERROR-LINE.
     .
     .
PROCEDURE DIVISION.
PURGE SECTION.
START-PARA.
    OPEN INPUT CARD-FILE, OLD-TAPE; OUTPUT NEW-TAPE, PRINT-FILE.
    READ OLD-TAPE RECORD AT END GO TO STOP-PARA.
    READ CARD-FILE RECORD AT END GO TO WRAP-UP.
COMPARE-SSN-PARA.
    IF SSN-OT = SSN-PC GO TO PURGE-PARA.
    IF SSN-OT < SSN-PC GO TO NO-PURGE-PARA.
ERROR-PARA.
    MOVE SSN-PC TO SSN-EL.
    WRITE PRINT-LINE FROM ERROR-LINE.
    READ CARD-FILE RECORD AT END GO TO WRAP-UP.
    GO TO COMPARE-SSN-PARA.
PURGE-PARA.
    READ OLD-TAPE RECORD AT END GO TO STOP-PARA.
    READ CARD-FILE RECORD AT END GO TO WRAP-UP.
    GO TO COMPARE-SSN-PARA.
NO-PURGE-PARA.
    WRITE NT-REC FROM OT-REC.
    READ OLD-TAPE RECORD AT END GO TO STOP-PARA.
    GO TO COMPARE-SSN-PARA.
WRAP-UP SECTION.
TRANSFER-REMAINING-RECS-PARA.
    WRITE NT-REC FROM OT-REC.
    READ OLD-TAPE RECORD AT END GO TO STOP-PARA.
    GO TO TRANSFER-REMAINING-RECS-PARA.
STOP-PARA.
    CLOSE CARD-FILE, OLD-TAPE, NEW-TAPE, PRINT-FILE.
    STOP RUN.
```

(handwritten note: perform purge / perform compare)

FIGURE 15.9   A Program to Purge Selected Records from a Tape File

purged. A purge operation is 90 percent the same as an update operation. It, too, involves the creation of a new tape. Each record to be purged must be searched for in exactly the same way you searched for the records to be updated, making sure as you search that the records you bypass are transferred to the new tape. You report the occurrence of erroneous key field values on data cards in exactly the same way you did in an update operation.

It's when you find a record that has to be purged that something different happens. In an update operation, when you find a record to be updated, you correct the appropriate field in the record and then write the corrected record on the new tape. When you find a record that is to be purged, you simply *do not transfer that record to the new tape*. When the purge operation is complete, the new tape contains all of the records from the old tape *except* those which you did not transfer to it from the old tape and therefore were purged.

Suppose the registrar wanted a program which would delete from his file the records of all students who have dropped out of school in the past term. He will give you a deck of data cards, each card containing the SSN of a student to be purged. Again, the cards will be in order by SSN.

The flowchart for this program is given in Figure 15.8. If you compare this flowchart with the one for a simple update given in Figure 15.6d, you'll be struck by how similar they are. In fact there's only one difference between them—in the left-hand column of steps (the branch taken when the record we've been searching for is found). In Figure 15.6d, the first two steps of that branch cause the record to be corrected and then written on the new tape. In a purge operation there is no correction to be made to the record. But most important of all, it is the *avoidance* of writing that record on the new tape that ultimately results in its being purged from the file. Therefore those first two steps of the left-hand branch of Figure 15.6d are absent from the corresponding spot in Figure 15.8.

In every other respect, however, the two flowcharts describe exactly the same logic.

Figure 15.9 shows the purge program which was written from the flowchart of Figure 15.8. (Since the ENVIRONMENT and DATA DIVISIONs of this purge program would be so similar to those shown in Figure 15.5 for the preceding update program, Figure 15.9 shows only the parts of those two divisions that are different from Figure 15.5. Dotted lines in Figure 15.9 indicate portions that are exactly the same as in Figure 15.5.)

15.4   File Maintenance: the Multiple Update Operation

As I mentioned before, there are many update operations in which more than one correction must be posted to each tape record being updated. Consider for example the problem of updating a bank account file. Very few people write only one check on their account in the course of a month. Most write several checks, and they make a few deposits as well. If it weren't for the multiple update operation, you'd have to run a simple update program 20 times to complete the update of the balance field in the record of a customer who'd written 20 checks.

In developing the logic for a multiple update, we drop the assumption that there will be only one update card in the data deck for every tape record that is to be updated; however, we do *not* drop the assumption that the cards in the data deck will be in the same order that the tape records are in. The result of this last assumption is that all update cards applying to the same tape record will be grouped together in the data deck.

The example to be used this time involves the inevitable requirement to post end-of-term grades to the registrar's file. The data cards for this multiple update will be in this form:

COLUMNS	INFORMATION	PICTURE
1–9	Student's SSN.	9(9)
10–15	Course number.	X(6)
16	Credit hours for this course.	9
17	Letter grade earned in this course.	A
18–80	Blank.	X(63)

For each student there will be one card in the data deck for each course she took during the term. As indicated above, each course card will contain the SSN of the student concerned, the number of the course, the number of credit hours the course was worth (up to a maximum of 4), and the letter grade earned by the student in that course (an A, B, C, D, or F). Most students will take four or five courses in a term, so for each of them there will be four or five cards in the deck. However, there will also be part-time students who've taken only one or two courses, and there'll only be one or two cards for them. There may even be an occasional student who took the term off and for whom there'll be no cards at all.

The point is that in a multiple update operation, there can be *any* number of update cards in the data deck for each record in the tape file—there will usually be more than one, but there *can* be only *one*, and sometimes there will be none at all. The program must be written to handle any of those possibilities.

The ultimate purpose of this program will be to update the grade point average of each student who has taken any courses this term. (The grade point average is important to a student, because many a future employer or graduate school will consider that average as an indicator of her potential for future success. Also, many schools will not promote a freshman, for example, to a sophomore unless her grade point average is above a certain level.)

In our fictitious (though typical) school, a student's grade point average is calculated by dividing the total number of grade points she has earned in all courses she has taken since the beginning of her freshman year, by the total number of credit hours those courses were worth.

To calculate the number of grade points earned in a course, you multiply the point value of the letter grade earned, by the number of credit hours the course is worth.

Letter Grade	Point Value
A	4 points
B	3 points
C	2 points
D	1 point
F	0 points

As an example, a student who'd earned a B in a 4 credit hour course would earn 12 grade points.

From what I have said so far, you can see that our program cannot be written to update just the grade point average. We must also keep track of the student's past grade point and credit hour totals, so those two fields will have to be updated as well.

First, let's consider the ENVIRONMENT and DATA DIVISIONs for this program. They're shown in Figure 15.10 below. Since these two DIVISIONs for a multiple update program would be so similar to those shown in Figure 15.5 for the simple update program, Figure 15.10 shows only the parts of those two DIVISIONs that are different from Figure 15.5. Dotted lines in Figure 15.10 indicate portions that are exactly the same as in Figure 15.5.

```
ENVIRONMENT DIVISION.
     •
     •
DATA DIVISION.
FILE SECTION.
FD   CARD-FILE; RECORD CONTAINS 80 CHARACTERS; LABEL RECORDS ARE
     OMITTED; DATA RECORD IS COURSE-CARD.
01   COURSE-CARD.
     02   SSN-CC              PICTURE 9(9).
     02   FILLER              PICTURE X(6).
     02   CRED-HRS-CC         PICTURE 9.
     02   LTR-GRADE-CC        PICTURE A.
     02   FILLER              PICTURE X(63).
FD   PRINT-FILE; . . . . . . . .
     •
     •
FD   OLD-TAPE; . . . . . . . . .
     •
     •
FD   NEW-TAPE; . . . . . . . . .
     •
     •
WORKING-STORAGE SECTION.
77   NUM-GRADE-WS            PICTURE 9.
77   GR-PTS-WS              PICTURE 99.
01   ERROR-LINE.
     •
     •
```

FIGURE 15.10   The ENVIRONMENT and DATA DIVISIONs of a Tape File Multiple Update Program

Now take a look at the flowchart of this multiple update operation in Figure 15.11. Again, it is in many ways similar to the simple update flowchart of Figure 15.6d. The principal difference lies once more in the left-hand column of steps (the branch taken when the record we've been searching for has been found). In a simple update operation, where we *know* that there will be no more than one change to be made to any record needing updating, as soon as the change is made we can immediately write that corrected record on the new tape and then read the next record off the old tape. Not so in a multiple update.

In a multiple update operation, you *don't* know how many changes are going to be made to each tape record. The left-hand branch, therefore, cannot include the writing of that corrected record on the new tape. You may not be finished posting corrections to that record, and you do not want to write it on the new tape until you are. Likewise, if you are not finished with that record, you will not yet be ready to get another record off the old tape either; so the reading of the next old tape record must also be eliminated from the left-hand branch.

In the left-hand branch there now remain only two steps we want the computer to take: we want it to post the latest update to the tape record and then we want it to get the next course card from the data deck. Notice that we then tell the computer to go back and check the SSN in the old tape record against the SSN on this latest course card it has read. The computer loops through this left-hand branch repeatedly as long as the SSN's it gets from subsequent course cards continue to agree with the SSN in the latest tape record it got off the old tape.

Only when the computer reads a card which contains a SSN that is greater than the one in the old tape record we've been updating (i.e., when SSN-CC > SSN-OT—or the equivalent condition SSN-OT < SSN-CC used in the flowchart) do we know that we have no more corrections to be posted to that record. When that happens we want the computer to write the updated record on the new tape and then get the next student's record off the old tape, so we tell it to take the right-hand branch to the GET-NEXT-STUDENT-PARA. In that branch of the flowchart, it is told to write the corrected record on the new tape and read the next record off the old tape. It then loops repeatedly through that right-hand branch as it searches for the student on the old tape whose SSN is the same as the one that appeared on the latest course card that was read. When that student is found, the computer then returns to looping repeatedly through the left-hand branch (the UPDATE-PARA) as it performs the multiple updates of that student's record.

And so it goes—back and forth between the UPDATE-PARA and the GET-NEXT-STUDENT-PARA (with a minimum number of trips through the ERROR-PARA, we hope)—until the end of the data deck is detected. A few loops through the WRAP-UP SECTION and the operation is finished.

Now study the program given in Figure 15.12 to see how this flowchart looks in COBOL. Notice especially the UPDATE-CALC-ROUTINE and how a PERFORM verb was used to call it into operation.

15.5   Tape File Maintenance Operations: One Last Point

This completes my discussion of the update and purge operations. Before we move on I want to make one last, practical point.

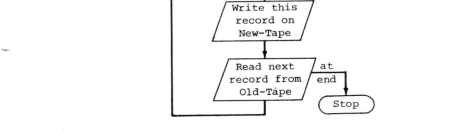

FIGURE 15.11   The Multiple Update Operation

ENVIRONMENT and DATA DIVISIONs shown in Figure 15.10

```
PROCEDURE DIVISION.
UPDATE SECTION.
START-PARA.
     OPEN INPUT CARD-FILE, OLD-TAPE; OUTPUT PRINT-FILE, NEW-TAPE.
     READ OLD-TAPE RECORD AT END GO TO STOP-PARA.
     READ CARD-FILE RECORD AT END GO TO WRAP-UP.
COMPARE-SSN-PARA.
     IF SSN-OT = SSN-CC GO TO UPDATE-PARA.
     IF SSN-OT < SSN-CC GO TO GET-NEXT-STUDENT-PARA.
ERROR-PARA.
     MOVE SSN-CC TO SSN-EL.
     WRITE PRINT-LINE FROM ERROR-LINE.
     READ CARD-FILE RECORD AT END GO TO WRAP-UP.
     GO TO COMPARE-SSN-PARA.
UPDATE-PARA.
     PERFORM UPDATE-CALC-ROUTINE.
     READ CARD-FILE RECORD AT END GO TO WRAP-UP.
     GO TO COMPARE-SSN-PARA.
GET-NEXT-STUDENT-PARA.
     WRITE NT-REC FROM OT-REC.
     READ OLD-TAPE RECORD AT END GO TO STOP-PARA.
     GO TO COMPARE-SSN-PARA.
UPDATE-CALC-ROUTINE.
     IF LTR-GRADE-CC = 'A' MOVE 4 TO NUM-GRADE-WS.
     IF LTR-GRADE-CC = 'B' MOVE 3 TO NUM-GRADE-WS.
     IF LTR-GRADE-CC = 'C' MOVE 2 TO NUM-GRADE-WS.
     IF LTR-GRADE-CC = 'D' MOVE 1 TO NUM-GRADE-WS.
     IF LTR-GRADE-CC = 'F' MOVE 0 TO NUM-GRADE-WS.
     MULTIPLY NUM-GRADE-WS BY CRED-HRS-CC GIVING GR-PTS-WS.
     ADD GR-PTS-WS TO TOTAL-GR-PTS-OT.
     ADD CRED-HRS-CC TO TOTAL-CR-HRS-OT.
     DIVIDE TOTAL-GR-PTS-OT BY TOTAL-CR-HRS-OT
          GIVING GR-PT-AVE-OT.
WRAP-UP SECTION.
TRANSFER-REMAINING-RECS-PARA.
     WRITE NT-REC FROM OT-REC.
     READ OLD-TAPE RECORD AT END GO TO STOP-PARA.
     GO TO TRANSFER-REMAINING-RECS-PARA.
STOP-PARA.
     CLOSE CARD-FILE, OLD-TAPE, NEW-TAPE, PRINT-FILE.
     STOP RUN.
```

FIGURE 15.12   The PROCEDURE DIVISION of a Tape File Multiple Update Program

Remember that when you write an update (or purge) program, you're not writing a program that will be run once and then forever retired to the shelf. An update program is one that is run on a regular basis—either monthly, weekly or sometimes even daily. The programmers in an installation which runs daily updates (for example) must keep this in mind: Monday's new tape will be used on Tuesday as the old tape; Tuesday's new tape will become Wednesday's old tape; Wednesday's new tape will become Thursday's old tape; etc.; etc.

That is the reason why I mentioned earlier that the format of an update program's new tape file must be exactly the same as its old tape file. The records of the two files must be in exactly the same formats, as well. If you created a new tape file in a format different from the old tape file, then today's new tape would *not* work as tomorrow's old tape.

Today's old tape was yesterday's new tape, so if you don't want to have to rewrite your DATA DIVISION every day, be sure your new tape is created in a format that duplicates the format of the old tape:

1. The size of their record blocks must be the same.

2. The size of their individual records must be the same.

3. The order of the data fields within their records must be the same.

4. The PICTURE clauses of their data fields must be the same.

15.6 The SORT Operation

When you have a tape file whose records are in some given order (say for example, numerical order by account number) and you wish to have the records rearranged into some different order (for example, alphabetical order by customer name), you must perform a sort operation on the file.

One of COBOL's real claims to fame is its remarkable SORT verb.

A program which uses the SORT verb must have three files:

1. An *input file* containing the records you want sorted;

2. A *sort file* to be used as a work file by the computer while it performs the sort; and

3. An *output file* upon which the computer will write the records after they have been sorted.

The ENVIRONMENT DIVISION must include SELECT sentences for all three of these files.

In the DATA DIVISION the input and output files are described with the usual FD entries. The sort file is described with a Sort-File Description (SD) entry. An SD entry contains only three elements:

```
SD   sort-file-name;
     RECORD CONTAINS integer CHARACTERS;
     DATA RECORD IS sort-record-name.
```

Note that there is no LABEL RECORDS clause in an SD entry.

Like an FD entry, an SD entry is followed by an 01 level record-name entry and the appropriate group and elementary item entries to describe the contents of the record. The format of the three files' records must be identical, i.e., the order of their fields as well as the PICTURE clauses of each of the corresponding fields must be exactly the same.

Suppose, for example, that the registrar wanted a listing of the contents of his tape file, not in its present arrangement (records in numerical order by SSN), but rather by class (with freshmen listed first and seniors last). Within classes he wants students arranged in alphabetical order.

Figure 15.13 shows the ENVIRONMENT DIVISION and DATA DIVISION for this program. Notice that we've declared the name of the sort file to be SORT-TAPE, and that there is a SELECT sentence in the ENVIRONMENT DIVISION and an SD entry in the DATA DIVISION to describe it. Notice that there is a PRINT-FILE and DETAIL-LINE for use in printing out the results of the sort. I am using duplicate data-names between the NT-REC and the DETAIL-LINE so I can use the MOVE CORResponding verb in transferring data from one to the other.

In the PROCEDURE DIVISION of a sort program, you use a SORT sentence to tell the computer how you want the sort performed.

```
ENVIRONMENT DIVISION.
CONFIGURATION SECTION.
SOURCE-COMPUTER.  HAL-2001.
OBJECT-COMPUTER.  HAL-2001.
INPUT-OUTPUT SECTION.
FILE-CONTROL.
     SELECT OLD-TAPE ASSIGN TO TAPE-1.
     SELECT SORT-TAPE ASSIGN TO TAPE-2.
     SELECT NEW-TAPE ASSIGN TO TAPE-3.
     SELECT PRINT-FILE ASSIGN TO LINE-PRINTER.
DATA DIVISION.
FILE SECTION.
FD   OLD-TAPE; BLOCK CONTAINS 20 RECORDS; RECORD CONTAINS 76 CHARA
-    CTERS; LABEL RECORDS ARE STANDARD; DATA RECORD IS OT-REC.
01   OT-REC.
     02  NAME-OT              PICTURE A(24).
     02  ADDR-OT              PICTURE X(28).
     02  SSN-OT               PICTURE 9(9).
     02  GRAD-YR-OT           PICTURE 99.
     02  MAJOR-OT             PICTURE AA.
     02  TOTAL-CR-HRS-OT      PICTURE 999.
     02  TOTAL-GR-PTS-OT      PICTURE 9999.
     02  GR-PT-AVE-OT         PICTURE 9V999.
FD   NEW-TAPE; BLOCK CONTAINS 20 RECORDS; RECORD CONTAINS 76 CHARA
-    CTERS; LABEL RECORDS ARE STANDARD; DATA RECORD IS NT-REC.
01   NT-REC.
     02  NAME                 PICTURE A(24).
     02  ADDR                 PICTURE X(28).
     02  SSN                  PICTURE 9(9).
     02  GRAD-YR              PICTURE 99.
     02  MAJOR                PICTURE AA.
     02  TOTAL-CR-HRS         PICTURE 999.
     02  TOTAL-GR-PTS         PICTURE 9999.
     02  GR-PT-AVE            PICTURE 9V999.
SD   SORT-TAPE; RECORD CONTAINS 76 CHARACTERS; DATA RECORD IS
     ST-REC.
01   ST-REC.
     02  NAME-ST              PICTURE A(24).
     02  ADDR-ST              PICTURE X(28).
     02  SSN-ST               PICTURE 9(9).
```

FIGURE 15.13   The ENVIRONMENT and DATA DIVISIONs of a Sort Program

```
    02  GRAD-YR-ST              PICTURE 99.
    02  MAJOR-ST                PICTURE AA.
    02  TOTAL-CR-HRS-ST         PICTURE 999.
    02  TOTAL-GR-PTS-ST         PICTURE 9999.
    02  GR-PT-AVE-ST            PICTURE 9V999.
FD  PRINT-FILE; RECORD CONTAINS 136 CHARACTERS; LABEL RECORDS ARE
    OMITTED; DATA RECORD IS PRINT-LINE.
01  PRINT-LINE                  PICTURE X(136).
WORKING-STORAGE SECTION.
01  DETAIL-LINE.
    02  NAME                    PICTURE BA(24)B(5).
    02  ADDR                    PICTURE X(28)B(5).
    02  SSN                     PICTURE 999B99B9999B(5).
    02  FILLER                  PICTURE XX              VALUE '19'.
    02  GRAD-YR                 PICTURE 99B(5).
    02  MAJOR                   PICTURE AAB(5).
    02  TOTAL-CR-HRS            PICTURE ZZ9B(5).
    02  TOTAL-GR-PTS            PICTURE ZZZ9B(5).
    02  GR-PT-AVE               PICTURE 9.999.
    02  FILLER                  PICTURE X(19)           VALUE SPACES.
```

FIGURE 15.13   (continued)

```
SORT sort-file-name

       ⎧ ASCENDING  ⎫
    ON ⎨    or      ⎬ KEY data-name-1, data-name-2, . . . . . . . . ,
       ⎩ DESCENDING ⎭           └──── Optional ────┘

       ⎧ ASCENDING  ⎫
    ON ⎨    or      ⎬ KEY data-name-3, data-name-4, . . . . . . . . ,
       ⎩ DESCENDING ⎭
       └──────────────── Optional ────────────────┘

    USING input-file-name

    GIVING output-file-name.
```

The data-names given in the SORT sentence must be those of the sort-record. They are referred to as sort keys. As an example of a correct SORT sentence, here is the sentence that will be used to obtain the order of records the registrar has asked us for:

```
SORT SORT-TAPE
     ON DESCENDING KEY GRAD-YR-ST
     ON ASCENDING KEY NAME-ST
     USING OLD-TAPE
     GIVING NEW-TAPE.
```

There only *has* to be one data-name given as a sort key, and you must specify whether you want the records sorted into ascending or descending order on that key. You may give as many additional sort keys as you wish, however; and you may specify each of those keys to be in either order (ascending or descending). When more than one sort key is given, the computer handles the first one named as the primary key, the second as the secondary key, the third as the tertiary key, etc., etc. In performing the sort, as long as the computer finds no two records' primary key values to be identical, it ignores all lower ranked keys. Only when it finds the values of two or more records' primary keys to be identical does it consider the values of the secondary keys in order to determine what the order of the records should be. It ignores the tertiary keys unless it finds two or more records whose primary keys' values are identical *and* whose secondary keys' values are identical. And so on, and so forth.

As another example, suppose the registrar wanted all students' records sorted into the following order:

1. All majors are to be grouped together, Anthropology first;
2. Within majors the students are to be arranged by class (seniors first);
3. Students with the same major who are also in the same class, are to be arranged so that those with the highest grade point averages will be first; and
4. If there are any with the same major who are in the same class and have the same grade point average, he wants them in alphabetical order.

This is the SORT sentence which would accomplish that rearrangement:

```
SORT SORT-TAPE
      ON ASCENDING KEY MAJOR-ST, GRAD-YR-ST
      ON DESCENDING KEY GR-PT-AVE-ST
      ON ASCENDING KEY NAME-ST
      USING OLD-TAPE
      GIVING NEW-TAPE.
```

Consider the remarkable amount of work done for you by the SORT sentence:

The SORT Sentence:

1. OPENs the Input-File for INPUT and the Sort-File for OUTPUT.
2. READs all Input-File records and WRITEs them into the Sort-File.
3. CLOSEs the Input- and Sort-Files.
4. SORTs the Sort-File's records according to the keys you specified.
5. OPENs the Sort-File for INPUT and the Output-File for OUTPUT.
6. READs all Sort-File records and WRITEs them into the Output-File.
7. CLOSEs the Sort- and Output-Files.

Notice from what's just been said that all three files involved in the sort are OPENed as a part of the sort procedure, and that before the procedure is finished they are all CLOSEd again. As a result, if any of those files are OPENed by you before you get to the SORT sentence, you must be sure to CLOSE them prior to the SORT. Likewise, if you have need to process the data in either the input file or the output file after the sort is completed, you will have to OPEN them again for INPUT or OUTPUT as appropriate.

ENVIRONMENT and DATA DIVISIONs shown in Figure 15.13.

```
PROCEDURE DIVISION.
SORT-THE-FILE SECTION.
SORT-PARA.
      SORT SORT-TAPE ON DESCENDING KEY GRAD-YR-ST
            ON ASCENDING KEY NAME-ST
            USING OLD-TAPE
            GIVING NEW-TAPE.
PRINT-RESULTS-OF-SORT SECTION.
OPEN-PARA.
      OPEN INPUT NEW-TAPE, OUTPUT PRINT-FILE.
READ-NEW-TAPE-AND-PRINT-PARA.
      READ NEW-TAPE RECORD AT END GO TO STOP-PARA.
      MOVE CORR NT-REC TO DETAIL-LINE.
      WRITE NT-REC FROM DETAIL-LINE.
      GO TO READ-NEW-TAPE-AND-PRINT-PARA.
STOP-PARA.
      CLOSE NEW-TAPE, PRINT-FILE.
      STOP RUN.
```

FIGURE 15.14   The PROCEDURE DIVISION of a Sort Program

The PROCEDURE DIVISION for our example program is given in Figure 15.14. Notice that none of the files involved in the sort were OPENed prior to the SORT sentence. Notice that after the SORT sentence, when it was desired to dump the contents of the NEW-TAPE to the line printer, we had to OPEN that tape for INPUT before reading from it.

15.7   The MERGE Operation

There often occurs a need to add new records to an established tape file (for example, the need to add the records of newly opened charge accounts to a department store's file of already active charge accounts). This would be a relatively simple task to perform, if it were not for one vital consideration—all records in any file must be in the proper location relative to all other records, according to the established order for that file. If any records were not in the proper order, the search, update and purge operations (whose logic was developed around the assumption that all records *would* be in order) would not work properly on that file.

In order to add new records to a file so that they will be in the proper locations among the file's original records, you perform a merge operation.

The COBOL MERGE verb is every bit as remarkable as the SORT verb. In fact, the two verbs have very much in common.

A program that uses the MERGE verb must have four files:

1. The *old input file* of original records;
2. The *new input file* of records to be merged with the records of the old input file;
3. The *merge file* to be used as a work file by the computer as it performs the merge operation; and
4. The *output file* which will receive the results of the merging of the two files.

The ENVIRONMENT DIVISION must include SELECT sentences for all four files.

In the DATA DIVISION, the old input file, the new input file, and the output file are described using the normal FD entries. The merge file is described using an SD entry (described in the last section). The format of the four files' records must be identical, i.e., the order of their fields as well as the PICTURE clauses of each of the corresponding fields must be exactly the same.

The MERGE sentence is in the following form:

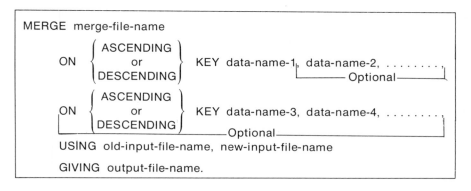

The keys given in the MERGE sentence, like those given in the SORT sentence, specify the order in which we want the records recorded in the output file. They must be data-names of the merge-record. Unlike the SORT sentence, however, the MERGE sentence requires that the records in each of the two input files be *already* in the order specified by those keys. If either input file (or both) were not already in that order, a SORT would have to be performed upon them before the MERGE.

The MERGE sentence, like the SORT, requires that all files involved in the merge operation be closed prior to starting the merge. It OPENs them as it needs to and CLOSEs them all again before it is through.

Figure 15.15 shows the ENVIRONMENT, DATA and PROCEDURE DIVISIONs of an example merge program. This time the registrar has asked us to prepare a program to merge into his tape file the records of new freshmen. The freshmen's records will be given to us as a deck of cards, so we'll use the card file as the new-input-file.

```
ENVIRONMENT DIVISION.
CONFIGURATION SECTION.
SOURCE-COMPUTER.  HAL-2001.
OBJECT-COMPUTER.  HAL-2001.
INPUT-OUTPUT SECTION.
FILE-CONTROL.
     SELECT OLD-TAPE ASSIGN TO TAPE-1.
     SELECT NEW-STUDENTS-FILE ASSIGN TO CARD-READER.
     SELECT MERGE-TAPE ASSIGN TO TAPE-2.
     SELECT NEW-TAPE ASSIGN TO TAPE-3.
DATA DIVISION.
FILE SECTION.
FD   OLD-TAPE; BLOCK CONTAINS 20 RECORDS; RECORD CONTAINS 76 CHARA
-    CTERS; LABEL RECORDS ARE STANDARD; DATA RECORD IS OT-REC.
 01  OT-REC.
     02  NAME-OT              PICTURE A(24).
     02  ADDR-OT              PICTURE X(28).
     02  SSN-OT               PICTURE 9(9).
     02  GRAD-YR-OT           PICTURE 99.
     02  MAJOR-OT             PICTURE AA.
     02  TOTAL-CR-HRS-OT      PICTURE 999.
     02  TOTAL-GR-PTS-OT      PICTURE 9999.
     02  GR-PT-AVE-OT         PICTURE 9V999.
FD   NEW-STUDENTS-FILE; RECORD CONTAINS 80 CHARACTERS; LABEL RECOR
-    DS ARE OMITTED; DATA RECORD IS NEW-STUDENT-CARD.
 01  NEW-STUDENT-CARD.
     02  NAME-NS              PICTURE A(24).
     02  ADDR-NS              PICTURE X(28).
     02  SSN-NS               PICTURE 9(9).
     02  GRAD-YR-NS           PICTURE 99.
     02  MAJOR-NS             PICTURE AA.
     02  TOTAL-CR-HRS-NS      PICTURE 999.
     02  TOTAL-GR-PTS-NS      PICTURE 9999.
     02  GR-PT-AVE-NS         PICTURE 9V999.
     02  FILLER               PICTURE X(4).
SD   MERGE-TAPE; RECORD CONTAINS 76 CHARACTERS; DATA RECORD IS
     MERGE-REC.
 01  MERGE-REC.
     02  NAME-MT              PICTURE A(24).
     02  ADDR-MT              PICTURE X(28).
     02  SSN-MT               PICTURE 9(9).
     02  GRAD-YR-MT           PICTURE 99.
     02  MAJOR-MT             PICTURE AA.
     02  TOTAL-CR-HRS-MT      PICTURE 999.
     02  TOTAL-GR-PTS-MT      PICTURE 9999.
     02  GR-PT-AVE-MT         PICTURE 9V999.
FD   NEW-TAPE; BLOCK CONTAINS 20 RECORDS; RECORD CONTAINS 76 CHARA
-    CTERS; LABEL RECORDS ARE STANDARD; DATA RECORD IS NT-REC.
 01  NT-REC.
     02  NAME-NT              PICTURE A(24).
     02  ADDR-NT              PICTURE X(28).
     02  SSN-NT               PICTURE 9(9).
     02  GRAD-YR-NT           PICTURE 99.
     02  MAJOR-NT             PICTURE AA.
     02  TOTAL-CR-HRS-NT      PICTURE 999.
```

FIGURE 15.15   A Merge Program

```
02   TOTAL-GR-PTS-NT      PICTURE 9999.
02   GR-PT-AVE-NT         PICTURE 9V999.
PROCEDURE DIVISION.
MERGE-PARA.
    MERGE MERGE-TAPE ON ASCENDING KEY SSN-MT
        USING OLD-TAPE, NEW-STUDENTS-FILE
        GIVING NEW-TAPE.
    STOP RUN.
```

FIGURE 15.15   (continued)

15.8   Multiple Reel Files

There are actually three types of tape files:

1. Single reel files;
2. Multiple reel files; and
3. Multiple file reels.

The file we've been discussing so far has been a single reel file—a file which will fit entirely on one reel of tape. In this section we'll discuss multiple reel files—files that are too large to fit on a single reel. In the next section we'll discuss how you load *more* than one file on a single reel (a multiple file reel).

When a file is contained on more than one reel, the system employs Beginning- and Ending-Reel-Labels in addition to the Beginning- and Ending-File-Labels we spoke of earlier. The placement of those labels is outlined in Figure 15.16.

Placing a file on more than one reel is a simple matter from the programmer's point of view. You simply include more than one device-name in the SELECT sentence for that file. For example, if your INVENTORY-TAPE-FILE were going to be placed on three reels of tape, and you'd loaded those reels on tape drives 4, 5, and 6; your SELECT sentence would say:

SELECT INVENTORY-TAPE-FILE ASSIGN TO TAPE-4, TAPE-5, TAPE-6.

	Begins With	Ends With
First Reel	Beginning-File-Label	Ending-Reel-Label
Each Intermediate Reel	Beginning-Reel-Label	Ending-Reel-Label
Final Reel	Beginning-Reel-Label	Ending-File-Label

FIGURE 15.16   The Arrangement of Labels in a Multiple Reel File

You write a COBOL program to create a multiple reel file in *exactly* the same way as you'd write it if it created a single reel file. In executing the program, the computer begins by recording the records on the first tape. When the trailer marker at the end of that first tape is detected, it records that tape's Ending-Reel-Label, and then performs what's called a "reel swap."—it switches its output channel over to the next tape drive indicated in the SELECT sentence. It records the second reel's Beginning-Reel-Label and then continues recording the contents of the file on that tape. The same thing happens when the end of the second tape is reached.

In COBOL, a program which reads a multiple reel file is also written exactly like one which reads from a single reel file (except for the file's SELECT sentence). Again, the computer automatically performs the reel swapping routines when it's time to do so—the programmer is completely free of that concern.

15.9   Multiple File Reels

When your file is too small to fill up a 2400 foot reel, it is possible to put it on a smaller reel. It is also possible to put it on a 2400 foot reel along with other short files, and when you do that you are said to be creating a multiple file reel. It does take a little more programming effort to create a multiple file reel.

The first new feature of a program that either creates or uses a multiple file reel occurs in the FILE-CONTROL paragraph of the ENVIRON-MENT DIVISION's INPUT-OUTPUT SECTION. You must have a SELECT sentence for each of the files in the reel. If, for example, you had (or were about to read) two files—an EXPIRED-CREDIT-CARD-FILE and a CUSTOMER-DISCOUNT-RATE-FILE—on the tape which is mounted on tape drive 4, you'd use these two SELECT sentences:

```
SELECT EXPIRED-CREDIT-CARD-FILE ASSIGN TO TAPE-4A.
SELECT CUSTOMER-DISCOUNT-RATE-FILE ASSIGN TO TAPE-4B.
```

(You're reminded that the device-names which appear in ASSIGN clauses are very much different on different computers. These are representative examples. You'll have to check at your computer center to find out what you should use for your system.)

A second new feature appearing in the ENVIRONMENT DIVISION is the I-O-CONTROL paragraph of the INPUT-OUTPUT SECTION. In that paragraph, you place a MULTIPLE FILE TAPE sentence of this form:

```
MULTIPLE FILE TAPE CONTAINS file-name-1, file-name-2, . . . . . . . .
```

The purpose of the MULTIPLE FILE TAPE sentence is to inform the computer of the order in which the files occur on the tape.

This is what the INPUT-OUTPUT SECTION would look like for the example files I mentioned above:

```
INPUT-OUTPUT SECTION.
FILE-CONTROL.
    SELECT EXPIRED-CREDIT-CARD-FILE ASSIGN TO TAPE-4A.
    SELECT CUSTOMER-DISCOUNT-RATE-FILE ASSIGN TO TAPE-4B.
    SELECT . . . . . . . . . . . .
I-O-CONTROL.
    MULTIPLE FILE TAPE CONTAINS EXPIRED-CREDIT-CARD-FILE,
    CUSTOMER-DISCOUNT-RATE-FILE.
```

(The incomplete third SELECT sentence is intended to represent the SELECTs for any other files used by the program.)

In the DATA DIVISION each file would have its own separate FD entry.

In the PROCEDURE DIVISION of the program that created these files, you'd include first a sentence to OPEN the first file:

```
OPEN OUTPUT EXPIRED-CREDIT-CARD-FILE.
```

Then you'd provide the sentences necessary to record the records of that file. After the first file was complete you'd say:

```
CLOSE EXPIRED-CREDIT-CARD-FILE WITHOUT REWIND.
```

The computer would record the Ending-File-Label on that file, but would *not* rewind the reel.

Next you'd command:

```
OPEN OUTPUT CUSTOMER-DISCOUNT-RATE-FILE WITHOUT REWIND.
```

(When you OPEN a file that for any reason wasn't fully rewound, the computer will rewind it first. That's why we have to specify here that we want this file OPENed WITHOUT REWIND.) The computer would now record the Beginning-File-Label for this second file immediately after the Ending-File-Label of the first file.

Next would come your sentences necessary to record the records of the second file on the tape. When the file was complete you'd tell the computer to:

```
CLOSE CUSTOMER-DISCOUNT-RATE-FILE.
```

The Ending-File-Label for that file would be recorded and the *entire reel* would be rewound.

In writing a program which would read either of the files, you'd simply OPEN the file you wanted to use. If you said:

```
OPEN INPUT EXPIRED-CREDIT-CARD-FILE.
```

the tape would be positioned at the beginning of the first file. If you said:

```
OPEN INPUT CUSTOMER-DISCOUNT-RATE-FILE.
```

the tape would be reeled forward and positioned at the beginning of the second file.

If you CLOSEd *either* file, the *entire reel* would be rewound all the way back to the load point marker (unless, of course, you CLOSEd WITH-OUT REWIND, and then there'd be no rewind at all).

There is this restriction—only one file from a multiple file reel may be OPEN at any one time.

What if you wrote a program which did not use all of the files in multiple file reel? Such a program would use this second version of the MULTI-PLE FILE TAPE sentence:

MULTIPLE FILE TAPE CONTAINS file-name-1 POSITION integer-1,

file-name-2 POSITION integer-2, ...
—————————Optional—————————

The POSITION clause is used to indicate the position of a file on the tape when all file names from that tape are not mentioned in the sentence.

A program, for example, which used only our second file, the CUSTOMER-DISCOUNT-RATE-FILE mentioned earlier, would have an INPUT-OUTPUT SECTION like this:

```
INPUT-OUTPUT SECTION.
FILE-CONTROL.
    SELECT CUSTOMER-DISCOUNT-RATE-FILE ASSIGN TO TAPE-4.
    SELECT . . . . . . . . .
I-O-CONTROL.
    MULTIPLE FILE TAPE CONTAINS CUSTOMER-DISCOUNT-RATE-FILE
    POSITION 2.
```

Notice that we only needed a SELECT sentence for the file we were actually going to use. None was required for the first file on that tape. For the same reason, we are now relieved of having to write DATA DIVISION FD entries for every file on the tape—only the file(s) we actually intend to use in a program will need FD entries in that program.

15.10 A Final Comment on Multiple Reel Files and Multiple File Reels

I have included these last two sections on Multiple Reel Files and Multiple File Reels only for the sake of the completeness of these Chapters on Magnetic Tape Files. The fact of the matter is that the overwhelming majority of tape files existent today are single reel files.

In order to avoid the complexities of multiple reel files, data processing managers normally opt to break a super-huge file down into smaller sub-files, each of which *can* be fit on a single reel. For example, our registrar's file could have been subdivided into a single reel freshman-file, a single reel sophomore-file, etc., if the all-encompassing student-file grew too large to fit on a single reel.

To avoid the complexities of multiple file reels, data processing managers will usually elect to place their smaller files on smaller reels.

For those reasons, I have chosen to dwell only minimally on these last two topics. In your study of magnetic tape operations, you should concentrate on Sections 14.1 through 15.7. Likewise, the Exercises, Example Program and Student's Program which follow this chapter will deal exclusively with single reel files.

EXERCISES

Answers to all exercises in this chapter are given in Appendix A.

15.1 Refer to the search program of Figure 15.1. Rewrite the PRINT-SELECTED-RECORDS-PARA so that the computer will list all members of the class of 1981 who are PE majors.

15.2 This is the DATA DIVISION of a search program:

```
DATA  DIVISION.
FILE  SECTION.
FD    CATALOG-TAPE-FILE; BLOCK CONTAINS 30 RECORDS; RECORD CONTAINS
      45 CHARACTERS; LABEL RECORDS ARE STANDARD; DATA RECORD IS
      CATALOG-REC.
01    CATALOG-REC.
      02  CATALOG-NUMBER    PICTURE 9(8).
      02  ITEM-NAME         PICTURE A(20).
      02  QUANTITY-ON-HAND  PICTURE 9999.
      02  UNIT-PRICE        PICTURE 999V99.
      02  REORDER-POINT     PICTURE 9999.
      02  REORDER-QUANTITY PICTURE 9999.
FD    PRINT-FILE; RECORD CONTAINS 136 CHARACTERS; LABEL RECORDS ARE
      OMITTED; DATA RECORD IS PRINT-LINE.
01    PRINT-LINE            PICTURE X(136).
WORKING-STORAGE SECTION.
01    REORDER-LINE.
      02  FILLER            PICTURE A(7)      VALUE ' ORDER '.
      02  REORDER-QUANTITY PICTURE ZZZ9.
      02  FILLER            PICTURE X(13)     VALUE ' OF PART NO. '.
      02  CATALOG-NUMBER    PICTURE 9(8).
      02  FILLER            PICTURE X(104)    VALUE SPACES.
```

The tape file contains records on every item stocked in a department store's catalog warehouse. The term "reorder point" refers to the level at or below which you wish to reorder the item from your supplier. The "reorder quantity" is the quantity you wish to order when you place that reorder. Write the PROCEDURE DIVISION of this search program: Have the computer go through the tape file and report every item that is at or below its reorder point. The report is to include the quantity of each item to be reordered in a line of this format:

ORDER 100 OF PART NO. 21746890

15.3 The company auditor needs a monthly report on the total value of the department store's catalog warehouse inventory. The value of each item in the inventory is calculated by multiplying the quantity of that item on hand by the unit price of the item. Using the FILE SECTION given in exercise 15.2 above, write the WORKING-STORAGE SECTION and the PROCEDURE DIVISION of a program that will calculate the total value of all items in the warehouse. Report the results of the calculation in a report line of this format (use floating $'s):

THE VALUE OF ALL ITEMS ON HAND IN THE WAREHOUSE IS $999,999,999.99

15.4 Every day the catalog warehouse manager needs to know the quantity of selected items on hand in the warehouse. Every morning she'll give you a deck of data cards, each card containing the catalog number of an item whose quantity she wants to know. The cards will be in numerical order. (Assume that the records in the tape file are also in numerical order by catalog number.) Refer back to the DATA DIVISION described in exercise 15.2. Consider this FD entry to have been added to the FILE SECTION:

```
FD   CARD-FILE; RECORD CONTAINS 80 CHARACTERS; LABEL RECORDS ARE
     OMITTED; DATA RECORD IS CAT-NO-CARD.
01   CAT-NO-CARD.
     02  DES-CAT-NO   PICTURE 9(8).
     02  FILLER       PICTURE X(72).
```

Consider the WORKING-STORAGE SECTION of exercise 15.2 to have been replaced by the following:

```
WORKING-STORAGE SECTION.
01   DETAIL-LINE.
     02  CATALOG-NUMBER    PICTURE B9(8)B(5).
     02  ITEM-NAME         PICTURE A(20)B(5).
     02  QUANTITY-ON-HAND  PICTURE ZZZ9.
     02  FILLER            PICTURE X(93)    VALUE ' ON HAND.'.
01   ERROR-LINE.
     02  CAT-NO-EL         PICTURE B9(8).
     02  FILLER            PICTURE X(127)   VALUE ' NOT IN FILE.'.
```

Write the PROCEDURE DIVISION of a program to search for each of the items the warehouse manager wants reported. The format of the report on each item will be as indicated in the DETAIL-LINE above. If an erroneous catalog number turns up in the data deck, report it using the ERROR-LINE given above.

15.5 These FD entries describe the two tape files that will be involved in an update operation:

```
FD   OLD-TAPE; BLOCK CONTAINS 25 RECORDS; RECORD CONTAINS 15 CHARA
     CTERS; LABEL RECORDS ARE STANDARD; DATA RECORD IS OT-REC.
01   OT-REC.
     02  PART-NO-OT     PICTURE 9(6).
     02  UNIT-PRICE-OT  PICTURE 999V99.
     02  QUANTITY-OT    PICTURE 9999.
FD   NEW-TAPE; BLOCK CONTAINS 30 RECORDS; RECORD CONTAINS 14 CHARA
     CTERS; LABEL RECORDS ARE STANDARD; DATA RECORD IS NT-REC.
01   NT-REC.
     02  PART-NO-NT     PICTURE 9(5).
     02  QUANTITY-NT    PICTURE 9999.
     02  UNIT-PRICE-NT  PICTURE 999V99.
```

Do you detect any potential problems from what you see in those two FD entries?

15.6 Refer to the simple update program of Figures 15.5 and 15.7. Consider this to have been substituted for the first FD entry in the DATA DIVISION:

```
FD  CARD-FILE; RECORD CONTAINS 80 CHARACTERS; LABEL RECORDS ARE
    OMITTED; DATA RECORD IS CHANGE-CARD.
01  CHANGE-CARD.
    02  SSN-CC                  PICTURE 9(9).
    02  CODE-CC                 PICTURE 9.
    02  NEW-ADDRESS             PICTURE X(28).
    02  NEW-MAJOR               PICTURE AA.
    02  FILLER                  PICTURE X(40).
```

The plan is to remodel the update program so that we're not limited to changing *just* the student's address. We now also want the ability to change her graduation year if she's dropped back, or her major if she's switched majors. To provide for this, we've first redesigned the CHANGE-CARD as shown above. It now has a field in which to place the new address and a separate one for the new major, which we'll use depending on which we want to change. A code field has been added to the card to indicate which field is to be changed:

A Code Value of	Means
1	Change the address.
2	Change the graduation year.
3	Change the major.

When a person's graduation year is to be changed, you simply add 1 to whatever the former year was. Rewrite the UPDATE-PARA of Figure 15.7 to incorporate these revisions to the simple update program.

15.7   Refer to the sort program of Figure 15.14. Rewrite the SORT-PARA so that the file will be sorted into this arrangement: (1) all classes together (freshmen first); (2) within each class, majors together (Anthropology first, Zoology last); (3) within each major, students in alphabetical order; and (4) should there be any students with the same name (two John Smith's, for example), put them in numerical order by SSN.

15.8   This is supposed to be a Sort-File Description entry. What's wrong with it?

```
FD  WORK-TAPE; BLOCK CONTAINS 25 RECORDS; RECORD CONTAINS 160 CHA
    RACTERS; LABEL RECORDS ARE STANDARD; DATA RECORD IS SORT-REC.
```

15.9   This is the PROCEDURE DIVISION of a program that is supposed to re-sort a file of old customers' records and a file of new customers' records and then to merge the two files into a MERGED-CUST-FILE. However, something is wrong with the program. What is it?

```
PROCEDURE DIVISION.
SORT-MERGE-PARA.
    SORT WORK-TAPE ON ASCENDING KEY ZIP-CODE-WT, TOWN-WT, NAME-WT
        USING OLD-CUSTOMERS-FILE GIVING SORTED-OLD-CUST-FILE.
    SORT WORK-TAPE ON ASCENDING KEY ZIP-CODE-WT, TOWN-WT, NAME-WT
```

```
        USING NEW-CUSTOMERS-FILE GIVING SORTED-NEW-CUST-FILE.
    MERGE WORK-TAPE ON ASCENDING KEY NAME-WT, TOWN-WT, ZIP-CODE-WT
        USING SORTED-OLD-CUST-FILE, SORTED-NEW-CUST-FILE
        GIVING MERGED-CUST-FILE.
    STOP RUN.
```

EXAMPLE PROGRAM

Checking Accounts Update

A bank has its checking accounts records in a magnetic tape file. Each account record in the tape file contains the following fields:

Field	PICTURE
Account number	9(5)
Name	A(20)
Balance	9(6)V99

The file was created with a blocking factor of 10.

Write a program to perform monthly updates of the checking accounts tape file. Input to the program will include the old tape file (containing the account records prior to the update) and a deck of transaction cards. The program will produce as output a new tape file (containing the account records after the update) and a listing on the line printer of "bounced checks" and illegitimate account numbers (account numbers which appeared on transaction cards but were not in the old tape file).

The transactions cards will be in this form:

COLUMNS	INFORMATION	PICTURE
1– 5	Account number	9(5)
6	Transaction code	9
7–12	Amount (if applicable)	9999V99
13–17	Check number (if applicable)	999
18–80	Blank	X(65)

A card containing a transaction code of 1 refers to a deposit made by the customer whose account number is on the card. On a code 1 card, the amount field refers to the amount deposited, and it should be added to the balance field in the account record from the tape. (On a code 1 card, the check number field is blank.)

A card containing a transaction code of 2 refers to a check written by the customer. On a code 2 card the amount field refers to the amount of check, and it should be subtracted from the balance field in the account record from the tape, *unless* there is an insufficient balance in the account. If there is an insufficient balance, report that fact in a BOUNCED-CHECK-LINE of this form:

CHECK NO. 123 ON ACCOUNT NO. 12345 NOT HONORED DUE TO INSUFFICIENT FUNDS.

The amount of a "bounced" check should not be subtracted from the balance in the account.

A card containing a transaction code of 3 is a card identifying an account which has been closed. The record on such an account should be purged from the file. (On a code 3 card, the amount and check number fields will be blank.)

Don't forget the requirement to report account numbers that turn up in the transaction deck which are not in the old tape file. Report such illegitimate account numbers in an ILLEGIT-ACCT-NO-LINE of this form:

ACCOUNT NO. 12345 IS ILLEGITIMATE.

As usual, you are to assume that all records in the old tape file are in numerical order by account number. The cards in the transaction deck are also in numerical order by account number. Because of the way you would have been adding cards to that deck as the month progressed, and because of the way the mechanical card sorter works, when there is more than one card in the deck which applies to a single account, they will be in order by the date on which they were received.

Suggested contents for a trial tape file:

```
00890ALEXANDER    ARMSTRONG 00002537
01710MURIEL  G     BAILEY       00104698
02515EVELYN  K     CASSARA      03739862
03420DAVID  A      DONOVAN      00000023
04020JOHN  A       EISENHOWER00732953
04690ELIZABETH     FINKENAUR   09275687
05945HOWARD  A     GOLDSMITH   02369783
06450TIMOTHY  H    HAYDEN       00008379
07060CHRISTINE     KENNEDY      00057203
07910TODD  A       KULIK        00063925
08460PHYLLIS  D    LEVESQUE     00000001
08920STEPHEN       NAWORSKI     00162371
09270MARTIN  G     PLASSMEYER09547633
11006KELLY  J      ROCK         00200503
12370JOHN  A       SZYPKO       12653279
```

Suggested contents for a trial transaction deck:

```
↓Col. 1                ↓Col. 1
017102004500761       079102063925872
017102052641762       079103
034201010000          079102010000873
034202007555491       084603000350
040202732953603       089202060000421
040203                089202045000422
051622050000226       089202092142423
064502009137041       089202102417424
```

Solution

IDENTIFICATION DIVISION omitted.

```
ENVIRONMENT DIVISION.
CONFIGURATION SECTION.
SOURCE-COMPUTER. HAL-2001.
OBJECT-COMPUTER. HAL-2001.
INPUT-OUTPUT SECTION.
FILE-CONTROL.
    SELECT TRANSACTION-CARD-FILE ASSIGN TO CARD-READER.
    SELECT PRINT-FILE ASSIGN TO LINE-PRINTER.
    SELECT OLD-TAPE-FILE ASSIGN TO TAPE-1.
    SELECT NEW-TAPE-FILE ASSIGN TO TAPE-2.
DATA DIVISION.
FILE SECTION.
FD   TRANSACTION-CARD-FILE; RECORD CONTAINS 80 CHARACTERS; LABEL
     RECORDS ARE OMITTED; DATA RECORD IS TRANSACTION-CARD.
01   TRANSACTION-CARD.
     02   ACCT-NO-TC          PICTURE 9(5).
     02   TRANS-CODE-TC        PICTURE 9.
     02   AMOUNT-TC            PICTURE 9999V99.
     02   CHECK-NO-TC          PICTURE 999.
     02   FILLER              PICTURE X(65).
FD   PRINT-FILE; RECORD CONTAINS 136 CHARACTERS; LABEL RECORDS ARE
     OMITTED; DATA RECORD IS PRINT-LINE.
01   PRINT-LINE               PICTURE X(136).
FD   OLD-TAPE-FILE; BLOCK CONTAINS 10 RECORDS; RECORD CONTAINS 33
     CHARACTERS; LABEL RECORDS ARE STANDARD; DATA RECORD IS
     OT-REC.
01   OT-REC.
     02   ACCT-NO-OT          PICTURE 9(5).
     02   NAME-OT             PICTURE A(20).
     02   BALANCE-OT          PICTURE 9(6)V99.
FD   NEW-TAPE-FILE; BLOCK CONTAINS 10 RECORDS; RECORD CONTAINS 33
     CHARACTERS; LABEL RECORDS ARE STANDARD; DATA RECORD IS
     NT-REC.
01   NT-REC                   PICTURE X(33).
WORKING-STORAGE SECTION.
01   BOUNCED-CHECK-LINE.
     02   FILLER              PICTURE X(11)   VALUE ' CHECK NO. '.
     02   CHECK-NO-BCL        PICTURE 999.
     02   FILLER              PICTURE X(16)
            VALUE ' ON ACCOUNT NO. '.
     02   ACCT-NO-BCL         PICTURE 9(5).
     02   FILLER                          PICTURE X(101)
            VALUE ' NOT HONORED DUE TO INSUFFICIENT FUNDS.'.
01   ILLEGIT-ACCT-NO-LINE.
     02   FILLER              PICTURE X(13)
            VALUE ' ACCOUNT NO. '.
     02   ILLEGIT-ACCT-NO     PICTURE 9(5).
     02   FILLER              PICTURE X(118)
            VALUE ' IS ILLEGITIMATE.'.
PROCEDURE DIVISION.
UPDATE SECTION.
START-PARA.
    OPEN INPUT TRANSACTION-CARD-FILE, OLD-TAPE-FILE;
```

```
         OUTPUT PRINT-FILE, NEW-TAPE-FILE.
    READ OLD-TAPE-FILE RECORD AT END GO TO STOP-PARA.
    READ TRANSACTION-CARD-FILE RECORD AT END GO TO WRAP-UP.
COMPARE-ACCT-NOS-PARA.
    IF ACCT-NO-OT = ACCT-NO-TC GO TO UPDATE-OR-PURGE-PARA.
    IF ACCT-NO-OT < ACCT-NO-TC GO TO GET-NEXT-ACCOUNT-PARA.
ERROR-PARA.
    MOVE ACCT-NO-TC TO ILLEGIT-ACCT-NO.
    WRITE PRINT-LINE FROM ILLEGIT-ACCT-NO-LINE.
    READ TRANSACTION-CARD-FILE RECORD AT END GO TO WRAP-UP.
    GO TO COMPARE-ACCT-NOS-PARA.
UPDATE-OR-PURGE-PARA.
    IF TRANS-CODE-TC = 3 GO TO PURGE-PARA.
UPDATE-PARA.
    PERFORM UPDATE-PROCEDURES.
    READ TRANSACTION-CARD-FILE RECORD AT END GO TO WRAP-UP.
    GO TO COMPARE-ACCT-NOS-PARA.
PURGE-PARA.
    READ OLD-TAPE-FILE RECORD AT END GO TO STOP-PARA.
    READ TRANSACTION-CARD-FILE RECORD AT END GO TO WRAP-UP.
    GO TO COMPARE-ACCT-NOS-PARA.
GET-NEXT-ACCOUNT-PARA.
    WRITE NT-REC FROM OT-REC.
    READ OLD-TAPE-FILE RECORD AT END GO TO STOP-PARA.
    GO TO COMPARE-ACCT-NOS-PARA.
UPDATE-PROCEDURES SECTION.
DEPOSIT-OR-CHECK-PARA.
    IF TRANS-CODE-TC = 2 GO TO CHECK-PARA.
DEPOSIT-PARA.
    ADD AMOUNT-TC TO BALANCE-OT.
    GO TO UPDATE-EXIT.
CHECK-PARA.
    IF AMOUNT-TC > BALANCE-OT GO TO BOUNCED-CHECK-PARA.
    SUBTRACT AMOUNT-TC FROM BALANCE-OT.
    GO TO UPDATE-EXIT.
BOUNCED-CHECK-PARA.
    MOVE CHECK-NO-TC TO CHECK-NO-BCL.
    MOVE ACCT-NO-TC TO ACCT-NO-BCL.
    WRITE PRINT-LINE FROM BOUNCED-CHECK-LINE.
UPDATE-EXIT.
    EXIT.
WRAP-UP SECTION.
TRANSFER-REMAINING-RECS-PARA.
    WRITE NT-REC FROM OT-REC.
    READ OLD-TAPE-FILE RECORD AT END GO TO STOP-PARA.
    GO TO TRANSFER-REMAINING-RECS-PARA.
STOP-PARA.
    CLOSE TRANSACTION-CARD-FILE, PRINT-FILE, OLD-TAPE-FILE,
        NEW-TAPE-FILE.
    STOP RUN.
```

Discussion

This program is based directly on the multiple update program of Figures 15.10 and 15.12. With only two exceptions, the logic of the program is exactly like the logic portrayed in the flowchart of Figure 15.11. (Refer back to that flowchart for a moment.)

The first exception results from the fact that this program incorporates features of the purge operation along with those of the multiple update operation. So the left (Update-Para) branch of the Figure 15.11 flowchart has to be modified to provide for the possibility that a record may need to be purged rather than updated. In order to provide for that possibility, we borrow the left (Purge-Para) branch of the purge flowchart in Figure 15.8. In this example program, whenever we find a record we've been searching for, we first check in the UPDATE-OR-PURGE-PARA to see if the record is to be updated or purged. If it's to be purged, the program branches to the PURGE-PARA, otherwise it simply drops to the UPDATE-PARA, and the appropriate steps are taken.

The second exception involves the update routine. In Figures 15.11 and 15.12, the update routine was simple enough to be contained in one paragraph. In this program the update routine is sufficiently complex that it could not have been contained in one paragraph. For that reason, it is written in several paragraphs and those paragraphs are grouped together into an UPDATE-PROCEDURES SECTION. Back in the UPDATE-PARA, we call for the execution of that section by saying PERFORM UPDATE-PROCEDURES.

Notice the UPDATE-EXIT paragraph with its EXIT statement at the end of the UPDATE-PROCEDURES SECTION. This is an example of the situation discussed in Section 13.5 where we want the ability to avoid under certain conditions the execution of some of the sentences in a section that is being PERFORMed. Remember, you *must* provide for the flow of a program to reach the last sentence of a section, paragraph, or series of paragraphs that are being PERFORMed, if you don't want to be guilty of "violating" the PERFORM software.

STUDENT'S PROGRAM

Inventory Update

In Chapter 14's Example Program, we created an inventory file on magnetic tape for the AC-DC Electronics Supply Company. Our requirement now is to write an update program that can be used to keep the inventory file up to date.

Input to the program will be the old inventory tape file and a deck of transaction cards. The program will produce as output the new (updated) inventory tape, a printed list of filled and unfilled orders, and a printed list of erroneous transaction cards found in the deck. The records in the inventory tape file are already in numerical order by part number. We'll be sure to sort the transaction cards into the same order before we run this program. Cards applying to the same part will be in the order that they were received.

The transaction cards are in this format:

COLUMNS	INFORMATION	PICTURE
1–10	Part number	9(10)
11	Transaction code	9
12–15	Quantity received or ordered by customer	9999
16–20	Order number (if applicable)	9(5)
21–25	New unit price (if applicable)	999V99
26–80	Blanks	X(55)

A card containing a transaction code of 1 refers to a shipment received. The quantity on a code 1 card should be added to the quantity-on-hand field in the tape record for the item whose part number appears on the transaction card. (On a code 1 card, the order number and new unit price fields are blank.)

A card containing a transaction code of 2 refers to an order placed by a customer. When we process a code 2 card, we must first assure ourselves that there is enough of the item on hand to enable us to fill the order. If there is not enough on hand, we will report that fact in an UNFILLED-ORDER-LINE of this form:

ORDER NO. 12345 NOT FILLED DUE TO INSUFFICIENT STOCK OF PART NO. 0123456789

When there *is* a sufficient quantity of an item to satisfy an order for that item, we will report that fact in a FILLED-ORDER-LINE of this form:

ORDER NO. 12345 FILLED. BILL CUSTOMER FOR $9,999,999.99

and then subtract the quantity of the item ordered from the quantity-on-hand field in the tape record for that item. The dollar amount for which the customer will be billed is computed by multiplying the quantity he ordered by the current unit price of the item. (On a code 2 card, the new unit price field is blank.)

A card containing a transaction code of 3 is a card indicating a revised unit price for an item. The new unit price is to be substituted for the former unit price in the tape record for that item. (A code 3 card is the *only* transaction card that will contain anything at all in the new unit price field. However, its quantity and order number fields will be blank.)

A card containing a transaction code of 4 is a card identifying an item which has been dropped from the inventory and will no longer be stocked. The record on such an item should be purged from the tape file. (A code 4 card is blank in all fields except the part number and transaction code.)

If a transaction card in the deck contains a part number which is not in the tape file, report that fact on the line printer in an ERROR-LINE of this form:

PART NO. 0123456789 NOT IN INVENTORY FILE.

Suggested contents for a trial tape file were given in the Chapter 14 Example Program. The following are suggested as contents for a trial transaction deck:

```
00357421692001000421
00357421693          01240
00357421692001000422
02492487702000600423
03670669522000900424
03670669524
05861840342002500425
105875166110075
17769338432010000426
17769338432008000427
```

Appendix A: Solutions to Exercises

Chapter 1:

1.1   Because computers can't understand any spoken languages.

1.2   The Stored Program Concept.

1.3   Input Unit, Central Processing Unit, and Output Unit.

1.4   Input Unit and Output Unit.

1.5   The card reader.

1.6   b.

1.7   Control Unit, Arithmetic Unit, and Memory Unit.

1.8   Add, subtract, multiply, and divide.

1.9   Instructions and data values.

1.10   b.

1.11   a. I/O b. I c. O d. O e. I/O f. I/O g. I/O h. I/O

1.12   a. data-name.   c. data-name.   e. data-value.
           b. data-value.   d. data-value.   f. data-name.

1.13   a. nondestructive read.   b. destructive write.

1.14   10101.

1.15   26.

1.16   Cores can store only one of two digits, 0 or 1.

1.17   In machine language: a. Each instruction is in binary form, and b. Each basic operation to be performed is stated explicitly in a separate instruction.

1.18   To translate it into machine language.

1.19   It must be translated by the compiler into machine language before it can be understood by the computer.

1.20   Yes. FORTRAN.

1.21   a. The program in COBOL.
           b. The program after its translation into machine language.

Chapter 2:

2.1   The computer receives and stores *all* instructions needed to solve a problem, while other calculators can only take one instruction at a time.

2.2   a.   Reading the instruction deck.
      b.   Translating instructions into machine language.
      c.   Storing instructions in memory.

2.3   Instruction deck.

2.4   END PROGRAM card.

2.5   Instruction deck ends.

2.6   Data deck.

2.7   Stored in memory.

2.8   READ instruction detects no more data cards.

2.9   STOP RUN instruction.

2.10   a. C b. E c. C d. E e. C f. E g. C h. E i. E j. E

2.11   a.   IDENTIFICATION DIVISION.   b.   ENVIRONMENT DIVISION.
       c.   DATA DIVISION.   d.   PROCEDURE DIVISION.

2.12   None.

2.13   False.

2.14   False.

2.15   The next instruction.

2.16   The first instruction in CALCULATIONS-PARAGRAPH.

2.17   ABLE: 24   BAKER: 08   CHARLIE: 24

2.18   ABLE: 78   BAKER: 08   CHARLIE: 70

Chapter 3:

3.1   x ÷ # & a : [Θ ½ π ≠ Ñ should have been X'd.

3.2   c.   ** are special characters.   d.   Periods are special characters.
      f.   % is not a COBOL character.   g.   Longer than 30 characters.
      h.   Embedded space.   i.   Reserved word.
      k.   Trailing hyphen.

3.3   e.   Decimal point on right.   g.   Comma is special character.
      h.   / is special character.   i. $ is special character.
      j.   Longer than 18 digits.   l.   Decimal point on right.
      m.   Contains letters.   n.   ' is special character.

3.4   c.   ¢ is not a COBOL character.   f.   & is not a COBOL character.
      g.   ' not permitted within literal.

3.5   ONE TWO THREE are not figurative constants.

3.6   False.

3.7   True.

3.8   True.

3.9   8 and 12.

3.10   a.   Sequence Number Field.   b.   Name Field.
       c.   Text Field.   d.   Identification Field.

3.11   To identify continuation cards (with a -) and to identify comment cards
       (with a *).

3.12 False.

3.13 True.

3.14 True.

3.15 False. You have *no* choice. You must continue to col. 72 and break at that point, no matter where you are in the literal.

3.16 4.

3.17 False.

3.18 False.

3.19

```
250      IF NUMBER-OF-PARTS-ON-HAND IS LESS THAN DESIRED-MINIMUM-STOCK
260-     AGE-LEVEL, THEN MOVE 'THE QUANTITY OF THIS PART IS TOO LOW; T
270-     'IME TO PLACE AN ORDER FOR MORE.' TO SUPERVISORS-MESSAGE.
```

— or —

```
250      IF NUMBER-OF-PARTS-ON-HAND IS LESS THAN
260      DESIRED-MINIMUM-STOCKAGE-LEVEL, THEN MOVE 'THE QUANTITY OF TH
270-     'IS PART IS TOO LOW; TIME TO PLACE AN ORDER FOR MORE.' TO
280      SUPERVISORS-MESSAGE.
```

Chapter 4:

4.1 False. Every computer model has its own COBOL Reference Manual.

4.2 False.

4.3 True.

4.4 True.

4.5 False. Only a small portion of the program will have to be changed.

4.6 a. Line 10: There should be no hyphen.
    b. Line 20: Hyphen missing in PROGRAM-ID.
    c. Line 30: Final period missing.
    d. Line 40: INSTALLATION is misspelled.
    e. Lines 50 & 60: Hyphens missing from paragraph-names.

4.7 a. PROGRAM-ID paragraph is missing. It is mandatory.
    b. Line 30: & is not a COBOL character.
    c. Line 40: REMARKS paragraph out of order. It should follow the DATE-COMPILED paragraph.

4.8 Line 20: Hyphen missing from program-name, SECOND-PROGRAM.

4.9 a. Line 70: ENVIRONMENT misspelled.
    b. Line 80: There should be no hyphen.
    c. Line 90: OBJECT-COMPUTER paragraph is out of order. It should follow the SOURCE-COMPUTER paragraph.
    d. Line 110: Hyphen missing in INPUT-OUTPUT.
    e. FILE-CONTROL paragraph header is missing.
    f. Lines 120 & 130: Seem to say that the same file will be on two different devices. A new name will have to be chosen for the second file.

4.10   a. Line 90: Period missing after SOURCE-COMPUTER.

          b. OBJECT-COMPUTER paragraph missing.

          c. Line 110: The word PARAGRAPH should not be in a paragraph heading.

4.11   False. There are no sections in the IDENTIFICATION DIVISION.

4.12   False. They're reserved-names.

4.13   Only in the PROCEDURE DIVISION.

4.14   Only the IDENTIFICATION DIVISION.

Chapter 5:

5.1   a. Organization.   b. Data-name; memory-location.

5.2   Data-names appearing in the FILE SECTION are associated with files external to the computer. Data-names in the WORKING-STORAGE SECTION have data-values which are generated within the program.

5.3   a. Record.   b. File.

5.4   Card 330 should say RECORD CONTAINS, not RECORDS CONTAIN.
Card 340 should not end in a period.
Card 350 should begin with DATA RECORD, not DATA-RECORD.
Card 360 should read 01 APPLICATION-CARD.

5.5   Hierarchy or relative rank.

5.6   Record-names.

5.7   False. The upper limit is 49, not 99.

5.8   False.

5.9   False. Usually, but not always.

5.10   420 G 450 E 480 E 510 E 540 G 570 E
430 E 460 E 490 G 520 E 550 G 580 E
440 G 470 G 500 E 530 E 560 E

5.11   Only h. Elementary-items.

5.12   Only g. Group-items.

5.13   Class: N AB N AN AN
Size: 4 15 2 35 24

5.14
```
01  BIRTH-RECORD.
    02  FAMILY-NAME        PICTURE A(20).
    02  BABYS-NAME.
        03  FIRST-NAME     PICTURE A(10).
        03  MIDDLE-NAME    PICTURE A(10).
    02  TIME-OF-BIRTH.
        03  AM-OR-PM       PICTURE AA.
        03  HOUR           PICTURE 99.
        03  MINUTES        PICTURE 99.
    02  DATE-OF-BIRTH.
        03  DAY            PICTURE 99.
        03  MONTH          PICTURE AAA.
        03  YEAR           PICTURE 99.
```

```
      02  SEX              PICTURE  A.
      02  WEIGHT.
          03  POUNDS       PICTURE  99.
          03  OUNCES       PICTURE  99.
      02  MOTHERS-ROOM.
          03  FLOOR        PICTURE  9.
          03  ROOM-NR      PICTURE  99.
      02  FILLER           PICTURE  X(19).
```

5.15 FD POLICY-HOLDER-FILE; RECORD CONTAINS 80 CHARACTERS; LABEL RECORDS ARE OMITTED; DATA RECORD IS POLICY-RECORD.

```
      01  POLICY-RECORD.
          02  FILLER           PICTURE  X(8).
          02  NAME-ON-POLICY   PICTURE  A(18).
          02  FILLER           PICTURE  X(25).
          02  ZIP-CODE         PICTURE  9(5).
          02  PHONE            PICTURE  9(10).
          02  FILLER           PICTURE  X(14).
```

5.16 FD PHONE-LISTING; RECORD CONTAINS 136 CHARACTERS; LABEL RECORDS ARE OMITTED; DATA RECORD IS PRINTER-LINE.

```
      01  PRINTER-LINE.
          02  FILLER               PICTURE  X(5).
          02  PHONE-TO-BE-LISTED   PICTURE  9(10).
          02  FILLER               PICTURE  X(5).
          02  NAME-TO-BE-LISTED    PICTURE  A(18).
          02  FILLER               PICTURE  X(98).
```

Chapter 6:

6.1   A statement contains one verb and directs that one operation to be performed; a sentence can contain one or more statements.

6.2   For INPUT: CARD-FILE, OLD-DISK-FILE.
      For OUTPUT: TAPE-FILE, PRINT-FILE, NEW-DISK-FILE.

6.3   CARD-FILE was never OPENed. DATA-FILE was not OPENed for input.

6.4   Should not include words INPUT and OUTPUT.

6.5   b.   6.6   False.   6.7   True.

6.8   You don't WRITE files; you WRITE records.

6.9   a.   OLD-DATA.   b.   DETAIL-LINE.

6.10 a.   In a SELECT sentence in the ENVIRONMENT DIVISION.
      b.   In an FD entry in the DATA DIVISION.
      c.   In an OPEN sentence in the PROCEDURE DIVISION.

6.11	a. 24th	b. 25th	c. 28th
6.12	HIS-PAY: 495	HER-PAY: 495	MY-PAY: 495
6.13	HIS-PAY: 495	HER-PAY: 495	MY-PAY: 250
6.14	HIS-PAY: 378	HER-PAY: 495	MY-PAY: 378
6.15	HIS-PAY: 650	HER-PAY: 378	MY-PAY: 495
6.16	HANDSOME: KIP	MORE-HANDSOME: JOE	MOST-HANDSOME: BOB
6.17	HANDSOME: BOB	MORE-HANDSOME: BOB	MOST-HANDSOME: BOB

6.18   720-730-740-800-810-760-770-780-830-840-850

6.19   720-730-740-830-840-850-790-800-810-760-770

6.20   Should be GO TO REQUIRED-CALCULATIONS.

Chapter 7:

7.1   a. Control Cards.   b. Instruction Deck.   c. END PROGRAM card.
       d. Data deck.   e. END OF FILE card.

7.2   a. Program listing. b. Error messages.   c. Output of the program.

7.3   a. S b. L c. L d. S e. L f. L

7.4   File-name; record-name.

7.5   True.

7.6   False.

7.7   a. Card reader reads one card.
       b. Data-values on that card are stored in appropriate memory locations.

7.8   When the card read is the END OF FILE card.

7.9   a. Data-values from appropriate memory locations are sent to the line printer.
       b. Line printer prints one line.

7.10 a. To indicate a portion of a data card or a printed line which contains spaces.
       b. To indicate a portion of a data card which contains data-values we don't need.

7.11 MR. SMITH
       MR. JONES
       MS. JONES
       MS. KULIK

Chapter 8:

8.1   a. 53$\hat{9}$ 3 d. 40632 5 g. 4260000 3 j. 999V99 5 m. PPP99 2
       b. 10$\hat{9}$5 4 e. 9$\hat{2}$7 3 h. $_\wedge$0000093 2 k. S99V9 3 n. 999 3
       c. 007$\hat{2}$1 5 f. 73.621 6 i. 9V9999 5 l. X(5) 5 o. V999 3

8.2   Prepares raw data for presentation to humans.

8.3   PICTURE; DATA; PROCEDURE; MOVE.

8.4   NE; AE; AE.   8.5   9 B 0

8.6   a. 03 HRS-EDIT PICTURE ZZZ.99.   c. Sending Field; Receiving Field.
       b. (1) 025$\hat{4}$9   (2) 25.49

8.7   a. +   b. Blank   c. Blank   d. Blank

8.8   a. –   b. –   c. CR   d. DB

8.9   a. V is not permitted in NE item; or $ is not permitted in N item.
       b. – may be in leading or trailing positions but not embedded.
       c. S is not permitted in NE item; or . is not permitted in N item.

d. $ is not permitted in AE item; or X is not permitted in NE item.
e.   Two floating string characters used.
f.   PICTURE misspelled.
g.   CR not in trailing position.
h.   Floating string character is not left-most character.

8.10   a.   5 3.04
       b.   7 −721.29
       c.   6 −6.71
       d.   5 38.9
       e.   5 +10.3
       f.   8   .00
       g.   6 SS AN
       h.   7 $29.18
       i.   9 $ 26.35
       j.   9 $1,184.06

k.   7 $.00
l.   5   −67
m.   5 XYZ
n.   11 $ 72.39CR
o.   6 $32.04
p.   11 $.94
q.   7 $**7.03
r.   10 $2,761.48-
s.   7 7700399
t.   7 $732.04

u.   6 $ZZ.99
v.   7 $$$$.99
w.   11 $$,$$$.99DB
x.   9 $(5).99-
y.   9 AAAABAAAA
z.   7 $$$$.99
aa. 6 ++9.99
bb. 6 ZZZ.99
cc. 9 $*(5).99
dd. 7 −$ZZ.99

Chapter 9:

9.1   MOVE ZERO TO FIELD-1, FIELD-2, FIELD-3.

9.2   False.   9.3   True.   9.4   True.   9.5   False.

9.6   a.   They're undisturbed.   b.   They're destroyed.

9.7   a.   N   N   N   d.   N   AE AN   g.   AB AE AN   j.   AN N AN
      b.   N NE   N   e.   N   NE   N   h.   AB AN AN
      c.   N AN AN   f.   NE AN AN   i.   AN AE AN

9.8   a.   N to AB is illegal.   e.   NE to N is illegal.
      d.   Non-integer N to AN is illegal.

9.9   a.   N   b.   AN   c.   B   d.   N   e.   AN   f.   N

9.10 a.   012345   h.   005.00   o.   COD
      b.   012340   i.   05.00   p.   124
      c.   78   j. $ 1,234.00   q.   NAME
      d.   7890   k.   56   r.   NAM
      e.   0135790   l.   56   s.   NAME
      f.   357   m.   056   t.   I. R.
      g.   135   n.   AB   u.   PA6 5000

9.11 NUM-1: 3794   NUM-2: 379   NUM-3: 7

9.12 c.   9.13   c.   9.14   True.   9.15   True.   9.16   False.

9.17 Qualify the data-name.

9.18 MOVE SPACES TO LAST-NAME IN NEW-REC.

9.19 a.   FIRST-N: JOHN   LAST-NAME: FINKENAUR   SSN: 081325549
      b.   FIRST-N: FINKE   LAST-NAME: NAUR JOHN   SSN: 310813255

Chapter 10:

10.1   a.   True.   b.   False.

10.2   a.   True.   b.   True.   c.   True.   d.   False.   e.   False.   f.   True.   g.   False.

10.3   a. True. b. False. c. True. d. False. e. True.

10.4
a. OK	f. VALUE 1975.	k. OK
b. OK	g. VALUE ZERO.	l. OK
c. OK	h. OK	m. PICTURE X(8)
d. PICTURE 999	i. PICTURE X(10)	n. VALUE '108'.
e. OK	j. OK	

10.5   False! Except for the initial values *you* provide, you may make no assumptions whatsoever about initial values stored in *any* memory locations.

10.6   a. WRITE PRINT-REC FROM PAGE-HEADING.
       b. MOVE PAGE-HEADING TO PRINT-REC. WRITE PRINT-REC.

10.7   a. 00001   b. 1 (and 4 spaces)

10.8   a. 1st.   b. Spaces.   c. At the top of the next page.

       d. It's unpredictable. Two carriage control functions are being attempted in a single output statement.

10.9   a. True.   b. False.

10.10   In the input area.

10.11   They are destroyed by the action of storing the contents of the 2nd data card in the input area.

10.12   MOVE them from the input area to a memory location in Working Storage.

Chapter 11:

11.1   a. True.   b. True.   c. False.   d. True.   e. False.

11.2   a. ADD A, B TO C.
       b. MULTIPLY 750.00 BY EXEMPTIONS.
       c. DIVIDE D INTO A.
       d. SUBTRACT 150.00 FROM GROSS-PAY.
       e. SUBTRACT A FROM C GIVING B.
       f. Correct.
       g. MULTIPLY EXEMPTIONS BY 750.00 GIVING EXEMPT-ALLOWANCE.
       h. DIVIDE A INTO D. DIVIDE B INTO D.
       i. ADD BONUS, PAY GIVING TOTAL-PAY.
       j. MULTIPLY 2.5 BY C GIVING D.
       k. ADD 10 TO HOURS-WORKED.
       l. ADD 10.0 TO HOURS-WORKED.
       m. MOVE TOTAL TO TOTAL-OUT. (The ROUNDED option is available for arithmetic statements only.)

11.3   a. A: 10   B: 20   C: 70   b. A: 10   B: 20   C: 30

11.4   DIVIDE B INTO A. —or— DIVIDE A BY B GIVING A.

11.5
a. A: 0000	B: 0000	C: 000	g. A: 0163	B: 3250	C: 565
b. A: 0000	B: 0000	C: 565	h. A: 0163	B: 3250	C: 005
c. A: 5650	B: 0000	C: 565	i. A: 0163	B: 6250	C: 005
d. A: 5650	B: 6500	C: 565	j. A: 0163	B: 6250	C: 021
e. A: 5650	B: 3250	C: 565	k. A: 2100	B: 6250	C: 021
f. A: 0325	B: 3250	C: 565	l. A: 2100	B: 1900	C: 021

11.6   a.   A: 100̬   B: 030̬15   C: 0000̬   D: 250̱5   E: 035̄
       b.   A: 100̬   B: 030̬15   C: 0000̬   D: 335̱7   E: 035̄
       c.   A: 025̄   B: 030̬15   C: 0000̬   D: 335̱7   E: 035̄
       d.   A: 035̄   B: 030̬15   C: 0000̬   D: 335̱7   E: 035̄
       e.   A: 035̄   B: 030̬15   C: 0004̬   D: 335̱7   E: 035̄
       f.   A: 035̄   B: 030̬15   C: 0370̬   D: 335̱7   E: 035̄
       g.   A: 035̄   B: 030̬15   C: 0370̬   D: 335̱7   E: 070̬
       h.   A: 035̄   B: 111̬90   C: 0370̬   D: 335̱7   E: 070̬
       i.   A: 105̄   B: 111̬90   C: 0370̬   D: 335̱7   E: 070̬

Chapter 12:

12.1   a.   IF A IS LESS THAN B NEXT SENTENCE, ELSE GO TO WRAP-UP.
       b.   IF X IS ALPHABETIC GO TO NEXT-PARA.
          IF X IS NUMERIC GO TO NEXT-PARA.
          MOVE C TO D.
       c.   IF TOTAL-HOURS IS GREATER THAN 40.0 GO TO OVER-TIME.
       d.   IF KODE = 'E' GO TO FINISH-ROUTINE.
       e.   Correct.
       f.   IF ALPHA IS EQUAL TO 'DONE' MOVE G TO H.
       g.   IF C IS GREATER THAN D NEXT SENTENCE, ELSE GO TO READ-LOOP.
       h.   IF FICA-TOTAL IS NOT < 778.20 GO TO PRINT-PARA.

12.2   a.   True.   b.   True.   c.   True.
       d.   False.   D IS EQUAL TO 33 would be True.
       e.   True.   f.   True.
       g.   False.   E IS EQUAL TO 'TEST' would be True.
       h.   False.   A IS EQUAL TO 17 would be True.

12.3   IF PRINT-REC IS EQUAL TO SPACES GO TO LOOP-PARA.

12.4   MOVE A TO LARGEST.
       IF B IS GREATER THAN LARGEST MOVE B TO LARGEST.
       IF C IS GREATER THAN LARGEST MOVE C TO LARGEST.

12.5   620-630-640-660-670-680-690-770-780-790-800-810-740-750

12.6   IF FINAL-AVERAGE > 90 GO TO A-PARA.
         IF FINAL-AVERAGE > 80 GO TO B-PARA.
         IF FINAL-AVERAGE > 70 GO TO C-PARA.
         IF FINAL-AVERAGE > 60 GO TO D-PARA.
         MOVE 'F' TO LETTER-GRADE. GO TO NEXT-PARA.
     A-PARA.
         MOVE 'A' TO LETTER-GRADE. GO TO NEXT-PARA.
     B-PARA.
         MOVE 'B' TO LETTER-GRADE. GO TO NEXT-PARA.
     C-PARA.
         MOVE 'C' TO LETTER-GRADE. GO TO NEXT-PARA.
     D-PARA.
         MOVE 'D' TO LETTER-GRADE. GO TO NEXT-PARA.
     NEXT-PARA.
         Etc.
       —Or—

MOVE 'F' TO LETTER-GRADE.
IF FINAL-AVERAGE > 60 MOVE 'D' TO LETTER-GRADE.
IF FINAL-AVERAGE > 70 MOVE 'C' TO LETTER-GRADE.
IF FINAL-AVERAGE > 80 MOVE 'B' TO LETTER-GRADE.
IF FINAL-AVERAGE > 90 MOVE 'A' TO LETTER-GRADE.

12.7 IF A IS LESS THAN B NEXT SENTENCE, ELSE GO TO PARA-2.
IF A IS LESS THAN C GO TO PARA-1, ELSE GO TO PARA-2.

12.8 TOTAL-SUM: 10   COUNTER: 5

12.9 IF TEST-NUMBER IS NEGATIVE MULTIPLY −1 BY TEST-NUMBER.

Chapter 13:

13.1 Should be DEPENDING ON not DEPENDENT UPON.

13.2 GO TO PARA-A, PARA-B, PARA-A, PARA-C DEPENDING ON COUNTER.

13.3 PRICE isn't an integer and it should be.

13.4 a. PARA-2. b. PARA-3. c. PARA-4. d. PARA-5. e. PARA-2. f. PARA-2.

13.5 SUBTRACT 3 FROM PREFIX.
GO TO RTN-1, RTN-2, RTN-3 DEPENDING ON PREFIX.
GO TO LAST-PARA.
—Or—
GO TO LAST-PARA, LAST-PARA, LAST-PARA, RTN-1, RTN-2, RTN-3
DEPENDING ON PREFIX.
GO TO LAST-PARA.

13.6 720-730-740-830-840-750-770-780-830-840-790-800-860-870-880.

13.7 720-730-740-810-820-830-860-870-840-750-770-780-790.

13.8 a. 1   b. 3   c. 1   d. 2   e. 2

13.9 PROCEDURE DIVISION.
RNT-A.
      Sentence.
      PERFORM RTN-C THRU EXIT-PARA.
RTN-B.
      Sentence.
RTN-C.
      Sentence.
      IF A > B GO TO EXIT-PARA.
      Sentence.
RTN-D.
      Sentence.
EXIT-PARA.
      EXIT.
RTN-E.
      Sentence.
      Etc.

13.10 A: 7   B: 33

Chapter 14:

14.1 a. False   b. False   c. True   d. True.

14.2 False

14.3 a. Available tape space is used more efficiently.
   b. Less total tape is required.
   c. The file can be read or written in less time.

14.4 a. $45,000 \times .1 + 45,000 \times .6 = 31500$ in. $= 2625$ ft.
   b. $45,000 \times .1 + (45,000/25) \times .6 = 5580$ in. $= 465$ ft.

14.5 $45,000 \times (40/80) \times .1 + (45,000/25) \times .6 = 3330$ in. $= 277.5$ ft.

14.6 $60,000 \times (160/80) \times .1 + (60,000/30) \times .6 = 13200$ in. $= 1100$ ft.

14.7 $R \times (160/80) \times .1 + (R/30) \times .6 = 2400 \times 12$ in.; $R = 130,909 \simeq 130,000$ recs.

14.8 $25,000 \times (C/80) \times .1 + 25,000 \times .6 = 2400 \times 12$ in.; $C = 441.6 \simeq 440$ ch.

14.9 a. $5 + 25 + 40 + 10 + 40 + 10 + 7 + 3 = 140$ characters
   b. $140/4 = 35$ words

14.10 a. $13,000 - 6,000 - 4,800 = 2200$ words
   b. $2200/2 = 1100$ words per buffer; $1100/35 = 31.4$ or 30 records per block

14.11 $5000/140 = 35.7$ or 35 records per block

14.12 The more restrictive—30 records per block

14.13 FD MORTGAGE-FILE; BLOCK CONTAINS 30 RECORDS; RECORD
   CONTAINS 140 CHARACTERS; LABEL RECORDS ARE STANDARD;
   DATA RECORD IS MORTGAGE-RECORD.

14.14 PROCEDURE DIVISION.
   OPEN-PARA.
   OPEN INPUT CARD-FILE; OUTPUT MORTGAGE-FILE.
   READ-CARDS-WRITE-TAPE-PARA.
   READ CARD-FILE RECORD AT END GO TO CLOSE-PARA.
   MOVE CORR FIRST-CARD TO MORTGAGE-RECORD.
   READ CARD-FILE RECORD AT END GO TO CLOSE-PARA.
   MOVE CORR SECOND-CARD TO MORTGAGE-RECORD.
   WRITE MORTGAGE-RECORD.
   GO TO READ-CARDS-WRITE-TAPE-PARA.
   CLOSE-PARA.
   CLOSE CARD-FILE, MORTGAGE-FILE.
   STOP RUN.

14.15 a. The tape is rewound, if necessary.
   b. The Beginning-File-Label is written on the tape.

14.16 a. The final buffer load is written on the tape as the last record block.
   b. The EOF mark is recorded on the tape.
   c. The Ending-File-Label is written on the tape.
   d. The tape is rewound.

14.17 a. The tape is rewound, if necessary.
   b. The Beginning-File-Label is read and checked to see if this is the correct tape file.
   c. The first record block is read and its contents are loaded into the buffer.

14.18 a. The Ending-File-Label is read and checked.
   b. The tape is rewound.

Chapter 15:

15.1 PRINT-SELECTED-RECORDS-PARA.
   IF GRAD-YR IN TAPE-REC IS NOT = 81 GO TO READ-TAPE-PARA.
   IF MAJOR IN TAPE-REC IS NOT = 'PE' GO TO READ-TAPE-PARA.
   MOVE CORR TAPE-REC TO DETAIL-LINE.
   WRITE PRINT-LINE FROM DETAIL-LINE.
   GO TO READ-TAPE-PARA.

15.2 PROCEDURE DIVISION.
   OPEN-PARA.
      OPEN INPUT CATALOG-TAPE-FILE, OUTPUT PRINT-FILE.
   READ-TAPE-PARA.
      READ CATALOG-TAPE-FILE RECORD AT END GO TO CLOSE-PARA.
   PRINT-ITEMS-FOR-REORDER-PARA.
      IF QUANTITY-ON-HAND > REORDER-POINT GO TO READ-TAPE-PARA.
      MOVE CORR CATALOG-REC TO REORDER-LINE.
      WRITE PRINT-LINE FROM REORDER-LINE.
      GO TO READ-TAPE-PARA.
   CLOSE-PARA.
      CLOSE CATALOG-TAPE-FILE, PRINT-FILE.
      STOP RUN.

15.3 WORKING-STORAGE SECTION.
   77 VALUE-OF-THIS-ITEM-WS   PICTURE 9(7)V99.
   77 TOTAL-VALUE-WS   PICTURE 9(8)V99   VALUE ZERO.
   01 REPORT-LINE.
      02 FILLER   PICTURE A(52)
            VALUE ' THE VALUE OF ALL ITEMS ON HAND IN THE WAREHOU
               ' SE IS '.
      02 TOTAL-VALUE-RL   PICTURE $$$$,$$$,$$$.99.
      02 FILLER   PICTURE X(69)   VALUE SPACES.
   PROCEDURE DIVISION.
   OPEN-PARA.
      OPEN INPUT CATALOG-TAPE-FILE, OUTPUT PRINT-FILE.
   READ-TAPE-AND-CALCULATE-PARA.
      READ CATALOG-TAPE-FILE RECORD AT END GO TO REPORT-PARA.
      MULTIPLY QUANTITY-ON-HAND BY UNIT-PRICE
            GIVING VALUE-OF-THIS-ITEM-WS.
      ADD VALUE-OF-THIS-ITEM-WS TO TOTAL-VALUE-WS.
      GO TO READ-TAPE-AND-CALCULATE-PARA.
   REPORT-PARA.
      MOVE TOTAL-VALUE-WS TO TOTAL-VALUE-RL.
      WRITE PRINT-LINE FROM REPORT-LINE.
      CLOSE CATALOG-TAPE-FILE, PRINT-FILE.
      STOP RUN.

15.4 PROCEDURE DIVISION.
   START-PARA.
      OPEN INPUT CARD-FILE, CATALOG-TAPE-FILE; OUTPUT PRINT-FILE.
      READ CARD-FILE RECORD AT END GO TO STOP-PARA.
      READ CATALOG-TAPE-FILE RECORD AT END GO TO STOP-PARA.
   COMPARE-CAT-NO-PARA.
      IF CATALOG-NUMBER IN CATALOG-REC = DES-CAT-NO
            GO TO FOUND-PARA.
      IF CATALOG-NUMBER IN CATALOG-REC < DES-CAT-NO
            GO TO CONTINUE-SEARCH-PARA.

```
ERROR-PARA.
    MOVE DES-CAT-NO TO CAT-NO-EL.
    WRITE PRINT-LINE FROM ERROR-LINE.
    READ CARD-FILE RECORD AT END GO TO STOP-PARA.
    GO TO COMPARE-CAT-NO-PARA.
FOUND-PARA.
    MOVE CORR CATALOG-REC TO DETAIL-LINE.
    WRITE PRINT-LINE FROM DETAIL-LINE.
    READ CARD-FILE RECORD AT END GO TO STOP-PARA.
    READ CATALOG-TAPE-FILE RECORD AT END GO TO STOP-PARA.
    GO TO COMPARE-CAT-NO-PARA.
CONTINUE-SEARCH-PARA.
    READ CATALOG-TAPE-FILE RECORD AT END GO TO STOP-PARA.
    GO TO COMPARE-CAT-NO-PARA.
STOP-PARA.
    CLOSE CARD-FILE, CATALOG-TAPE-FILE, PRINT-FILE.
    STOP RUN.
```

15.5   The format of the new tape should be the same as the format of the old tape, but it isn't:
         a.   The blocking factors are different.
         b.   The PICTURE of part number is not the same on both tapes.
         c.   The order of the fields is different.

15.6   UPDATE-PARA.

```
    IF CODE-CC = 1 MOVE NEW-ADDRESS TO ADDR-OT.
    IF CODE-CC = 2 ADD 1 TO GRAD-YR-OT.
    IF CODE-CC = 3 MOVE NEW-MAJOR TO MAJOR-OT.
    WRITE NT-REC FROM OT-REC.
    READ CARD-FILE RECORD AT END GO TO WRAP-UP.
    READ OLD-TAPE RECORD AT END GO TO STOP-PARA.
    GO TO COMPARE-SSN-PARA.
```

15.7   SORT-PARA.

```
    SORT SORT-TAPE
        ON DESCENDING KEY GRAD-YR-ST
        ON ASCENDING KEY MAJOR-ST, NAME-ST, SSN-ST
        USING OLD-TAPE
        GIVING NEW-TAPE.
```

15.8   a.   FD should be SD.
         b.   There should be no BLOCK CONTAINS clause.
         c.   There should be no LABEL RECORDS clause.

15.9   The MERGE's two input files must already be in the order specified by the merge keys in the MERGE statement. In this example they are not.

Appendix B: COBOL Reserved Word List

The following is the list of COBOL Reserved Words as adopted by the American National Standards Institute, Inc., on May 10, 1974.

ACCEPT	CODE-SET	DELIMITER
ACCESS	COLLATING	DEPENDING
ADD	COLUMN	DESCENDING
ADVANCING	COMMA	DESTINATION
AFTER	COMMUNICATION	DETAIL
ALL	COMP	DISABLE
ALPHABETIC	COMPUTATIONAL	DISPLAY
ALSO	COMPUTE	DIVIDE
ALTER	CONFIGURATION	DIVISION
ALTERNATE	CONTAINS	DOWN
AND	CONTROL	DUPLICATES
ARE	CONTROLS	DYNAMIC
AREA	COPY	
AREAS	CORR	EGI
ASCENDING	CORRESPONDING	ELSE
ASSIGN	COUNT	EMI
AT	CURRENCY	ENABLE
AUTHOR		END
	DATA	END-OF-PAGE
BEFORE	DATE	ENTER
BLANK	DATE-COMPILED	ENVIRONMENT
BLOCK	DATE-WRITTEN	EOP
BOTTOM	DAY	EQUAL
BY	DE	ERROR
	DEBUG-CONTENTS	ESI
CALL	DEBUG-ITEM	EVERY
CANCEL	DEBUG-LINE	EXCEPTION
CD	DEBUG-NAME	EXIT
CF	DEBUG-SUB-1	EXTEND
CH	DEBUG-SUB-2	
CHARACTER	DEBUG-SUB-3	FD
CHARACTERS	DEBUGGING	FILE
CLOCK-UNITS	DECIMAL-POINT	FILE-CONTROL
CLOSE	DECLARATIVES	FILLER
COBOL	DELETE	FINAL
CODE	DELIMITED	FIRST

FOOTING
FOR
FROM

GENERATE
GIVING
GO
GREATER
GROUP

HEADING
HIGH-VALUE
HIGH-VALUES

I-O
I-O-CONTROL
IDENTIFICATION
IF
IN
INDEX
INDEXED
INDICATE
INITIAL
INITIATE
INPUT
INPUT-OUTPUT
INSPECT
INSTALLATION
INTO
INVALID
IS

JUST
JUSTIFIED

KEY

LABEL
LAST
LEADING
LEFT
LENGTH
LESS
LIMIT
LIMITS
LINAGE
LINAGE-COUNTER
LINE
LINE-COUNTER
LINES
LINKAGE
LOCK
LOW-VALUE
LOW-VALUES

MEMORY
MERGE
MESSAGE
MODE
MODULES
MOVE
MULTIPLE
MULTIPLY

NATIVE
NEGATIVE
NEXT
NO
NOT
NUMBER
NUMERIC

OBJECT-COMPUTER
OCCURS
OF
OFF
OMITTED
ON
OPEN
OPTIONAL
OR
ORGANIZATION
OUTPUT
OVERFLOW

PAGE
PAGE-COUNTER
PERFORM
PF
PH
PIC
PICTURE
PLUS
POINTER
POSITION
POSITIVE
PRINTING
PROCEDURE
PROCEDURES
PROCEED
PROGRAM
PROGRAM-ID

QUEUE
QUOTE
QUOTES

RANDOM
RD
READ

RECEIVE
RECORD
RECORDS
REDEFINES
REEL
REFERENCES
RELATIVE
RELEASE
REMAINDER
REMOVAL
RENAMES
REPLACING
REPORT
REPORTING
REPORTS
RERUN
RESERVE
RESET
RETURN
REVERSED
REWIND
REWRITE
RF
RH
RIGHT
ROUNDED
RUN

SAME
SD
SEARCH
SECTION
SECURITY
SEGMENT
SEGMENT-LIMIT
SELECT
SEND
SENTENCE
SEPARATE
SEQUENCE
SEQUENTIAL
SET
SIGN
SIZE
SORT
SORT-MERGE
SOURCE
SOURCE-COMPUTER
SPACE
SPACES
SPECIAL-NAMES
STANDARD
STANDARD-1
START
STATUS

STOP	THRU	WHEN
STRING	TIME	WITH
SUB-QUEUE-1	TIMES	WORDS
SUB-QUEUE-2	TO	WORKING-STORAGE
SUB-QUEUE-3	TOP	WRITE
SUBTRACT	TRAILING	
SUM	TYPE	ZERO
SUPPRESS		ZEROES
SYMBOLIC	UNIT	ZEROS
SYNC	UNSTRING	
SYNCHRONIZED	UNTIL	+
	UP	−
TABLE	UPON	*
TALLYING	USAGE	/
TAPE	USE	**
TERMINAL	USING	
TERMINATE		>
TEXT	VALUE	<
THAN	VALUES	=
THROUGH	VARYING	

The following is a selected list of "non-standard" reserved words used by several computer manufacturers. Because they are widely used, you ought to make a habit of avoiding them despite the fact that they are not recognized by the A. N. S. I. These words were selected because they appear to be the type programmers would most likely be tempted to use as programmer-invented-names:

ADDRESS	DIRECT	LIBRARY	PROCESS
CHECK	DOLLAR	LOCATION	SKIP
CLASS	EJECT	MAJOR	SUPERVISOR
CONSTANT	ENTRY	OWNER	TALLY
CURRENT-DATE	ERROR-CODE	PERCENT	TIME-OF-DAY
DAY-OF-WEEK	EXHIBIT	PLACES	TODAYS-DATE
DEPTH	FLOAT	PRIORITY	VOLUME

Appendix C: Operation of the I.B.M. 29 Card Punch

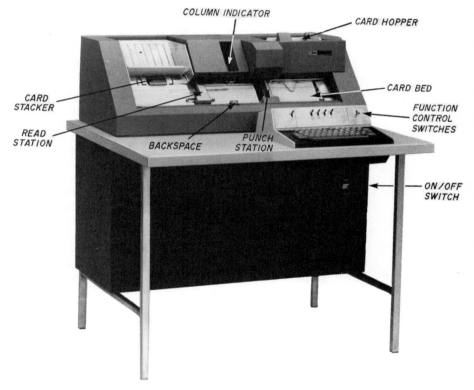

COLUMN INDICATOR

CARD HOPPER

CARD STACKER

CARD BED

READ STATION

FUNCTION CONTROL SWITCHES

BACKSPACE

PUNCH STATION

ON/OFF SWITCH

FIGURE C.1   The IBM 29 Card Punch

Courtesy of IBM Corp.

I. Your Initial Attempts

1. Turn on the Card Punch.
2. While it's warming up, load the Card Hopper.
3. Turn all Function Control Switches *off* except PRINT. Leave PRINT on or no characters will be printed along the top edge of the card to tell you what you've punched.

4. Locate the RELease, FEED, and REGister keys on the keyboard.
5. Push FEED. A card will be fed down from the Hopper into the Card Bed.
6. Push REGister. The card will be moved left to the Punch Station and aligned (registered) with its first column under the punches.
7. Punch the card (see the discussion of the keyboard below).
8. When you've punched all you're going to punch on that card, push RELease, and the card will be moved left along the Card Bed and out of the Punch Station.
9. Push FEED. Another card will be fed down from the Hopper.
10. Push REGister. Punch the card.
11. Push RELease, FEED, REGister. Punch the card. (Notice that the first card you punched has now reached the Card Stacker. All cards you punch will be automatically stacked for you in this way.)
12. Push RELease, FEED, REGister. Punch the card.
13. Push RELease, FEED, REGister. Punch the card.
14. Continue repeating these steps until your entire deck is punched.
15. When you've completed punching your deck, push the CLEAR Function Control Switch upward once and all the cards in the Card Bed will be moved to the Card Stacker.

II. The Keyboard

The keyboard of the Card Punch has its letters in the same arrangement as the letters on a typewriter. The digits are in an arrangement similar to those on a calculator (except that the lower digits are on the top keys and the higher digits are on the bottom).

All letters punched are capital letters, so we don't speak of upper and lower case letters per se. There *are* upper and lower case characters, however. All the letters and several of the special characters are in the "lower case" position on the keys. All the digits and the remaining special characters are in the "upper case" position. On a typewriter you use the Shift key to get upper case characters. Located on the card punch keyboard in the same position as a typewriter's *left* Shift key is the NUMERIC key. It is your "Shift" key on the card punch. You hold down the NUMERIC key whenever you're punching digits or "upper case" special characters. (You'll notice an ALPHA key located in the same position as a typewriter's right Shift key. Unfortunately, however, the ALPHA key is *not* a "Shift" key. You must always use the NUMERIC key to get digits and "upper case" special characters on the card punch.)

A word of caution—if you ever mistakenly hit your REL, FEED or REG keys out of the proper sequence, the keyboard will lock up. To unlock the keyboard, start the cycle over again from REL or hit the ERROR RESET key.

III. Other Useful Features

1. *The Column Indicator* indicates the card column which is aligned under the punches. It tells you the column in which you are *about to* punch.

FIGURE C.2   The Keyboard of the IBM 29 Card Punch (seé also Figure 3.8)

Courtesy of IBM Corp.

As you have noticed, because the card is partially hidden under the Punch Station, you cannot see the characters you have just punched. If you lose track of where you are while punching a card, look at the Column Indicator and note the number of the column you're aligned on. You can then look at that column on your coding form to see where you are and what should be punched next.

2. *Error Correction with the DUPlicate Key.* Although the DUP key can be used to duplicate an entire card, it is most often used in correcting errors. If in the process of punching your deck you make an error on a card by hitting an incorrect key, note the column number where the error was made, and continue punching the card. When you're finished punching that card, RELease it as usual. This will move the card to the left, past the Punch Station and toward the Read Station. FEED down a blank card, and then hit the REG key. Both cards will be simultaneously registered—the punched card at the Read Station and the blank card at the Punch Station. When you hold down the DUPlicate key, the Card Punch advances both cards in unison, reading the holes in the punched card at the Read Station, while simultaneously punching a duplicate of those holes in the blank card at the Punch Station. Hold the DUP key down until you see on the Column Indicator that you have reached the column where the error is. Hit the correct key for that column, and then DUPlicate the rest of the card. If your error was one of having left something out, then the DUPlicate feature is useful only up to the column where the omission was made. You'll have to repunch the remainder of the card from the keyboard.

3. *The BACKSPACE Button* can be used if you've hit the space bar too many times and you want to back up to the column where you should have stopped.

IV. Manual Insertion and DUPlication of Individual Cards

1. *Manual Insertion.* You may occasionally need to punch an individual card, such as a control card or an instruction card you forgot while punching your deck. When that's all you want to do, don't waste time loading the Card Hopper. You can simply insert a single blank card by hand into the Card Bed through the slots at its right end. Slide it along the Card Bed, stopping just short of the Punch Station. REGister the card, punch it, and CLEAR it.

2. *Manual DUPlication.* You may discover an error you made in punching a card after you've finished punching the deck. There are slots just to the *left* of the Punch Station. Slide the punched card into the Card Bed through those slots, stopping just short of the Read Station. Insert a blank card as described under Manual Insertion, above, and REGister both cards *simultaneously.* DUPlicate the columns that were correct; repunch those that were incorrect; and CLEAR.

V. After You've Been At It Awhile—Using the AUTO-FEED Option

Don't attempt this until you're completely at home with all the operations described in I through IV, above.

Use of the AUTO-FEED Option relieves you of always having to hit the REL, FEED, and REG keys between every card. Turn the AUTO-FEED switch on. Hit the FEED key once. A card will be fed down into the Card Bed in the pre-registration position. Hit the FEED key again. The first card will be registered at the Punch Station and a second card will be fed down into the Card Bed behind the first, but in the pre-registration position.

You are now ready to begin punching your deck. Since you are using AUTO-FEED, when you are finished punching a card, simply hit the RELease key. Three things will happen automatically when you hit REL: (1) the card you were punching will be released from the Punch Station; (2) the card that was in the pre-registration position will be registered; and (3) a new card will be fed down from the Hopper into the pre-registration position in the Card Bed.

When you're finished punching your deck, hit the CLEAR, and *turn off the AUTO-FEED switch.*

VI. After You've Become a Real Pro—Using the Program Drum

There are a large number of automatic features available to you on the Card Punch which haven't been discussed here. You may be interested in knowing about them, because in one way or another, they all serve to make your card punching job easier. Borrow a copy of your Computer Center's

Reference Manual on the I.B.M. 29 Card Punch if you wish to learn about them.

If you have access to a Program Drum, learning how to use it should be your first priority. Punching COBOL Instruction Cards is made *much* easier with a Program Drum. With a Program Drum, for example, you can "program" the Card Punch to register each card at column 8 (Margin A) rather than column 1. You can even "program" the Card Punch to execute an automatic release if you ever attempt to type beyond column 72. Although "Tab Stops" are not available on a Card Punch, with the Program Drum you can make the Card Punch act as if it had them.

Although I will leave you to dig out the particulars of the use of the Program Drum on your own, I will give you this general description: You specify the automatic functions you want by punching certain characters on a blank card and wrapping that card around the Program Drum before installing the Drum in the Card Punch. The following is a recommended arrangement of punches on a Program Drum Card to use when punching a COBOL Instruction Deck:

Card Columns	Characters to be Punched	Function
1	–	
2– 7	All &'s	Provides for Automatic Skip to Margin A.
8	1	
9–11	All A's	
12	1	Provides "Tab Stop" at Margin B.
13–15	All A's	
16	1	Provides "Tab Stop" for 03 level entries.
17–19	All A's	
20	1	Provides "Tab Stop" for PICTURE clauses.
21–72	All A's	
73	/	Provides for Automatic Duplication of the Identification Field.
74–80	All A's	

(Leave column 1 blank if you're going to use sequence numbers. Punch a - in column 73 if you're not going to use the Identification Field.) Set the PROGram SELect switch to ONE, and the AUTO SKIP/DUP switch to ON. The SKIP key is your "Tab" key for use with the "Tab Stops" established by the Program Drum Card.

VII.   The I.B.M. 026 Card Punch

The older Model 26 Card Punches are still available at many Computer Centers. All features described in this appendix for the Model 29 are available on the Model 26, with two exceptions:

1.   There is no CLEAR switch. To clear the Card Bed after you've punched your deck, turn off the AUTO FEED switch and hit RELease - REGister - RELease - REGister.

2. The COBOL special characters "less than" (<), "greater than" (>), and the semi-colon (;) are not available on the keyboard. You *can* punch the holes which represent these characters through the use of the MULT PCH key, but my recommendation is that you simply spell out IS LESS THAN and IS GREATER THAN, and that you use a comma wherever you might have used a semi-colon since the two characters may be used interchangeably, or leave it out altogether since the semi-colon is always optional.

Appendix D: The COMPUTE Verb and COBOL Arithmetic-Expressions

The COMPUTE verb gives you the ability to combine several arithmetic operations all in one statement. The form of a COMPUTE statement is as follows:

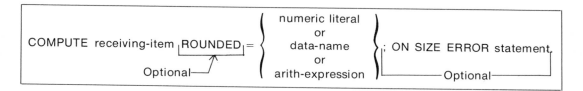

The computer reacts to a COMPUTE statement by first determining the value of whatever is on the right side of the equals sign and then storing that value in the memory location of the receiving-item.

Here is an example of a COMPUTE statement which uses a numeric literal on the right side of the equals sign:

COMPUTE MINIMUM-AGE = 18.

It is equivalent to:

MOVE 18 TO MINIMUM-AGE.

Here is an example which uses a data-name on the right of the equals sign:

COMPUTE NUM-ON-HAND = NUM-ORDERED.

It is equivalent to:

MOVE NUM-ORDERED TO NUM-ON-HAND.

This example demonstrates the use of an arithmetic-expression on the right of the equals sign:

COMPUTE TOTAL-PAY = REG-PAY + OVT-PAY.

It is equivalent to:

ADD REG-PAY, OVT-PAY GIVING TOTAL-PAY.

Here's another example using a somewhat more complex arithmetic-expression and the ROUNDED option:

COMPUTE OVT-PAY ROUNDED = (TOTAL-HOURS − 40) * PAY-RATE * 1.5.

It would take *three* simple COBOL arithmetic statements to write the equivalent of that COMPUTE statement:

SUBTRACT 40 FROM TOTAL-HOURS GIVING TEMP.
MULTIPLY PAY-RATE BY TEMP.
MULTIPLY 1.5 BY TEMP GIVING OVT-PAY, ROUNDED.

The counting statement ADD 1 TO COUNTER would be expressed this way using the COMPUTE statement:

COMPUTE COUNTER = COUNTER + 1.

For students of COBOL who have never programmed in FORTRAN, the really new and unfamiliar element of the COMPUTE statement is the arithmetic-expression. An arithmetic-expression is a combination of data-names and numeric-literals connected by arithmetic operators:

Arithmetic Operator	Means
+	Plus
−	Minus
*	Multiplied by
/	Divided by
**	Raised to the power of

Here are some examples of simple COBOL arithmetic-expressions and their mathematical equivalents:

COBOL Arithmetic-Expression	Mathematical Equivalent
C − D + E	$c - d + e$
1.5 * B	$1.5 \times b$ or $1.5b$
A * B	$a \times b$ or ab
A / 4	$\dfrac{a}{4}$ or $a \div 4$
A * B * C / D	$\dfrac{abc}{d}$
A * B / C * D	$\dfrac{abd}{c}$
C ** 2	c^2 or $c \times c$
D ** 3	d^3 or $d \times d \times d$
B ** 0.5 + C	$\sqrt{b} + c$

Don't forget that in COBOL all elements of a statement must be separated by spaces (this applies to arithmetic-expressions, as well), and that a statement must be ended by a period. This would be an *incorrect* COMPUTE statement:

    COMPUTE W=X*Y+10.

Its elements are not separated by spaces. This would also be an *incorrect* COMPUTE statement:

    COMPUTE W = X * Y + 2.5

because it is not ended by a period. This is a *correct* COMPUTE statement:

    COMPUTE W = X * Y + 2.5.

Its elements are separated by spaces and it ends in a period.

When computing the value of an arithmetic-expression, the computer does not necessarily execute the arithmetic operators in order from left to right. It follows a strict set of rules called the "Hierarchy of Operations."

Hierarchy of Operations

Order of Execution	Operation
1st	Unary $-$[1]
2nd	**
3rd	* or /
4th	+ or $-$

When there are operators of equal hierarchical rank in an arithmetic-expression, the computer *will* execute *them* in order from left to right.

The Hierarchy of Operations is what causes this arithmetic-expression

$$A - B / C + D$$

to be evaluated as if it had been written this way in math:

$$a - \frac{b}{c} + d \text{ and } not \ \frac{a-b}{c+d}$$

Likewise, this arithmetic-expression:

$$C ** 2 / 3$$

[1] A unary minus is seldom used in COBOL. It is a minus sign used with a single data-name rather than as a connector between two data-names and/or numeric literals. Consider the statement COMPUTE X = $-$ Y * Z. The minus before the Y is a unary minus. The computer responds to a unary minus in the same way as if you had multiplied the value of Y by the numeric literal -1.

would be evaluated as if it had been written this way in math:

$$\frac{c^2}{3}$$ and *not* c raised to the two-thirds power.

Parentheses[2] are used whenever you wish to have some order of execution other than that specified in the Hierarchy. For example, if you wanted this evaluation:

$$\frac{a - b}{c + d}$$

you would have to write:

$$(A - B) / (C + D)$$

If you wanted the cube root of C (which is the same as C raised to the one-third power) you'd have to write:

$$C ** (1 / 3)$$

You may even "nest" parentheses if you need to. When you do, the computer will evaluate the inner parentheses first. For example, suppose you wanted this evaluation:

$$\left(\frac{a + b}{c}\right)^2$$

This expression would be *incorrect:*

$$A + B / C ** 2$$

because it would be evaluated like this:

$$a + \frac{b}{c^2}$$

This expression would also be *incorrect:*

$$(A + B) / C ** 2$$

because it would be evaluated like this:

$$\frac{a + b}{c^2}$$

---

[2] There is a long-standing COBOL punctuation rule which was dropped in the 1974 American National Standard, but may still be in effect on many computers—a left parenthesis must not be followed by a space, and a right parenthesis must not be preceded by a space. Check at your computer center to see if you must observe that rule.

This is the only expression that would give you the evaluation you wanted:

$$((A + B) / C) ** 2$$

If you have taken a course in algebra, you are accustomed to being able to imply multiplication in expressions like these:

$$ab \quad \text{and} \quad 2(a + b)$$

In COBOL, these are *incorrect* as arithmetic-expressions:

$$A\,B \quad \text{and} \quad 2 (A + B)$$

You must always include the multiplication operator in such expressions. Those two would have to be written like this:

$$A * B \quad \text{and} \quad 2 * (A + B)$$

Don't forget a rule that's been with you since Chapter 11—any item that will be involved in an arithmetic operation must be a numeric literal or a Class Numeric data-name. That rule applies to everything that appears on the right of the equals sign in a COMPUTE statement.

Since the receiving-item of a COMPUTE statement is *not* involved in the arithmetic operation but only receives its result, it may be either a Class Numeric or Numeric-Edited data-name (but, of course, it *must* be a data-name).

Finally, here is an example of a COMPUTE statement that uses the ON SIZE ERROR option:

```
COMPUTE SAVINGS = DEPOSIT * ( 1 + INT ) ** YEARS; ON SIZE ERROR GO TO
    BANK-PARA.
```

Appendix E: Logic Diagramming with Flowcharts

Flowcharting provides programmers with a graphic means of displaying for themselves and others the flow of the logic in their programs. Although a finished flowchart is valuable as documentation for an already completed program, its biggest value to *you* will be as a visual aid in your development of complex program logic.

As the programs you write grow in complexity, it becomes more and more important that your first step in designing a program involve some graphic device such as a flowchart in developing the logic you plan to employ. One reason graphic development is so important is that it allows you to actually *see* the branches you intend to incorporate in the program. In a coded program, the branches are no longer visual—they are (for example) GO TO statements which you must first read and comprehend and whose destination-paragraphs you then must search for and find.

Another problem a flowchart alleviates is the distracting effect of having to keep track of so many grammar rules, punctuation rules, spelling rules, format rules, etc., while coding a COBOL program. With so much trivia absorbing your powers of concentration, there's very little mental energy left to devote to logic development. Since the computer will never have to comprehend your flowchart, you can write it free of concern for COBOL's myriad of style restrictions and hence devote nearly all of your mental energies to the design of sound program logic. (Why, in a flowchart you can even read records instead of files, if you want to!)

Flowcharts are made up of a group of symbols connected by arrows. The symbols represent the steps of the program. The arrows represent the path you wish the computer to follow as it progresses through the steps and hence the order in which you desire each step to be executed. Since flowcharts are written by so many different people and must be understood by so many other people, the American National Standards Institute has stepped in to establish a standardized set of flowcharting symbols:

Symbol	Meaning
⬭	The starting or ending point of the program.

370

A data processing step, such as a MOVE or arithmetic statement.

An input or output step; represents a READ or WRITE statement.

A conditional step; represents an IF statement in the program.

A separately defined procedure is to be executed; represents a PERFORM statement in the program.

Flow arrows; represent the flow of logic in the program; used also to visually represent branches caused by GO TO statements.

A connector; used to indicate the connect point between separated portions of the flowchart.

The only portion of a program which is represented by a flowchart is the PROCEDURE DIVISION. Figure E.1 is a simple flowchart that demonstrates the use of the symbols introduced above. We want a program to calculate the average weight of all males over 40 in a given company. The program is to take as input a file of data cards which give the name, sex, age, and weight of every employee in the company. It is to produce a listing of the names and weights of all men over 40, and in a single page-footing line, the average weight of all men listed.

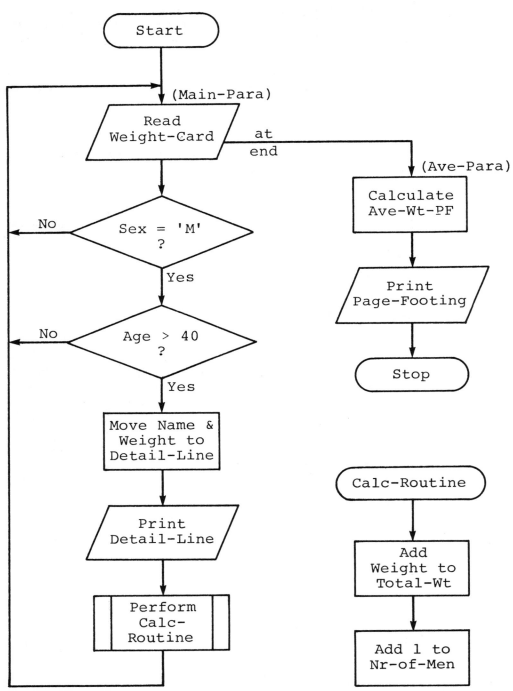

FIGURE E.1 The Flowchart of a COBOL Program

Notice the labelling of selected symbols with paragraph-names. This facilitates the translation of the flowchart into COBOL. Notice also the notation used to indicate the AT END clause of the READ statement.

This is what that flowchart would look like in COBOL:

```
PROCEDURE DIVISION.
START-PARA.
        OPEN INPUT CARD-FILE, OUTPUT PRINT-FILE.
MAIN-PARA.
        READ CARD-FILE RECORD AT END GO TO AVE-PARA.
        IF SEX IS NOT = 'M' GO TO MAIN-PARA.
        IF AGE IS NOT > 40 GO TO MAIN-PARA.
        MOVE NAME TO NAME-DL.
        MOVE WEIGHT TO WEIGHT-DL.
        WRITE PRINT-LINE FROM DETAIL-LINE.
        PERFORM CALC-ROUTINE.
        GO TO MAIN-PARA.
AVE-PARA.
        DIVIDE TOTAL-WT BY NR-OF-MEN GIVING AVE-WT-PF.
        WRITE PRINT-LINE FROM PAGE-FOOTING.
STOP-PARA.
        CLOSE CARD-FILE, PRINT-FILE.
        STOP RUN.
CALC-ROUTINE.
        ADD WEIGHT TO TOTAL-WT.
        ADD 1 TO NR-OF-MEN.
```

The message of this appendix is that the design of your PROCEDURE DIVISION should be accomplished in two phases: (1) the flowcharting phase during which you concentrate on logic development while giving very little thought to the countless small details of COBOL grammar, and (2) the coding phase during which you concentrate on translating the flowchart into COBOL in a relaxed frame of mind, knowing that your logic is in good shape.

Appendix F: Basic Environment Division Elements for Selected Computer Systems

Burroughs 1700, 2500, 3500, 5500

```
CONFIGURATION  SECTION.
SOURCE-COMPUTER.   B-1700.      B-2500.      B-3500.      B-5500.
OBJECT-COMPUTER.    B-1700.  or  B-2500.  or  B-3500.  or  B-5500.
INPUT-OUTPUT  SECTION.
FILE-CONTROL.
        SELECT file-name ASSIGN TO  READER.       (card reader)
                                    PRINTER.       (line printer)
                                    TAPE.          (magnetic tape)
                                    SORT-TAPES.    (sort-tape—B-5500 only)
```

Control Data 3300, 6400, 6500, 6600, 6700

```
CONFIGURATION  SECTION.
SOURCE-COMPUTER.   3300.      6400.      6500.      6600.      6700.
OBJECT-COMPUTER.   3300.  or  6400.  or  6500.  or  6600.  or  6700.
INPUT-OUTPUT  SECTION.
FILE-CONTROL.
        SELECT file-name ASSIGN TO  INPUT.     (card reader)
                                    OUTPUT.    (line printer)
                                    TAPE01.    (magnetic tape)
```

Digital Equipment System 10

```
CONFIGURATION  SECTION.
SOURCE-COMPUTER.   DECSYSTEM-10.
OBJECT-COMPUTER.    DECSYSTEM-10.
SPECIAL-NAMES.   CHANNEL (1) IS NEXT-PAGE.*
INPUT-OUTPUT  SECTION.
FILE-CONTROL.
        SELECT file-name ASSIGN TO  CDR.    (card reader)
                                    LPT.    (line printer)
                                    MTA.    (magnetic tape)
```

* Allows you to advance to the top of the next page by ending your WRITE statement with AFTER ADVANCING NEXT-PAGE.

Honeywell 200

```
CONFIGURATION SECTION.
SOURCE-COMPUTER.   H-200.
OBJECT-COMPUTER.   H-200.
SPECIAL-NAMES.  PAGE IS NEXT-PAGE.**
INPUT-OUTPUT SECTION.
FILE-CONTROL.
      SELECT file-name ASSIGN TO  CARD-READER.   (card reader)
                                  PRINTER.       (line printer)
                                  TAPE-UNIT.     (magnetic tape)
```

Honeywell 600/6000 Series*

```
CONFIGURATION SECTION.
SOURCE-COMPUTER.   H-600.  or  H-6000.
OBJECT-COMPUTER.   H-600.      H-6000.
INPUT-OUTPUT SECTION.
FILE-CONTROL.
      SELECT file-name ASSIGN TO  dc FOR CARDS.    (card reader)
                                  dc FOR LISTING.  (line printer)
                                  dc.              (magnetic tape)
```

The dc is a two-character device-code (either two letters or a letter and a digit). It is programmer-invented and established by being included on the $DATA control card for the card reader, on the $SYSOUT control card for the line printer, and the $TAPE control card(s) for the tape(s).

IBM 360, 370

```
CONFIGURATION SECTION.
SOURCE-COMPUTER.   IBM-360.  or  IBM-370.
OBJECT-COMPUTER.   IBM-360.      IBM-370.
SPECIAL-NAMES.  C01 IS NEXT-PAGE.**
INPUT-OUTPUT SECTION.
FILE-CONTROL.
      SELECT file-name
           ASSIGN TO    UR-2501-S-ddname.   (card reader)     ⎫
                        UR-1403-S-ddname.   (line printer)    ⎬ Under OS.
                        UT-2400-S-ddname.   (magnetic tape)   ⎭
                        SYSnnn-UR-2501-S.   (card reader)      ⎫
                        SYSnnn-UR-1403-S.   (line printer)     ⎬ Under DOS.
                        SYSnnn-UT-2400-S.   (magnetic tape)    ⎭
```

* On Honeywell 600 and 6000 series computers, you advance to the top of the next page by ending your WRITE statement with AFTER ADVANCING TO TOP OF PAGE.

** Allows you to advance to the top of the next page by ending your WRITE statement with AFTER ADVANCING NEXT-PAGE.

The ddname is a programmer-invented external file-name defined on the DD control card. The ddname may be 1 to 8 characters long. The nnn is a number between 000 and 221 called the system number. Each peripheral device will have its own unique system number assigned by the local computer center:

IBM 1130

```
CONFIGURATION SECTION.
SOURCE-COMPUTER.  IBM-1130.
OBJECT-COMPUTER.  IBM-1130.
SPECIAL-NAMES.  C01 IS NEXT-PAGE*
INPUT-OUTPUT SECTION.
FILE-CONTROL.
     SELECT file-name ASSIGN TO  RD-2501.  (card-reader)
                                 PR-1403.  (line printer)
                                 (magnetic tapes not available)
```

IBM System 3

```
CONFIGURATION SECTION.
SOURCE-COMPUTER.  IBM-S3.
OBJECT-COMPUTER.  IBM-S3.
SPECIAL-NAMES.  C01 IS NEXT-PAGE.*
INPUT-OUTPUT SECTION.
FILE-CONTROL.
     SELECT file-name ASSIGN TO  UR-2501-RD.    (card reader)
                                 UR-1403-3.     (line printer)
                                 UT-3400-F-fname.  (magnetic tape)
```

The fname is a programmer-invented external file name given on the FILES control card. The fname may be 1 to 8 characters long.

NCR Century 8200**

```
CONFIGURATION SECTION.
SOURCE-COMPUTER.  NCR-CENTURY-8200.
OBJECT-COMPUTER.  NCR-CENTURY-8200.
INPUT-OUTPUT SECTION.
FILE-CONTROL.
     SELECT file-name ASSIGN TO  CARD-READER.  (card reader)
                                 PRINTER.      (line printer)
                                 (magnetic tapes not available)
```

* Allows you to advance to the top of the next page by ending your WRITE statement with AFTER ADVANCING NEXT-PAGE.
** On the NCR Century 8200, you advance to the top of the next page by ending your WRITE statement with AFTER ADVANCING PAGE.

UNIVAC 1106, 1108

```
CONFIGURATION  SECTION.
SOURCE-COMPUTER.   UNIVAC-1106.  or  UNIVAC-1108.
OBJECT-COMPUTER.   UNIVAC-1106.      UNIVAC-1108.
SPECIAL-NAMES.  TOP-OF-PAGE  IS  NEXT-PAGE.*
INPUT-OUTPUT  SECTION.
FILE-CONTROL.
      SELECT file-name ASSIGN  TO  CARD-READER.  (card reader)
                                   PRINTER.       (line printer)
                                   UNISERVO.      (magnetic tape)
```

XDS Sigma

```
CONFIGURATION  SECTION.
SOURCE-COMPUTER.   XDS-SIGMA.
OBJECT-COMPUTER.   XDS-SIGMA.
INPUT-OUTPUT  SECTION.
FILE-CONTROL.
      SELECT file-name ASSIGN  TO  CARD-READER.    (card reader)
                                   PRINTER.         (line printer)
                                   MAGNETIC-TAPE.   (magnetic tape)
```

---

* Allows you to advance to the top of the next page by ending your WRITE statement with AFTER ADVANCING NEXT-PAGE.

Epilog: Where Do I Go From Here?

This text has discussed roughly half of the most commonly used features of the COBOL language. Its intent was to help you through what for many students is a troublesome experience—their first contact with a computer. The text started out at 10 miles per hour, picked up speed as it went along, and finished at 40 miles per hour. This book was written to answer the need for a more gradual approach. Far too many COBOL programming texts now available start out at 60 miles per hour and finish at 90, dropping their beginning student readers in confused heaps along the side of the road as they speed along.

Having brought you this far, I would be remiss if I left you with the impression that you are in command of the entire COBOL language. You are not. You *are,* as I mentioned above, in command of roughly half of its most used features, and you *are* now far better prepared to deal with the "high speed" books in order to learn the remaining elements of the language. The principal features which remain, and which you should now move on to study, are these:

1. The use of compound conditionals in IF statements, and the nesting of IF statements.
2. The move advanced versions of the PERFORM statement.
3. The establishment of tables using the OCCURS clause in the DATA DIVISION, and the manipulation of the data in those tables using subscripts or indexes in the PROCEDURE DIVISION.
4. The creation and use of sequential, indexed, and relative (or direct) data files on magnetic disk.
5. The REPORT WRITER feature.
6. Structured COBOL programming.

These more advanced topics are discussed in most of the "high speed," complete COBOL programming texts available. They should be mastered if you plan to become a serious COBOL programmer.

Index